LSAT®

READING

COMPREHENSION

STRATEGIES AND TACTICS

SECOND EDITION

100% OFFICIAL LSAT PrepTest® Questions

Scott Emerson

© 2013 Kaplan, Inc.

Published by Kaplan Publishing, a division of Kaplan, Inc.
395 Hudson Street
New York, NY 10014

Printed in the United States of America

10 9 8 7 6 5 4 3 2 1

ISBN: 978-1-60978-685-4

Kaplan Publishing books are available at special quantity discounts to use for sales promotions, employee premiums, or educational purposes. For more information or to purchase books, please call the Simon & Schuster special sales department at 866-506-1949.

Contents

About the Author

Scott Emerson began his work with Kaplan in 2004 after achieving a 99th percentile LSAT score. He is a veteran classroom instructor, an experienced and highly demanded private tutor, and a trainer of excellent Kaplan instructors. In his seven years with Kaplan he has helped over 2,000 students achieve LSAT success, with nearly 200 of those students reporting scores above the 90th percentile. He has been actively involved in the evolution of Kaplan's proven approach to the LSAT, bringing his expertise to the research and development of a cutting-edge curriculum that has made Reading Comprehension approachable to students around the world. He currently teaches and resides in the Los Angeles area.

Introduction to the LSAT

The Law School Admissions Test (LSAT) is probably unlike any other test you've taken in your academic career. Most tests you've encountered in high school and college have been content based—that is, they have required you to recall facts, formulas, theorems, or other acquired knowledge.

The LSAT, however, is a skills-based test. It doesn't ask you to repeat memorized facts or to apply learned formulas to specific problems. In fact, all you'll be asked to do on the LSAT is think—thoroughly, quickly, and strategically. There's no required content to study.

But the lack of specific content to memorize is one of the things that makes preparing for the LSAT so challenging. Before you get the idea that you can skate into the most important test of your life without preparing, remember that learning skills and improving performance take practice. You can't cram for the test.

ABOUT THE LSAT

The LSAT is a standardized test written by the Law School Admissions Council (LSAC) and administered four times each year. The test is a required component of your application to all American Bar Association–approved law schools as well as some others.

The LSAT is designed to measure the skills necessary (according to the governing bodies of law schools) for success in your first year of law school, such as strategic reading, analyzing arguments, understanding formal logic, and making deductions. Because these skills will serve you well throughout law school and your professional life, consider your LSAT preparation an investment in your career.

You may already possess some level of proficiency with LSAT-tested skills. However, you probably haven't yet mastered how to use those skills to your best advantage in the context of a standardized, skills-based test that requires careful time management.

The LSAT is also a test of endurance—five 35-minute blocks of multiple-choice testing plus a 35-minute writing sample. Add in the administrative tasks at both ends of the test and a 10- to 15-minute break midway through, and you can count on being in the test room for at least four and a half hours. It's a grueling experience, but it's not as bad if you are familiar with the test and ready to handle every section. You want to approach the test with confidence so that you can maintain your focus, limit your stress, and get your highest score on test day. That's why it's so important to take control of the test, just as you will take control of the rest of the application process.

Our material is as up-to-date as possible at the time of this printing, but test specifications may change at any time. Please visit our website at http://kaptest.com/LSAT for the latest news and updates.

How Do I Register for the LSAT?

The LSAT is administered by the Law School Admissions Council (LSAC). Be sure to register as soon as possible, as your preferred test site can fill up quickly. You can register for the LSAT in three ways:

- Online: Sign up at http://lsac.org.
- Telephone: Call LSAC at (215) 968-1001.
- Email: Contact LSAC for a registration packet at lsacinfo@lsac.org.

If you have additional questions about registration, contact the LSAC by phone or by email.

The LSAT Sections

The LSAT consists of five multiple-choice sections: two Logical Reasoning sections, one Logic Games section, one Reading Comprehension section, and one unscored "experimental" section that looks exactly like one of the other multiple-choice sections. At the end of the test, there is a Writing Sample section during which you'll write a short essay. Here's how the sections break down:

Section	Number of Questions	Minutes
Logical Reasoning	24–26	35
Logical Reasoning	24–26	35
Logic Games	22–24	35
Reading Comprehension	26–28	35
"Experimental"	22–28	35
Writing Sample	n/a	35

The five multiple-choice sections can appear in any order, but the Writing Sample is always last. You will also get a 10- or 15-minute break between the third and fourth sections of the test.

You'll be answering roughly 125 multiple-choice questions (101 of which are scored) over the course of three intense hours. Taking control of the LSAT means increasing your test speed only to the extent that you can do so without sacrificing accuracy.

First, just familiarize yourself with the sections and the kinds of questions asked in each one.

Logical Reasoning

WHAT IT IS: The two Logical Reasoning sections each consist of 24–26 questions that reward your ability to analyze a "stimulus" (a paragraph or a dialogue between two speakers) and make judgments accordingly. You will evaluate the logic and structure of arguments and make inferences from the statements as well as find underlying assumptions, strengthen and weaken arguments, determine logical flaws, and identify parallel argument structures.

WHY IT'S ON THE TEST: Law schools want to see whether you can understand, analyze, evaluate, and manipulate arguments, and draw reliable conclusions—as every law student and attorney must. This question type makes up half of your LSAT score, which means this is a valuable skill to master.

Logic Games

WHAT IT IS: In the Logic Games (aka Analytical Reasoning) section, you'll find four games (aka critical-thinking puzzles) with five to seven questions each for a total of 22–24 questions. They reward your ability to make valid deductions from a set of rules or restrictions in order to determine what can, must, or cannot be true in various circumstances.

WHY IT'S ON THE TEST: In law school, your professors will have you read dozens of cases, extract their rules, and apply them to or distinguish them from hypothetical cases. The Logic Games section rewards the same skill set: attention to detail, rigorous deductive reasoning, an understanding of how rules limit and order behavior (the very definition of law), and the ability to discern the conditions under which those rules do and do not apply.

Reading Comprehension

WHAT IT IS: The Reading Comprehension section consists of three passages, each 450–550 words, and a set of two short passages that total 450–550 words. Each passage is followed by five to eight questions. The topics may range from areas of social science, humanities, natural science, and law. Because content isn't tested, you won't need any outside knowledge.

WHY IT'S ON THE TEST: The Reading Comprehension section tests your ability to quickly understand the gist and structure of long, difficult prose—just as you'll have to do in law school and throughout your career.

The Writing Sample

WHAT IT IS: During the Writing Sample section, you will read a paragraph that presents a problem and lists two possible solutions. Each solution will have strengths and weaknesses; you must argue in favor of one based on the given criteria. There is no right or wrong answer, and the writing sample is unscored. However, law schools will receive a copy of your essay along with your LSAT score.

WHY IT'S ON THE TEST: The Writing Sample shows law schools your ability to argue for a position while attacking an opposing argument under timed conditions. In addition, it may be used to verify that your writing style is similar to that in your personal statement.

How the LSAT Is Scored

You'll receive one score for the LSAT ranging between 120 and 180 (no separate scores for Logical Reasoning, Logic Games, and Reading Comprehension). There are roughly 101 scored multiple-choice questions on each exam:

- About 52 from the two Logical Reasoning sections
- About 22 from the Logic Games section
- About 27 from the Reading Comprehension section

Your **raw score**, the number of questions that you answer correctly, will be multiplied by a complicated scoring formula (different for each test, to accommodate differences in difficulty level) to yield the **scaled score**—the one that will fall somewhere in that 120–180 range—which is reported to the schools.

Because the test is graded on a largely preset curve, the scaled score will always correspond to a certain percentile, also indicated on your score report. A score of 160, for instance, corresponds roughly to the 80th percentile, meaning that 80 percent of test takers scored at or below your level. The percentile figure is important because it allows law schools to see where you fall in the pool of applicants.

All scored questions are worth the same amount—one raw point—and there's no penalty for guessing. That means that you should always fill in an answer for every question, whether you get to that question or not.

What's a "Good" LSAT Score?

What you consider a "good" LSAT score depends on your own expectations and goals, but here are a few interesting statistics.

If you got about half of all of the scored questions right (a raw score of roughly 50), you would earn a scaled score of roughly 147, putting you in about the 30th percentile—not a great performance. But on the LSAT, a little improvement goes a long way. In fact, getting only one additional question right every 10 minutes would give you a raw score of about 64, pushing you into the 60th percentile—a huge improvement.

| **Sample Percentiles** | | |
| **Approx. Scaled Score** | | |
Percentile	**(Range 120–180)**	**Approx. Raw Score**
99th percentile	174	~94 correct out of 101
95th percentile	168	~88 correct out of 101
90th percentile	164	~82 correct out of 101
80th percentile	160	~76 correct out of 101
75th percentile	157	~71 correct out of 101
50th percentile	152	~61 correct out of 101

Note: Exact percentile-to-scaled-score relationships vary from test to test.

As you can see, you don't have to be perfect to do well. On most LSATs, you can get as many as 28 questions wrong and still remain in the 80th percentile or as many as 20 wrong and still be in the 90th percentile. Most students who score 180 get a handful of questions wrong.

Although many factors play a role in admissions decisions, the LSAT score is usually one of the most important. And—generally speaking—being average won't cut it. The median LSAT score is somewhere around 152. If you're aiming for the top, you've got to do even better.

By using the strategies in this book, you'll learn how to approach—and master—the test in a general way. As you'll see, knowing specific strategies for each type of question is only part of your task. To do your best, you have to approach the entire test with the proactive, take-control kind of thinking it inspires—the LSAT mindset.

For more information on the LSAT experience, see Part IV of this book.

Good luck!

PART I

HOW READING COMPREHENSION WORKS

CHAPTER 1

LSAT READING IS CRITICAL READING

Many of the students I've worked with over the years have been surprised by the difficulties they've encountered when trying to complete the Reading Comprehension section of the LSAT. Perhaps you feel the same way. After all, this is a job you've faced before: You are given a brief passage and tasked with reading it, understanding it, and then answering a series of questions. You've been doing this in one form or another throughout your scholastic career, and now that you're preparing to go to law school you're undoubtedly expecting to do more of the same. So why does such a familiar task suddenly seem so daunting? Once you understand the answer to this question, you'll be ready to learn the correct approach to LSAT Reading Comprehension and ultimately raise your LSAT score.

YOU CAN MASTER LSAT READING COMPREHENSION

Although the challenges of LSAT Reading Comprehension haven't changed much over the years, different test takers approach the section with their own specific problems and concerns. I'll walk you through a few of the more common ones.

"I've Always Been a Slow Reader."

Perhaps you're concerned about the speed at which you read. How can you be expected to read so much information in so little time? If this is one of your worries, I have great news for you: The LSAT rewards test takers who read for the right information, not those who dwell on every sentence. Read the following excerpt from a previously released LSAT passage and do your best to understand precisely what it is saying:

> Although philanthropy—the volunteering of
> private resources for humanitarian purposes—reached
> its apex in England in the late nineteenth century,
> modern commentators have articulated two major
> (5) criticisms of the philanthropy that was a mainstay of
> England's middle-class Victorian society.[1]

Now, without looking back at the excerpt, can you remember when philanthropy reached its apex in England? On the LSAT, it actually doesn't matter whether you can or not, because this information probably won't be useful in answering any of the questions. In fact, the test makers rarely expect you to take notice of the minor details in the passage and instead reward you for staying focused on the big ideas. I'll discuss these concepts in greater detail very soon, but for now, remember that the LSAT isn't designed to reward fast reading, but rather strategic reading—a Kaplan skill that anyone can learn.

"I'm Intimidated by Complicated Language and Topics."

Every LSAT Reading Comprehension section will contain four passages, one from each of four broad subject areas: Humanities, Natural Sciences, Social Sciences, and Law. When I teach in the classroom, I always ask my students if they have one subject in particular that makes them nervous. Invariably their hands fly up as they confess their fears of arcane-seeming scientific jargon or dense, abstract legal theory. Usually at the root of this fear is a lack of familiarity with the subject. How can you be expected to answer questions about Victorian philanthropy if you haven't studied it? Here's an example:

23. Which one of the following best describes the
     attitude of the author of the passage toward the
     "Whig" interpretation of Victorian philanthropy?

     (A)   strong disagreement
     (B)   mild skepticism
     (C)   cynical amusement
     (D)   bland indifference
     (E)   unqualified support[2]

---

[1]PrepTest 41, Sec 4, Passage 4

[2]PrepTest 41, Sec 4, Q 23

How familiar is the average reader with the Whig interpretation of Victorian philanthropy? At a glance this question might seem intimidating or unfair. But look a little more carefully:

23. Which one of the following best describes the attitude of the author of the passage toward the "Whig" interpretation of Victorian philanthropy?

   (A) strong disagreement
   (B) mild skepticism
   (C) cynical amusement
   (D) bland indifference
   (E) unqualified support[3]

The question isn't really asking about the Whig interpretation at all, but rather the author's opinion of it. Read the LSAT passage excerpt below and try to find the information that provides the correct answer.

(35)   Modern critics of Victorian philanthropy often use
          the words "amateurish" or "inadequate" to describe
          Victorian philanthropy, as though Victorian charity can
          only be understood as an antecedent to the era of state-
          sponsored, professionally administered charity. This
(40) assumption is typical of the "Whig fallacy": the
          tendency to read the past as an inferior prelude to an
          enlightened present.[4]

The author of the passage clearly refers to the Whig interpretation as a fallacy, explaining that she regards it as incorrect. The only answer that states this correctly is choice (A).

I hope you have already realized what this example reveals about LSAT Reading Comprehension: The LSAT is not designed to test content, and it requires absolutely no outside knowledge of the topics addressed in the passages. Every question has only one correct answer, and all the information you need to find that correct answer is right there in the passage. Once again, you can see that the test makers reward those who stay focused on important information and use it to score points.

"There Just Isn't Enough Time. I Can Never Finish all Four Passages!"

This is the most common problem that my students have. You've probably encountered this problem as well. Maybe you can confidently tackle the first two passages, but you begin to feel rushed as you begin the third, and you just don't have time to read the fourth. I know how discouraging it can feel to desperately read and re-read the text of the passage in the hopes of scoring a needed point, all the while knowing that time is ticking away. Consider a very common type of question:

[3]PrepTest 41, Sec 4, Q 23
[4]PrepTest 41, Sec 4, Passage 4

21. Which one of the following best summarizes the main idea of the passage?

    (A) While the motives of individual practitioners have been questioned by modern commentators, Victorian philanthropy successfully dealt with the social ills of nineteenth-century England.

    (B) Philanthropy, inadequate to deal with the massive social and economic problems of the twentieth century, has slowly been replaced by state-sponsored charity.

    (C) The practice of reading the past as a prelude to an enlightened present has fostered revisionist views of many institutions, among them Victorian philanthropy.

    (D) Although modern commentators have perceived Victorian philanthropy as either inadequate or self-serving, the theoretical bias behind these criticisms leads to an incorrect interpretation of history.

    (E) Victorian philanthropists, aware of public resentment of their self-congratulatory attitude, used devious methods to camouflage their self-serving motives.[5]

The question asks you to identify the main idea of the passage, but the author presented many different ideas. How are you supposed to find the correct answer among these five long, dense choices? The answer is simple: If you employ the Kaplan Method as you read the passage, by the time you come to this question, you've already predicted the correct response. You won't need to re-read the passage, and you'll score this point in less than 30 seconds! There are only five commonly occurring question types within the LSAT Reading Comprehension section, and the Kaplan Method will help you identify and answer them accurately and efficiently.

I'll come back to question 21 in a short while. Before I move on, I want to revisit what I've covered so far. You don't have to be a fast reader to master LSAT Reading Comprehension. You don't need a background in law or science. Once you've mastered the Kaplan Method, on test day you'll never have to ask yourself, "What do I do next?" It will take time, patience, practice, and careful study, but if you dedicate yourself to learning the proper approach, you can master LSAT Reading Comprehension.

LSAT READING IS NOT CASUAL READING
Active Reading vs. Passive Reading

Take a moment to imagine yourself in your first year of law school. Think about what academic challenges are sure to await you. Regardless of what other images come to your mind, reading

---

[5]PrepTest 41, Sec 4, Q 21

should certainly be one of them. You are likely to find yourself reading and briefing hundreds of cases in preparation for in-depth discussion in your classes. That's a lot of reading, and it can easily amount to 300 pages per week.

Now think about the way you read a magazine or a novel. When you read for leisure, you probably read casually. You're not in any particular hurry, you linger over interesting details, and you follow along wherever the author leads you. If you become distracted or feel that you didn't understand something completely, you may go back and re-read a paragraph or two.

It's probably obvious at this point that leisure reading and law school reading are very, very different. When you read for pleasure or to pass the time, you're reading passively. To succeed in law school, you must prepare to read actively.

As an active reader you will engage with the passage and seek out the most important ideas in each paragraph. Details are of less importance, so you'll read them quickly to keep from getting bogged down in them. With time and practice, you'll even be able to predict the direction that a passage is likely to take as you read it, using clues the test makers provide for you. Unsurprisingly, the LSAT is designed to reward those who have mastered this crucial skill, so your first step toward a great LSAT score is to learn how to read actively.

Using the Clues

Take a look at the first paragraph of another LSAT Reading Comprehension passage. Read it as quickly as you can:

> Countee Cullen (Countee Leroy Porter,
> 1903–1946) was one of the foremost poets of the
> Harlem Renaissance, the movement of African
> American writers, musicians, and artists centered in the
> (5)   Harlem section of New York City during the 1920s.
> Beginning with his university years, Cullen strove to
> establish himself as an author of romantic poetry on
> abstract, universal topics such as love and death.
> Believing poetry should consist of "lofty thoughts
> (10) beautifully expressed," Cullen preferred controlled
> poetic forms. He used European forms such as sonnets
> and devices such as quatrains, couplets, and
> conventional rhyme, and he frequently employed
> classical allusions and Christian religious imagery,
> (15) which were most likely the product both of his
> university education and of his upbringing as the
> adopted son of a Methodist Episcopal reverend.[6]

This paragraph is a good example of the kind of writing you will see on test day. After introducing Countee Cullen, the author describes several defining aspects of Cullen's poetry. Chances

---

[6]PrepTest 41, Sec 4, Passage 2

are good that you remember a few details, but you've probably already forgotten a lot of what you just read. Don't worry! This doesn't mean that you're a poor reader. It simply means that you read the paragraph passively. Take another look at the first few sentences, and be sure to pay close attention to the circled words:

> Countee Cullen (Countee Leroy Porter,
> 1903–1946) was one of the (foremost) poets of the
> Harlem Renaissance, the movement of African
> American writers, musicians, and artists centered in the
> (5) Harlem section of New York City during the 1920s.
> (Beginning with) his university years, Cullen (strove) to
> establish himself as an author of romantic poetry on
> abstract, universal topics such as love and death.
> (Believing) poetry should consist of "lofty thoughts
> (10) beautifully expressed," Cullen (preferred) controlled
> poetic forms.[7]

Why are these particular words so important? Examine each one and think about what it tells you:

- "Foremost" emphasizes that Cullen was a notable figure in American literature.
- "Beginning with" identifies the start of a sequence of potentially important ideas.
- "Strove" points to a key element of Cullen's poetic style.
- "Believing" indicates that you're about to get more insight into Cullen's ideas about poetry.
- "Preferred" points to another element of Cullen's style.

Notice that none of these words contain much information by themselves, but every one of them indicates that an important fact is to follow. Not only do they help you to better understand the structure of the author's ideas, but they also help you to find the information that is likely to be tested when you get to the questions. And the test makers place these kinds of clues in *every single passage*. From now on I will refer to them as Keywords.

Take a look at this LSAT question:

10. The passage suggests which one of the following about Cullen's use of controlled poetic forms?[8]

Don't worry about the lack of answer choices; I'll present them momentarily. For now, refer back to the circled Keywords and see whether you can find information you can use to answer this question:

---

[7]PrepTest 41, Sec 4, Passage 2
[8]PrepTest 41, Sec 4, Q 10

Countee Cullen (Countee Leroy Porter,
1903–1946) was one of the (foremost) poets of the
Harlem Renaissance, the movement of African
American writers, musicians, and artists centered in the
(5)   Harlem section of New York City during the 1920s.
(Beginning with) his university years, Cullen (strove) to
establish himself as an author of romantic poetry on
abstract, universal topics such as love and death.
(Believing) poetry should consist of "lofty thoughts
(10) beautifully expressed," Cullen (preferred) controlled
poetic forms.[9]

You probably went directly to the final sentence. By referring to the Keywords, you can easily see that this is where Cullen's preference for "controlled poetic forms" is mentioned. Why did Cullen express this preference? The answer immediately follows the Keyword "believing." Try to summarize that part of the text in your mind before reading on.

Whether you realize it or not, you have just made an extremely important step toward Reading Comprehension mastery. By coming up with your summary, you have effectively predicted what the answer to question 10 is likely to be. Now all you have to do is look at the answer choices and pick the one that resembles your summary. Try it:

(A)   Cullen used controlled poetic forms because
      he believed they provided the best means to
      beautiful poetic expression.
(B)   Cullen's interest in religious themes naturally
      led him to use controlled poetic forms.
(C)   Only the most controlled poetic forms allowed
      Cullen to address racial issues in his poems.
(D)   Cullen had rejected the less controlled poetic
      forms he was exposed to prior to his
      university years.
(E)   Less controlled poetic forms are better suited
      to poetry that addresses racial or political issues.[10]

Hopefully you spotted choice (A) as the correct answer and scored the point. Most test takers waste a lot of time on test day reading the answer choices over and over again, letting the choices guide their thinking. As you'll learn, this is a very poor approach to the LSAT; it wastes precious time, and it is likely to lead you to an incorrect answer. You, on the other hand, just took a very active approach to this question. You paid attention to the Keywords in the passage that pointed to important information, you predicted what the correct answer would look like, and you selected it with confidence.

At this point you may be wondering how to find Keywords on your own. You'll learn about this in great detail in chapter 2. For now, take a brief look at how you can use Keywords to make an entire passage easier to understand.

---

[9]PrepTest 41, Sec 4, Passage 2
[10]PrepTest 41, Sec 4, Q 10

ANATOMY OF AN LSAT PASSAGE
Reading the Kaplan Way

Earlier in this chapter you saw selected fragments of an LSAT passage about Victorian-era philanthropy. Now take a look at the passage in its entirety:

Although philanthropy—the volunteering of private resources for humanitarian purposes—reached its apex in England in the late nineteenth century, modern commentators have articulated two major
(5) criticisms of the philanthropy that was a mainstay of England's middle-class Victorian society. The earlier criticism is that such philanthropy was even by the later nineteenth century obsolete, since industrialism had already created social problems that were beyond the
(10) scope of small, private voluntary efforts. Indeed, these problems required substantial legislative action by the state. Unemployment, for example, was not the result of a failure of diligence on the part of workers or a failure of compassion on the part of employers, nor
(15) could it be solved by well-wishing philanthropists.

The more recent charge holds that Victorian philanthropy was by its very nature a self-serving exercise carried out by philanthropists at the expense of those whom they were ostensibly serving. In this view,
(20) philanthropy was a means of flaunting one's power and position in a society that placed great emphasis on status, or even a means of cultivating social connections that could lead to economic rewards. Further, if philanthropy is seen as serving the interests
(25) of individual philanthropists, so it may be seen as serving the interests of their class. According to this "social control" thesis, philanthropists, in professing to help the poor, were encouraging in them such values as prudence, thrift, and temperance, values perhaps

(30) worthy in themselves but also designed to create more productive members of the labor force. Philanthropy, in short, was a means of controlling the labor force and ensuring the continued dominance of the management class.
(35) Modern critics of Victorian philanthropy often use the words "amateurish" or "inadequate" to describe Victorian philanthropy, as though Victorian charity can only be understood as an antecedent to the era of state-sponsored, professionally administered charity. This
(40) assumption is typical of the "Whig fallacy": the tendency to read the past as an inferior prelude to an enlightened present. If most Victorians resisted state control and expended their resources on private, voluntary philanthropies, it could only be, the argument
(45) goes, because of their commitment to a vested interest, or because the administrative apparatus of the state was incapable of coping with the economic and social needs of the time.

This version of history patronizes the Victorians,
(50) who were in fact well aware of their vulnerability to charges of condescension and complacency, but were equally well aware of the potential dangers of state-managed charity. They were perhaps condescending to the poor, but—to use an un-Victorian metaphor—they
(55) put their money where their mouths were, and gave of their careers and lives as well.[11]

---

[11]PrepTest 41, Sec 4, Passage 4

This lengthy, dense passage poses a formidable challenge to passive readers. It deals with an unfamiliar subject, it is rife with jargon, and it explores abstract concepts while providing very few concrete examples to illustrate them. Perhaps you felt a little overwhelmed while you were reading it. If so, you probably don't feel ready to answer the six questions that follow it.

Fortunately, this won't happen to you on test day, because you will know how to read actively. Figure 1.1 shows the same passage after I've applied the Kaplan Method to it.

Vict.
philanthropy
def.

(Although) philanthropy—the volunteering of private resources for humanitarian purposes—reached its apex in England in the late nineteenth century, (modern commentators) have articulated two major
(5) (criticisms) of the philanthropy that was a mainstay of England's middle-class Victorian society. The (earlier)

Early crit.

criticism is that such philanthropy was even by the later nineteenth century obsolete, (since) industrialism had

Philanthropy
obsolete

already created social problems that were beyond the
(10) scope of small, private voluntary efforts. (Indeed,) these problems required substantial legislative action by the state. Unemployment, (for example,) was not the result of a failure of diligence on the part of workers (or) a failure of compassion on the part of employers, (nor)
(15) could it be solved by well-wishing philanthropists.

Modern
crit.

The (more recent) charge holds that Victorian philanthropy was by its very nature a self-serving exercise carried out by philanthropists at the expense of those whom they were ostensibly serving. (In) this view,
(20) philanthropy was a means of flaunting one's power and

Philanthropy
self serving

position in a society that placed (great emphasis) on status, or (even) a means of cultivating social connections that could (lead to) economic rewards. (Further,) if philanthropy is seen as serving the interests
(25) of individual philanthropists, (so) it may be seen as serving the interest of their class. (According to) this "social control" thesis, philanthropists, in professing to help the poor, were encouraging in them such values as prudence, thrift, and temperance, values perhaps
(30) worthy in themselves (but also) designed to create more productive members of the labor force. Philanthropy, in short, was a means of controlling the labor force and ensuring the continued dominance of the management class.

Author:
Modern crit.
wrong

(35) Modern critics of Victorian philanthropy often use
the words "amateurish" or "inadequate" to describe
Victorian philanthropy, as though Victorian charity can
only be understood as an antecedent to the era of state-
sponsored, professionally administered charity. This
(40) assumption is typical of the "Whig fallacy": the
tendency to read the past as an inferior prelude to an
enlightened present. If most Victorians resisted state
control and expended their resources on private,
voluntary philanthropies, it could only be, the argument
(45) goes, because of their commitment to a vested interest,
or because the administrative apparatus of the status was
incapable of coping with the economic and social
needs of the time.

Critics
incorrect

This version of history patronizes the Victorians,
(50) who were in fact well aware of their vulnerability to
charges of condescension and complacency, but were
equally well aware of the potential dangers of state-
managed charity. They were perhaps condescending to
the poor, but—to use an un-Victorian metaphor—they
(55) put their money where their mouths were, and gave of
their careers and lives as well.[12]

Quite a difference! First, notice that I circled important Keywords throughout the passage. Just as in the Countee Cullen passage, Keywords are vital to your ability to make sense of what you're reading. I'll explain a couple of specific ones.

The phrase "For example" in line 12 helps you to return to this bit of illustrative text easily if you need to answer a question about it. When you read an LSAT passage using the Kaplan Method, you won't dwell on examples and details. You *do* read them, and you always circle the Keywords surrounding them, but you don't make any effort to memorize or completely understand them. This idea might make you a bit nervous at first, but there are two very good reasons why you must do it. First, while specific details are often necessary to answer questions, there's no guarantee that this particular example will show up in the question set. If you dwell on details that aren't tested, you waste your time. Second, if it turns out that you do need this detail in order to answer a question, you're going to have to come back to the passage to look it up anyway. The test makers reward those who research the right information at the right time, and they set out answer traps for those who try to rely on memorization. In any case, if you need this example later, you'll be able to find it very easily, thanks to your attention to Keywords.

Now look at a particularly important set of Keywords at the beginning of the third paragraph. I circled "Modern critics" in line 35 because the ideas that follow are those of the critics, and *not* necessarily the author's. On test day, on every passage, you will encounter questions that relate to the author's viewpoint. It is therefore very important that you differentiate between

[12]PrepTest 41, Sec 4, Passage 4

the author's opinions and those of other parties mentioned in the passage. Most passages contain multiple points of view, and the test makers will write questions that reward you for knowing which is which.

Scan over the other Keywords and think about why they are important. It's good practice for chapter 2.

The Roadmap

The Keywords I circled in the previous example probably looked familiar to you, but what about the notes written in the margins beside each paragraph? Read them carefully. They're brief, but they're extremely important. Each one of those notes is a summary of all the major ideas present in the associated paragraph. Look at the notes next to the first paragraph shown in Figure 1.2.

Vict.
philanthropy
def.

Early crit.

Philanthropy
obsolete

(Although) philanthropy—the volunteering of private resources for humanitarian purposes—reached its apex in England in the late nineteenth century, (modern commentators) have articulated two major
(5)   (criticisms) of the philanthropy that was a mainstay of England's middle-class Victorian society. The (earlier) criticism is that such philanthropy was even by the later nineteenth century obsolete, (since) industrialism had already created social problems that were beyond the
(10)   scope of small, private voluntary efforts. (Indeed,) these problems required substantial legislative action by the state. Unemployment, (for example,) was not the result of a failure of diligence on the part of workers (or) a failure of compassion on the part of employers, (nor)
(15)   could it be solved by well-wishing philanthropists.[13]

The first note simply says, "Vict. philanthropy def." This shorthand tells you that the first paragraph began by defining Victorian philanthropy. The second note, "Early crit," reminds you that a criticism is being leveled against the philanthropists, and that it's the earlier of the two presented. Take a moment to read over the rest of the margin notes and get a sense for how each one summarizes the key information in each paragraph.

I call this series of notes a Roadmap. I'd like you to take particular note of two very important aspects of the Roadmap: It's succinct, and yet it spells out every major idea the author presents in this passage. In other words, all of this dense text can be summarized in a few simple lines of shorthand, and as you will learn, every single LSAT passage can be summarized in this way, no matter how complicated it may appear at first glance.

As you become proficient in the Kaplan Method, you will learn to create Roadmaps of your own. The Roadmap serves a number of important purposes. It helps you to keep track of the

[13]PrepTest 41, Sec 4, Passage 4

author's primary ideas and the structure of the passage as a whole, both of which will be the subject of test questions. It also gives you a handy index to use when you scan the passage for information. Even the act of writing down the Roadmap is useful, as it helps you to clarify your thoughts. I'll come back to Roadmaps in greater detail in chapter 3. For now, I'd like to present one more element of the Kaplan Method to you before you tackle a couple of questions.

The Big Picture

So far, I've explained how you can use Keywords and the Roadmap to avoid dwelling on details and to keep your focus where it belongs: on the larger themes of the text. In order to make sure you've really captured the essence of the author's big ideas, there are four attributes of the passage that you should think about before you move on. You won't see them written down anywhere in Figure 1.1, and that's because on test day you shouldn't write them down either. Instead, you will develop the habit of working them out in your mind. I'll define each one of them for you in brief:

- Topic: A very general description of its subject matter
- Scope: The narrower area of interest within the Topic that the author explores
- Purpose: A description of *why* the author wrote the passage
- Main Idea: A summary of the author's primary point

I'll walk you through the topic, scope, purpose, and main idea of the Victorian philanthropy passage. Actually, I've already named the topic: Victorian philanthropy. So what about philanthropy is the author interested in exploring? She spends most of the passage examining the merits of the two criticisms that have been leveled against it. That's the scope: criticisms of Victorian philanthropy.

In order to decide on the purpose, refer to the Roadmap for guidance. Going paragraph by paragraph, you can see that the author wrote this passage in order to describe two specific criticisms of Victorian philanthropy and then to refute those criticisms; that's the purpose. Finally, articulate the main idea. If you could summarize the entire passage in a sentence or two, what would you say? Think about it before reading on.

You probably came up with something like this: "Various critics have described the Victorian philanthropists as inadequate and self-serving, but these critics are incorrect." Your version of the main idea may have been a bit briefer or more detailed than mine, but as long as you came up with something similar you're on the right track. I'll discuss topic, scope, purpose, and main idea more thoroughly in chapter 4, but for now you might be asking, "Why do I need to bother thinking about this?" The answer is simple: It helps you earn points on the LSAT.

Pulling It All Together

Now use your new skills to answer a couple of questions. Begin by returning to question 21:

21. Which one of the following best summarizes the
    main idea of the passage?

    (A)   While the motives of individual practitioners
            have been questioned by modern
            commentators, Victorian philanthropy
            successfully dealt with the social ills of
            nineteenth-century England.
    (B)   Philanthropy, inadequate to deal with the
            massive social and economic problems of the
            twentieth century, has slowly been replaced
            by state-sponsored charity.
    (C)   The practice of reading the past as a prelude to
            an enlightened present has fostered
            revisionist views of many institutions, among
            them Victorian philanthropy.
    (D)   Although modern commentators have
            perceived Victorian philanthropy as either
            inadequate or self-serving, the theoretical bias
            behind these criticisms leads to an incorrect
            interpretation of history.
    (E)   Victorian philanthropists, aware of public
            resentment of their self-congratulatory
            attitude, used devious methods to camouflage
            their self-serving motives.[14]

The question is asking for the main idea of the passage, and you've already worked out what
it is. Which answer choice matches the prediction you just made? Perhaps choice (A) looks
tempting at first, but if you compare it to your prediction, you can see that it's incorrect; at
no point did the author claim that the Victorian philanthropists successfully dealt with the ills
of their time. (When you see a clever wrong answer trap like this one, it's very important that
you stick to your prediction.) Of the remaining choices, choice (D) matches your prediction
note for note. It's a bit wordier than what you may have come up with, but that will almost
always be the case. You don't need to look for the same words, but rather the same concept.

Look at another question:

24. Which one of the following best describes the
    primary purpose of the passage?

    (A)   providing an extended definition of a key term
    (B)   defending the work of an influential group of
            theorists
    (C)   narrating the chronological development of a
            widespread practice
    (D)   examining modern evaluations of a historical
            phenomenon
    (E)   analyzing a specific dilemma faced by workers
            of the past[15]

---

[14]PrepTest 41, Sec 4, Q 21

[15]PrepTest 41, Sec 4, Q 24

This question asks for the primary purpose, and once again you've already made a prediction. Only choice (D) matches your prediction, and it's the correct answer. If you had encountered this passage on test day, you would have already scored two quick points simply by understanding and identifying the author's purpose and main idea. Try one more:

26. Which one of the following best describes the organization of the passage?

    (A)   Two related positions are discussed, then both are subjected to the same criticism.
    (B)   Two opposing theories are outlined, then a synthesis between the two is proposed.
    (C)   A position is stated, and two differing evaluations of it are given.
    (D)   Three examples of the same logical inconsistency are given.
    (E)   A theory is outlined, and two supporting examples are given.[16]

Questions that ask for passage structure can appear baffling, but you've got exactly what you need to answer this question quickly and correctly: your Roadmap. Look back over the structure of the passage as described in the Roadmap and you'll see that the only answer choice that matches is choice (A). The other choices may tempt you if you haven't analyzed the passage structure carefully, but with the aid of the Kaplan Method, they won't fool you. All three of these questions demonstrate something very important about LSAT Reading Comprehension as a whole. The test makers reward those who think about the big issues and don't allow themselves to get mired in the details.

Congratulations are in order! You've made it this far and have already learned many important LSAT concepts. I've also introduced you to the basics of the Kaplan Method. To conclude chapter 1, I'll explain the Kaplan Method in more detail.

THE KAPLAN METHOD

As you know, LSAT Reading Comprehension is timed, and 35 minutes may not seem like a generous amount of time to work with. In order to master Reading Comprehension you must not only be accurate, but efficient as well. One of the biggest fears my students have on their first day of class is imagining opening their booklets on test day, looking at the page, and having no idea what to do next as time slips away. Perhaps you have the same fear. Fortunately, there is a solution: If you follow a methodical approach, you'll always know what to do next. Here is the Kaplan Method:

---

[16]PrepTest 41, Sec 4, Q 26

KAPLAN'S METHOD FOR READING COMPREHENSION

STEP 1 **Read the Passage Strategically.**
Read for Topic, Scope, Purpose, and Main Idea and build your Roadmap.

STEP 2 **Identify the Question Type.**
Look for clues to identify the question and help you find the answer in the passage.

STEP 3 **Research the Relevant Text.**
Use your Roadmap to guide your research.

STEP 4 **Make a Prediction.**
Make effective predictions to help you get the right answer quickly and efficiently.

STEP 5 **Evaluate the Answer Choices.**
Evaluate each choice and eliminate those that don't match your prediction, keeping your eye out for common wrong answer traps.

You've already executed each step of the Kaplan Method at various stages. For now, I'll discuss each step briefly and then expand on them in subsequent chapters.

Step 1: Read the Passage Strategically

I've already introduced you to all of the important aspects of Step 1. I've discussed Keywords, building a Roadmap, and the importance of determining Topic, Scope, Purpose, and Main Idea. I'll explore all of these ideas in greater detail moving forward, but for now I want to emphasize the importance of practicing this new way of reading. It may not be easy at first and will certainly require a good deal of practice to master, but the benefit of mastery is a higher LSAT score. Part I of this book will primarily focus on strategic reading.

Step 2: Identify the Question Type

There are only five common question types in LSAT Reading Comprehension, and the Kaplan Method will allow you to master each one of them. In Part II of this book, I'll teach you how to identify each type and introduce you to those strategies. I'll also show you how to use clues in the question stem to quickly determine where in the passage you should look to find the answer.

Step 3: Research the Relevant Text

Most Reading Comprehension questions require you to reference specific information from the passage. This step is crucial in answering those questions correctly. One of the biggest mistakes I see students make is to over-rely on memory. This is a terrible habit, one that I want to prevent you from forming. As you begin to apply the Kaplan Method to every question, you'll soon learn to use your Roadmap to correctly identify which text is relevant to a given question. That way you can answer the question quickly without sacrificing accuracy.

Step 4: Make a Prediction

You've already seen the power of making predictions before you look at the answer choices. Nevertheless, this approach may seem counterintuitive to you initially, and you might fear that it's too time-consuming to apply. With practice, you will make predictions quickly and accurately, saving time and allowing you to eliminate wrong answer traps with ease. Once you've made it a habit, you will enjoy a boost to your confidence and, in turn, your score. The answer to most Reading Comprehension questions can be predicted, making this a particularly vital skill to master.

Step 5: Evaluate the Answer Choices

Most of the time, this means seeking out a choice that matches the prediction you made in Step 4. For questions less amenable to prediction, you will learn to apply alternative ways of evaluating the choices. You will also become familiar with the most common types of wrong answer that appear on the LSAT so that you are less likely to be enticed by them.

When you follow the steps of the Kaplan Method, you will always know what to do on test day, and you can be sure that you're always approaching the test the right way. That brings me right back to the main point of chapter 1.

YOU CAN MASTER LSAT READING COMPREHENSION

LSAT Reading Comprehension can be challenging, intimidating, and confusing. It can also be a fantastic opportunity to improve your score and take a big step forward on the road to law school. Keep this in mind as you learn more about the Kaplan Method and begin to practice. I know from experience that while it's sometimes difficult to keep a positive outlook when taking on a big challenge, it's also absolutely essential. You won't master the methods overnight, and you'll make some mistakes along the way. I'll do my best to help you see those mistakes for what they are: opportunities to learn. And as you start to attain mastery, you'll begin to wonder why you were ever intimidated by Reading Comprehension at all. For now, let's continue with a more thorough discussion of Keywords in chapter 2.

CHAPTER 2

ALL ABOUT KEYWORDS

WHY KEYWORDS MATTER

In the last chapter I introduced you to Keywords, and I hope I convinced you that learning to make use of them is vital to your LSAT success. But just to be certain, I'll begin with a brief discussion of why Keywords are so important.

Keywords Make Reading Easier

LSAT Reading Comprehension is designed to be challenging to all readers. The test makers purposefully choose subjects that are diverse, nuanced, and sometimes complex. They gravitate toward formal, scholarly language that can be dense, dull, and laden with complex details or abstract ideas. Such language can be difficult to comprehend even when you have plenty of time to read it; the LSAT rachets up the difficulty level by adding the pressure of the clock.

Fortunately, Keywords are there to help. They provide structure to the passage, allowing you to discern one idea from another and to organize important information as you read. Let me show you what I mean. Read the following:

Charlie sat down. He took a pencil out of his pocket. He wanted to work through some sample questions. His pencil wasn't sharpened. He had a spare pencil. It was sharpened. He was ready to get to work.

If that seemed confusing or odd, that's because it was completely lacking in useful Keywords. No one ever writes like this, at least not in formal writing. You would instead expect to see something more like this:

(First) Charlie sat down, (and then) he took a pencil out of his pocket. He wanted to work through some sample questions, (but) his pencil wasn't sharpened. (Fortunately,) he had a spare pencil, (and) (since) it was sharpened, he was ready to get to work.

It still isn't Shakespeare, but it's certainly much easier to follow. Notice that the highlighted Keywords provide bits of information that assist us in linking the various ideas together. The guidance that Keywords provide is helpful in a simple example, and they become absolutley crucial in a more challenging passage:

>   Drilling a well
>   creates a conduit connecting all the formations that it
> (30) has penetrated. (Consequently,) without appropriate
>   safeguards, wells that penetrate both groundwater and
>   oil or saline water formations (inevitably) contaminate
>   the groundwater. (Initial) attempts to prevent this
>   contamination (consisted of) sealing off the
> (35) groundwater formations with some form of protective
>   barrier to prevent the oil flowing up the well from
>   entering or mixing with the natural groundwater
>   reservoir. This method, which is still in use today,
>   (initially) involved using hollow trees to seal off the
> (40) groundwater formations; (now,) (however,) large metal
>   pipe casings, set in place with cement, are used.[1]

In this LSAT passage excerpt, you are bombarded with information. The provided Keywords help you to understand the logic of what the author is saying. Words like "initially," "consequently," and "however" provide the sequence of events and their relationship to one another. Hopefully it has occurred to you that everything you've ever read that was written in formal English contained dozens of Keywords. Because they're so ubiquitous, you may tend to take them for granted, rarely noticing them at all. As part of your Kaplan training, I will teach you to re-acquaint yourself with these useful words and to use them to become a more confident and efficient reader.

Keywords Denote Emphasis

There are different kinds of Keywords that guide us in a variety of ways, and I'll explain all of them in this chapter. LSAT passages invariably contain Keywords that denote emphasis, and any emphasized idea is likely to be important when you proceed to the questions. Sometimes emphatic Keywords are quite obvious, but they can be subtle as well. See whether you can spot the emphasis Keywords in this sentence:

---

[1]PrepTest 43, Sec 1, Passage 1

Because the well was drilled in a channel
accessing the ocean, not only was the area's
(60)   groundwater completely contaminated, but widespread
coastal contamination also occurred, prompting
international concern over oil exploration and
initiating further attempts to refine regulations.[2]

Hopefully you recognized a number of Keywords, but here are the ones I want you to pay particular attention to:

Because the well was drilled in a channel
(60)   accessing the ocean, (not only) was the area's
groundwater completely contaminated, (but) widespread
coastal contamination (also) occurred, prompting
international concern over oil exploration and
initiating further attempts to refine regulations.[3]

In this sentence, the author describes two consequences of the drilling of a well. The Keyword pairing "not only . . . but also" helps you keep track of them. It also implies that the second consequence, the coastal contamination, is the one that the author is most interested in. If you're not sure why, think about the way these Keywords are used in everyday life:

The senator was contrite in his remarks, not only apologizing for his mistakes, but also announcing his resignation to his constituents.

The senator did two things, and one of them was more important or more surprising than the other. If he gave a contrite speech, you would expect him to issue apologies. You wouldn't necessarily expect him to abandon his post. You can see that with this particular Keyword pairing, whatever follows the "not only" is generally less emphatic, and what follows the "but also" is usually more emphatic.

Understanding which ideas the author emphasizes is extremely important, because the majority of the questions you see when you take your LSAT will reference those ideas. Put simply: Knowing what has been emphasized will earn you points. If it's important to the author, it's important to you as well.

Keywords Are Always There

To conclude this overview of Keywords, I want to restate something I mentioned in the first chapter of this book: *Every single LSAT passage is loaded with Keywords.* This, above all, is the reason that they are so important. The test makers deliberately provide you with all the Keywords you need because they want to reward you for noticing them and using them correctly. The ability to navigate dense language quickly and understand its structure and core ideas is

---

[2]PrepTest 43, Sec 1, Passage 1

[3]PrepTest 43, Sec 1, Passage 1

an imperative for law school students. That's why Reading Comprehension is on the LSAT, and that's why the Keywords are always there.

In order to read strategically, you must learn to identify Keywords. Now I'll introduce the most common Keywords you should expect to see on test day, broken down into six categories.

Contrast Keywords

Contrast Keywords indicate that the passage is about to move in a different direction. Here's an example:

> Most of what has been written about Thurgood
> Marshall, a former United States Supreme Court justice
> who served from 1967 to 1991, has just focused on his
> judicial record and on the ideological content of his
> (5)   earlier achievements as a lawyer pursuing civil rights
> issues in the courts. But when Marshall's career is
> viewed from a technical perspective, his work with the
> NAACP (National Association for the Advancement of
> Colored People) reveals a strategic and methodological
> (10) legacy to the field of public interest law.[4]

The author begins this passage with a description of what has generally been written about Marshall's work. But she's actually more interested in examining aspects of his work with the NAACP. In order to alert the reader to this change, she uses the Keyword "but." Here's another example from an excerpt you examined previously:

> This method, which is still in use today,
> initially involved using hollow trees to seal off the
> (40) groundwater formations; now, however, large metal
> pipe casings, set in place with cement, are used.[5]

In this case, the author uses contrast Keywords to indicate a shift from what was previously true to what is true now.

Contrast Keywords are important because LSAT passages tend to involve conflict. Science passages frequently pit one theory or model against another, and Law passages will often feature debates between legal scholars or schools of thought. You will almost certainly encounter

---

[4]PrepTest 42, Sec 3, Passage 1
[5]PrepTest 43, Sec 1, Passage 1

passages on test day that introduce multiple points of view and then demonstrate how and why they differ. Any time a conflict is present in a passage, you should take heed; it will probably be the subject of at least one question. To illustrate:

> (In addition,) Marshall used sociological (and) psychological statistics—presented in expert testimony, (for example,) about the psychological impact of enforced segregation—(as a means) of transforming constitutional law by persuading the courts that certain discriminatory laws produced public harms in violation
> (40) of constitutional principles. This tactic, (while) often effective, has been (criticized) by (some legal scholars) as a pragmatic attempt to give judges nonlegal material with which to fill gaps in their justifications for decisions where the purely legal principles appear
> (45) inconclusive.[6]

In the first sentence, the author describes one of Marshall's tactics. The Keyword "while" in the second sentence points to a contrast. Even though the tactic is effective, certain scholars have criticized it.

Here is the final question from this passage:

7. According to the passage, some legal scholars have criticized which one of the following?

   (A) the ideology Marshall used to support his goals
   (B) recent public interest campaigns
   (C) the use of Marshall's techniques by politically conservative lawyers
   (D) the use of psychological statistics in court cases
   (E) the set of criteria for selecting public interest litigants[7]

You can find support for correct answer (D) in the text immediately following the Keywords "in addition" at the paragraph's beginning. It's worth noting that these critics are not mentioned anywhere else in the passage; the test makers regarded this sole bit of critique to be important enough to warrant a question. Careful attention to Keywords makes this an easy point to earn. Among the most common contrast Keywords are "not," "although," "while," "even though," "despite," and "however." Be on the lookout for them, but know that you don't need to memorize long lists of Keywords to improve your LSAT score. Most of them you will recognize instinctively, and with practice you'll soon identify them by habit.

---

[6]PrepTest 42, Sec 3, Passage 1

[7]PrepTest 42, Sec 3, Q 7

Continuation Keywords

Continuation Keywords are the opposites of contrast Keywords. They indicate that the author is continuing ahead in the same vein:

> The effects of groundwater bacteria, traffic
> vibrations, and changing groundwater chemistry are
> (50) likewise unassessed. Further, there is no guarantee that
> wells drilled in compliance with existing regulations will
> not expose a need for research in additional areas: on the
> west coast of North America, a major disaster recently
> occurred because a well's location was based on a poor
> (55) understanding of the area's subsurface geology.[8]

Here's one more:

> In addition, Marshall used sociological
> and psychological statistics—presented in expert
> testimony, for example, about the psychological
> impact of enforced segregation—as a means of
> (40) transforming constitutional law by persuading the
> courts that certain discriminatory laws produced
> public harms in violation of constitutional
> principles.[9]

Continuation Keywords are useful for breaking up long chains of ideas and for anticipating the structure of a passage quickly. In the first example above, the word "Further" helps us quickly see where one concept ends and where another related concept begins. Taking note of this now will help immensely if you need to re-examine these examples quickly while answering a question. The sentence in the second example is the first of a new paragraph. LSAT passages frequently begin paragraphs with Keywords; pay special heed to them, because they provide invaluable information about the structure of the passage.

Conclusion Keywords and Evidence Keywords

The Logical Reasoning section of the LSAT requires that you become very skillful at identifying an argument's conclusion and its evidence. That same skill is also useful in Reading Comprehension. For the purposes of Reading Comprehension, a conclusion Keyword indicates an important

---

[8]PrepTest 43, Sec 1, Passage 1
[9]PrepTest 42, Sec 3, Passage 1

opinion being expressed, and an evidence Keyword denotes any type of supporting information, including examples. Since these types of Keywords often work in pairs, I'll examine them together. Begin with a passage excerpt:

> (Because) the market system enables entrepreneurs
> and investors who develop new technology to reap
> financial rewards from their risk of capital, it may seem
> that the primary (result) of this activity is that some
> (5)   people who have spare capital accumulate more.[10]

The conclusion Keyword "result" points directly to a conclusion that the author wishes to discuss. The evidence Keyword "because" at the beginning of the sentence indicates the evidence provided for this conclusion.

Evidence and conclusion Keywords don't always have to be directly paired with one another. For instance:

> When commercial drilling for oil began in North
> America in the mid-nineteenth century, regulations
> reflected the industry's concern for the purity of the
> wells' oil. In 1893, (for example,) regulations were
> (15)   enacted specifying well construction requirements to
> protect oil and gas reserves from contamination by
> fresh water.[11]

Here is a very common evidence Keyword: "for example." The author uses the example to illustrate the industry concerns mentioned in the first sentence. There aren't any obvious conclusion Keywords, but the presence of the example informs you that a conclusion is nearby. This is important to remember: The examples in a passage exist primarily to substantiate conclusions, so any time you see examples, you should also be on the lookout for a key idea.

Common evidence Keywords include "since," "because," and "for example." There is an abundance of conclusion Keywords, but some of the most common are "thus," "therefore," "as a result," and "in conclusion." Note that conclusions may also be identified by field-specific Keywords such as "hypothesis," "theory," and "interpretation." These are particularly common in natural science and law passages.

POV Keywords

POV (point of view) Keywords indicate that a point of view is about to be expressed, and they help you to differentiate one opinion from another in the passage. Since most passages contain

---

[10]PrepTest 42, Sec 3, Passage 3

[11]PrepTest 43, Sec 1, Passage 1

multiple viewpoints (including the author's), you must be careful not to confuse them. Here's an example that should look familiar:

(40)   This tactic, while often
effective, has been criticized by some legal scholars as
a pragmatic attempt to give judges nonlegal material
with which to fill gaps in their justifications for
decisions where the purely legal principles appear
(45)   inconclusive.[12]

It is very common for the author to present a criticism from a third party. Because this is the case, take care to note which opinions are the author's and which are not. In the above example, note that the author is stating that the tactic is effective, while the legal scholars are providing the criticism. Does the author agree with the critics? I hope your answer was, "I don't know." The author has neither disputed nor endorsed the critics' stance. Perhaps she will render an opinion at a later time, but for now, you should not make any assumptions beyond what is presented to us in the text of the passage.

POV Keywords generally appear as short phrases such as "according to," "the critics claim," "scholars agree," and "scientists hypothesize." Note that these phrases not only indicate that a claim is being made, but also who is making the claim.

Emphasis Keywords

At the beginning of this chapter I told you that one of the most important functions that Keywords serve is to denote emphasis. Look at one more example of an emphasis Keyword:

An essential element in the success of this tactic was
the explicit recognition that in a public interest legal
campaign, choosing the right plaintiff can mean the
(30)   difference between success and failure.[13]

Emphasis Keywords are extremely varied, and it would be almost impossible to list them all. This doesn't mean they're difficult to identify; they're simply words or phrases that indicate that a given concept is important or interesting. Common examples include "crucial," "essential," "vital," "of course," "interesting," and "important." The author may also use qualifying words and phrases to denote emphasis, such as "the most influential" or "the greatest reason." These are all just different ways the author might indicate the importance of an idea. And as I said before, anything that's important to the author is likely to be the subject of questions.

---

[12]PrepTest 42, Sec 3, Passage 1

[13]PrepTest 42, Sec 3, Passage 1

A slight variation on the emphasis Keyword is the opinion Keyword:

(50)
This version of history (patronizes) the Victorians, who were (in fact) well aware of their vulnerability to charges of condescension and complacency, but were equally well aware of the potential dangers of state-managed charity.[14]

In this example, the author uses the opinion Keyword "patronizes" to express disapproval of a particular historical viewpoint. He then introduces his contrary opinion with the phrase "in fact." Opinion Keywords usually indicate that the author is taking sides in a debate.

Please remember that these categories don't perfectly encapsulate every possible Keyword that you might encounter on the LSAT, and there are some Keywords that may seem to fit into multiple categories. But that's fine; on test day, you don't identify Keywords to categorize them. You identify them to break down the passage more efficiently and to answer the questions more easily.

---

[14] PrepTest 41, Sec 4, Passage 4

DRILL: IDENTIFYING KEYWORDS

Now try the following exercise. In each of the five excerpts below, identify and circle every Keyword you can find. Take your time; right now your goal is accuracy, not speed. Complete answers and explanations follow the drill. Be sure to read them carefully before you move on.

1.

Most Internet communication
(5)   consists of sending electronic mail or exchanging ideas
on electronic bulletin boards; however, a growing
number of transmissions are of copyrighted works—
books, photographs, videos and films, and sound
recordings.[15]

2.

But while many muralist works express populist or
nationalist ideas, it is a mistake to attempt to reduce
Mexican mural painting to formulaic, official
government art.[16]

3.

Moreover, while they shared a common interest in
rediscovering their Mexican national identity, they
(35)   developed their own distinct styles. Rivera, for
example, incorporated elements from pre-Columbian
sculpture and the Italian Renaissance fresco into his
murals and used a strange combination of mechanical
shapes to depict the faces and bodies of people.[17]

4.

Some experts propose simply adding unauthorized
digitalization to the list of activities proscribed under
current law, to make it clear that copyright holders own
(35)   electronic reproduction rights just as they own rights to
other types of reproduction. But criminalizing
digitalization raises a host of questions.[18]

5.

One fundamental assumption of wave
theory was that as the length of a wave of radiation
shortens, its energy increases smoothly—like a volume
(10)   dial on a radio that adjusts smoothly to any setting—
and that any conceivable energy value could thus occur
in nature.[19]

---

[15] PrepTest 39, Sec 3, Passage 4

[16] PrepTest 39, Sec 3, Passage 1

[17] PrepTest 39, Sec 3, Passage 1

[18] PrepTest 39, Sec 3, Passage 4

[19] PrepTest 39, Sec 3, Passage 3

Answer Explanations follow on the next page.

Explanations

Now compare your work to the explanations. Don't worry if you didn't find every Keyword, or if you identified Keywords that aren't listed here. Detecting Keywords isn't an exact science. Your goal is simply to understand which Keywords are the most important ones.

1.

(Most) Internet communication
(5) consists of sending electronic mail or exchanging ideas
on electronic bulletin boards; (however,) a growing
number of transmissions are of copyrighted works—
books, photographs, videos and films, and sound
recordings.[20]

The Keyword "most" suggests that a contrast is coming up, and sure enough, you soon see "however." This pair of Keywords allows you to quickly see that the author is pointing out an exception to the rule that will probably be discussed in greater detail.

2.

(But) while many muralist works express populist or
nationalist ideas, it is (a mistake) to attempt to reduce
Mexican mural painting to formulaic, official
government art.[21]

The sentence begins with a common contrast Keyword, "but," which tells you that this part of the passage is in opposition to what came before it. "A mistake" conveys the author's disapproval of the opinion that follows.

3.

(Moreover,) (while) they shared a common interest in
rediscovering their Mexican national identity, they
(35) developed their own (distinct) styles. Rivera, (for
example,) incorporated elements from pre-Columbian
sculpture and the Italian Renaissance fresco into his
murals and used a strange combination of mechanical
shapes to depict the faces and bodies of people.[22]

"Moreover" is a continuation Keyword and tells you that the author is extending whatever ideas were presented immediately before the excerpt. "While" sets up a potentially important contrast, leading to the emphasis that the author places on "distinct" styles; this is a great example

---

[20]PrepTest 39, Sec 3, Passage 4

[21]PrepTest 39, Sec 3, Passage 1

[22]PrepTest 39, Sec 3, Passage 1

of how Keywords work together to bracket an important idea. Finally, "for example" tells you that the author is mentioning Rivera in order to illustrate the distinct styles already mentioned.

4.

> (Some experts) propose simply adding unauthorized
> digitalization to the list of activities proscribed under
> current law, to make it clear that copyright holders own
> (35) electronic reproduction rights just as they own rights to
> other types of reproduction. (But) criminalizing
> digitalization raises a host of questions.[23]

Here is an excellent illustration of a common LSAT passage structure. The author introduces the opinion of "some experts" in the first sentence and then quickly raises doubts about their ideas by starting the next sentence with the contrast/opinion indicator "but."

5.

> One (fundamental) assumption of wave
> theory was that as the length of a wave of radiation
> shortens, its energy increases smoothly—(like) a volume
> (10) dial on a radio that adjusts smoothly to any setting—
> and that any conceivable energy value could (thus) occur
> in nature.[24]

Keywords are especially helpful in passages that feature technical language or abstract ideas. In this excerpt from a natural science passage, "fundamental" gives emphasis to the assumption described by the author. "Like" points to a useful illustration, and "thus" leads you to the assumption's conclusion.

WHAT KEYWORDS TELL YOU
Keywords Establish Context

So far I've shown you how to identify Keywords and encouraged you to circle them when you see them. This is an important habit to learn, so be sure to circle every Keyword you find in every passage you read, from now until test day. But merely identifying Keywords isn't enough.

When I first began to teach for Kaplan, I counseled a student who was experiencing a lot of frustration with strategic reading. I asked him to execute the first step of the Kaplan Method on a passage and I observed him while he worked, trying to pinpoint the problem. Within a few minutes he had read the passage and dutifully circled every Keyword. When he had finished, I asked him if he could tell me the Topic, Scope, Purpose, and Main Idea of the passage. He

---

[23] PrepTest 39, Sec 3, Passage 4
[24] PrepTest 39, Sec 3, Passage 3

replied, "No. I'm sorry, but I have no idea what I just read." I realized at that instant what his problem was: He was identifying the Keywords, but he wasn't thinking about what they were telling him. I was able to help him correct the problem, but I'd like you to avoid it altogether by thinking about the context of Keywords from day one.

Fortunately, you've already made good progress toward understanding this important concept. In the first half of this chapter, you learned that Keywords come in a variety of types. Now I'll show you how to use the Keywords to guide your reading.

The Two-Part Process

The process is very simple: First, every time you spot a Keyword, circle or underline it. Second, think about what the Keyword is telling you before reading on. By doing this, you keep focused on the most important information in the passage.

I want you to take a moment to think about what this really means. You can actually use the clues provided by the test maker to predict what is coming next in the passage, sentence by sentence and paragraph by paragraph. You can instantly separate crucial information from details likely to be untested. And you'll never become bogged down in a dense, difficult passage, because all of the clues you need are there to guide you. Does this sound too good to be true? Let me show you what I mean. Examine the first paragraph of a previously released passage and put this strategy to work.

> The myth persists that in 1492 the Western
> Hemisphere was an untamed wilderness and that it was
> European settlers who harnessed and transformed its
> ecosystems.[25]

This passage starts off with a great Keyword. "Myth" indicates that the author disagrees with the notion that an untamed wilderness existed prior to European settlement. So you know that the author holds a contrary opinion, and that he thinks the wilderness was already being transformed.

---

[25]PrepTest 38, Sec 3, Passage 1

(5) (But) scholarship shows that forests, (in) (particular,) had been altered to varying degrees well before the arrival of Europeans. Native populations had converted much of the forests to successfully cultivated stands, (especially) by means of burning. (Nevertheless,) (some researchers) have maintained that the extent,
(10) frequency, and impact of such burning was minimal. (One geographer claims) that climatic change could have accounted for some of the changes in forest composition; (another) (argues) that burning by native populations was done only sporadically, to augment the
(15) effects of natural fires.[26]

Unsurprisingly, the next sentence begins with a contrast Keyword. The author reveals that, contrary to the myth, native populations had been altering the environment. Also note the emphasis Keyword "especially." The passage will probably go into greater detail about the burning of forests as it proceeds.

"Nevertheless" immediately signals that a contrary opinion is about to be presented. You can even predict what it will be: Since the author believes that the native population *did* frequently burn forests, the opposing opinion must suggest that it did not. And that's exactly what you are told: Some researchers believe burning was minimal.

Next you reach the geographer's claim. Since there are no Keywords of contrast, you should expect this claim to support the "minimal burning" theory. Sure enough, that's what happens. The same goes for the other geographer. The geographers aren't really presenting any important new ideas; their claims are simply evidence in support of the broader claim that was made at the beginning of the first sentence.

Let me take a moment to summarize what a few well-placed Keywords told you about this paragraph. You were presented with a myth that the author disagreed with. Then several supporters of the original myth were cited. In all of the text of the first paragraph, *that's all that really happened!* This is the true power of strategic reading. You just broke an entire paragraph down into two simple sentences, a skill that you will further hone in chapter 3. But first, try out your Keyword skills with a brief exercise:

---

[26]PrepTest 38, Sec 3, Passage 1

DRILL: WORKING WITH KEYWORDS

In this exercise, I'll present you with excerpts from two Reading Comprehension passages. Read each one, circle any Keywords you identify, and answer the questions in your own words. The questions will help you think about what the Keywords are telling you and what you should expect as a consequence. Take your time with this exercise and make sure you understand each example. I've provided explanations after the drill.

1.

> Because the memoirs were written so long after the events they describe, some historians question their reliability. Certainly,[27]

Whose point of view is presented here?

_____

What is the author likely to describe next?

_____

2.

> Certainly, memory is subject to the loss or
> confusion of facts and, more to the point in these
> (20) partisan accounts, to the distortions of a mind intent on
> preserving its particular picture of the past. But[28]

On which idea does the author place the most emphasis?

_____

What will happen next?

_____

3.

> But other
> scholars have shown that close inspection of these
> documents resolves such doubts on two scores.[29]

What Keywords should we expect immediately after this sentence?

_____

---

[27]PrepTest 35, Sec 2, Passage 1
[28]PrepTest 35, Sec 2, Passage 1
[29]PrepTest 35, Sec 2, Passage 1

The following three exercises are from a tougher passage, one that deals with abstract natural science concepts. But don't worry; you can apply the same thinking to simplify complex ideas!

4.

(15) Philosophers of science have not been alone in claiming that science must consist of universal laws.[30]

Whose point of view does the author describe?

_____

What point of view will be described next?

_____

5.

Some evolutionary biologists have also acceded to the general intellectual disdain for the merely particular and tried to emulate physicists, constructing their
(20) science as a set of universal laws. In formulating the notion of a universal "struggle for existence" that is the engine of biological history or in asserting that virtually all DNA evolves at a constant clocklike rate, they have attempted to find their own versions of the
(25) law of gravity. Recently, however,[31]

Use the context of what you've read so far to write a simplified version of the first sentence.

_____

What purpose does the second sentence serve?

_____

What will the author describe next?

_____

6.

(25) Recently, however, some biologists have questioned whether biological history is really the necessary unfolding of universal laws of life, and they have raised the possibility that historical contingency is an integral factor in biology.[32]

What does the phrase "historical contingency" mean in the context of this sentence?

_____

_____

[30] PrepTest 35, Sec 2, Passage 3
[31] PrepTest 35, Sec 2, Passage 3
[32] PrepTest 35, Sec 2, Passage 3

Explanations

1.

> (Because) the memoirs were written so long after the
> events they describe, (some historians) question their
> reliability. (Certainly,)[33]

Whose point of view is presented here?

The point of view of "some historians" is being described in this sentence. Be sure to note that you can't yet ascertain whether the author agrees with the historians.

What is the author likely to describe next?

In order to know what's coming next, think about the Keyword, "certainly." What idea did the author present immediately prior to this Keyword? It was the opinion of the historians, that the memoirs may not be reliable. Since "certainly" is a Keyword of continuation, you should expect the author to provide some details concerning this lack of reliability. You should similarly expect that the author will agree to some extent with the historians.

2.

> (Certainly,) memory is subject to the loss or
> confusion of facts and, (more to)(the point) in these
> (20)   partisan accounts, to the distortions of a mind intent on
> preserving its particular picture of the past. (But)[34]

On which idea does the author place the most emphasis?

As predicted, the author is now describing ways in which a memoir might be unreliable. He describes two main reasons: faulty memory and deliberate distortion. Of these two, the second is more central to the author's argument. Why? Because it is signaled by the Keywords "more to the point," which indicate clear emphasis. When several similar ideas are presented to you in a passage, look for any clues that may tell you which are most important.

What will happen next?

Once again, you've got an excellent Keyword to help you stay one step ahead of the author. The contrast word "but" tells you that the author is going to change course. Here's an important question to consider: In the context of what you've read so far, do you think the author will disagree with the details you just read (reasons for unreliability) or with the historians' conclusion presented in exercise 1 (the memoirs may be unreliable)? Since the details are only there to support the conclusion, the conclusion is more important. Hence, the author will probably argue that the memoirs are reliable after all.

---

[33]PrepTest 35, Sec 2, Passage 1
[34]PrepTest 35, Sec 2, Passage 1

3.

> (But) (other)
> (scholars) have shown that close inspection of these
> documents resolves such doubts on (two scores).[35]

What Keywords should we expect immediately after this sentence?

When a sentence ends with a clear indicator of structure like "two scores," you should be on the alert for Keywords that will help you easily find each one of the arguments that the author is preparing to introduce. Incidentally, here is the text that follows, with two expected Keywords identified:

> (First)
> for major public happenings, there are often multiple
> (25) accounts, allowing for cross-verification. (Second)
> regarding the truth of personal events known only to
> the author, more subjective guidelines must be used:[36]

Once again, you can see that Keywords work together in order to help you easily break down the structure of a passage.

4.
(15) (Philosophers of science) have not been alone in
      (claiming) that science must consist of universal laws.[37]

Whose point of view does the author describe?

The author describes a central claim of the "philosophers of science" in this sentence. Even though this passage contains potentially intimidating subject matter, the same common Keywords are there to help guide you through the text.

What point of view will be described next?

Hopefully you clued in on the words "have not been alone." They indicate that another party is about to be introduced to the conversation, one that will express agreement with the philosophers. In an abstract passage like this one, it's a good idea to make sure you're comfortable with the primary point of agreement before you move on. In this case, the philosophers claim that science consists of universal laws. If you don't yet understand what that means, don't worry. You'll probably get a more detailed description when the author introduces the next point of view.

_____

[35] PrepTest 35, Sec 2, Passage 1
[36] PrepTest 35, Sec 2, Passage 1
[37] PrepTest 35, Sec 2, Passage 3

5.

> (Some) evolutionary biologists have (also) acceded to the
> general intellectual disdain for the (merely) particular
> and tried to emulate physicists, constructing their
> (20) science as a set of universal laws. (In formulating) the
> notion of a universal "struggle for existence" that is the
> engine of biological history or in asserting that
> virtually all DNA evolves at a constant clocklike rate,
> they have (attempted) to find their own versions of the
> (25) law of gravity. (Recently,) (however,)[38]

Use the context of what you've read so far to write a simplified version of the first sentence. This might have been a little tricky. Take a look at the clues you have to work with. The author is now describing the views of the evolutionary biologists. You know that their views are in accordance with the philosophers from the previous sentence. Both groups seem to be interested in describing science as "universal" in some way. Whenever you see a term like this one repeated in a passage, it's sure to be important. So you could simplify this sentence like so: "The biologists want their science to be universal." Your answer may have included some other details, and that's fine. The main thing I'm pointing out in this example is that LSAT passages will frequently bury simple ideas in piles of complex text. As you master the Kaplan Method, you'll become better and better at looking beyond the jargon.

What purpose does the second sentence serve?

The second sentence is long and complex and deals with abstract ideas. But why is it really here? The Keywords "in formulating" probably indicate continuation, so this entire sentence is likely to be a long example that backs up what you already know: The biologists want their science to be universal. Since you never want to get bogged down in the details of a passage, you should read through this example quickly without trying to understand it in depth. It's more important to know *why* the evidence is here than to know exactly what it's saying. Thinking this way will keep you focused on the big picture as you read and save you time as you proceed toward the question set.

What will the author describe next?

"However" at the end of the excerpt tells you that dissenting opinions are about to appear. What are they likely to say? That science *doesn't* have to be universal. This prediction will help you understand the next sentence.

---

[38]PrepTest 35, Sec 2, Passage 3

6.

> ⟨Recently,⟩⟨however,⟩ some ⟨biologists⟩
> have ⟨questioned⟩ whether biological history is really the
> necessary unfolding of universal laws of life, and they
> (30) have ⟨raised the⟩⟨possibility⟩ that historical contingency is
> an integral factor in biology.[39]

What does the phrase "historical contingency" mean in the context of this sentence?

Here's your opportunity to pull it all together and clear up this dense passage. The prediction was correct: The author introduces some new biologists who question the ideas of the other biologists. What idea do they challenge? As you know, they must be against the idea of universal laws in their science. So when you see an unfamiliar phrase like "historical contingency," you can use what you've already learned to make sense of it. It must be the opposite of universal laws. From the clues in the previous sentences, you've probably deduced that universal laws refer to laws that are true all the time. Historical contingency must therefore relate somehow to laws that *aren't* always true. Once again, strategic reading helps you simplify the structure and meaning of complex ideas.

KEYWORDS RAISE YOUR SCORE

You now have a good idea about what Keywords are, how to identify them, and what they tell you about the structure and meaning of a passage. This is very important, because they form the foundation of strategic reading. You may be worried at this point that circling the Keywords and thinking about the structure they provide will be too time consuming to be useful on test day. As with any other new skill that you learn, this one may not be easy at first. But with practice, you'll soon find that working with Keywords becomes a natural and automatic part of your approach to Reading Comprehension. And since Keywords clue you in to the most important ideas in the passage, mastery of Keywords will raise your LSAT score. I'll show you how in chapter 3.

---

[39]PrepTest 35, Sec 2, Passage 3

CHAPTER 3

BUILDING A ROADMAP

THE ROADMAP DEFINED
How Do You Get Where You're Going?

Imagine that you're in Dallas and you need to drive to Chicago. You're on a very tight schedule, and you need to get there as quickly as possible . . . and as luck would have it, you've never even been to Chicago before. How do you ensure a successful trip?

You probably know that Chicago is somewhere northeast of Dallas, so perhaps you could just start driving north, getting hints from whatever signs you happen to see on your way, and work out your route as you go. But this is clearly a flawed plan. You may or may not actually end up at your destination, and even if you do, you're not likely to make very good time. Imagine the anxiety you would feel if your were actually in this situation. You would never do this in real life, except as a last resort.

An alternative would be to get a detailed map of North America and consult it as you drive. This is a better approach, but it still has some problems. Certainly it may help you stay on course city by city as you make your way to Chicago, but it's also likely to contain a lot of distracting information that isn't directly relevant to your goal. It will likely present you with a number of different possible routes you could take, while providing little or no information about which route is the fastest. If you choose this solution you're probably going to reach your destination, but not as efficiently as you might like.

Now imagine what you almost certainly *would* do in this situation. You would probably use a GPS or an online navigation service that would show you precisely which route to take. You could specify that you want to take the fastest route available and be sure that the information you receive is accurate and up to date. In addition to detailed directions, you'll also get a roadmap displaying the specific route you wish to take. This is definitely the way to travel; you'll reach your destination, and you'll get there at top speed.

So the answer to the original question should be clear: To ensure a successful trip, you don't set off at random, and you don't consult useless information. You use a Roadmap.

Reading Without Direction

I'm sure you've already realized that the above example is illustrative of the way you should approach Reading Comprehension on the LSAT, but I'd like to break down the analogy a little before moving on.

The first approach I asked you to consider in the Chicago scenario was that of driving off in the general direction of your destination with no guidance except for a vague notion of where you think you should go. This is obviously a bad idea, and yet it is the approach that most of my students initially employ when faced with Reading Comprehension. I had one student in particular who, before starting her class, was absolutely convinced that it was impossible to complete all four passages in the alotted 35 minutes. It didn't take me long to discover why.

I observed her as she attempted to read a passage and answer its questions. She skimmed the passage, taking no notes, and then began to grapple with the questions. Each time she came to a new question she would go back to the passage and carefully re-read entire paragraphs from beginning to end. She often repeated this exercise for each answer choice. By the time she answered all of the questions nearly fifteen minutes had elapsed. Even if she answered every question correctly she would almost certainly have to guess at an equal number as time began to run out. It's no wonder she was frustrated.

When my students get into time trouble, it's usually because they aren't reading with any direction, and therefore are constantly lost. They're lost when they read the passage, they're lost when they read a question, and they're lost when they try to evaluate the answer choices. And since we know that the LSAT awards efficiency, being lost is big trouble. If this sounds like you, don't worry. In this chapter I'm going to show you how to take control of the passage and provide yourself with the guidance you need.

Reading Without a Goal

Think back to the second solution to the Chicago travel problem, referring to a detailed map of North America. In the context of the example, you can easily see why that's not the ideal solution. But once again, this is exactly the type of approach that unprepared test takers often use.

My students are very aware that after they read a passage, they're going to have to answer a series of questions based on its content. With that awareness comes a very strong desire to thoroughly understand everything in the passage. So their initial inclination is to read each sentence with great care, absorbing every example, parsing each jargon-laden sentence, struggling with all the concepts. If they don't understand something, they read it again and again until it makes sense. This is a time-consuming process, but it makes them feel prepared for anything the question set may happen to throw at them.

But a strange thing happens. Despite all that careful reading, they find they still don't really have a clear understanding of what the passage was all about. Questions about the author's opinions are challenging because those opinions got lost in the barrage of ideas they encountered. Most frustrating of all, when they try to answer questions about the very details they spent so much time reading, they find that they have to go right back to the passage and read them all over again. If they try to rely on memory, they lose points because their recollection of the material isn't as complete as they think it is. In short, test takers who try to read for total comprehension become mired in unimportant details, and as a result they waste time and they score fewer points.

If this sounds like you, take heart. You've already learned about the importance of Keywords, and you're using them to help you read more actively. Now you're ready to take your mastery of strategic reading to the next level.

Reading the Kaplan Way

Returning one final time to our Chicago trip, it's easy to see that the third solution, the one that you almost certainly came up with on your own, is clearly superior to the others. A specific, guided roadmap keeps you from wandering aimlessly. At the same time, it helps you stay focused on the goal and avoid wasteful digressions.

Most LSAT Reading Comprehension questions test your understanding of the major themes contained in the passage, but some simply ask for specific details. You therefore must read the passage in a very focused way. You've got to understand the big ideas, while at the same time knowing where crucial details can be found if you need them. Let me emphasize this extremely important concept: You absolutely do not have time to dwell on the details of the passage the first time you read, because when questions ask for them, you're going to have to revisit the passage and examine the relevant text anyway.

This brings me to the solution, which I introduced you to briefly in chapter 1. The test makers don't provide you with a Roadmap to guide you through the passage. So in this chapter, I'll show you how to create one yourself, and how it will help you score more points in less time.

BUILDING A ROADMAP

I'll begin with an experiment. Try reading this LSAT passage without taking any notes. Read as quickly as you are able.

Wherever the crime novels of P. D. James are discussed by critics, there is a tendency on the one hand to exaggerate her merits and on the other to castigate her as a genre writer who is getting above
(5) herself. Perhaps underlying the debate is that familiar, false opposition set up between different kinds of fiction, according to which enjoyable novels are held to be somehow slightly lowbrow, and a novel is not considered true literature unless it is a tiny bit dull.

(10) Those commentators who would elevate James's books to the status of high literature point to her painstakingly constructed characters, her elaborate settings, her sense of place, and her love of abstractions: notions about morality, duty, pain, and
(15) pleasure are never far from the lips of her police officers and murderers. Others find her pretentious and tiresome; an inverted snobbery accuses her of abandoning the time-honored conventions of the detective genre in favor of a highbrow literary style.
(20) The critic Harriet Waugh wants P. D. James to get on with "the more taxing business of laying a tricky trail and then fooling the reader"; Philip Oakes in *The Literary Review* groans, "Could we please proceed with the business of clapping the handcuffs on the
(25) killer?"

James is certainly capable of strikingly good writing. She takes immense trouble to provide her characters with convincing histories and passions. Her descriptive digressions are part of the pleasure of her
(30) books and give them dignity and weight. But it is equally true that they frequently interfere with the story; the patinas and aromas of a country kitchen receive more loving attention than does the plot itself. Her devices to advance the story can be shameless and
(35) thin, and it is often impossible to see how her detective arrives at the truth; one is left to conclude that the detective solves crimes through intuition. At this stage in her career P. D. James seems to be less interested in the specifics of detection than in her characters'
(40) vulnerabilities and perplexities.

However, once the rules of a chosen genre cramp creative thought, there is no reason why an able and interesting writer should accept them. In her latest book, there are signs that James is beginning to feel
(45) constrained by the crime-novel genre. Here her determination to leave areas of ambiguity in the solution of the crime and to distribute guilt among the murderer, victim, and bystanders points to a conscious rebellion against the traditional neatness of detective
(50) fiction. It is fashionable, though reprehensible, for one writer to prescribe to another. But perhaps the time has come for P. D. James to slide out of her handcuffs and stride into the territory of the mainstream novel.[1]

[1]PrepTest 19, Sec 3, Passage 1

Now think about what you just read. Test your memory of the passage with a few questions. Can you describe the primary complaint leveled against James by her critics? Did the author agree or disagree with the critics? What was the primary purpose of the second paragraph of the passage?

Some of these questions may be easier to answer than others, but taken together, they present a daunting challenge. Your first instinct is probably to review the text of the passage to find the answers, but where do you start? The confusion that you experience when you read a passage quickly rather than efficiently is a liability to your LSAT score. Fortunately, there's a better way. It's time to build your first Roadmap. Building a good Roadmap is a natural extension of the thinking you apply when you seek out Keywords As you identify important ideas, jot down a couple of brief notes in the margins of the paragraph summarizing them. Your notes should include authorial opinion, key conclusions, and alternating points of view. I'm going to guide you through the process paragraph by paragraph.

Read the following excerpt, noting the circled Keywords and thinking about what they mean. The author begins by describing critics' different views of P.D. James's works. It's not unusual for the first paragraph of a passage to introduce conflicting ideas; they tend to form the basis for what is to follow. Since this is structurally important, jot down some brief notes in the margin of the paragraph summarizing the dichotomy:

Critics: Praise
James or
attack her

Wherever the crime novels of P. D. James are discussed by critics, there is a tendency on the one hand to exaggerate her merits and on the other to castigate her as a genre writer who is getting above
(5) herself. Perhaps underlying the debate is that familiar, false opposition set up between different kinds of fiction, according to which enjoyable novels are held to be somehow slightly lowbrow, and a novel is not considered true literature unless it is a tiny bit dull.[2]

Notice that the notes do not restate in detail information that is already in the passage; they simply point the way to it. You should follow this principle when building your own Roadmaps. In general, keep your annotations as concise as possible. Abbreviations and other forms of shorthand are useful, as long as you can clearly understand what you've written. Note also that I've indicated that it is the critics who are attacking or praising James as opposed to the author.

As you move on through the paragraph, you should pay particular attention to the opinion/emphasis keyword "false." The author tells you that the debate is based on a false opposition. This is *extremely* important, as it's your first clue about the author's attitude. You should annotate this as well.

---

[2]PrepTest 19, Sec 3, Passage 1

Critics: Praise
James or
attack her

Auth: False
opp.

(Wherever) the crime novels of P. D. James are discussed by (critics,) there is a tendency (on the one) hand to exaggerate her merits and (on the other) to castigate her as a genre writer who is getting above
(5) herself. Perhaps (underlying) the debate is that familiar (false) opposition set up (between) different kinds of fiction, (according to) which enjoyable novels are held to be somehow slightly lowbrow, (and) a novel is not considered true literature unless it is a tiny bit dull.[3]

And with that, you've successfully Roadmapped paragraph 1. Take a moment to appreciate this accomplishment: When you write a Roadmap, you pare down an entire paragraph into a few words, and you give yourself exactly the guidance you need if a question directs you back to these concepts. On test day, this kind of guidance will improve both your timing and your accuracy.

Now read the next paragraph. Again, take note of the Keywords, but this time try to summarize the main ideas yourself before reading on.

(10) Those (commentators) who would (elevate) James's books to the status of high literature (point to) her painstakingly constructed characters, her elaborate settings, her sense of place, and her love of (abstractions:) notions about morality, duty, pain, and
(15) pleasure are never far from the lips of her police officers and murderers. (Others) find her pretentious and tiresome; an inverted snobbery (accuses) her of abandoning the time-honored conventions of the detective genre (in favor of) a highbrow literary style.
(20) The (critic) Harriet Waugh wants P. D. James to get on with "the more taxing business of laying a tricky trail and then fooling the reader"; Philip Oakes in *The Literary Review* (groans,) "Could we please proceed with the business of clapping the handcuffs on the
(25) killer?"[4]

A good question to stay in the habit of asking yourself when you read is, "Why is the author telling me this?" You recall from the first paragraph that various critics are at odds with one another regarding James's work. All this paragraph does is flesh out that idea by giving examples. Should you attempt to memorize all of these examples? Absolutely not! Just note that if a question requires in-depth knowledge of the critics' opinions, this is the paragraph you should come to.

---

[3]PrepTest 19, Sec 3, Passage 1
[4]PrepTest 19, Sec 3, Passage 1

Critics:
opinions about
James

(10)   Those commentators who would elevate James's
books to the status of high literature point to her
painstakingly constructed characters, her elaborate
settings, her sense of place, and her love of
abstractions: notions about morality, duty, pain, and
(15)   pleasure are never far from the lips of her police
officers and murderers. Others find her pretentious and
tiresome; an inverted snobbery accuses her of
abandoning the time-honored conventions of the
detective genre in favor of a highbrow literary style.
(20)   The critic Harriet Waugh wants P. D. James to get on
with "the more taxing business of laying a tricky trail
and then fooling the reader"; Philip Oakes in *The
Literary Review* groans, "Could we please proceed
with the business of clapping the handcuffs on the
(25)   killer?"[5]

You might be thinking, "Is that really all I should be writing down?" The answer: probably. All of my students have their own Roadmapping styles, and while there are good principles to follow, there are few definitive rules. For instance, perhaps you would rather write your Roadmap for paragraph two more like this:

Critics: who
like James

(10)   Those commentators who would elevate James's
books to the status of high literature point to her
painstakingly constructed characters, her elaborate
settings, her sense of place, and her love of
abstractions: notions about morality, duty, pain, and
(15)   pleasure are never far from the lips of her police

Critics: who
dislike James

officers and murderers. Others find her pretentious and
tiresome; an inverted snobbery accuses her of
abandoning the time-honored conventions of the
detective genre in favor of a highbrow literary style.
(20)   The critic Harriet Waugh wants P. D. James to get on
with "the more taxing business of laying a tricky trail
and then fooling the reader"; Philip Oakes in *The
Literary Review* groans, "Could we please proceed
with the business of clapping the handcuffs on the
(25)   killer?"[6]

Is one way better than the other? Not really. As long as your Roadmap is clear, concise, accurate, and useful, you're doing it correctly.

---

[5]PrepTest 19, Sec 3, Passage 1

[6]PrepTest 19, Sec 3, Passage 1

Ready for paragraph three? As before, try to come up with your own notes as you read:

> James is certainly capable of (strikingly) good
> writing. She takes (immense) trouble to provide her
> characters with convincing histories and passions. Her
> descriptive digressions are part of the pleasure of her
> (30) books (and) give them dignity and weight. (But) it is
> equally true that they frequently interfere with the
> story; the patinas and aromas of a country kitchen
> receive more loving attention (than) does the plot itself.
> Her devices to advance the story can be (shameless) and
> (35) thin, (and) it is often impossible to see how her detective
> arrives at the truth; one is left to (conclude) that the
> detective solves crimes through intuition. At (this stage)
> in her career P. D. James seems to be (less) interested in
> the specifics of detection (than) in her characters'
> (40) vulnerabilities and perplexities.[7]

I hope you noticed right away whose opinion is presented in this paragraph. When the author speaks, it's time to pay attention. Has the author sided with one group of critics over the other? To the contrary, she's in agreement to some extent with both camps, noting toward the end of the paragraph that James's most recent work shows a preference for character development over plot.

> **Auth: James is striking writer**
>
> James is certainly capable of (strikingly) good
> writing. She takes (immense) trouble to provide her
> characters with convincing histories and passions. Her
> descriptive digressions are part of the pleasure of her
> (30) books (and) give them dignity and weight. (But) it is
> equally true that they frequently interfere with the
> story; the patinas and aromas of a country kitchen
> receive more loving attention (than) does the plot itself.
> Her devices to advance the story can be (shameless) and
> **Sometimes bad**
> **for plot** (35) thin, (and) it is often impossible to see how her detective
> arrives at the truth; one is left to conclude that the
> detective solves crimes through intuition. At (this stage)
> in her career P. D. James seems to be (less) interested in
> the specifics of detection (than) in her characters'
> (40) vulnerabilities and perplexities.[8]

Now you have a nice summary of the author's attitudes, and you know exactly where to do your research if you need to examine them in detail.

One more paragraph to go. Another common pattern you should expect to encounter in LSAT passages is a final paragraph that summarizes the author's primary viewpoint, sometimes going in directions you didn't necessarily see coming. The author ultimately supports James's

---

[7]PrepTest 19, Sec 3, Passage 1
[8]PrepTest 19, Sec 3, Passage 1

"rebellion" against the norms of the crime novel and even suggests that she should consider leaving it behind:

Auth: James not limited by genre

(45)

(50)

Auth: James maybe go mainstr.

(However,) once the rules of a chosen genre cramp creative thought, there is (no reason) why an able and interesting writer should accept them. In her (latest) book, there are signs that James is beginning to (feel) constrained by the crime-novel genre. Here her (determination) to leave areas of ambiguity in the solution of the crime (and) to distribute guilt among the murderer, victim, and bystanders (points to) a conscious (rebellion) against the (traditional) neatness of detective fiction. It is fashionable, (though reprehensible,) for one writer to prescribe to another. (But) perhaps the time has come for P. D. James to slide out of her handcuffs (and) stride into the territory of the mainstream novel.[9]

Well done. You've just completed your first Roadmap. By thinking through the core ideas of every paragraph, you accomplish a number of goals: You give yourself points of reference, you elucidate the structure of the passage, and you solidify your own understanding of what the passage is saying. With careful practice, creating Roadmaps will become second nature to you, and in a moment I'll give you a drill to get some practice. But first, take a look at how a good Roadmap helps you to answer questions quickly and correctly:

3. The second paragraph serves primarily to

    (A) propose an alternative to two extreme opinions described earlier
    (B) present previously mentioned positions in greater detail
    (C) contradict an assertion cited previously
    (D) introduce a controversial interpretation
    (E) analyze a dilemma in greater depth[10]

This question type requires you to quickly summarize the purpose of the second paragraph. You need look no further than your Roadmap to predict the correct answer:

Critics: Praise James or attack her

(5)

Auth: False opp.

(Wherever) the crime novels of P. D. James are discussed by (critics,) there is a tendency (on the one) hand to exaggerate her merits and (on the other) to castigate her as a genre writer who is getting above herself. Perhaps (underlying) the debate is that familiar, (false) opposition set up (between) different kinds of fiction, (according to) which enjoyable novels are held to be somehow slightly lowbrow, (and) a novel is not considered true literature unless it is a tiny bit dull.

Critics: who like James

(10)   Those commentators who would elevate James's books to the status of high literature point to her painstakingly constructed characters, her elaborate settings, her sense of place, and her love of abstractions: notions about morality, duty, pain, and

(15) pleasure are never far from the lips of her police

Critics: who dislike James

officers and murderers. Others find her pretentious and tiresome; an inverted snobbery accuses her of abandoning the time-honored conventions of the detective genre in favor of a highbrow literary style.

(20) The critic Harriet Waugh wants P. D. James to get on with "the more taxing business of laying a tricky trail and then fooling the reader"; Philip Oakes in *The Literary Review* groans, "Could we please proceed with the business of clapping the handcuffs on the

(25) killer?"

Auth: James very descriptive

James is certainly capable of strikingly good writing. She takes immense trouble to provide her characters with convincing histories and passions. Her descriptive digressions are part of the pleasure of her

(30) books and give them dignity and weight. But it is equally true that they frequently interfere with the story; the patinas and aromas of a country kitchen receive more loving attention than does the plot itself.

Auth: Sometimes bad for plot

Her devices to advance the story can be shameless and

(35) thin, and it is often impossible to see how her detective arrives at the truth; one is left to conclude that the detective solves crimes through intuition. At this stage in her career P. D. James seems to be less interested in the specifics of detection than in her characters'

(40) vulnerabilities and perplexities.

Auth: James not limited by genre

However, once the rules of a chosen genre cramp creative thought, there is no reason why an able and interesting writer should accept them. In her latest book, there are signs that James is beginning to feel

(45) constrained by the crime-novel genre. Here her determination to leave areas of ambiguity in the solution of the crime and to distribute guilt among the murderer victim, and bystanders points to a conscious rebellion against the traditional neatness of detective

(50) fiction. It is fashionable, though reprehensible, for one

Auth: James maybe go mainstr.

writer to prescribe to another. But perhaps the time has come for P. D. James to slide out of her handcuffs and stride into the territory of the mainstream novel.[11]

---

[11]PrepTest 19, Sec 3, Passage 1

The Roadmap reminds you that this paragraph supplies examples of the critics mentioned in the first paragraph. Armed with this prediction, the correct answer must be choice (B). The Roadmap allows you to score this point in a matter of seconds. Try one more question:

2. The author refers to the "patinas and aromas of a country kitchen" (line 32) most probably in order to

    (A) illustrate James's gift for innovative phrasing
    (B) highlight James's interest in rural society
    (C) allow the reader to experience the pleasure of James's books
    (D) explain how James typically constructs her plots
    (E) exemplify James's preoccupation with descriptive writing[12]

At first you might think that the Roadmap isn't particularly useful in answering this question. After all, you've already got a specific line reference. But be careful: The test maker is asking you to explain *why* the author used this example, and this requires you to read for context. The Roadmap is exceptionally useful for providing such context:

Auth: James is striking writer

> James is certainly capable of (strikingly) good writing. She takes (immense) trouble to provide her characters with convincing histories and passions. Her descriptive digressions are part of the pleasure of her
> (30) books (and) give them dignity and weight. (But) it is equally true that they frequently interfere with the story; the patinas and aromas of a country kitchen receive more loving attention (than) does the plot itself.

Auth: Sometimes bad for plot

> Her devices to advance the story can be (shameless) and
> (35) thin, (and) it is often impossible to see how her detective arrives at the truth; one is left to conclude that the detective solves crimes through intuition. At (this stage) in her career P. D. James seems to be (less) interested in the specifics of detection (than) in her characters'
> (40) vulnerabilities and perplexities.[13]

At the point in which the quote from the question appears, you noted that the author was agreeing with the critics who find James overly expressive. A quick glance at the surrounding text confirms this prediction, and you should confidently choose choice (E), the correct answer.

Now that you understand how to construct a Roadmap and how to put it to good use, it's time for some practice.

---

[12]PrepTest 19, Sec 3, Q 2

[13]PrepTest 19, Sec 3, Passage 1

DRILL: CONSTRUCTING A ROADMAP

Part 1: Read the following passage, circling Keywords as you go. As you discover major ideas and key examples, note them in your Roadmap. When you've finished, carefully compare your Roadmap to the one I provide in the explanations. Take your time, and don't worry if this first Roadmap is a little tough to build. You'll have plenty of opportunities to practice as you continue to prepare for the LSAT.

Even in the midst of its resurgence as a vital tradition, many sociologists have viewed the current form of the powwow, a ceremonial gathering of native Americans, as a sign that tribal culture is in decline.
(5) Focusing on the dances and rituals that have recently come to be shared by most tribes, they suggest that an intertribal movement is now in ascension and claim the inevitable outcome of this tendency is the eventual dissolution of tribes and the complete assimilation of
(10) native Americans into Euroamerican society. Proponents of this "Pan-Indian" theory point to the greater frequency of travel and communication between reservations, the greater urbanization of native Americans, and, most recently, their increasing
(15) politicization in response to common grievances as the chief causes of the shift toward intertribalism.

Indeed, the rapid diffusion of dance styles, outfits, and songs from one reservation to another offers compelling evidence that intertribalism has been
(20) increasing. However, these sociologists have failed to note the concurrent revitalization of many traditions unique to individual tribes. Among the Lakota, for instance, the Sun Dance was revived, after a forty-year hiatus, during the 1950's. Similarly, the Black Legging
(25) Society of the Kiowa and the Hethuska Society of the Ponca—both traditional groups within their respective tribes—have gained new popularity. Obviously, a more complex societal shift is taking place than the theory of Pan-Indianism can account for.

(30) An examination of the theory's underpinnings may be critical at this point, especially given that native Americans themselves chafe most against the Pan-Indian classification. Like other assimilationist theories with which it is associated, the Pan-Indian view is
(35) predicated upon an a priori assumption about the nature of cultural contact: that upon contact minority societies immediately begin to succumb in every respect—biologically, linguistically, and culturally—to the majority society. However, there is no evidence
(40) that this is happening to native American groups.

Yet the fact remains that intertribal activities are a major facet of native American culture today. Certain dances at powwows, for instance, are announced as intertribal, others as traditional. Likewise, speeches
(45) given at the beginnings of powwows are often delivered in English, while the prayer that follows is usually spoken in a native language. Cultural borrowing is, of course, old news. What is important to note is the conscious distinction native Americans
(50) make between tribal and intertribal tendencies.

Tribalism, although greatly altered by modern history, remains a potent force among native Americans: It forms a basis for tribal identity, and aligns music and dance with other social and cultural
(55) activities important to individual tribes. Intertribal activities, on the other hand, reinforce native American identity along a broader front, where this identity is directly threatened by outside influences.[14]

[14]PrepTest 25, Sec 1, Passage 3

Answer Explanations follow on the next page.

Explanations

Compare your Roadmap to mine, paragraph by paragraph:

Soc: gatherings mean tribal decline

(5)

(10)

Pan-Indian theory, evidence

(15)

(Even) in the midst of its (resurgence) as a vital tradition, many (sociologists) have viewed the current form of the powwow, a ceremonial gathering of native Americans, (as a sign) that tribal culture is in decline. (Focusing) on the dances and rituals that have (recently) come to be shared by most tribes, they (suggest) that an intertribal movement is now in ascension and (claim) the (inevitable) outcome of this tendency is the eventual dissolution of tribes and the complete assimilation of native Americans into Euroamerican society. (Proponents) of this "Pan-Indian" theory (point to) the greater frequency of travel and communication between reservations, the greater urbanization of native Americans, (and,) most (recently,) their increasing politicization in (response) to common grievances as the chief causes of the shift toward intertribalism.[15]

This first paragraph is a little wordy, but there were plenty of Keywords to guide you. The author is describing the proponents of a "Pan-Indian" theory that suggests tribal culture is in decline. Notice that the author is using several different terms to describe the same idea: "Pan-Indian" theory and "intertribalism" in particular. I hope you noted that the last sentence of this paragraph gives a list of reasons why the proponets support this theory; such key evidence may be the subject of questions.

Auth: Intertribalism on rise

(20)

Unique traditions rising too

(25)

Auth: P.I.T doesn't explain

(Indeed,) the rapid diffusion of dance styles, outfits, and songs from one reservation to another offers (compelling evidence) that intertribalism has been increasing. (However,) these (sociologists) have (failed) to note the concurrent revitalization of many traditions unique to individual tribes. (Among) the Lakota, for (instance,) the Sun Dance was revived, after a forty-year hiatus, during the 1950's. (Similarly,) the Black Legging Society of the Kiowa and the Hethuska Society of the Ponca—(both) traditional groups within their respective tribes—have gained (new popularity.) (Obviously,) a more complex societal shift is taking place (than) the theory of Pan-Indianism can account for.[16]

The Keyword "Indeed" at the beginning of this paragraph signals continuation, but you should really focus on the text following "However" in the second sentence. This contrast alerts you to the author's true intent: To indicate that individual tribes have revitalized their own traditions, a fact that the sociologists from paragraph 1 have overlooked. (I've used the abbreviation P.I.T. to refer to the sociologists' Pan-Indian Theory. Remember, shorthand can streamline the

---

[15]PrepTest 25, Sec 1, Passage 3

[16]PrepTest 25, Sec 1, Passage 3

Roadmapping process as long as it doesn't interfere with clarity.) This idea is reinforced in the final sentence, introduced by the emphasis Keyword "Obviously."

Auth: must
examine theory

Theory based on
wrong assump.

(30)   An (examination) of the theory's underpinnings may
be (critical) at this point, (especially) given that native
Americans themselves (chafe most) against the Pan-
Indian classification. (Like) other assimilationist theories
with which it is associated, the Pan-Indian view is
(35)   (predicated upon) an a priori assumption about the nature
of cultural contact: that (upon) contact minority
societies (immediately) begin to succumb in every
respect—biologically, linguistically, and culturally—to
the majority society. (However,) there is (no evidence)
(40)   that this is happening to native American groups.[17]

Look at the profusion of emphasis Keywords that begin this sentence: A look at the theory is "critical," "especially" because native Americans aren't fans of it. When the author is this clear about the intent of the paragraph you should start Roadmapping right away. Don't worry about potentially unfamiliar terms like "assimilationist" and "a priori." Remember, you're not reading for total comprehension, just the central ideas. When you encounter complex language like this, sift though it for ideas that are more plainly stated. Following the emphasis Keyword "immediately" you get a nice, simple summary of what the author is really getting at: The sociologists think that all minority cultures immediately succumb to majority cultures. And the author is quick to point out that this isn't happening in the case of the native Americans discussed in the passage. Your passage map should clearly point out these conflicting opinions.

Auth: Intertribal
act. still
important

Tribal and
Intertribal
distinct

(Yet) the fact remains that intertribal activities are a
(major facet) of native American culture today. Certain
dances at powwows, (for instance,) are announced as
intertribal, (others) as traditional. (Likewise,) speeches
(45)   given at the beginnings of powwows are (often)
delivered in English, (while) the prayer that follows is
(usually) spoken in a native language. Cultural
borrowing is, (of course,) old news. What is (important) to
note is the conscious (distinction) native Americans
(50)   make (between) tribal and intertribal tendencies.[18]

The author immediately prepares us for a shift with "Yet" at the beginning. Most of what follows are examples of intertribal practices. Once again, the author provides emphasis words to highlight the main point: "What is important to note" couldn't be any clearer. Take the author's advice and note this important information, the distinction between tribal and intertribal activites.

---

[17]PrepTest 25, Sec 1, Passage 3
[18]PrepTest 25, Sec 1, Passage 3

Auth: Both are
important

Tribalism, (although greatly altered) by modern
history, (remains) a (potent) force among native
Americans: It forms a (basis) for tribal identity, (and)
aligns music and dance with other social and cultural
(55) activities (important) to individual tribes. Intertribal
activities, on the (other hand,) (reinforce) native American
identity along a broader front, (where) this identity is
directly threatened by outside influences.[19]

The passage wraps up nicely with a summary of the dichotomy that the author has been examining. While tribalism remains a "potent" force in native American communities, "on the other hand" intertribal communities serve an important role as well. If you found this to be a predictable ending for the passage, congratulations! You'll find as you develop your strategic reading skills that most LSAT passages *are* very predictable in structure. I'll elaborate on this idea more in chapter 6.

Part 2: You've completed your first Roadmap, and that's an important accomplishment. Now it's time to put it to use. Answer the following selected questions, using your Roadmap to guide you back to the passage as necessary. *Do not rely on your memory of the text.* This is a bad habit and will rob you of crucial points if you adopt it. Read each question carefully, determine what it is asking, and do your research. As always, complete explanations follow.

---

[19]PrepTest 25, Sec 1, Passage 3

17. The primary function of the third paragraph is to
    (A) search for evidence to corroborate the basic
         assumption of the theory of Pan-Indianism
    (B) demonstrate the incorrectness of the theory of
         Pan-Indianism by pointing out that native
         American groups themselves disagree with the theory
    (C) explain the origin of the theory of Pan-Indianism
         by showing how it evolved from other
         assimilationist theories
    (D) examine several assimilationist theories in order
         to demonstrate that they rest on a common
         assumption
    (E) criticize the theory of Pan-Indianism by pointing
         out that it rests upon an assumption for which
         there is no supporting evidence[20]

18. Which one of the following most accurately describes
    the author's attitude toward the theory of Pan-Indianism?
    (A) critical of its tendency to attribute political
         motives to cultural practices
    (B) discomfort at its negative characterization of
         cultural borrowing by native Americans
    (C) hopeful about its chances for preserving tribal
         culture
    (D) offended by its claim that assimilation is a
         desirable consequence of cultural contact
    (E) skeptical that it is a complete explanation of
         recent changes in native American society[21]

20. Which one of the following situations most clearly
    illustrates the phenomenon of intertribalism, as that
    phenomenon is described in the passage?
    (A) a native American tribe in which a number of
         powerful societies attempt to prevent the revival
         of a traditional dance
    (B) a native American tribe whose members attempt
         to learn the native languages of several other
         tribes
    (C) a native American tribe whose members attempt
         to form a political organization in order to
         redress several grievances important to that tribe
    (D) a native American tribe in which a significant
         percentage of the members have forsaken their
         tribal identity and become assimilated into
         Euroamerican society
    (E) a native American tribe whose members often
         travel to other parts of the reservation in order to
         visit friends and relatives[22]

---

[20]PrepTest 25, Sec 1, Q 17

[21]PrepTest 25, Sec 1, Q 18

[22]PrepTest 25, Sec 1, Q 20

Explanations

17. **(E)**

The primary function of the third paragraph is to

(A)   search for evidence to corroborate the basic assumption of the theory of Pan-Indianism

(B)   demonstrate the incorrectness of the theory of Pan-Indianism by pointing out that native American groups themselves disagree with the theory

(C)   explain the origin of the theory of Pan-Indianism by showing how it evolved from other assimilationist theories

(D)   examine several assimilationist theories in order to demonstrate that they rest on a common assumption

(E)   criticize the theory of Pan-Indianism by pointing out that it rests upon an assumption for which there is no supporting evidence[23]

When a question asks you to provide the primary purpose of a paragraph, the answer always lies right in the Roadmap. A review of your notes should give you a good prediction for the correct answer: The author critiqued the sociologists' theory and demonstrated that it didn't really apply to Native Americans. That prediction matches the correct answer, choice (E), spot-on. Choices (A) and (C) are both out of scope; your Roadmap reminds you that this paragraph is written to critique, not to explain or provide evidence, and in any case choice (A) says that the author gives support to the Pan-Indian theory, which never happens. Choice (B) wrongly states that the author demonstrates the incorrectness of Pan-Indianism, which does not occur in the third paragraph. Finally, choice (D) also wanders out of scope. The author's goal is to critique Pan-Indianism, not to examine numerous theories.

18. **(E)**

Which one of the following most accurately describes the author's attitude toward the theory of Pan-Indianism?

(A)   critical of its tendency to attribute political motives to cultural practices

(B)   discomfort at its negative characterization of cultural borrowing by native Americans

(C)   hopeful about its chances for preserving tribal culture

(D)   offended by its claim that assimilation is a desirable consequence of cultural contact

(E)   skeptical that it is a complete explanation of recent changes in native American society[24]

Where does your Roadmap tell you to look for the author's attitude toward Pan-Indianism? The second paragraph introduced authorial point of view. Keywords should guide you right back

---

[23]PrepTest 25, Sec 1, Q 17
[24]PrepTest 25, Sec 1, Q 18

to lines 27–29 in order to find a good summary: Something more complex is happening than the Pan-Indian theory can account for. Going to the choices, notice that (A), (B), (C), and (D) all bring outside ideas into the passage; they are all out of scope. Only correct choice (E) remains, and it matches your prediction perfectly by pointing out that Pan-Indianism is incomplete.

20. **(B)**

Which one of the following situations most clearly illustrates the phenomenon of intertribalism, as that phenomenon is described in the passage?

(A)   a native American tribe in which a number of powerful societies attempt to prevent the revival of a traditional dance

(B)   a native American tribe whose members attempt to learn the native languages of several other tribes

(C)   a native American tribe whose members attempt to form a political organization in order to redress several grievances important to that tribe

(D)   a native American tribe in which a significant percentage of the members have forsaken their tribal identity and become assimilated into Euroamerican society

(E)   a native American tribe whose members often travel to other parts of the reservation in order to visit friends and relatives[25]

This question asks you to provide an illustration of intertribalism *as it is described in the passage*. Your Roadmap may have guided you either to paragraph one or two, and you can find similar definitions in either location: Intertribalism involves the sharing of cultural traditions among different tribes. Which answer choice describes this? Only the correct answer, choice (B). Choice (A) introduces the completely unsupported notion of the suppression of cultural revival. Choice (C) is a distortion of what the passage is truly saying; while political action is mentioned at the end of the first paragraph, it is presented as evidence that the Pan-Indian theory may be true, not as a definition of intertribalism. Choices (D) and (E) are incorrect for the same reason, presenting the sociologists' evidence for their theory.

Even if you struggled with these questions, be sure to notice that each correct answer was supported by text from the passage and that your Roadmap provided you with an efficient way to sort through the information.

ROADMAPPING RULES OF THUMB

Earlier in this chapter I mentioned that all of my students Roadmap their passages a little bit differently. It will almost certainly take a little experimentation to learn exactly what

---

[25]PrepTest 25, Sec 1, Q 20

information to put in your Roadmap and how to write it. That said, there are a few good general principles you should follow.

Keep It Simple

Your Roadmap will only be useful insofar as it makes the passage easier to navigate. If you include too many details, you begin to defeat the purpose of having a Roadmap at all, and you'll find yourself in one of the bad situations I presented to you at the beginning of this chapter. As an illustration, take another look at this paragraph:

Auth: James is
striking writer

James is certainly capable of (strikingly) good writing. She takes (immense) trouble to provide her characters with convincing histories and passions. Her descriptive digressions are part of the pleasure of her (30) books (and) give them dignity and weight. (But) it is equally true that they frequently interfere with the story; the patinas and aromas of a country kitchen receive more loving attention (than) does the plot itself.

Auth: Sometimes
bad for plot (35)

Her devices to advance the story can be (shameless) and thin, (and) it is often impossible to see how her detective arrives at the truth; one is left to conclude that the detective solves crimes through intuition. At (this stage) in her career P. D. James seems to be (less) interested in the specifics of detection (than) in her characters' (40) vulnerabilities and perplexities.[26]

Remember that this paragraph is composed mostly of details. You were able to sum up its purpose in just a few words. But what if your Roadmap looked more like this?

James writes
strikingly

characters w/
stories give (30)
dignity

Kitchen vs. plot/
story too thin

(35)

crimes solved by
intuition / char.
more than plot

James is certainly capable of (strikingly) good writing. She takes (immense) trouble to provide her characters with convincing histories and passions. Her descriptive digressions are part of the pleasure of her (30) books (and) give them dignity and weight. (But) it is equally true that they frequently interfere with the story; the patinas and aromas of a country kitchen receive more loving attention (than) does the plot itself. Her devices to advance the story can be (shameless) and thin, (and) it is often impossible to see how her detective arrives at the truth; one is left to conclude that the detective solves crimes through intuition. At (this stage) in her career P. D. James seems to be (less) interested in the specifics of detection (than) in her characters' (40) vulnerabilities and perplexities.[27]

This Roadmap restates practically everything that the passage already says. Your goal isn't to rewrite the passage, a time-consuming and wasteful approach. Trust in a simple Roadmap, and remember that you've still got all those Keywords to help you narrow down your search

---

[26]PrepTest 19, Sec 3, Passage 1

[27]PrepTest 19, Sec 3, Passage 1

to a specific detail should you need it. Keywords are the foundation of your Roadmap, and you should use both tools together when answering the questions.

Note Important Examples

The Roadmap's primary goal is to allow you to see, at a glance, each paragraph's main ideas. But if the paragraph contains emphasized supporting examples you can call attention to them with a couple of simple annotations, like this:

Hart's theory of hard cases	H. L. A. Hart's *The Concept of Law* is still the clearest and most persuasive statement of both the
	(10) standard theory of hard cases and the standard theory of law on which it rests. For Hart, the law consists of legal rules formulated in general terms;
Core and penumbra →	these terms he calls "open textured," which means that they contain a "core" of settled meaning and a
	(15) "penumbra" or "periphery" where their meaning is not determinate. For example, suppose an ordinance prohibits the use of vehicles in a park.
Ex: Vehicle →	"Vehicle" has a core of meaning which includes cars and motorcycles. But, Hart claims, other
	(20) vehicles, such as bicycles, fall within the peripheral meaning of "vehicle," so that law does not establish whether they are prohibited. There will always be cases not covered by the core meaning of
Ex is legally indeterm.	legal terms within existing laws; Hart considers
	(25) these cases to be legally indeterminate. Since courts cannot decide such cases on legal grounds, they must consider nonlegal (for example, moral and political) grounds, and thereby exercise judicial discretion to make, rather than apply, law.[28]

The Roadmap doesn't actually restate the key example or attempt to break it down. It simply provides you with a simple way to find this part of the text in case you need it. If it doesn't always seem clear to you which examples are most likely to show up in the questions, never fear; with practice and close attention to Keywords of emphasis the distinction will become clearer, and this is a subject that I'll revisit in future chapters.

Denote Differing Points of View

You know that the author's voice is of paramount importance in any LSAT passage, but other viewpoints are likely to be tested as well. You've already learned to circle Keywords that indicate shifting points of view. Now you should get into the habit of denoting point of view in your Roadmap as well:

---

[28]PrepTest 17, Sec 4, Passage 2

Diff. between
groups

(30) To illustrate the difference between biologists
favoring universal, deterministic laws of evolutionary
development and those leaving room for historical
contingency, consider two favorite statements of
philosophers (both of which appear, at first sight, to be
(35) universal assertions): "All planets move in ellipses"

Ex of universal
law

and "All swans are white." The former is truly
universal because it applies not only to those planets
that actually do exist, but also to those that could
exist—for the shape of planetary orbits is a necessary
(40) consequence of the laws governing the motion of
objects in a gravitational field.

Bio Determ:
swans =
universal

Biological determinists would say that "All swans
are white" is universal in the same way, since, if all
swans were white, it would be because the laws of
(45) natural selection make it impossible for swans to be
otherwise: natural selection favors those
characteristics that increase the average rate of

Bio non-determ:
swans = historical

offspring production, and so traits that maximize
flexibility and the ability to manipulate nature will
(50) eventually appear. Nondeterminist biologists would
deny this, saying that "swans" is merely the name of a
finite collection of historical objects that may happen

Auth: undecided

all to be white but not of necessity. The history of
evolutionary theory has been the history of the struggle
(55) between these two views of swans.[29]

In these two paragraphs, we have three separate voices. The determinist biologists are discussed in the first paragraph, nondeterminist biologists take the floor in the second, and the author summarizes the debate in the final sentence. The test makers will reward you for recognizing and differentiating the different opinions present in the passage; one of the easiest ways to keep track of them is to clearly mark them in your Roadmap.

Strategic Reading Requires a Roadmap

I'll close this chapter by encouraging you to Roadmap every single passage you read in your practice from now until test day. Creating Roadmaps may feel awkward and time-consuming at first, and this is to be expected. As you become more proficient with this skill, it will become second nature to you. Since everyone maps a little differently, don't be alarmed if the Roadmaps you create aren't exactly like the ones you see in Kaplan's answers and explanations. Getting the major ideas down on paper is the most important thing.

When you're ready, proceed to chapter 4, where your Roadmapping skills will come in handy once again.

---

[29]PrepTest 35, Sec 2, Passage 3

CHAPTER 4

TOPIC, SCOPE, PURPOSE, AND MAIN IDEA

Now that you understand the importance of Keywords and have learned how to Roadmap passages, you are almost fully conversant with Step 1 of Kaplan's Method for Reading Comprehension. I'd like to congratulate you for making it this far. It isn't necessarily easy to change the way you read, but strategic reading isn't just useful on the LSAT—it's indispensable.

In this chapter, I'm going to reintroduce you to your final task when reading a passage strategically. After you've created your Roadmap, you should think through four key attributes that you will use to describe the passage: Topic, Scope, Purpose, and Main Idea. Put simply, every passage can be defined in terms of these four ideas, and knowing them will lead you directly to correct answers—and a higher score—while helping you steer clear of wrong answer traps.

TOPIC AND SCOPE

I'll start by introducing the two more general ideas, Topic and Scope. These are two fairly generalized descriptions of the passage, and over the years I've seen far too many students fail to grasp their importance. Because I don't want you to make that mistake, I'm going to define each of these important concepts and explain why understanding them will improve your LSAT score.

Topic: Broad Subject Area

Every passage you read addresses a generally defined Topic. The Topic of a passage is simply the broad, general subject that the passage describes. The author's Topic is usually very easy to determine, and it is generally obvious by the time you've finished reading the first paragraph. Take another look at the first paragraph from the P. D. James passage:

Critics: Praise James or attack her

Auth: False opp.

(Wherever) the crime novels of P. D. James are discussed by (critics,) there is a tendency (on the one) hand to exaggerate her merits and (on the other) to castigate her as a genre writer who is getting above
(5) herself. Perhaps (underlying) the debate is that familiar (false) opposition set up (between) different kinds of fiction, (according to) which enjoyable novels are held to be somehow slightly lowbrow, (and) a novel is not considered true literature unless it is a tiny bit dull.[1]

Once you've read this paragraph strategically, there's little doubt that the passage is going to explore some aspect of James's work. That's as far as you need to go in determining the Topic; the only real rule to follow is to keep it very general. For this passage the Topic is simply the works of P. D. James.

Look at another opening paragraph from the previous chapter and try to determine the Topic of the passage:

Soc: gatherings mean tribal decline

Pan-Indian theory, evidence

(Even) in the midst of its (resurgence) as a vital tradition, many (sociologists) have viewed the current form of the powwow, a ceremonial gathering of native Americans, (as a sign) that tribal culture is in decline.
(5) (Focusing) on the dances and rituals that have (recently) come to be shared by most tribes, they (suggest) that an intertribal movement is now in ascension and (claim) the (inevitable) outcome of this tendency is the eventual dissolution of tribes (and) the complete assimilation of
(10) native Americans into Euroamerican society. (Proponents) of this "Pan-Indian" theory (point to) the greater frequency of travel and communication between reservations, the greater urbanization of native Americans, (and,) most (recently,) their increasing
(15) politicization in (response) to common grievances as the chief causes of the shift toward intertribalism.[2]

In this paragraph, many ideas are presented to you: the powwow, the "Pan-Indian" theory, and intertribalism. Fortunately, with a good Roadmap you've cut through some of the jargon. Just as with the last exercise, keep the Topic very broad. Hopefully you came up with something along the lines of "Native American culture" or "theories about tribal life." These two topics

---

[1]PrepTest 19, Sec 3, Passage 1

[2]PrepTest 25, Sec 1, Passage 3

may seem very different, but they're both perfectly good descriptions of the broad subject that the author will go on to address in the passage.

Given the very general nature of the Topic, you may already be wondering why you should bother thinking about it at all. The primary reason is that the Topic guides you naturally to the Scope, and as I will show you, knowing the Scope of the passage is crucial to understanding the passage.

Scope: The Author's Focus

The Scope of the passage can be defined in a couple of ways, and I'll describe them both in this section. Put plainly, the Scope of the passage is the narrower area of specific interest within the Topic that the author wishes to explore. Returning to the P. D. James passage:

Critics: Praise James or attack her

Wherever the crime novels of P. D. James are discussed by critics, there is a tendency on the one hand to exaggerate her merits and on the other to castigate her as a genre writer who is getting above

(5) herself. Perhaps underlying the debate is that familiar

Auth: False opp.

false opposition set up between different kinds of fiction, according to which enjoyable novels are held to be somehow slightly lowbrow, and a novel is not considered true literature unless it is a tiny bit dull.

(10) Those commentators who would elevate James's

Critics who like James

books to the status of high literature point to her painstakingly constructed characters, her elaborate settings, her sense of place, and her love of abstractions: notions about morality, duty, pain, and

(15) pleasure are never far from the lips of her police

Critics who dislike James

officers and murderers. Others find her pretentious and tiresome; an inverted snobbery accuses her of abandoning the time-honored conventions of the detective genre in favor of a highbrow literary style.

(20) The critic Harriet Waugh wants P. D. James to get on with "the more taxing business of laying a tricky trail and then fooling the reader"; Philip Oakes in *The Literary Review* groans, "Could we please proceed with the business of clapping the handcuffs on the

(25) killer?"[3]

I've presented the first two paragraphs this time because, while the Scope can often be gleaned from the first paragraph alone, you'll sometimes need to read a bit further before it becomes clear. Earlier I identified the Topic of this passage as the works of P. D. James. As you dig a little deeper into the passage, it becomes clear that the author's focus is not on the works in general, but on the various criticisms that have been leveled against them. That's the Scope: criticisms of James's work.

---

[3]PrepTest 19, Sec 3, Passage 1

Another way to think about the Scope is to ask yourself, "What question about the Topic is the author interested in answering?" If you think about it this way, you might define the Scope as "What are some common criticisms of James's work?" or "Are James's critics correct in their views?" The second of these two questions is a bit more specific than the first, but by the end of the passage you definitely know that the author evaluates the critics' position. This raises an important point: You may make a prediction about the author's Scope toward the beginning of the passage only to revise it as you learn more about the author's primary motives. This is perfectly fine. The further you read into a passage, the more clearly defined the Scope will become.

As I hinted at above, knowing the Scope of the passage is of immediate pragmatic value to you on test day. The reason is simple: Many of the incorrect answers you encounter on the LSAT will be wrong because they fall *outside the author's Scope*. As a demonstration, look carefully at the following answer choices removed from their associated question:

(A) Critics of literature must acknowledge that they are less talented than creators of literature.
(B) Critics should hesitate to disparage popular authors.
(C) P. D. James's novels should focus less on characters from the English landed gentry.
(D) Detective fiction should be content to remain an unambitious literary genre.
(E) P. D. James should be less fastidious about portraying violence.[4]

Examine each answer choice and try to determine whether it falls within the author's Scope. Choice (A) does mention critics, but it isn't discussing their individual criticisms, but rather their own talent or lack thereof. It is likely to be out of scope. Choice (B) doesn't really address the critics' views either, instead suggesting that they shouldn't be critics at all. Choice (C) does mention a specific criticism of James, but take a moment to tighten the Scope by reviewing the actual claims made by the critics: That James is either too highbrow as a writer or too lowbrow. Choice (C) therefore is out of Scope. Skipping ahead to choice (E): Once again, this is not one of the criticisms that the author explores, placing choice (E) out of Scope, too.

What's left? Only choice (D) is within the author's Scope. It addresses a specific criticism mentioned in the passage, and it matches the passage's established dichotomy of highbrow literature vs. popular genre writing. Choice (D) must therefore be the right answer.

---

[4]PrepTest 19, Sec 3, Q 7

Just for context, take a look at the entire question:

7. The author characterizes the position of some critics as "inverted snobbery" (line 17) because they hold which one of the following views?

 (A) Critics of literature must acknowledge that they are less talented than creators of literature.
 (B) Critics should hesitate to disparage popular authors.
 (C) P. D. James's novels should focus less on characters from the English landed gentry.
 (D) Detective fiction should be content to remain an unambitious literary genre.
 (E) P. D. James should be less fastidious about portraying violence.[5]

I want to be very clear about something: This exercise is in no way meant to suggest that on test day you should answer the questions using this process of elimination. To the contrary, as you advance through this book and learn more about Steps 2–5 of the Kaplan Method, you will find that it is generally possible to know exactly what the right answer will look like before you evaluate the choices, which is a much more efficient approach to the questions. Regardless, adherence to the author's Scope remains a powerful method of discerning which choices are possible candidates for selection and which should be eliminated immediately. It also gives you a focused approach to the passage, making you less likely to misunderstand the author's Purpose.

Purpose: Why Is the Author Writing This?

As you reach the end of a passage, your careful attention to structure should give you a clear understanding of the author's motivations. When defining the Purpose of the passage, your task is to summarize each of the author's goals as they relate to the structure of the passage as a whole. A demonstration will probably make this concept easier to understand. Take a moment to review the full James passage:

Critics: Praise
James or
attack her

Wherever the crime novels of P. D. James are discussed by critics, there is a tendency on the one hand to exaggerate her merits and on the other to castigate her as a genre writer who is getting above
(5) herself. Perhaps underlying the debate is that familiar,

Auth: False
opp.

false opposition set up between different kinds of fiction, according to which enjoyable novels are held to be somehow slightly lowbrow, and a novel is not considered true literature unless it is a tiny bit dull.

_____
[5] PrepTest 19, Sec 3, Q 7

Critics who like James
(10)   Those commentators who would elevate James's books to the status of high literature point to her painstakingly constructed characters, her elaborate settings, her sense of place, and her love of abstractions; notions about morality, duty, pain, and
(15) pleasure are never far from the lips of her police officers and murderers. Others find her pretentious and

Critics who dislike James
tiresome; an inverted snobbery accuses her of abandoning the time-honored conventions of the detective genre in favor of a highbrow literary style.
(20)   The critic Harriet Waugh wants P. D. James to get on with "the more taxing business of laying a tricky trail and then fooling the reader"; Philip Oakes in *The Literary Review* groans, "Could we please proceed with the business of clapping the handcuffs on the
(25) killer?"

Auth: James very descriptive
James is certainly capable of strikingly good writing. She takes immense trouble to provide her characters with convincing histories and passions. Her descriptive digressions are part of the pleasure of her
(30) books and give them dignity and weight. But it is equally true that they frequently interfere with the story; the patinas and aromas of a country kitchen receive more loving attention than does the plot itself.

Auth: Sometimes bad for plot
Her devices to advance the story can be shameless and
(35) thin, and it is often impossible to see how her detective arrives at the truth; one is left to conclude that the detective solves crimes through intuition. At this stage in her career P. D. James seems to be less interested in the specifics of detection than in her characters'
(40) vulnerabilities and perplexities.

Auth: James not limited by genre
However, once the rules of a chosen genre cramp creative thought, there is no reason why an able and interesting writer should accept them. In her latest book, there are signs that James is beginning to feel
(45) constrained by the crime-novel genre. Here her determination to leave areas of ambiguity in the solution of the crime and to distribute guilt among the murderer victim, and bystanders points to a conscious rebellion against the traditional neatness of detective
(50) fiction. It is fashionable, though reprehensible, for one

Auth: James maybe go mainstr.
writer to prescribe to another. But perhaps the time has come for P. D. James to slide out of her handcuffs and stride into the territory of the mainstream novel.[6]

To define the Purpose of this passage, review your Roadmap carefully and ask of each paragraph, "Why did the author write this? What was the intended goal?" Then summarize your thoughts in a brief sentence. You should work through it like this:

Paragraph 1: The author begins by describing a debate that surrounds the works of P. D. James.
Paragraph 2: She then describes several specific criticisms of James's work.

[6]PrepTest 19, Sec 3, Passage 1

Paragraph 3: She acknowledges that there is some legitimacy in the critics' claims.

Paragraph 4: She suggests that James's writing surpasses the restrictions of her chosen genre.

Summarizing the entire passage structure is very easy to do once you've become proficient at Roadmapping , which is another reason why you should continue to practice and perfect that vital skill. Now all you need to do is combine those statements to come up with the author's Purpose: to examine several criticisms of a writer and to suggest that the writer rise above those criticisms.

Notice that I've used simple, general language as well as specific action verbs in describing the Purpose of the passage: The author wrote to examine, to describe, to suggest. These are the kinds of words you should use as well. In fact, you'll find that certain common actions will show up again and again as you continue to practice. LSAT passages are very predictable and the range of possible motivations for their authors isn't terribly wide. Here are some common examples. The author may write to:

- Describe a theory or idea
- Explain a phenomenon
- Compare one explanation to another
- Support a given theory
- Refute a claim made about an artist's work
- Defend an assumption against critics

Again, because the passages are limited in Scope, there are only so many Purposes that an author can pursue. This is great news because it demonstrates that no passage will ever be too complex to summarize in a sentence or two. For practice, take another look at the Intertribalism passage and try to define its primary Purpose using the process I just described.

Soc: gatherings mean tribal decline

Pan-Indian theory, evidence

(Even) in the midst of its (resurgence) as a vital tradition, many (sociologists) have viewed the current form of the powwow, a ceremonial gathering of native Americans, (as a sign) that tribal culture is in decline.
(5) (Focusing) on the dances and rituals that have (recently) come to be shared by most tribes, they (suggest) that an intertribal movement is now in ascension and (claim) the (inevitable) outcome of this tendency is the eventual dissolution of tribes and the complete assimilation of
(10) native Americans into Euroamerican society. (Proponents) of this "Pan-Indian" theory (point to) the greater frequency of travel and communication between reservations, the greater urbanization of native Americans, (and) most (recently,) their increasing
(15) politicization in (response) to common grievances as the chief causes of the shift toward intertribalism.

Auth: Intertribalism on rise

(Indeed,) the rapid diffusion of dance styles, outfits, and songs from one reservation to another offers (compelling evidence) that intertribalism has been
(20) increasing. (However,) these (sociologists) have (failed) to note the concurrent revitalization of many traditions unique to individual tribes. (Among) the Lakota, for (instance,) the Sun Dance was revived, after a forty-year hiatus, during the 1950's. (Similarly,) the Black Legging
(25) Society of the Kiowa and the Hethuska Society of the Ponca—(both) traditional groups within their respective tribes—have gained (new popularity.) (Obviously) a more complex societal shift is taking place(than) the theory of Pan-Indianism can account for.

Unique traditions rising too

P.I.T doesn't explain

(30)   An (examination) of the theory's underpinnings may be (critical) at this point, (especially) given that native Americans themselves (chafe most) against the Pan-Indian classification. (Like) other assimilationist theories with which it is associated, the Pan-Indian view is
(35) (predicated upon) an a priori assumption about the nature of cultural contact: that (upon) contact minority societies (immediately) begin to succumb in every respect—biologically, linguistically, and culturally—to the majority society. (However,) there is (no evidence)
(40) that this is happening to native American groups.

Auth: must examine theory

Theory based on wrong assump.

(Yet) the fact remains that intertribal activities are a (major facet) of native American culture today. Certain dances at powwows, (for instance,) are announced as intertribal, (others) as traditional. (Likewise,) speeches
(45) given at the beginnings of powwows are (often) delivered in English, (while) the prayer that follows is (usually) spoken in a native language. Cultural borrowing is, (of course,) old news. What is(important) to note is the conscious (distinction) native Americans
(50) make (between) tribal and intertribal tendencies.

Auth: Intertribal act. still important

Tribal and Intertribal distinct

Tribalism, (although greatly altered) by modern history, (remains) a (potent) force among native Americans: It forms a (basis) for tribal identity, (and) aligns music and dance with other social and cultural
(55) activities (important) to individual tribes. Intertribal activities, on the (other hand,) (reinforce) native American identity along a broader front, (where) this identity is directly threatened by outside influences.[7]

Auth: Both are important

Hopefully you thought about the passage like this:

Paragraph 1: The author explains the views of sociologists who believe that intertribalism is on the rise and that tribal culture is fading.

Paragraph 2: He points out that these sociologists overlook the revitalization of specific cultural traditions.

---

[7]PrepTest 25, Sec 1, Passage 3

Paragraph 3: He demonstrates possible weaknesses in the Pan-Indian theory.

Paragraph 4: He shows that Native Americans distinguish between tribal and intertribal activities.

Paragraph 5: He suggests that tribal culture is actually strengthened by intertribal activities.

Purpose: The author wrote this passage to examine claims made by sociologists about declining tribal life and to demonstrate that the opposite is true.

Understanding and articulating the author's primary Purpose will lead to immediate rewards on test day, since many of the questions will directly test your knowledge of it. In fact, take a look at this question:

21. In the passage, the author is primarily concerned with
     doing which one of the following?[8]

Before I reveal the answer choices, I want you to recognize that this is a "Global" question type, one that is specifically asking for the Purpose we just summarized. (I'll discuss the different Reading Comprehension question types in greater detail in Part 2 of this book). Recall the Purpose you just defined. Now look at the answer choices and find the one that matches your prediction:

(A) identifying an assumption common to various assimilationist theories and then criticizing these theories by showing this assumption to be false

(B) arguing that the recent revival of a number of tribal practices shows sociologists are mistaken in believing intertribalism to be a potent force among native American societies

(C) questioning the belief that native American societies will eventually be assimilated into Euroamerican society by arguing that intertribalism helps strengthen native American identity

(D) showing how the recent resurgence of tribal activities is a deliberate attempt to counteract the growing influence of intertribalism

(E) proposing an explanation of why the ascension of intertribalism could result in the eventual dissolution of tribes and complete assimilation of native Americans into Euroamerican society[9]

You can quickly see that the correct answer is choice (C), which restates the primary Purpose.

There is a clever wrong answer trap here that is worth taking a moment to examine. Perhaps you thought at first that choice (B) was the proper match for your prediction. But recall from your analysis of the passage that while the author does claim that the sociologists are mistaken,

---

[8]PrepTest 25, Sec 1, Q 21
[9]PrepTest 25, Sec 1, Q 21

he doesn't say that intertribalism fails to be a potent force in Native American society. To the contrary, he claims that intertribalism is alive and well, and that it points to a strengthening of tribal culture rather than a weakening of it. Don't be disheartened if you picked choice (B) over choice (C). This is a one of the most common traps that occur regularly on the LSAT, and I'll discuss them all in greater detail later in this book.

You are very likely to encounter a question or two on test day that will be exactly like the one you just examined. For this reason alone, determining the author's Purpose is extremely important. As you continue to practice, you'll learn that some questions that don't directly ask you to identify the Purpose will still rely upon your understanding of it to find the credited answer among the traps. Bottom line: To be successful on Reading Comprehension, you must determine the Purpose of every passage you read from now until test day.

Main Idea: What's It All About?

Once you've determined the author's Topic, Scope, and Purpose, the Main Idea isn't far behind. In essence, it's the simplest, most direct summary of the author's primary conclusion that you can come up with. When trying to articulate the Main Idea of a passage, ask yourself, "If the author wanted me to come away from this text believing only *one* thing, what would it be?" The answer to this question is the Main Idea.

You'll find that as you become adept at defining the Purpose of the passage, the Main Idea is usually a natural extension of it. For example, you determined that the primary Purpose of the James passage was to examine several criticisms of a writer and to suggest that the writer rises above those criticisms. To get the Main Idea, you simply go from this general description of the passage's goals to a more specific and declarative one. The Main Idea of the passage is: James's work surpasses the limits of the crime-novel genre in spite of the claims of her critics. Again, notice that the difference is primarily one of specificity. Instead of referring to a writer who "rises above . . . criticisms" as I did in the Purpose, in the Main Idea I provide the specifics: James is the writer, and she breaks the conventions of a particular genre.

The difference may seem minor, but it's extremely important:

1. Which one of the following best states the author's main conclusion?[10]

---

[10]PrepTest 19, Sec 3, Q 1

This question is not asking for structure. It's asking for the Main Idea. Think over your prediction, then look at the choices:

(A)   Because P. D. James's potential as a writer is stifled by her chosen genre, she should turn her talents toward writing mainstream novels.

(B)   Because the requirements of the popular novel are incompatible with true creative expression, P. D. James's promise as a serious author has been diminished.

(C)   The dichotomy between popular and sophisticated literature is well illustrated in the crime novels of P. D. James.

(D)   The critics who have condemned P. D. James's lack of attention to the specifics of detection fail to take into account her carefully constructed plots.

(E)   Although her plots are not always neatly resolved, the beauty of her descriptive passages justifies P. D. James's decision to write in the crime-novel genre.[11]

Hopefully this time you found the match with no difficulty: Choice (A) matches the author's ultimate recommendation perfectly and is a good match for our prediction as well.

The majority of LSAT passages will immediately be followed by a question that asks for the Main Idea. And as with Purpose, even those questions that don't ask for the Main Idea directly will often require that you demonstrate a clear understanding of it. Because Main Idea is so important, I'd like you to try one more exercise. Take a moment to review the primary Purpose of the Intertribalism Passage: to examine claims made by sociologists about declining tribal life, and to demonstrate that the opposite is true.

[11]PrepTest 19, Sec 3, Q 1

Now take a minute to articulate the Main Idea. Then try to answer this question:

14. Which one of the following best summarizes the main idea of the passage?

   (A) Despite the fact that sociologists have only recently begun to understand its importance, intertribalism has always been an influential factor in native American culture.

   (B) Native Americans are currently struggling with an identity crisis caused primarily by the two competing forces of tribalism and intertribalism.

   (C) The recent growth of intertribalism is unlikely to eliminate tribalism because the two forces do not oppose one another but instead reinforce distinct elements of native American identity.

   (D) The tendency toward intertribalism, although prevalent within native American culture, has had a minimal effect on the way native Americans interact with the broader community around them.

   (E) Despite the recent revival of many native American tribal traditions, the recent trend toward intertribalism is likely to erode cultural differences among the various native American tribes.[12]

The Main Idea of this passage could be stated as: Intertribalism isn't causing a decline in tribal life, but rather strengthening it. As always, don't worry if your prediction didn't exactly match mine; little differences are to be expected. Armed with this prediction, there's no doubt that the correct answer to this question is choice (C).

Topic, Scope, Purpose, Main Idea: A Summary

Although Topic, Scope, Purpose, and Main Idea may appear to be four very different concepts, I hope you can see that there's a binding relationship among them. Topic gives you a sense of general context, and helps lead you to the Scope. Purpose allows you to summarize passage structure, and the Main Idea is the central theme that ties everything together. Understanding these four attributes of every Reading Comprehension passage is the final stage of strategic reading and will allow you to approach the question set with confidence. I can't stress this enough: The majority of the questions that you will encounter on test day will require you to understand these ideas, either directly or indirectly, and the test makers will reward you for doing so. For this reason, you should *always* make sure you understand the Topic, Scope, Purpose, and Main Idea of every LSAT passage. Don't write them down (this can take more time than it's worth), but do clearly identify them in your mind before attempting any of the questions. With this in mind, it's time for some practice.

---

[12]PrepTest 25, Sec 1, Q 14

DRILL: IDENTIFYING TOPIC, SCOPE, PURPOSE, AND MAIN IDEA

Part 1: This will be your first attempt at applying Step 1 of the Kaplan Method in its entirety. As in the previous chapter, this Drill will be split into two separate tasks. First, read the passage strategically, noting Keywords, creating your Roadmap, and noting the Topic, Scope, Purpose, and Main Idea of the passage. (As I mentioned earlier, you won't write the Topic, Scope, Purpose, and Main Idea down on test day, but it's a good idea to do so now, as it gets you in the habit of thinking about them.) This passage is full of intricate details, but don't let them distract you. Also, remember that your Roadmap will be particularly helpful as you formulate the Purpose and Main Idea of the passage, so refer to it as needed. Explanations will follow. Read them carefully and double-check your work before you move on to Part 2 of the Drill.

In England before 1660, a husband controlled his wife's property. In the late seventeenth and eighteenth centuries, with the shift from land-based to commercial wealth, marriage began to incorporate certain features
(5) of a contract. Historians have traditionally argued that this trend represented a gain for women, one that reflects changing views about democracy and property following the English Restoration in 1660. Susan Staves contests this view; she argues that whatever
(10) gains marriage contracts may briefly have represented for women were undermined by judicial decisions about women's contractual rights.

Shifting through the tangled details of court cases, Staves demonstrates that, despite surface changes, a
(15) rhetoric of equality, and occasional decisions supporting women's financial power, definitions of men's and women's property remained inconsistent—generally to women's detriment. For example, dower lands (property inherited by wives after their husbands'
(20) deaths) could not be sold, but "curtesy" property (inherited by husbands from their wives) could be sold. Furthermore, comparatively new concepts that developed in conjunction with the marriage contract, such as jointure, pin money, and separate maintenance,
(25) were compromised by peculiar rules. For instance, if a woman spent her pin money (money paid by the husband according to the marriage contract for the wife's personal items) on possessions other than clothes she could not sell them; in effect they belonged
(30) to her husband. In addition, a wife could sue for pin money only up to a year in arrears—which rendered a suit impractical. Similarly, separate maintenance allowances (stated sums of money for the wife's support if husband and wife agreed to live apart) were

(35) complicated by the fact that if a couple tried to agree in a marriage contract on an amount, they were admitting that a supposedly indissoluble bond could be dissolved, an assumption courts could not recognize. Eighteenth-century historians underplayed these inconsistencies,
(40) calling them "little contrarieties" that would soon vanish. Staves shows, however, that as judges gained power over decisions on marriage contracts, they tended to fall back on pre-1660 assumptions about property.

(45) Staves' work on women's property has general implications for other studies about women in eighteenth-century England. Staves revises her previous claim that separate maintenance allowances proved the weakening of patriarchy; she now finds that
(50) an oversimplification. She also challenges the contention by historians Jeanne and Lawrence Stone that in the late eighteenth century wealthy men married widows less often than before because couples began marrying for love rather than for financial reasons.
(55) Staves does not completely undermine their contention, but she does counter their assumption that widows had more money than never-married women. She points out that jointure property (a widow's lifetime use of an amount of money specified in the marriage contract)
(60) was often lost on remarriage.[13]

Topic:_____

Scope:_____

Purpose:_____

Main Idea:_____

---

[13]PrepTest 26, Sec 4, Passage 4

Explanations

In England (before) 1660, a husband controlled his wife's property. (In) the late seventeenth and eighteenth centuries, (with) the shift from land-based to commercial wealth, marriage (began) to incorporate certain features (5) of a contract. (Historians) have (traditionally argued) that this trend (represented) a gain for women, one that reflects (changing views) about democracy and property (following) the English Restoration in 1660. Susan Staves (contests) this view; (she argues) that whatever (10) gains marriage contracts may briefly have represented for women were (undermined) by judicial decisions about women's contractual rights.

(Shifting) through the tangled details of court cases, Staves (demonstrates) that, (despite) surface changes, a (15) rhetoric of equality, and occasional decisions supporting women's financial power, (definitions) of men's and women's property (remained) inconsistent— (generally) to women's detriment. For (example,) dower lands (property inherited by wives after their husbands' (20) deaths) could not be sold, (but) "curtesy" property (inherited by husbands from their wives) could be sold. (Furthermore,) comparatively (new concepts) that developed in conjunction with the marriage contract, (such as) jointure, pin money, and separate maintenance, (25) were compromised by (peculiar) rules. (For instance,) if a woman spent her pin money (money paid by the husband according to the marriage contract for the wife's personal items) on possessions (other than) clothes she could not sell them; (in effect) they belonged (30) to her husband. (In addition,) a wife could sue for pin money (only) up to a year in arrears—(which) rendered a suit impractical. (Similarly,) separate maintenance allowances (stated sums of money for the wife's support if husband and wife agreed to live apart) were (35) (complicated) by the fact that if a couple tried to agree in a marriage contract on an amount, they were (admitting) that a supposedly indissoluble bond could be dissolved, an (assumption) courts could not recognize. Eighteenth-century historians (underplayed) these inconsistencies, (40) calling them "little contrarieties" that would soon vanish. Staves (shows, however,) that as judges gained power over decisions on marriage contracts, they (tended) to fall back on pre-1660 assumptions about property.

(margin notes)

Marriage = Contract

Hist: gain for women

Staves: no gain

Staves: legal definitions didn't help women

Examples →

Implications of
Staves' work

(45)   Staves' work on women's property has general
       (implications) for other studies about women in
       eighteenth-century England. Staves (revises) her
       (previous) claim that separate maintenance allowances
       proved the weakening of patriarchy; she (now finds) that
(50)   an (oversimplification.) She (also) challenges the
       contention by historians Jeanne and Lawrence Stone
       (that) in the late eighteenth century wealthy men married
       widows less often than before (because) couples began
       marrying for love (rather) than for financial reasons.
(55)   Staves does (not) completely (undermine) their contention,
       (but) she does (counter) their assumption that widows had
       more money than never-married women. She (points)
       out that jointure property (a widow's lifetime use of an
       amount of money specified in the marriage contract)
(60)   was (often) lost on remarriage.[14]

Paragraph Structure: **Paragraph 1** gives you a brief introduction to the subject matter (and some excellent clues to guide you toward the Topic and Scope). The author describes a traditional view held by historians: that womens' rights were generally improved in the seventeenth and eighteenth centuries by the shift toward contract-based marriages. This view is challenged by Susan Staves, who asserts the opposite. Your Roadmap should reflect this conflict.

Paragraph 2 unsurprisingly provides evidence for Staves's claim; it's always a plus when you see a Keyword like "demonstrates" right away. This paragraph is comparatively long, and it is packed with detailed examples of how marriage contracts and legal definitions often worked to the detriment of women's property rights. Such a paragraph gives you an excellent opportunity to do the right thing and refuse to dwell on these examples in depth. The terminology and definitions in this paragraph can easily become confusing, but never forget that active reading means recognizing the difference between main points and supporting evidence (and giving the latter less of your attention). By judiciously circling Keywords, you can research any of this evidence if a question requires you to. For now, take note of the primary reason why all of that information is provided: to shore up Staves's assertion that the legal definitions of the time worked against the interests of women.

Paragraph 3 starts with a clue right off the bat: When you see a Keyword like "implications" in line 46, pay close attention. The author widens the Scope of the passage somewhat by describing how Staves' work affects the studies of others. What follows are, of course, examples that illustrate how this is so. Please note the presence of several important tone Keywords in this paragraph. In line 55, the author states that Staves doesn't "completely undermine" the work of Jeanne and Lawrence Stone, but that she does counter one of their assumptions. This is very different from asserting that Staves *disproves* others' work, and the test makers always reward those who recognize the difference.

---

[14]PrepTest 26, Sec 4, Passage 4

Topic: The opening paragraph introduces us to the Topic right away: the rights of English women after 1660. As always, keep the Topic very general.

Scope: What about women's rights did the author explore? From the beginning, he seems more interested in the work of Susan Staves and her assertion that the laws of the time did not contribute to the betterment of women, than in the traditional views mentioned in lines 5–8. There are many ways you might have phrased this, such as, "The failure of contract law to protect women's property rights," or "Why didn't marriage contracts advance women's rights?" As long as you stayed close to these concepts you're on the right track.

Purpose: Stay in the habit of using simple active verbs to define the Purpose. In this passage, the author wrote to *describe* how Susan Staves undermines a commonly held view of history and what some of the implications of her work are. Note that the author doesn't directly agree or disagree with Staves, but is content to simply describe her point of view.

Main Idea: Your Main Idea should always be simple, declarative, and very tightly focused, so boil it all down to one simple sentence: Susan Staves challenges the assumption that changes in marriage law after 1660 worked to the benefit of English women.

Part 2: Now that you've executed Step 1 of the Kaplan Method, try three practice questions. Use your Roadmap and your knowledge of the passage's Topic, Scope, Purpose, and Main Idea to predict the answer to each question before you select your answer choice.

1. Which one of the following best expresses the main idea of the passage?
   (A) As notions of property and democracy changed in late seventeenth- and eighteenth-century England, marriage settlements began to incorporate contractual features designed to protect women's property rights.
   (B) Traditional historians have incorrectly identified the contractual features that were incorporated into marriage contracts in late seventeenth- and eighteenth-century England.
   (C) The incorporation of contractual features into marriage settlements in late seventeenth- and eighteenth-century England did not represent a significant gain for women.
   (D) An examination of late seventeenth- and eighteenth-century English court cases indicates that most marriage settlements did not incorporate contractual features designed to protect women's property rights.
   (E) Before marriage settlements incorporated contractual features protecting women's property rights, women were unable to gain any financial power in England.[15]

---

[15]PrepTest 26, Sec 4, Q 22

2. Which one of the following best describes the function of the last paragraph in the context of the passage as a whole?

(A) It suggests that Staves' recent work has caused significant revision of theories about the rights of women in eighteenth-century England.

(B) It discusses research that may qualify Staves' work on women's property in eighteenth-century England.

(C) It provides further support for Staves' argument by describing more recent research on women's property in eighteenth-century England.

(D) It asserts that Staves' recent work has provided support for two other hypotheses developed by historians of eighteenth-century England.

(E) It suggests the implications Staves' recent research has for other theories about women in eighteenth-century England.[16]

3. The primary purpose of the passage is to

(A) compare two explanations for the same phenomenon

(B) summarize research that refutes an argument

(C) resolve a long-standing controversy

(D) suggest that a recent hypothesis should be reevaluated

(E) provide support for a traditional theory[17]

---

[16]PrepTest 26, Sec 4, Q 23
[17]PrepTest 26, Sec 4, Q 24

Explanations

1. **(C)**

   Which one of the following best expresses the main idea
   of the passage?
   (A)   As notions of property and democracy changed in
         late seventeenth- and eighteenth-century
         England, marriage settlements began to
         incorporate contractual features designed to
         protect women's property rights.
   (B)   Traditional historians have incorrectly identified
         the contractual features that were incorporated
         into marriage contracts in late seventeenth- and
         eighteenth-century England.
   (C)   The incorporation of contractual features into
         marriage settlements in late seventeenth- and
         eighteenth-century England did not represent a
         significant gain for women.
   (D)   An examination of late seventeenth- and
         eighteenth-century English court cases indicates
         that most marriage settlements did not
         incorporate contractual features designed to
         protect women's property rights.
   (E)   Before marriage settlements incorporated
         contractual features protecting women's
         property rights, women were unable to gain any
         financial power in England.[18]

You've seen this type of question before, and you have just the tool with which to answer it. The
only choice that matches the Main Idea of the passage is the correct answer, choice (C). Choice
(A) focuses far too narrowly on details presented in the first paragraph. Choices (B) and (D) are
both too narrow and they also distort the passage; the author never asserted that historians
incorrectly identified contractual features or that settlements failed to incorporate them. Finally,
choice (E) is far too extreme and very much out of scope. The passage provides very little specific
information about women's property rights prior to the incorporation of contractual features.

2. **(E)**

   Which one of the following best describes the function
   of the last paragraph in the context of the passage as a
   whole?
   (A)   It suggests that Staves' recent work has caused
         significant revision of theories about the rights
         of women in eighteenth-century England.
   (B)   It discusses research that may qualify Staves'
         work on women's property in eighteenth-century
         England.
   (C)   It provides further support for Staves' argument
         by describing more recent research on women's
         property in eighteenth-century England.

---

[18]PrepTest 26, Sec 4, Q 22

(D)   It asserts that Staves' recent work has provided
        support for two other hypotheses developed by
        historians of eighteenth-century England.
(E)   It suggests the implications Staves' recent
        research has for other theories about women in
        eighteenth-century England.

Here's a great example of good preparation yielding results. Because the correct answer must mention the implications of Staves's research, a quick glance at your Roadmap should give you exactly what you need to earn this point. On the basis of this prediction, you can eliminate choices (B) and (C) immediately. Choice (D) mentions the relationship between Staves's work and the work of others, but describes this relationship incorrectly—Staves did not support the historians' hypotheses. Choice (A) is also incorrect; it makes claims that are extreme. Staves may have revised one of her own claims, and she has challenged the work of others, but that isn't the same as asserting that her work caused the "significant revision" of other theories as well. This kind of wrong answer trap is designed to ensnare those who fail to take tone into account, a bad habit that you've learned to avoid. The correct answer, choice (E), is a direct match of your prediction.

3.   **(B)**

The primary purpose of the passage is to
(A)   compare two explanations for the same
        phenomenon
(B)   summarize research that refutes an argument
(C)   resolve a long-standing controversy
(D)   suggest that a recent hypothesis should be
        reevaluated
(E)   provide support for a traditional theory

Which answer choice matches the Purpose? Choice (A) distorts the Purpose; the author isn't comparing two theories, but rather describing the implications of one for the other. Choice (C) is out because nothing is resolved, only described. The author never makes the suggestion described by choice (D), and choice (E) is the opposite of our prediction. That leaves choice (B), the correct answer, and the only choice that mentions Staves's challenge to a commonly held assumption.

THE FINAL PIECE OF THE BIG PICTURE

You now have a basic understanding of every component of Step 1 of the Kaplan Method. You've learned how to use Keywords to create a sense of context. You've begun to break down passage structure into a succinct and useful Roadmap. And now you've learned how to identify Topic, Scope, Purpose, and Main Idea, and how to use them to improve your LSAT score. You might be thinking that Purpose and Main Idea are primarily useful for answering questions that directly ask for them, but as you will soon learn, these ideas are so powerful and far-ranging that you will find yourself referring back to them again and again as you work through test questions. You should get into the habit of identifying them every time you read an LSAT passage. Mastery of these concepts will come only with practice, but with patience and diligence Kaplan's Method will become an instinctive part of your approach to the LSAT.

Because the skills I've taught you so far are vitally important, I'll encourage you to take a cue from the last couple of drills you completed and practice in the following way: Whenever you read a passage, start by executing Step 1 of the Kaplan Method, and then go immediately to the Explanations and check your work *before* you begin answering questions. Be certain you've understood the big picture before you proceed, and make sure your Roadmap is solid and that your understanding of the Main Idea is accurate. If you struggled with the passage, or if you find significant discrepancies between your reading and ours, take the time to reexamine your work. After you're confident that you've read the passage correctly, *then* attempt the question set. You'll find that this compartmentalized approach will allow you to master these core skills much more quickly than if you try to do everything at once. You shouldn't practice this way forever, but try it on your next few practice passages, and return to it whenever you need to.

CHAPTER 5

THE AUTHOR'S VOICE

UNDERSTANDING THE AUTHOR'S VOICE: A COMMON PROBLEM

A very specific problem crops up in every LSAT class I teach. It doesn't always happen during the same lesson or while the class is examining a particular passage. But it always comes up.

For the purposes of demonstration, read the following passage excerpt passively without applying the Kaplan Method:

> One of the greatest challenges facing medical students today, apart from absorbing volumes of technical information and learning habits of scientific thought, is that of remaining empathetic to the needs of
> (5) patients in the face of all this rigorous training. Requiring students to immerse themselves completely in medical coursework risks disconnecting them from the personal and ethical aspects of doctoring, and such strictly scientific thinking is insufficient for grappling
> (10) with modern ethical dilemmas. For these reasons, aspiring physicians need to develop new ways of thinking about and interacting with patients. Training in ethics that takes narrative literature as its primary subject is one method of accomplishing this.[1]

The author describes what he considers to be a great challenge facing medical students, the ability to remain empathetic toward patients. The strictly scientific nature of medical course-

---

[1]PrepTest 38, Sec 3, Passage 4

work is insufficient to prepare students to deal with ethical problems. The author then proposes that one method of dealing with this problem is the study of narrative literature. So far the author's intent seems fairly clear. The second paragraph goes on to explore the problem in greater detail:

(15)   Although training in ethics is currently provided by medical schools, this training relies heavily on an abstract, philosophical view of ethics. Although the conceptual clarity provided by a traditional ethics course can be valuable, theorizing about ethics
(20)   contributes little to the understanding of everyday human experience or to preparing medical students for the multifarious ethical dilemmas they will face as physicians. A true foundation in ethics must be predicated on an understanding of human behavior that
(25)   reflects a wide array of relationships and readily adapts to various perspectives, for this is what is required to develop empathy. Ethics courses drawing on narrative literature can better help students prepare for ethical dilemmas precisely because such literature attaches its
(30)   readers so forcefully to the concrete and varied world of human events.[2]

The author describes some of the deficiencies in the ethical training provided by medical schools, suggesting that the theoretical nature of such training is inadequate to prepare students for the real-life situations they will eventually face. Unsurprisingly, he once again suggests that the study of narrative literature may help remedy these shortcomings. The passage presents a clear dichotomy between these two approaches: if you encountered this passage on test day, you probably wouldn't be too surprised to see the following question:

27. The author's attitude regarding the traditional method of teaching ethics in medical school can most accurately be described as

You know from a quick examination of the first two paragraphs that the author considers traditional ethics training to be inadequate. With this in mind, examine the answer choices.

(A)   unqualified disapproval of the method and disapproval of all of its effects
(B)   reserved judgment regarding the method and disapproval of all of its effects
(C)   partial disapproval of the method and clinical indifference toward its effects
(D)   partial approval of the method and disapproval of all of its effects
(E)   partial disapproval of the method and approval of some of its effects[3]

[2]PrepTest 38, Sec 3, Passage 4
[3]PrepTest 38, Sec 3, Passage 4, Q 27

Do any of these choices stand out as clearly correct? Each of them mentions some degree of disapproval, so how do you know which one accurately reflects the author's attitude? The challenge presented by this question exemplifies the common problem I referred to earlier. When you read passively, you run the risk of developing an incorrect or incomplete understanding of the author's point of view. This is a costly mistake to make on the LSAT, because you will invariably be tested on your knowledge of the author's opinions.

THREE COMMON TRAPS TO AVOID

I began by saying that the problem of misunderstanding authorial intent is one that nearly all of my students encounter. Furthermore, it's the kind of mistake that any student can make, regardless of skill and experience. Since you are now on the path to LSAT mastery, I would very much like to see you avoid this mistake. In this chapter I will help you do so with a brief discussion of three common errors to watch out for: structural misunderstanding, distortion of tone, and multiple points of view.

Structural Misunderstanding

I already alluded to this common error with the example at the beginning of this chapter. Structural misunderstanding most often occurs when you either fail to take notice of a vital Keyword or neglect to think about what it tells you in the context of what you've already learned. Examine the opening of the second paragraph once more, this time with the Keywords identified:

> Although training in ethics is currently provided by medical schools, this training relies heavily on an abstract, philosophical view of ethics. Although the conceptual clarity provided by a traditional ethics course can be valuable, theorizing about ethics contributes little to the understanding of everyday human experience or to preparing medical students for the multifarious ethical dilemmas they will face as physicians.[4]

The contrast Keyword "although" at the beginning of the paragraph prepares you for the critique that follows it: Even though ethics training is provided, it relies too much on abstraction. Now, pay very close attention to the second "although" in line 17. The author makes a concession, then contrasts this with another criticism. This structural nuance is extremely important, because it reveals the full extent of the author's opinion—while there is some benefit in traditional ethics courses, there are also problematic gaps.

[4]PrepTest 38, Sec 3, Passage 4

Bearing this in mind, revisit question 27:

27. The author's attitude regarding the traditional method of teaching ethics in medical school can most accurately be described as

    (A)   unqualified disapproval of the method and disapproval of all of its effects

    (B)   reserved judgment regarding the method and disapproval of all of its effects

    (C)   partial disapproval of the method and clinical indifference toward its effects

    (D)   partial approval of the method and disapproval of all of its effects

    (E)   partial disapproval of the method and approval of some of its effects[5]

Choices (A), (B), and (D) each indicate that the author disapproves of *all* the effects of traditional ethics training. This is in direct opposition to the text, in which the author declares that such training "can be valuable" (line 19). Choice (C) is similarly flawed, since the author's concession can't be interpreted as indifference. Only correct Choice (E) properly characterizes both the author's reservations and partial approval.

This question can be confusing and time-consuming if you don't pay close attention to the structural clues in the passage. A passive reader is likely to overlook the contrast Keywords that inform the strategic reader of the author's intent, and even a test taker who is familiar with the Kaplan Method might notice the two occurrences of "although" at the paragraph's onset but fail to take note of the opinions they highlight.

You might be nodding your head at this point, thinking, "That sounds exactly like something I would do." Or perhaps you're wondering how anyone could make such a mistake. The fact is, no matter how skilled you become at strategic reading, this is an easy error to make, and it usually occurs when you rely on Keywords to do the thinking for you. Remember that in chapter 2, I pointed out that working with Keywords is a two-part process: You must identify the Keyword, but you must also understand what it is telling you in relation to the surrounding text.

Another contributor to structural misunderstanding is a shortage of Keywords pointing to the author's voice. You know from previous lessons that the author doesn't always present strong opinions in a passage. You also know that any opinions the author *does* present are usually tested, and you have learned to watch out for them. Try a little experiment: Read the following excerpt from an LSAT social science passage as quickly as you can, and see whether you can spot any authorial opinion:

---

[5]PrepTest 38, Sec 3, Passage 4, Q 27

Bettelheim interprets all fairy tales as driven by children's fantasies of desire and revenge, and in doing so suppresses the true nature of parental behavior ranging from abuse to indulgence. Fortunately, these
(50) characterizations of selfish children and innocent adults have been discredited to some extent by recent psychoanalytic literature. The need to deny adult evil has been a pervasive feature of our society, leading us to position children not only as the sole agents of evil
(55) but also as the objects of unending moral instruction, hence the idea that a literature targeted for them must stand in the service of pragmatic instrumentality rather than foster an unproductive form of playful pleasure.[6]

The paragraph primarily discusses the view of Bettelheim and those who agree with him, but did you spot the one crucial keyword that gives the author's opinion? Here it is:

(Fortunately,) these
(55) characterizations of selfish children and innocent adults have been discredited to some extent by recent psychoanalytic literature.[7]

This lone, vital Keyword is the means by which you know that the author finds it "fortunate" that Bettelheim's views have been partially discredited. Without it, the author's attitude would remain neutral; he would simply tell you that Bettelheim's ideas are under attack, and then go on to further explore the significance of those ideas in society as a whole.

How important is this one word and its implications?

11. Which one of the following is the most accurate description of the author's attitude toward Bettelheim's view of fairy tales?

(A) concern that the view will undermine the ability of fairy tales to provide moral instruction
(B) scorn toward the view's supposition that moral tenets can be universally valid
(C) disapproval of the view's depiction of children as selfish and adults as innocent
(D) anger toward the view's claim that children often improve as a result of deserved punishment
(E) disappointment with the view's emphasis on the manifest content of a tale[8]

---

[6]PrepTest 39, Sec 3, Passage 2
[7]PrepTest 39, Sec 3, Passage 2
[8]PrepTest 39, Sec 3, Passage 2, Q 11

All of the answer choices are to some degree negatively connotated, but only one matches point for point the author's opinion and the reasons he provides in the quoted paragraph: choice (C), the correct answer.

The LSAT is full of examples like that. In order to avoid a structural misunderstanding, you must always note Keywords of opinion, and you must always think about them in the context of the passage as a whole.

Distortion of Tone

Another common error is to misunderstand the author's tone. This is a problem I've presented to you before, but it's important enough to warrant a brief review. As a quick illustration, think for a moment about the incorrect answer choices in the question you just examined:

11. Which one of the following is the most accurate description of the author's attitude toward Bettelheim's view of fairy tales?

 (A) concern that the view will undermine the ability of fairy tales to provide moral instruction
 (B) scorn toward the view's supposition that moral tenets can be universally valid
 (C) disapproval of the view's depiction of children as selfish and adults as innocent
 (D) anger toward the view's claim that children often improve as a result of deserved punishment
 (E) disappointment with the view's emphasis on the manifest content of a tale[9]

Choice (A) is contrary to the author's opinion, and choice (B) is out of the scope of this question. Pay particular attention to the verbs used in choices (D) and (E). In the paragraph you read, did the author ever use language that indicated he was angry or disappointed with Bettelheim's hypothesis? Not at all. He did clearly state the disapproval mentioned in correct choice (C), but to confuse disapproval with anger or disappointment is to distort the author's tone.

Since the test makers will reward you for understanding the author's tone, they will provide correct answer choices that fall perfectly in line with it, but they will also list incorrect answer choices that vary from it in ways that can be quite nuanced.

Here's another example that often catches my students off guard. This time you'll read a short excerpt from a passage detailing a specific criticism and the author's response to it. Read strategically, paying attention to Keywords, and note the author's opinion (don't worry if the context of the excerpt isn't totally clear; for now all you really need to understand is the author's point of view):

---

[9]PrepTest 39, Sec 3, Passage 2, Q 11

This brand of criticism has
met opposition from the formalists, who study the
text alone and argue that reader-response theory can
(15)   encourage and even validate fragmented views of a
work, rather than the unified view acquired by
examining only the content of the text. However,
since no theory has a monopoly on divining meaning
from a text, the formalists' view appears
(20)   unnecessarily narrow.[10]

Now, take a moment to articulate in your mind the author's attitude toward the formalists, then answer the following question:

14.   Which one of the following most accurately describes
the author's attitude toward formalism as expressed in
the passage?

(A)   scholarly neutrality
(B)   grudging respect
(C)   thoughtless disregard
(D)   cautious ambivalence
(E)   reasoned dismissal[11]

The author declares the formalists' view to be "unnecessarily narrow" (line 20). An opinion has been provided, specifically a negative one. This makes it simple to rule out choices (A), (B), and (D), since the author is neither neutral nor respectful. This leaves (C) and (E) to choose from. Was the author's disapproval of formalism "thoughtless" or "reasoned"?

Many students choose incorrect choice (C) because they're uncomfortable with the word "dismissal" in correct choice (E). In the excerpt above, the author does indeed *dismiss* the formalists' claim, and does so "since" (line 18) no theory can completely describe the meaning of a text. This *must* be described as reasoned "dismissal", since a specific reason was provided.

Even at this relatively early stage of your LSAT training you've probably learned to be wary of language in the answer choices that seems too extreme, and rightfully so—many wrong answer traps do contain such language. When in doubt, research the relevant text and let the passage be your guide; the answer is always there.

Multiple Points of View

The final common trap I want to point out occurs when numerous viewpoints are presented in the passage. In such a situation, the pressure of the clock may cause you to rush through the passage and mistake one viewpoint for another or to confuse a third-party viewpoint with the

---

[10]PrepTest 43, Sec 1, Passage 3
[11]PrepTest 43, Sec 1, Passage 3, Q 14

author's. The best response to this situation is, as always, strategic reading. When numerous viewpoints are presented to you, take note of them right away in your Roadmap.

Read the following opening paragraph and based on your analysis of it, predict how many viewpoints at a minimum will be presented in the passage:

> Two impressive studies have reexamined Eric Williams' conclusion that Britain's abolition of the slave trade in 1807 and its emancipation of slaves in its colonies in 1834 were driven primarily by economic
> (5) rather than humanitarian motives. Blighted by depleted soil, indebtedness, and the inefficiency of coerced labor, these colonies, according to Williams, had by 1807 become an impediment to British economic progress.[12]

I hope you were keeping count. This paragraph tells you to expect no fewer than four different opinions in the passage. You have Eric Williams' conclusion, you're told about "two impressive studies" that comment on his opinions, and you should always be on the lookout for the author's point of view as well.

I'm going to come back to this passage and discuss various ways of staying ahead of multiple viewpoints in general in the next chapter. But for now, I want you to remember one important tip: When a passage clues you in to the presence of multiple opinions, actively prepare to seek them out and add them to your Roadmap; they will undoubtedly be crucial to scoring points in the question set. As a preview, take a look at a few of the questions:

23. Which one of the following best states Williams' view of the primary reason for Britain's abolition of the slave trade and the emancipation of slaves in its colonies?

24. According to Eltis, low wages and Draconian vagrancy laws in Britain in the seventeenth and eighteenth centuries were intended to

25. It can be inferred that the author of the passage views Drescher's presentation of British traditions concerning liberty as

26. The information in the passage suggests that Eltis and Drescher agree that[13]

A quick glance at these questions confirms that there are, indeed, at least four opinions to keep track of: Williams, Eltis, Drescher, and the author. Note how questions 23 and 24 each ask for some specific aspect of a single viewpoint, while question 25 asks for the author's opinion of Drescher's ideas, and question 26 asks you to find common ground between Eltis and Drescher. Not only must you understand each viewpoint separately, but you must be prepared to compare and contrast them as well in order to score these points.

[12]PrepTest 19, Sec 3, Passage 4
[13]PrepTest 19, Sec 3, Qs 23–26

Here's the good news. While a passage like this may appear intimidating, there is one thing you can be absolutely certain of: With so many opinions present, there will be a wealth of Keywords to help you keep track of them. And remember, your goal isn't to completely understand or memorize them, but only to summarize them, add them to your Roadmap, and be prepared to research them as necessary. Incidentally, most of my students find that passages containing definite opinions, even if there are several of them, tend to seem less abstract, and therefore less difficult, than passages that do not.

In any case, my purpose here is to remind you that you must always be aware, not just of what opinions are present in a passage, but to whom they belong as well.

DRILL: UNDERSTANDING THE AUTHOR

Now for some practice. Read and Roadmap the following passage, and then answer the questions that follow. I've chosen a passage that illustrates some of the traps I've described in this chapter, so watch for them as you work. When you've finished, carefully read the explanations that follow.

It has recently been discovered that many attributions of paintings to the seventeenth-century Dutch artist Rembrandt may be false. The contested paintings are not minor works, whose removal from the
(5) Rembrandt corpus would leave it relatively unaffected: they are at its very center. In her recent book, Svetlana Alpers uses these cases of disputed attribution as a point of departure for her provocative discussion of the radical distinctiveness of Rembrandt's approach to
(10) painting.

Alpers argues that Rembrandt exercised an unprecedentedly firm control over his art, his students, and the distribution of his works. Despite Gary Schwartz's brilliant documentation of Rembrandt's
(15) complicated relations with a wide circle of patrons, Alpers takes the view that Rembrandt refused to submit to the prevailing patronage system. He preferred, she claims, to sell his works on the open market and to play the entrepreneur. At a time when Dutch artists were
(20) organizing into professional brotherhoods and academies, Rembrandt stood apart. In fact, Alpers' portrait of Rembrandt shows virtually every aspect of his art pervaded by economic motives. Indeed, so complete was Rembrandt's involvement with the
(25) market, she argues, that he even presented himself as a commodity, viewing his studio's products as extensions of himself, sent out into the world to earn money. Alpers asserts that Rembrandt's enterprise is found not just in his paintings, but in his refusal to limit
(30) his enterprise to those paintings he actually painted. He marketed Rembrandt.

Although there may be some truth in the view that Rembrandt was an entrepreneur who made some aesthetic decisions on the basis of what he knew the
(35) market wanted, Alpers' emphasis on economic factors sacrifices discussion of the aesthetic qualities that make Rembrandt's work unique. For example, Alpers asserts that Rembrandt deliberately left his works unfinished so as to get more money for their revision and
(40) completion. She implies that Rembrandt actually wished the Council of Amsterdam to refuse the great *Claudius Civilis*, which they had commissioned for

their new town hall, and she argues that "he must have calculated that he would be able to get more money by
(45) retouching [the] painting." Certainly the picture is painted with very broad strokes but there is no evidence that it was deliberately left unfinished. The fact is that the look of a work like *Claudius Civilis* must also be understood as the consequence of
(50) Rembrandt's powerful and profound meditations on painting itself. Alpers makes no mention of the pictorial dialectic that can be discerned between, say, the lessons Rembrandt absorbed from the Haarlem school of painters and the styles of his native Leiden.
(55) The trouble is that while Rembrandt's artistic enterprise may indeed not be reducible to the works he himself painted, it is not reducible to marketing practices either.

1. Which one of the following best summarizes the main conclusion of the author of the passage?

   (A) Rembrandt differed from other artists of his time both in his aesthetic techniques and in his desire to meet the demands of the marketplace.

   (B) The aesthetic qualities of Rembrandt's work cannot be understood without consideration of how economic motives pervaded decisions he made about his art.

   (C) Rembrandt was one of the first artists to develop the notion of a work of art as a commodity that could be sold in an open marketplace.

   (D) Rembrandt's artistic achievement cannot be understood solely in terms of decisions he made on the basis of what would sell in the marketplace.

   (E) Rembrandt was an entrepreneur whose artistic enterprise was not limited to the paintings he actually painted himself.

2. According to the passage, Alpers and Schwartz disagree about which one of the following?

   (A)   the degree of control Rembrandt exercised over the production of his art

   (B)   the role that Rembrandt played in organizing professional brotherhoods and academies

   (C)   the kinds of relationships Rembrandt had with his students

   (D)   the degree of Rembrandt's involvement in the patronage system

   (E)   the role of the patronage system in seventeenth-century Holland

3. It can be inferred that the author of the passage and Alpers would be most likely to agree on which one of the following?

   (A)   Rembrandt made certain aesthetic decisions on the basis of what he understood about the demands of the marketplace.

   (B)   The Rembrandt corpus will not be affected if attributions of paintings to Rembrandt are found to be false.

   (C)   Stylistic aspects of Rembrandt's painting can be better explained in economic terms than in historical or aesthetic terms.

   (D)   Certain aesthetic aspects of Rembrandt's art are the result of his experimentation with different painting techniques.

   (E)   Most of Rembrandt's best-known works were painted by his students, but were sold under Rembrandt's name.[14]

---

[14]PrepTest 23, Sec 4, Passage 1, Qs 1, 2, 5

Explanations

Paragraph Structure:

Paragraph 1 begins with a brief discussion of potential forgeries in Rembrandt's body of work. You must be careful, however, as the author quickly takes the passage in a very different direction. In lines 6–10, the true scope of the passage is revealed: Susan Alpers uses the questionable paintings as a "point of departure" for her discussion of Rembrandt's approach to painting.

Paragraph 2 describes Aplers' view, that Rembrandt was driven primarily by economic motives. Note the abundance of Keywords of emphasis and tone in this paragraph. In line 22 Alpers claims that "virtually every aspect" of Rembrandt's work was influenced by these motives, and line 24 begins with, "Indeed, so complete was Rembrandt's involvement with the market" before going on to further describe Alpers' claim. I hope you also noticed the brief (but important) mention of a conflicting point of view beginning in line 13. Alpers claims that Rembrandt did not submit to the prevailing patronage system of his time "despite" Schwatz's "brilliant" claim to the contrary.

Paragraph 3 signals the author's opinion immediately, beginning with the contrast Keyword "although." Note that the author's tone is very clear: There may be "some truth" in Alpers' claim, but her work sacrifices a discussion of Rembrandt's aesthetic concerns. There follows a lengthy discussion of *Claudius Civilis*, an easy place to get bogged down in details, but "for example" in line 37 forewarns you that the following text is evidence for the conclusion already stated. The author returns to the main point at the end of the paragraph, identifying the "trouble" with Alpers' analysis in lines 55–58: Rembrandt can't be understood solely as an entrepreneur.

Topic: The work of Rembrandt

Scope: Alpers' view of Rembrandt as an entrepreneur

Purpose: To describe a study about Rembrandt's approach to art and to refute its central assumption

Main Idea: Rembrandt cannot be understood simply as an entrepreneur as Alpers claims.

1. **(D)**

    Which one of the following best summarizes the
    main conclusion of the author of the passage?
    (A)   Rembrandt differed from other artists of his
          time both in his aesthetic techniques and in
          his desire to meet the demands of the
          marketplace.
    (B)   The aesthetic qualities of Rembrandt's work
          cannot be understood without consideration
          of how economic motives pervaded decisions
          he made about his art.
    (C)   Rembrandt was one of the first artists to
          develop the notion of a work of art as a
          commodity that could be sold in an open
          marketplace.
    (D)   Rembrandt's artistic achievement cannot be
          understood solely in terms of decisions he
          made on the basis of what would sell in the
          marketplace.
    (E)   Rembrandt was an entrepreneur whose artistic
          enterprise was not limited to the paintings he
          actually painted himself.[15]

This type of question should be very familiar to you by now, and correct choice (D) perfectly
matches the author's Main Idea. Choice (B) contains a common wrong answer trap; it describes
Alpers' central assertion rather than the author's. Choices (A) and (C) distort the facts by claiming that Rembrandt's techniques were exclusive to his work, something the passage never
claims. Choice (E) focuses on a single aspect of Alpers' thesis without ever addressing the
author's central claim.

2. **(D)**

    According to the passage, Alpers and Schwartz
    disagree about which one of the following?
    (A)   the degree of control Rembrandt exercised
          over the production of his art
    (B)   the role that Rembrandt played in organizing
          professional brotherhoods and academies
    (C)   the kinds of relationships Rembrandt had with
          his students
    (D)   the degree of Rembrandt's involvement in the
          patronage system
    (E)   the role of the patronage system in
          seventeenth-century Holland[16]

Question 2 reminds you that conflicting points of view are usually tested. The only opinion
attributed to Schwartz appears in lines 13–15. Schwartz claims that Rembrandt worked within
the patronage system, and Alpers disagrees. Only choice (D) falls within this scope.

---

[15]PrepTest 23, Sec 4, Passage 1, Q 1

[16]PrepTest 23, Sec 4, Passage 1, Q 2

3.   **(A)**

It can be inferred that the author of the passage and Alpers would be most likely to agree on which one of the following?

(A)   Rembrandt made certain aesthetic decisions on the basis of what he understood about the demands of the marketplace.

(B)   The Rembrandt corpus will not be affected if attributions of paintings to Rembrandt are found to be false.

(C)   Stylistic aspects of Rembrandt's painting can be better explained in economic terms than in historical or aesthetic terms.

(D)   Certain aesthetic aspects of Rembrandt's art are the result of his experimentation with different painting techniques.

(E)   Most of Rembrandt's best-known works were painted by his students, but were sold under Rembrandt's name.[17]

Approach a question like this one with the author's tone in mind. Remember that the author didn't completely reject Alpers' claim, but instead insisted that it was inappropriately one-sided. Since both Alpers and the author did agree that Rembrandt made decisions that were to some extent influenced by the marketplace, choice (A) must be correct. Choice (C) describes a view that Alpers would probably agree with but that is contrary to the author's Main Idea. Choices (B), (D), and (E) are all out of scope.

LISTEN CAREFULLY TO THE AUTHOR

I can't say it often enough: The test makers reward those who understand the author's main ideas. This is a concept that you're very familiar with by now, but common pitfalls do exist. In summary, please remember the following:

- Don't just read and circle opinion Keywords; think about what they tell you, and pay close attention to the context in which they appear.
- Take note of *every* opinion Keyword, especially when they are scarce.
- Keep an eye out for qualifiers that help you understand the nuances of the author's opinions.
- Trust the text. The language you need to understand the author's voice is always there.
- When the passage contains multiple viewpoints, be sure to take note of who is saying what. Don't confuse the author's opinion with the opinions of others.

I've watched a lot of students learn these lessons the hard way, and you've probably made some of these mistakes yourself at one time or another. That's fine; in fact, it's an important part of the learning process. Keep these concepts in mind as you become more confident in your mastery of the Kaplan Method.

---

[17]PrepTest 23, Sec 4, Passage 1, Q 5

CHAPTER 6

READING PREDICTIVELY

THE PASSAGES ARE PREDICTABLE
Why Does LSAT Reading Seem Difficult?

I'd like you to think about a question that I haven't raised prior to this chapter, but that you may have already considered yourself: Why are certain LSAT Reading Comprehension passages so much harder to read than anything else you've read in your life? You might have thought of several answers right away, and I'll mention a few of the more common ones that I hear from my students.

Most of my students say that the Reading Comprehension passages are difficult because they contain difficult terminology and dense linguistic construction, especially law and science passages. They mention their own discomfort and lack of familiarity with these subjects as a further complication. Sometimes they complain that the passages don't follow any discernible logic, seeming to randomly jump from idea to idea without warning. Finally, what they all mention without fail is that if it weren't for the ticking of the clock (combined with the impending questions), LSAT reading wouldn't be any more challenging than any other reading they've already done.

You most likely agreed with some, possibly all, of these points. But if you take a moment to think about each one in the context of what you've learned so far, you'll make an important discovery.

The Real Challenge

The final point, that it's really the ticking clock that makes Reading Comprehension challenging, by its very definition weakens all the other points. Here's what I mean. The first complaint is that the text is dense and unfamiliar. That's a fair point, and very few test takers will get through a Reading Comprehension section without running into some unfamiliar words or concepts. But haven't you run into the same problem when reading in school, at work, or in your leisure time? Do you have to reach for a dictionary every time you encounter a new word? Most likely not; you can use the context of what you're reading to work out what the word means, or the author provides a definition a short while later. In any case, encountering one difficult word doesn't sabotage your ability to understand what you're reading.

The second point is only marginally different. Certainly, LSAT passages may wander into territory that you don't personally find familiar. But once again, think back to your prior reading experiences and you'll realize that you've been reading about unfamiliar topics your entire life. After all, there isn't much to be gained from reading the same thing over and over again. Clearly, then, you know how to grapple with unfamiliar ideas and learn what they mean.

The third problem—that the passages don't follow a logical path—should seem instinctively wrong to you now that you've learned the Kaplan Method. After all, every passage you've read thus far has been peppered with Keywords that spelled out the author's intent every step of the way. You know that the passages occasionally go in a direction that is surprising, but such a move will always be within the author's scope. Ultimately, you've learned that very little of what you encounter in the Reading Comprehension section will be surprising, because you've learned to read actively by predicting where the author is going to go next.

So that leaves the final point, and it bears repeating: It is the time limit, combined with the pressure of the question set, that makes LSAT reading challenging. This is, for the vast majority of test takers, unequivocally true. You've already demonstrated in various contexts your ability to deal with tough language, new subjects, and unusual structure. It's being forced to do these things under time constraints that makes the LSAT challenging. And the one thing you can't do is add minutes to the clock.

Staying One Step Ahead of the Author

The solution, as always, is to become a more skillful reader. Not merely faster, but more efficient. The next step is for you to begin reading predictively.

Reading predictively is a simple process, one that derives directly from ideas I've already introduced in earlier chapters. In fact, you've already begun to form the habit of reading predictively by learning to identify and analyze the Keywords in passages. Now you must simply take the process a step further: As you read a passage, you must actively predict the main ideas that are likely to occur next.

To illustrate this concept, I'll present you with an LSAT passage and walk you through the process of predictive reading. As you read, you should stop periodically and ask yourself: What is the author likely to do next?

> The debate over the environmental crisis is not
> new; anxiety about industry's impact on the
> environment has existed for over a century.[1]

The author begins by introducing the Topic, the environmental crisis. He asserts that the debate has been going on for over a century. Since passages usually focus on recent developments rather than well-established facts, you should immediately ask: **Are there any recent developments?**

> What is new is the extreme polarization of views.[2]

Perfect. The Scope of the passage is the polarization of views on the subject. You've probably already guessed what question you should ask next: **What are these polarized views?**

> Mounting
> (5) evidence of humanity's capacity to damage the
> environment irreversibly coupled with suspicions that
> government, industry, and even science might be
> impotent to prevent environmental destruction have
> provoked accusatory polemics on the part of
> (10) environmentalists. In turn, these polemics have elicited
> a corresponding backlash from industry. The sad effect
> of this polarization is that it is now even more difficult
> for industry than it was a hundred years ago to respond
> appropriately to impact analyses that demand action.[3]

As predicted, the author presents the polarized views. Notice the emphasis Keywords that help you spot them easily; words like "accusatory," "polemics," and "backlash" all indicate that there is a debate between environmentalists and industry. Your Roadmap should look something like this:

Auth: Env.
debate is
now polarized

> The debate over the environmental crisis is not
> new; anxiety about industry's impact on the
> environment has existed for over a century. What is
> new is the extreme polarization of views. Mounting
> (5) evidence of humanity's capacity to damage the
> environment irreversibly coupled with suspicions that
> government, industry, and even science might be
> impotent to prevent environmental destruction have
> provoked accusatory polemics on the part of
> (10) environmentalists. In turn, these polemics have elicited
> a corresponding backlash from industry. The sad effect
> of this polarization is that it is now even more difficult
> for industry than it was a hundred years ago to respond
> appropriately to impact analyses that demand action.[4]

[1]PrepTest 23, Sec 4, Passage 3
[2]PrepTest 23, Sec 4, Passage 3
[3]PrepTest 23, Sec 4, Passage 3
[4]PrepTest 23, Sec 4, Passage 3

You may be wondering why it's helpful to go through the trouble of asking these questions. The answer: If you can predict what is likely to come next, then you always have context for what you are reading. No matter how dense the language may become, you stay one step ahead of the author, and when she makes her main point you're already prepared to see it and understand it.

What is likely to happen in the next paragraph? Since the debate is between polarized points of view, the author will likely elaborate on those viewpoints.

(15)   Unlike today's adversaries, earlier ecological
         reformers shared with advocates of industrial growth a
         confidence in timely corrective action.[5]

The author presents the viewpoint of a group of "earlier" ecological reformers. This Keyword-laden sentence is extremely important, because it allows you to predict a slight twist in this passage that might otherwise catch you by surprise. **What is the author likely to discuss next?** Undoubtedly she will describe the earlier reformers, but the Keyword "unlike" tells you that soon after she will almost certainly contrast them with a more recent group.

This insight is extremely valuable; the first paragraph may have led you to believe that the author would primarily discuss the differences between ecological reformers and their industrial foes. That might still be true, but now you are prepared to see a different conflict, in this case between two separate groups of reformers. Being prepared for what comes next gives you an *enormous* advantage on test day. Less-alert readers may become confused when the author begins to discuss this secondary debate, thinking that the passage has thrown them a curveball. You, on the other hand, know it is going to happen.

To continue with paragraph two:

         George P.
         Marsh's pioneering conservation tract *Man and Nature*
         (1864) elicited wide acclaim without embittered
(20)   denials. *Man and Nature* castigated Earth's despoilers
         for heedless greed, declaring that humanity "has
         brought the face of the Earth to a desolation almost as
         complete as that of the Moon." But no entrepreneur or
         industrialist sought to refute Marsh's accusation, to
(25)   defend the gutting of forests or the slaughter of wildlife
         as economically essential, or to dismiss his ecological
         warnings as hysterical. To the contrary, they generally
         agreed with him.[6]

The author elaborates on one particular early reformer, then points out that industrialists tended to agree with him. This may seem surprising in light of your earlier predictions. Didn't the first paragraph indicate that the views of reformers and industry were polarized? Don't

[5]PrepTest 23, Sec 4, Passage 3

[6]PrepTest 23, Sec 4, Passage 3

worry; if you continue to read strategically the author's purpose will become clear. For now, review the Roadmap for the first two paragraphs, then predict what is likely to come next:

Auth: Env. debate is now polarized

The (debate) over the environmental crisis is not new; anxiety about industry's impact on the environment has existed for over a century. What is (new) is the (extreme) polarization of views. Mounting (5) (evidence) of humanity's capacity to damage the environment irreversibly (coupled with) suspicions that government, industry, and even science might be impotent to prevent environmental destruction have (provoked) accusatory (polemics) on the part of (10) environmentalists. In turn, these (polemics) have elicited a corresponding (backlash) from industry. The (sad effect) of this polarization is that it is now even (more difficult) for industry than it was a hundred years ago to respond appropriately to impact analyses that demand action.

Earlier reformers

(15) (Unlike) today's adversaries, (earlier) ecological reformers (shared) with advocates of industrial growth a confidence in timely corrective action. George P. Marsh's pioneering conservation tract *Man and Nature* (1864) (elicited) wide acclaim (without) embittered (20) denials. *Man and Nature* (castigated) Earth's despoilers for heedless greed, (declaring) that humanity "has brought the face of the Earth to a desolation almost as complete as that of the Moon." (But) no entrepreneur or industrialist sought to (refute) Marsh's accusation, to

Industry agreed

(25) defend the gutting of forests or the slaughter of wildlife as economically essential, (or) to dismiss his ecological warnings as hysterical. To the (contrary,) they generally agreed with him.[7]

What will happen next? The author is likely to explain why industry tended to agree with the earlier reformers. It is also likely that the author will soon discuss the more modern reformers. Either could occur in the next paragraph. Read on with these predictions in mind:

Why? Marsh and his followers took environmental (30) improvement and economic progress as givens; they disputed not the desirability of conquering nature but the bungling way in which the conquest was carried out. Blame was not personalized; Marsh denounced general greed rather than particular entrepreneurs, and (35) the media did not hound malefactors. Further, corrective measures seemed to entail no sacrifice, to demand no draconian remedies. Self-interest underwrote most prescribed reforms. Marsh's emphasis on future stewardship was then a widely accepted ideal (40) (if not practice). His ecological admonitions were in keeping with the Enlightenment premise that humanity's mission was to subdue and transform nature.[8]

---

[7]PrepTest 23, Sec 4, Passage 3
[8]PrepTest 23, Sec 4, Passage 3

The third paragraph explains why Marsh and the industrialists weren't in conflict; they shared many common views. The Roadmap should look something like this:

Why ind.
didn't
dispute
Marsh

(Why?)Marsh and his followers took environmental
(30)   improvement and economic progress as givens; they
        (disputed) not the desirability of conquering nature(but)
        the bungling way in which the conquest was carried
        out. Blame was not personalized; (Marsh denounced)
        general greed rather than particular entrepreneurs, (and)
(35)   the media did not hound malefactors. (Further,)
        corrective measures seemed to entail no sacrifice, to
        demand no draconian remedies. Self-interest
        underwrote most prescribed reforms. (Marsh's emphasis)
        on future stewardship was then a widely accepted ideal
(40)   (if not practice). His ecological admonitions were in
        (keeping with) the Enlightenment premise that
        humanity's mission was to subdue and transform
        nature.[9]

What will happen next? Using the context of what you've read so far, you can be fairly certain you'll soon encounter the modern ecological reformers. You can take this prediction a step further. **How do the new reformers differ from the old ones?** Since the earlier reformers were at least partially in agreement with industry, it must be that the modern reformers are in conflict with industry. You can make this prediction confidently; the author has been preparing you for it since the first paragraph. Reading on:

        Not until the 1960s did a gloomier perspective gain
(45)   popular ground. Frederic Clements' equilibrium model
        of ecology, developed in the 1930s, seemed consistent
        with mounting environmental disasters. In this view,
        nature was most fruitful when least altered. Left
        undisturbed, flora and fauna gradually attained
(50)   maximum diversity and stability. Despoliation
        thwarted the culmination or shortened the duration of
        this beneficent climax; technology did not improve
        nature but destroyed it.[10]

Notice how your predictions allow you to cut through the jargon of this paragraph and easily place it within the overall context of the passage. The author describes the "gloomier" perspective of the modern reformers. These reformers believe that nature should remain untouched and are in opposition to technology. This is precisely what you expected to read.

---

[9]PrepTest 23, Sec 4, Passage 3
[10]PrepTest 23, Sec 4, Passage 3

New view:
industry
bad for
environ.

(45) Not until the 1960s did a gloomier perspective gain
popular ground. Frederic Clements' equilibrium model
of ecology, developed in the 1930s, seemed consistent
with mounting environmental disasters. In this view,
nature was most fruitful when least altered. Left
undisturbed, flora and fauna gradually attained
(50) maximum diversity and stability. Despoliation
thwarted the culmination or shortened the duration of
this beneficent climax; technology did not improve
nature but destroyed it.[11]

What will the author conclude with? A better way to think about this might be, "What is the only major point introduced by the author that has yet to be discussed?" Since the author still hasn't explicitly discussed the debate between industry and environmentalists, you can confidently predict that the final paragraph will elaborate on this debate.

With this prediction in mind, read the final paragraph:

The equilibrium model became an ecological
(55) mystique: environmental interference was now taboo,
wilderness adored. Nature as unfinished fabric
perfected by human ingenuity gave way to the image of
nature debased and endangered by technology. In
contrast to the Enlightenment vision of nature,
(60) according to which rational managers construct an ever
more improved environment, twentieth-century
reformers' vision of nature calls for a reduction of
human interference in order to restore environmental
stability.[12]

Without a good sense of context, a paragraph like this one can be alarming. It shifts back and forth between two viewpoints, providing a healthy dose of jargon along the way. Terminology like "ecological mystique" and the "Enlightenment vision of nature" may not be helpful. Still, predictive reading provides clarity: The author is elaborating on the ways in which the modern reformers differ from their predecessors. You've already become acquainted with these two views, and this paragraph merely confirms what you already know; the modern reformers consider human encroachment on nature "taboo," and instead desire a "reduction of human interference." Your Roadmap should reflect this difference:

[11]PrepTest 23, Sec 4, Passage 3
[12]PrepTest 23, Sec 4, Passage 3

The equilibrium model (became) an ecological
(55) mystique: environmental interference was now taboo,
wilderness adored. Nature as unfinished fabric
perfected by human ingenuity (gave way) to the image of
nature debased and endangered by technology. In
(contrast) to the Enlightenment vision of nature,
(60) (according to) which rational managers construct an ever
more improved environment, twentieth-century
reformers' vision of nature (calls for) a reduction of
human interference in order to restore environmental
stability.[13]

New view:
no human
interference
w/ nature

With the Roadmap complete, take a moment to identify the author's Purpose and Main Idea before reading on.

Since the author didn't provide much strong opinion language, the Purpose of this passage could best be termed descriptive: The author describes polarized viewpoints. The Main Idea was laid out in the opening paragraph: A new group of environmental reformers who clash with both past reformers and modern industry have emerged.

This is the essence of predictive reading. Each time you reach a key idea or a new paragraph, take a moment to predict what is likely to happen next. Ask specific questions that help you understand the author's intent. Use the context of your predictions and your Roadmap as a guide when you encounter difficult paragraphs, and don't worry if the passage takes a turn that you didn't expect; simply adjust your Roadmap and proceed.

Predictive reading is a skill that takes some time to build, but with a strong foundation in strategic reading it will quickly become second nature to you. The advantages of this nuanced form of reading are tremendous: By staying one step ahead of the author at all times, you will read more efficiently and with greater confidence, and you will avoid becoming bogged down in challenging details. Predictive reading translates directly into saved time, an indispensable part of LSAT success.

PREDICTIVE READING IN CHALLENGING PASSAGES

In the last example, you used predictive reading to help you keep track of assorted viewpoints and make sense of a "twisty" science passage. While the passage certainly presented some challenges, its content and structure were probably familiar to you. Now I'll show you another passage, this one with a more challenging structure.

---

[13]PrepTest 23, Sec 4, Passage 3

> In recent years, a growing belief that the way
> society decides what to treat as true is controlled
> through largely unrecognized discursive practices has
> led legal reformers to examine the complex
> (5) interconnections between narrative and law.[14]

Don't let phrases like "unrecognized discursive practices" intimidate you. Read strategically and stay focused on the Keywords. The phrase "has led" points you to the author's main concern, a growing interest in the relationship between narrative and law. **What is coming next?** Most likely some detail describing this relationship. Keep this in mind as you read on.

> In many
> legal systems, legal judgments are based on competing
> stories about events. Without having witnessed these
> events, judges and juries must validate some stories as
> true and reject others as false. This procedure is rooted
> (10) in objectivism, a philosophical approach that has
> supported most Western legal and intellectual systems
> for centuries.[15]

Simplified, the author is discussing the stories upon which judgments are made. It isn't important for you to understand exactly what the author is saying here; notice instead that the author *is* providing details about narratives and law, matching the prediction, and has yet to divulge his main point. **Are there any Keywords here that help you predict what's coming next?** "Rooted in" emphasizes the idea of objectivism. The author is likely to describe objectivism in greater detail.

> Objectivism holds that there is a single
> neutral description of each event that is unskewed by
> any particular point of view and that has a privileged
> (15) position over all other accounts. The law's quest for
> truth, therefore, consists of locating this objective
> description, the one that tells what really happened, as
> opposed to what those involved thought happened. The
> serious flaw in objectivism is that there is no such thing
> (20) as the neutral, objective observer.[16]

Spot on. The author provided a wordy description of objectivism. Hopefully you stayed strategic and focused on that last sentence, wherein the author provided some excellent opinion and emphasis Keywords: he sees a "serious flaw" in objectivism. **What will the author discuss next?** Since objectivism is so problematic, he will likely present a more viable alternative. Read strategically, and keep an eye out for the alternative if it occurs.

---

[14]PrepTest 22, Sec 1, Passage 2

[15]PrepTest 22, Sec 1, Passage 2

[16]PrepTest 22, Sec 1, Passage 2

    As psychologists
have demonstrated, all observers bring to a situation a
set of expectations, values, and beliefs that determine
what the observers are able to see and hear. Two
individuals listening to the same story will hear
(25)   different things, because they emphasize those aspects
that accord with their learned experiences and ignore
those aspects that are dissonant with their view of the
world. Hence there is never any escape in life or in law
from selective perception, or from subjective
(30)   judgments based on prior experiences, values, and
beliefs.[17]

Did the author present an alternative to objectivism here? No. The expected contrast Keywords never arrived, and this text simply gave a more thorough description of the flaw in objectivism. Be prepared for this to happen occasionally as you read passages on test day. This doesn't mean that your prediction was incorrect or badly made, but it does remind you not to let your prediction take precedence over what the author is actually saying. You're only one paragraph into the passage and there's still plenty of time for the alternative to make an appearance. Before moving on, examine the Roadmap so far:

    In recent years, a growing belief that the way
society decides what to treat as true is controlled
through largely unrecognized discursive practices has
led legal reformers to examine the complex
(5)   interconnections between narrative and law. In many
legal systems, legal judgments are based on competing
stories about events. Without having witnessed these
events, judges and juries must validate some stories as
true and reject others as false. This procedure is rooted

Objectivism: one version of truth

(10)   in objectivism, a philosophical approach that has
supported most Western legal and intellectual systems
for centuries. Objectivism holds that there is a single
neutral description of each event that is unskewed by
any particular point of view and that has a privileged
(15)   position over all other accounts. The law's quest for
truth, therefore, consists of locating this objective
description, the one that tells what really happened, as
opposed to what those involved thought happened. The

Flaw: there isn't a neutral POV

serious flaw in objectivism is that there is no such thing
(20)   as the neutral, objective observer. As psychologists
have demonstrated, all observers bring to a situation a
set of expectations, values, and beliefs that determine
what the observers are able to see and hear. Two
individuals listening to the same story will hear
(25)   different things, because they emphasize those aspects
that accord with their learned experiences and ignore

---

[17]PrepTest 22, Sec 1, Passage 2

those aspects that are dissonant with their view of the
world. (Hence) there is never any escape in life or in law
from selective perception, or from subjective
(30) judgments based on prior experiences, values, and
beliefs.[18]

What is likely to occur next? Possibly the alternative, or possibly a continued discussion of objectivism. You should be prepared for either so you won't be taken by surprise.

Auth: Harm
caused by
objectivism

The societal harm (caused by) the assumption of
objectivist principles in traditional legal discourse is
that, historically, the stories judged to be objectively
(35) true are those told by people who are trained in legal
discourse, (while) the stories of those who are not fluent
in the language of the law are rejected as false.[19]

The author discussed the harm caused by objectivism. There's nothing surprising about that. Before moving on to the final paragraph, think about what you already know and revise your prediction:

What is likely to occur next? You still haven't heard from the reformers that the author mentioned at the beginning of the passage. The most logical next step for the author is to finally present an alternative to objectivism.

Legal scholars such as Patricia Williams, Derrick
Bell, and Mari Matsuda have sought empowerment for
(40) the latter group of people through the construction of
alternative legal narratives. Objectivist legal discourse
systematically disallows the language of emotion and
experience by focusing on cognition in its narrowest
sense. These legal reformers propose replacing such
(45) abstract discourse with powerful personal stories. They
argue that the absorbing, nonthreatening structure and
tone of personal stories may convince legal insiders for
the first time to listen to those not fluent in legal
language. The compelling force of personal narrative
(50) can create a sense of empathy between legal insiders
and people traditionally excluded from legal discourse
and, hence, from power. Such alternative narratives can
shatter the complacency of the legal establishment and
disturb its tranquility. Thus, the engaging power of
(55) narrative might play a crucial, positive role in the
process of legal reconstruction by overcoming
differences in background and training and forming a
new collectivity based on emotional empathy.[20]

---

[18]PrepTest 22, Sec 1, Passage 2

[19]PrepTest 22, Sec 1, Passage 2

[20]PrepTest 22, Sec 1, Passage 2

At last! The author introduces the reformers and provides an alternative to objectivism, which he refers to as "alternative legal narratives." He then goes on to provide evidence for the superiority of the alternative, contrasting it with objectivism every step of the way. This long, detail-laden paragraph becomes much easier to understand when you know exactly what it's going to say before you ever see it.

Alternative:
personal
stories

Auth: Possible
benefits

Legal scholars such as Patricia Williams, Derrick
Bell, and Mari Matsuda have sought empowerment for
(40) the latter group of people through the construction of
alternative legal narratives. Objectivist legal discourse
systematically disallows the language of emotion and
experience by focusing on cognition in its narrowest
sense. These legal reformers propose replacing such
(45) abstract discourse with powerful personal stories. They
argue that the absorbing, nonthreatening structure and
tone of personal stories may convince legal insiders for
the first time to listen to those not fluent in legal
language. The compelling force of personal narrative
(50) can create a sense of empathy between legal insiders
and people traditionally excluded from legal discourse
and, hence, from power. Such alternative narratives can
shatter the complacency of the legal establishment and
disturb its tranquility. Thus, the engaging power of
(55) narrative might play a crucial, positive role in the
process of legal reconstruction by overcoming
differences in background and training and forming a
new collectivity based on emotional empathy.[21]

In order to truly appreciate the true scope of predictive reading, I'd like you to take a quick look at the passage presented as a whole. Don't read it in detail. Just take a moment to examine its appearance on the page:

In recent years, a growing belief that the way
society decides what to treat as true is controlled
through largely unrecognized discursive practices has
led legal reformers to examine the complex
(5) interconnections between narrative and law. In many
legal systems, legal judgments are based on competing
stories about events. Without having witnessed these
events, judges and juries must validate some stories as
true and reject others as false. This procedure is rooted
(10) in objectivism, a philosophical approach that has
supported most Western legal and intellectual systems
for centuries. Objectivism holds that there is a single
neutral description of each event that is unskewed by
any particular point of view and that has a privileged
(15) position over all other accounts. The law's quest for
truth, therefore, consists of locating this objective

---

description, the one that tells what really happened, as
opposed to what those involved thought happened. The
serious flaw in objectivism is that there is no such thing

(20) as the neutral, objective observer. As psychologists
have demonstrated, all observers bring to a situation a
set of expectations, values, and beliefs that determine
what the observers are able to see and hear. Two
individuals listening to the same story will hear

(25) different things, because they emphasize those aspects
that accord with their learned experiences and ignore
those aspects that are dissonant with their view of the
world. Hence there is never any escape in life or in law
from selective perception, or from subjective

(30) judgments based on prior experiences, values, and
beliefs.

  The societal harm caused by the assumption of
objectivist principles in traditional legal discourse is
that, historically, the stories judged to be objectively

(35) true are those told by people who are trained in legal
discourse, while the stories of those who are not fluent
in the language of the law are rejected as false.

  Legal scholars such as Patricia Williams, Derrick
Bell, and Mari Matsuda have sought empowerment for

(40) the latter group of people through the construction of
alternative legal narratives. Objectivist legal discourse
systematically disallows the language of emotion and
experience by focusing on cognition in its narrowest
sense. These legal reformers propose replacing such

(45) abstract discourse with powerful personal stories. They
argue that the absorbing, nonthreatening structure and
tone of personal stories may convince legal insiders for
the first time to listen to those not fluent in legal
language. The compelling force of personal narrative

(50) can create a sense of empathy between legal insiders
and people traditionally excluded from legal discourse
and, hence, from power. Such alternative narratives can
shatter the complacency of the legal establishment and
disturb its tranquility. Thus, the engaging power of

(55) narrative might play a crucial, positive role in the
process of legal reconstruction by overcoming
differences in background and training and forming a
new collectivity based on emotional empathy.[22]

---

[22]PrepTest 22, Sec 1, Passage 2

This passage presents an intimidating appearance. Three paragraphs, two of them very long, and plenty of jargon throughout. Compare this with the summary provided by a solid Roadmap:

In (recent) years, a growing (belief) that the way
society decides what to treat as true is controlled
through largely unrecognized discursive practices has
(led) legal (reformers) to examine the complex
(5) interconnections between narrative and law. In many
legal systems, legal judgments are (based on) competing
stories about events. (Without) having witnessed these
events, judges and juries (must) validate some stories as
true (and) reject others as false. This procedure is (rooted)

Objectivism:
one version
of truth
(10) in objectivism, a philosophical approach that has
(supported) most Western legal and intellectual systems
for centuries. Objectivism (holds) that there is a single
neutral description of each event that is unskewed by
any particular point of view (and) that has a privileged
(15) position over all other accounts. The law's quest for
truth, (therefore,) consists of locating this objective
description, the one that tells what really happened, as
(opposed to) what those involved thought happened. The
(serious flaw) in objectivism is that there is no such thing

Flaw: there
isn't a
neutral
POV
(20) as the neutral, objective observer. (As) psychologists
have demonstrated, all observers bring to a situation a
set of expectations, values, and beliefs that determine
what the observers are able to see and hear. Two
individuals listening to the same story will hear
(25) different things, (because) they emphasize those aspects
that accord with their learned experiences (and) ignore
those aspects that are dissonant with their view of the
world. (Hence) there is never any escape in life or in law
from selective perception, or from subjective
(30) judgments based on prior experiences, values, and
beliefs.[23]

Auth: Harm
caused by
objectivism
The societal harm (caused by) the assumption of
objectivist principles in traditional legal discourse is
that, historically, the stories judged to be objectively
(35) true are those told by people who are trained in legal
discourse, (while) the stories of those who are not fluent
in the language of the law are rejected as false.

(Legal scholars) such as Patricia Williams, Derrick
Bell, and Mari Matsuda have (sought) empowerment for
(40) the latter group of people (through) the construction of
alternative legal narratives. Objectivist legal discourse

Alternative:
personal
stories
systematically disallows the language of emotion and
experience (by focusing) on cognition in its narrowest
sense. These legal reformers (propose) replacing such
(45) abstract discourse with (powerful) personal stories. They
(argue) that the absorbing, nonthreatening structure and
tone of personal stories may (convince) legal insiders for

Auth: possible
benefits

the first time to listen to those not fluent in legal
language. The (compelling) force of personal narrative
(50) can create a sense of empathy (between) legal insiders
(and) people traditionally excluded from legal discourse
and, (hence,) from power. Such alternative narratives can
shatter the complacency of the legal establishment and
disturb its tranquility. (Thus,) the engaging power of
(55) narrative might play a (crucial) positive role in the
process of legal reconstruction (by) overcoming
differences in background and training (and) forming a
new collectivity based on emotional empathy.

Notice how few ideas there actually were in this passage. By reading strategically, and by actively predicting the nature of the author's main points, you can reduce this dense, difficult passage to the following Main Idea: Objectivism is flawed, but personal narrative is a good alternative. Use this simple prediction to answer the following LSAT question:

9. Which one of the following best states the main idea of
    the passage?

    (A) Some legal scholars have sought to empower
        people historically excluded from traditional
        legal discourse by instructing them in the forms
        of discourse favored by legal insiders.
    (B) Some legal scholars have begun to realize the
        social harm caused by the adversarial
        atmosphere that has pervaded many legal
        systems for centuries.
    (C) Some legal scholars have proposed alleviating the
        harm caused by the prominence of objectivist
        principles within legal discourse by replacing
        that discourse with alternative forms of legal
        narrative.
    (D) Some legal scholars have contended that those
        who feel excluded from objectivist legal systems
        would be empowered by the construction of a
        new legal language that better reflected
        objectivist principles.
    (E) Some legal scholars have argued that the basic
        flaw inherent in objectivist theory can be
        remedied by recognizing that it is not possible to
        obtain a single neutral description of a particular
        event.[24]

The only choice that matches your prediction is choice (C).

This is how predictive reading translates into points on test day; it keeps you focused on the big picture, helps you sift through the details, and saves you crucial time that you can spend on the question set. Furthermore, while predictive reading is very helpful on a simple passage, it is absolutely indispensable on a tougher example like this one.

---

[24]PrepTest 22, Sec 1, Passage 2, Q 9

DRILL: READING PREDICTIVELY

Now it's time for you to practice predictive reading. I'd like to return to a passage that you examined partially in the last chapter. This passage contains multiple viewpoints and a dense paragraph structure, but, like all LSAT passages, it contains the clues you need to map out its structure. I've broken down the passage into small portions, each followed by predictive-reading questions. As always, circle Keywords as you spot them, and answer each question as you reach it. Be sure to keep your predictions in mind as you continue to read; the insight they provide will help you untangle the author's main ideas more quickly and easily.

Paragraph 1

Two impressive studies have reexamined Eric Williams' conclusion that Britain's abolition of the slave trade in 1807 and its emancipation of slaves in its colonies in 1834 were driven primarily by economic
(5)   rather than humanitarian motives. Blighted by depleted soil, indebtedness, and the inefficiency of coerced labor, these colonies, according to Williams, had by 1807 become an impediment to British economic progress.[25]

1. Whose opinions are likely to be presented in the coming paragraphs?

   _____

2. How might they differ from Williams' conclusion?

   _____

Paragraph 2

(10)   Seymour Drescher provides a more balanced view. Rejecting interpretations based either on economic interest or the moral vision of abolitionists, Drescher has reconstructed the populist characteristics of British abolitionism, which appears to have cut across lines of class, party, and religion.[26]

3. What is likely to follow the presentation of Drescher's idea?

   _____

---

[25]PrepTest 19, Sec 3, Passage 4
[26]PrepTest 19, Sec 3, Passage 4

Noting that between 1780
(15)   and 1830 antislavery petitions outnumbered those on
any other issue, including parliamentary reform,
Drescher concludes that such support cannot be
explained by economic interest alone, especially when
much of it came from the unenfranchised masses. Yet,
(20)   aside from demonstrating that such support must have
resulted at least in part from widespread literacy and a
tradition of political activism, Drescher does not finally
explain how England, a nation deeply divided by class
struggles, could mobilize popular support for
(25)   antislavery measures proposed by otherwise
conservative politicians in the House of Lords and
approved there with little dissent.[27]

4.   What is the author's opinion of Drescher's work?

_____

5.   Based on the author's opinion of Drescher, combined with what you know so far, what is
likely to come next?

_____

Paragraph 3

David Eltis' answer to that question actually
supports some of Williams' insights.[28]

6.   What was Williams' main idea?

_____

7.   What ideas will likely appear in Eltis' answer?

_____

Eschewing
Drescher's idealization of British traditions of liberty,
(30)   Eltis points to continuing use of low wages and
Draconian vagrancy laws in the seventeenth and
eighteenth centuries to ensure the industriousness of
British workers. Indeed, certain notables even called
for the enslavement of unemployed laborers who
(35)   roamed the British countryside—an acceptance of
coerced labor that Eltis attributes to a preindustrial
desire to keep labor costs low and exports competitive.[29]

_____

[27]PrepTest 19, Sec 3, Passage 4
[28]PrepTest 19, Sec 3, Passage 4
[29]PrepTest 19, Sec 3, Passage 4

8. What is likely to happen next?

_____

      By the late eighteenth century, however, a growing
home market began to alert capitalists to the
(40)   importance of "want creation" and to incentives such
as higher wages as a means of increasing both worker
productivity and the number of consumers.
Significantly, it was products grown by slaves, such as
sugar, coffee, and tobacco, that stimulated new wants
(45)   at all levels of British society and were the forerunners
of products intended in modern capitalist societies to
satisfy what Eltis describes as "nonsubsistence or
psychological needs." Eltis concludes that in an
economy that had begun to rely on voluntary labor to
satisfy such needs, forced labor necessarily began to
(50)   appear both inappropriate and counterproductive to
employers.[30]

9. Whose point of view is the author discussing?

_____

10. What is likely to follow?

_____

      Eltis thus concludes that, while Williams
(55)   may well have underestimated the economic viability
of the British colonies employing forced labor in the
early 1800s, his insight into the economic motives for
abolition was partly accurate. British leaders became
committed to colonial labor reform only when they
became convinced, for reasons other than those cited
by Williams, that free labor was more beneficial to the
imperial economy.[31]

11. What is the main difference between the viewpoints of Eltis and Williams?

_____

---

[30]PrepTest 19, Sec 3, Passage 4

[31]PrepTest 19, Sec 3, Passage 4

Explanations

Paragraph 1

> Two impressive studies have reexamined Eric Williams' conclusion that Britain's abolition of the slave trade in 1807 and its emancipation of slaves in its colonies in 1834 were driven primarily by economic
> (5) rather than humanitarian motives. Blighted by depleted soil, indebtedness, and the inefficiency of coerced labor, these colonies, according to Williams, had by 1807 become an impediment to British economic progress.[32]

1. Whose opinions are likely to be presented in the coming paragraphs?

The first paragraph begins with excellent Keywords you can use to make an immediate prediction: Since "two impressive studies" have reexamined Williams's work, you should expect to see those studies appear in subsequent paragraphs, and you should be prepared to pick out the thesis of each one. This prediction may seem rather obvious, but remember that one of the key advantages of predictive reading is focus: You know what important ideas are coming next and you will be prepared for them when you see them.

2. How might they differ from Williams's conclusion?

I hope you were careful to note the gist of Williams' conclusion, that the abolition of British slavery was primarily motivated by economics. Since the two upcoming studies "reexamine" his work, you should expect them to contrast in some way with Williams's conclusion.

Paragraph 2

> (10) Seymour Drescher provides a more balanced view. Rejecting interpretations based either on economic interest or the moral vision of abolitionists, Drescher has reconstructed the populist characteristics of British abolitionism, which appears to have cut across lines of class, party, and religion.[33]

3. What is likely to follow the presentation of Drescher's idea?

According to the author, Drescher's view is more "balanced," and involves an examination of the British population at large. You should expect to see support for this idea in the following sentences. Be prepared to read these ideas quickly, without getting lost in them.

---

[32]PrepTest 19, Sec 3, Passage 4
[33]PrepTest 19, Sec 3, Passage 4

(15)   Noting that between 1780
and 1830 antislavery petitions outnumbered those on
any other issue, including parliamentary reform,
Drescher concludes that such support cannot be
explained by economic interest alone, especially when
much of it came from the unenfranchised masses. Yet,
(20)   aside from demonstrating that such support must have
resulted at least in part from widespread literacy and a
tradition of political activism, Drescher does not finally
explain how England, a nation deeply divided by class
struggles, could mobilize popular support for
(25)   antislavery measures proposed by otherwise
conservative politicians in the House of Lords and
approved there with little dissent.[34]

4. What is the author's opinion of Drescher's work?

True to the prediction, the next two sentences expand upon Drescher's main point. But the contrast Keyword "yet" signals a contrast, and in line 23 the author indicates that Drescher does not adequately make clear how his explanation could have been possible.

5. Based on the author's opinion of Drescher, combined with what you know so far, what is likely to come next?

Here you can make a more sophisticated predication, one that can provide needed context for the final paragraph. You know that the author intends to present *two* examinations of Williams's work, and so far you've only seen one. You also know that the author believes that Drescher's ideas were inadequate to explain abolition. It's therefore extremely plausible that the author is preparing not only to introduce a second review of Williams, but also to indicate whether it provides a better explanation than Drescher's. Taking a few seconds to prepare yourself in this way for the detail-rich third paragraph begins to pay off almost immediately.

Paragraph 3

        David Eltis' answer to that question actually
(30)   supports some of Williams' insights.[35]

6. What was Williams's main idea?

As predicted, the second review of Williams appears, and the author states that it answers the question that Drescher didn't address. The author also points out that Eltis supports some of Williams's original ideas. You should take a moment to review what those ideas were before proceeding, and it doesn't take long: The crux of Williams's conclusion was that abolition was primarily the result of economic pressures.

---

[34]PrepTest 19, Sec 3, Passage 4
[35]PrepTest 19, Sec 3, Passage 4

7. What ideas will likely appear in Eltis's answer?

Since Eltis must partially support Williams, you can therefore expect Eltis's explanation to involve economic issues as well.

(30)   Eschewing
         Drescher's idealization of British traditions of liberty,
         Eltis points to continuing use of low wages and
         Draconian vagrancy laws in the seventeenth and
         eighteenth centuries to ensure the industriousness of
(35)   British workers. Indeed, certain notables even called
         for the enslavement of unemployed laborers who
         roamed the British countryside—an acceptance of
         coerced labor that Eltis attributes to a preindustrial
         desire to keep labor costs low and exports competitive.[36]

8. What is likely to happen next?

Predictably, the author is now explaining Eltis' view in earnest, and it centers on issues related to the British economy, specifically the problems of low wages and unemployment. Don't get bogged down in these details. At this point, since there are no Keywords to indicate a change in direction, you should expect the explanation to continue.

(40)   By the late eighteenth century, however, a growing
         home market began to alert capitalists to the
         importance of "want creation" and to incentives such
         as higher wages as a means of increasing both worker
         productivity and the number of consumers.
(45)   Significantly, it was products grown by slaves, such as
         sugar, coffee, and tobacco, that stimulated new wants
         at all levels of British society and were the forerunners
         of products intended in modern capitalist societies to
         satisfy what Eltis describes as "nonsubsistence or
(50)   psychological needs." Eltis concludes that in an
         economy that had begun to rely on voluntary labor to
         satisfy such needs, forced labor necessarily began to
         appear both inappropriate and counterproductive to
         employers.[37]

9. Whose point of view is the author discussing?

The author is still discussing Eltis and continues to do so right through to his conclusion. Don't be thrown by the presence of the Keyword "however." While you should certainly circle it and note that the author is demonstrating a contrast, it is a contrast within his continuing description of Eltis's ideas.

---

[36]PrepTest 19, Sec 3, Passage 4
[37]PrepTest 19, Sec 3, Passage 4

10. What is likely to follow?

Now that Eltis's conclusion has been revealed, the author is likely to reveal his final evaluation.

(55) Eltis thus concludes that, while Williams may well have underestimated the economic viability of the British colonies employing forced labor in the early 1800s, his insight into the economic motives for abolition was partly accurate. British leaders became committed to colonial labor reform only when they
(60) became convinced, for reasons other than those cited by Williams, that free labor was more beneficial to the imperial economy.[38]

11. What is the main difference between the viewpoints of Eltis and Williams?

Eltis is in partial agreement with Williams, acknowledging that economic forces did play an important role in the abolition of slavery, but he disagrees with the reasons that Williams provides.

[38]PrepTest 19, Sec 3, Passage 4

DRILL: ANSWERING THE QUESTIONS

Now use your understanding of the passage to answer a few questions. I'll provide a sample Roadmap to assist your research. Be sure to write down the Topic, Scope, Purpose, and Main Idea in the blanks provided before attempting to answer the questions. When you're finished, review the explanations carefully.

Williams: abolition for economic reasons.

Two impressive studies have reexamined Eric Williams' conclusion that Britain's abolition of the slave trade in 1807 and its emancipation of slaves in its colonies in 1834 were driven primarily by economic
(5) rather than humanitarian motives. Blighted by depleted soil, indebtedness, and the inefficiency of coerced labor, these colonies, according to Williams, had by 1807 become an impediment to British economic progress.

Drescher: more balanced

(10) Seymour Drescher provides a more balanced view. Rejecting interpretations based either on economic interest or the moral vision of abolitionists, Drescher has reconstructed the populist characteristics of British abolitionism, which appears to have cut across lines of
(15) class, party, and religion. Noting that between 1780 and 1830 antislavery petitions outnumbered those on any other issue, including parliamentary reform,

Not just economics.

Drescher concludes that such support cannot be explained by economic interest alone, especially when
(20) much of it came from the unenfranchised masses. Yet, aside from demonstrating that such support must have resulted at least in part from widespread literacy and a tradition of political activism, Drescher does not finally

Auth: Drescher doesn't fully explain

explain how England, a nation deeply divided by class
(25) struggles, could mobilize popular support for antislavery measures proposed by otherwise conservative politicians in the House of Lords and approved there with little dissent.

Eltis: partly agrees w/ Williams

David Eltis' answer to that question actually
(30) supports some of Williams' insights. Eschewing Drescher's idealization of British traditions of liberty, Eltis points to continuing use of low wages and Draconian vagrancy laws in the seventeenth and eighteenth centuries to ensure the industriousness of
(35) British workers. Indeed, certain notables even called for the enslavement of unemployed laborers who roamed the British countryside—an acceptance of coerced labor that Eltis attributes to a preindustrial desire to keep labor costs low and exports competitive.
(40) By the late eighteenth century, however, a growing home market began to alert capitalists to the importance of "want creation" and to incentives such as higher wages as a means of increasing both worker productivity and the number of consumers.

voluntary
labor leads to
abolition

(45) (Significantly,) it was products grown by slaves, such as sugar, coffee, and tobacco, that stimulated new wants at all levels of British society (and) were the forerunners of products intended in modern capitalist societies to satisfy what (Eltis describes) as "nonsubsistence or
(50) psychological needs." (Eltis concludes) that in an economy that had begun to rely on voluntary labor to satisfy such needs, forced labor (necessarily) began to appear (both) inappropriate (and) counterproductive to employers. Eltis (thus concludes) that, (while) Williams

Eltis on
Williams

(55) may well have underestimated the economic viability of the British colonies employing forced labor in the early 1800s, his insight into the economic motives for abolition was (partly accurate.) British leaders became committed to colonial labor reform (only when) they
(60) became (convinced,) for reasons (other than) those cited by Williams, that free labor was more beneficial to the imperial economy.[39]

Topic: _____

Scope: _____

Purpose: _____

Main Idea: _____

1. Which one of the following best describes the main idea of the passage?

    (A)   Although they disagree about the degree to which economic motives influenced Britain's abolition of slavery, Drescher and Eltis both concede that moral persuasion by abolitionists was a significant factor.

    (B)   Although both Drescher and Eltis have questioned Williams' analysis of the motivation behind Britain's abolition of slavery, there is support for part of Williams' conclusion.

    (C)   Because he has taken into account the populist characteristics of British abolitionism, Drescher's explanation of what motivated Britain's abolition of slavery is finally more persuasive than that of Eltis.

    (D)   Neither Eltis nor Drescher has succeeded in explaining why support for Britain's abolition of slavery appears to have cut across lines of party, class, and religion.

    (E)   Although flawed in certain respects, Williams' conclusions regarding the economic condition of British slave colonies early in the nineteenth century have been largely vindicated.[40]

---

[39]PrepTest 19, Sec 3, Passage 4
[40]PrepTest 19, Sec 3, Passage 4, Q 21

2. Which one of the following best states Williams' view of the primary reason for Britain's abolition of the slave trade and the emancipation of slaves in its colonies?

    (A)   British populism appealed to people of varied classes, parties, and religions.
    (B)   Both capitalists and workers in Britain accepted the moral precepts of abolitionists.
    (C)   Forced labor in the colonies could not produce enough goods to satisfy British consumers.
    (D)   The operation of colonies based on forced labor was no longer economically advantageous.
    (E)   British workers became convinced that forced labor in the colonies prevented paid workers from receiving higher wages.[41]

3. It can be inferred that the author of the passage views Drescher's presentation of British traditions concerning liberty as

    (A)   accurately stated
    (B)   somewhat unrealistic
    (C)   carefully researched
    (D)   unnecessarily tentative
    (E)   superficially convincing[42]

[41]PrepTest 19, Sec 3, Passage 4, Q 23
[42]PrepTest 19, Sec 3, Passage 4, Q 25

Explanations

Topic: The abolition of the slave trade in Britain, as introduced in the first paragraph

Scope: Various explanations for British abolition

Purpose: To examine an explanation of abolition, and to evaluate two responses to the original explanation

Main Idea: Williams' ideas are partially vindicated by Eltis' conclusions.

1. **(B)**

   Which one of the following best describes the main idea of the passage?
   (A)   Although they disagree about the degree to which economic motives influenced Britain's abolition of slavery, Drescher and Eltis both concede that moral persuasion by abolitionists was a significant factor.
   (B)   Although both Drescher and Eltis have questioned Williams' analysis of the motivation behind Britain's abolition of slavery, there is support for part of Williams' conclusion.
   (C)   Because he has taken into account the populist characteristics of British abolitionism, Drescher's explanation of what motivated Britain's abolition of slavery is finally more persuasive than that of Eltis.
   (D)   Neither Eltis nor Drescher has succeeded in explaining why support for Britain's abolition of slavery appears to have cut across lines of party, class, and religion.
   (E)   Although flawed in certain respects, Williams' conclusions regarding the economic condition of British slave colonies early in the nineteenth century have been largely vindicated.[43]

Recall that when you read the passage predictively you were careful to actively anticipate differing viewpoints. When the author presented (and favorably evaluated) Eltis's conclusion at the beginning of paragraph 3, he was careful to point out that Eltis was in partial agreement with Williams. Only choice (B) matches the author's opinion.

---

[43]PrepTest 19, Sec 3, Passage 4, Q 21

2. **(D)**

   Which one of the following best states Williams' view of the primary reason for Britain's abolition of the slave trade and the emancipation of slaves in its colonies?
   - (A) British populism appealed to people of varied classes, parties, and religions.
   - (B) Both capitalists and workers in Britain accepted the moral precepts of abolitionists.
   - (C) Forced labor in the colonies could not produce enough goods to satisfy British consumers.
   - (D) The operation of colonies based on forced labor was no longer economically advantageous.
   - (E) British workers became convinced that forced labor in the colonies prevented paid workers from receiving higher wages.[44]

The Roadmap reminds you that Williams' central assertion appears in the first paragraph, and as you read the passage predictively you consistently came back to Williams in order to provide context for Eltis and Drescher. What was Williams' main idea? That abolition ultimately came about as a result of economic considerations. Choice (D) is correct.

3. **(B)**

   It can be inferred that the author of the passage views Drescher's presentation of British traditions concerning liberty as
   - (A) accurately stated
   - (B) somewhat unrealistic
   - (C) carefully researched
   - (D) unnecessarily tentative
   - (E) superficially convincing[45]

The author states that Drescher's viewpoint is not sufficiently explanatory in lines 23–28. You used this information to provide context for the third paragraph and, hence, for the Main Idea of the passage. As it happens, this question rewards you for being alert to the author's voice. The only two choices that disparage Drescher's scholarship are (B) and (D). Choice (D) is out of scope, while correct choice (B) matches the author's evaluation perfectly.

PREDICTIVE READING IN REVIEW

I want to close this chapter by reinforcing the major concepts presented in this chapter. Since the LSAT demands efficiency from you as a reader, you absolutely must stay a step ahead of the author whenever you can. The presence of Keywords and predictable passage structures provide you with the tools you need to do so.

---

[44]PrepTest 19, Sec 3 Passage 4, Q 23

[45]PrepTest 19, Sec 3 Passage 4, Q 25

As you practice, get into the habit of pausing after each major idea and paragraph break to predict what is likely to occur next in the passage. Use the context of what you've already read to help you make accurate predictions, and don't be afraid to review earlier portions of your Roadmap if necessary. Remember that predictive reading is a fluid process; if you encounter something unexpected in the passage, continue reading strategically and adjust your predictions accordingly. Be confident in your ability to stay ahead of the author, but don't let your expectations blind you to what the author is really saying. Finally, remember that predictive reading is a tool to help you focus on the right things. You're likelier to spot and incorporate the author's primary ideas into your Roadmap more quickly and accurately if you already have a good idea about what those ideas will be.

This skill can be challenging to develop at first. As always, practice slowly and methodically until you feel the process begin to feel more natural. With dedication, you'll find that you're soon asking anticipatory questions of every passage by reflex. This level of mastery will come with repetition. It will also come with familiarity; LSAT passages tend to follow a small number of predictable structural patterns, and once you learn to recognize them, the art of predictive reading becomes even easier. I'll explain this idea further in the next chapter.

CHAPTER 7

COMMON PASSAGE STRUCTURES

PATTERNS IN THE PASSAGES

By this point you should feel fairly comfortable with Kaplan's Method for strategic reading. You've read and Roadmapped a number of passages and you've gotten into the habit of identifying the Topic, Scope, Purpose, and Main Idea. In the last chapter I illustrated the predictable nature of LSAT Reading Comprehension passages and showed you how to read predictively.

Through practice and repetition you may have begun to notice that there are only a limited number of passage structures that tend to occur regularly, and that sometimes the Purpose of one passage is very much like the Purpose of another. Of course, you've been exposed to many different Topics in your practice—so far you've read passages about Victorian philanthropy, objectivist legal discourse, and environmentalist doctrines, just to mention a few. But now that you're reading strategically and focusing on structure, you've learned that these passages aren't really as diverse as they seem.

Take a moment to think through the last passage you read. Try to remember the author's Purpose and what you wrote in your Roadmap. The passage probably presented several points of view, some of which were in conflict. Perhaps the author supported one viewpoint over another, or perhaps she presented an original argument. Even if you can't remember precisely what the passage was about, you can probably recall the presence of these broader ideas in the passage structure because you used them to formulate the author's Purpose.

I've already demonstrated that the skill of prediction is one of your greatest advantages in Reading Comprehension. Knowing that the passages are predictable will boost your confidence as well as your score. To supplement the skills you've already learned, I'll now illustrate the most common Purposes in the passages.

THREE COMMON PURPOSES

Although the passages will vary widely in their content, there are three common Purposes that the author will pursue:

- To support or refute an opinion other than his own
- To argue in favor of his own opinion
- To describe a series of ideas without taking sides

As I describe each Purpose in greater detail, please keep in mind that they are not inflexible categories that must exclude one another in every passage. For example, authors will frequently refute others' opinions before presenting their own opinions. But as you determine the author's primary Purpose, you'll often find that it primarily follows one of these three basic patterns, and knowing which one will make all the difference as you answer the questions.

Support or Refute an Opinion

You know from previous chapters that when the author presents outside viewpoints in a passage, you should seek the author's evaluations of them. Because LSAT passages tend to be argumentative in tone (the LSAT is designed for law schools, after all), the authors usually voice strong opinions. Review the following passage and its Roadmap:

Soc: gatherings mean tribal decline

Even in the midst of its resurgence as a vital tradition, many sociologists have viewed the current form of the powwow, a ceremonial gathering of native Americans as a sign that tribal culture is in decline.
(5) Focusing on the dances and rituals that have recently come to be shared by most tribes, they suggest that an intertribal movement is now in ascension and claim the inevitable outcome of this tendency is the eventual dissolution of tribes and the complete assimilation of
(10) native Americans into Euroamerican society.

Pan-Indian theory, evidence

Proponents of this "Pan-Indian" theory point to the greater frequency of travel and communication between reservations, the greater urbanization of native Americans, and, most recently, their increasing
(15) politicization in response to common grievances as the chief causes of the shift toward intertribalism.

Intertribalism on rise

Indeed the rapid diffusion of dance styles, outfits, and songs from one reservation to another offers compelling evidence that intertribalism has been

Unique
traditions
rising too

(20) increasing. (However,) these (sociologists) have (failed) to note the concurrent revitalization of many traditions unique to individual tribes. (Among) the Lakota, for (instance,) the Sun Dance was revived, after a forty-year hiatus, during the 1950's. (Similarly) the Black Legging

(25) Society of the Kiowa and the Hethuska Society of the Ponca—(both) traditional groups within their respective tribes—have gained (new popularity.) (Obviously,) a more complex societal shift is taking place (than) the theory of Pan-Indianism can account for.

P.I.T doesn't
explain

Auth: must
examine theory

(30) An (examination) of the theory's underpinnings may be (critical) at this point, (especially) given that native Americans themselves (chafe most) against the Pan-Indian classification. (Like) other assimilationist theories with which it is associated, the Pan-Indian view is

(35) (predicated upon) an a priori assumption about the nature of cultural contact: that (upon) contact minority societies (immediately) begin to succumb in every respect—biologically, linguistically, and culturally—to the majority society. (However,) there is (no evidence)

Theory based
on wrong
assump.

(40) that this is happening to native American groups.

Intertribal act.
Still important

(Yet) the fact remains that intertribal activities are a (major facet) of native American culture today. Certain dances at powwows (for instance) are announced as intertribal, (other) as traditional. (Likewise,) speeches

(45) given at the beginnings of powwows are (often) delivered in English, (while) the prayer that follows is (usually) spoken in a native language. Cultural borrowing is (of course,) old news. What is (important) to note is the conscious (distinction) native Americans

Tribal and
Intertribal
distinct

(50) make (between) tribal and intertribal tendencies.

Tribalism, (although greatly altered) by modern history, (remains) a (potent) force among native Americans: It forms a (basis) for tribal identity, (and) aligns music and dance with other social and cultural

Auth: Both are
important

(55) activities (important) to individual tribes. Intertribal activities, on the (other hand) (reinforce) native American identity along a broader front, (where) this identity is directly threatened by outside influences.[1]

Think about the structure of the passage and try to define the author's Purpose. In the first paragraph, the author introduces the proponents of the "Pan-Indian" theory, who state that tribalism is in decline. Does the author agree with them?

No. In the final three paragraphs, the author demonstrates that the theory's predictions have failed to come true, and concludes in line 52 that tribalism "remains a potent force among native Americans." Does the author provide an alternative theory? Again, no. The author's primary Purpose is to refute the theory that tribalism is in decline. It's true that in doing so

---

[1]PrepTest 25, Sec 1, Passage 3

the author provides evidence that intertribal activities strengthen tribal communities rather than weaken them, but the discussion is still centered around the theory put forward by the sociologists in the first paragraph.

This may seem like a minor distinction, but it can be a very important concept to be aware of before answering the questions. Take a look at this one:

21. In the passage, the author is primarily concerned with doing which one of the following?

   (A) identifying an assumption common to various assimilationist theories and then criticizing these theories by showing this assumption to be false

   (B) arguing that the recent revival of a number of tribal practices shows sociologists are mistaken in believing intertribalism to be a potent force among native American societies

   (C) questioning the belief that native American societies will eventually be assimilated into Euroamerican society by arguing that intertribalism helps strengthen native American identity

   (D) showing how the recent resurgence of tribal activities is a deliberate attempt to counteract the growing influence of intertribalism

   (E) proposing an explanation of why the ascension of intertribalism could result in the eventual dissolution of tribes and complete assimilation of native American into Euroamerican society[2]

Choices (D) and (E) fail to mention the author's core disagreement with the sociologists. Choice (A) might look tempting at first, but its scope is far too broad—the author is primarily concerned with refuting a single theory. Choice (B) distorts the author's viewpoint—she clearly believes that intertribalism *is* a potent force in tribal life. That leaves choice (C), the correct choice. As in your prediction, the author's Purpose is to question a given belief by presenting counter evidence. Your understanding of the author's goal guides you past the traps to score the point.

Try another question:

---

[2]PrepTest 25, Sec 1, Q 21

16. The author of the passage would most likely agree with which one of the following assertions?

(A) Though some believe the current form of the powwow signals the decline of tribal culture, the powwow contains elements that indicate the continuing strength of tribalism.

(B) The logical outcome of the recent increase in intertribal activity is the eventual disappearance of tribal culture.

(C) Native Americans who participate in both tribal and intertribal activities usually base their identities on intertribal rather than tribal affiliations.

(D) The conclusions of some sociologists about the health of native American cultures show that these sociologists are in fact biased against such cultures.

(E) Until it is balanced by revitalization of tribal customs, intertribalism will continue to weaken the native American sense of identity.[3]

The correct answer, choice (A), explicitly references the author's Purpose by asserting that her conclusion is true despite the fact that "some believe" that tribal culture is in decline. Note that even though this question didn't explicitly ask for the author's Purpose, understanding it was instrumental in scoring the point.

The LSAT is riddled with passages in which the author's primary goal is to support or refute a given theory. Here's another variation. Review this passage and Roadmap from the previous chapter:

> In recent years, a growing belief that the way society decides what to treat as true is controlled through largely unrecognized discursive practices has
> (5) led legal reformers to examine the complex interconnections between narrative and law. In many legal systems, legal judgments are based on competing stories about events. Without having witnessed these events, judges and juries must validate some stories as true and reject others as false. This procedure is rooted
>
> *Objectivism: one version of truth*
>
> (10) in objectivism, a philosophical approach that has supported most Western legal and intellectual systems for centuries. Objectivism holds that there is a single neutral description of each event that is unskewed by any particular point of view and that has a privileged
> (15) position over all other accounts. The law's quest for truth, therefore, consists of locating this objective description, the one that tells what really happened, as opposed to what those involved thought happened. The serious flaw in objectivism is that there is no such thing

---

Flaw-
there isn't
a neutral
POV

(20) as the neutral, objective observer. (As) psychologists
have demonstrated, all observers bring to a situation a
set of expectations, values, and beliefs that determine
what the observers are able to see and hear. Two
individuals listening to the same story will hear
(25) different things, (because) they emphasize those aspects
that accord with their learned experiences (and) ignore
those aspects that are dissonant with their view of the
world. (Hence) there is never any escape in life or in law
from selective perception, or from subjective
(30) judgments based on prior experiences, values, and
beliefs.

Harm
caused by
objectivism

The societal harm (caused by) the assumption of
objectivist principles in traditional legal discourse is
that, historically, the stories judged to be objectively
(35) true are those told by people who are trained in legal
discourse, (while) the stories of those who are not fluent
in the language of the law are rejected as false.

Alternative:
personal
stories

(Legal scholars) such as Patricia Williams, Derrick
Bell, and Mari Matsuda have (sought) empowerment for
(40) the latter group of people (through) the construction of
alternative legal narratives. Objectivist legal discourse
systematically disallows the language of emotion and
experience (by focusing) on cognition in its narrowest
sense. These legal reformers (propose) replacing such
(45) abstract discourse with (powerful) personal stories. They
(argue) that the absorbing, nonthreatening structure and
tone of personal stories may (convince) legal insiders for
the first time to listen to those not fluent in legal
language. The (compelling) force of personal narrative
(50) can create a sense of empathy (between) legal insiders
(and) people traditionally excluded from legal discourse
and, (hence,) from power. Such alternative narratives can
shatter the complacency of the legal establishment and
disturb its tranquility. (Thus,) the engaging power of
(55) narrative might play a (crucial) positive role in the
process of legal reconstruction (by) overcoming
differences in background and training (and) forming a
new collectivity based on emotional empathy.[4]

In this passage, the author begins by describing the principles of objectivism and then refutes them. Next, she introduces the alternative theory of the legal scholars listed in lines 38–39 and supports it, noting in line 55 that it "might play a crucial, positive role" in our legal system.

Notice how similar the structure of this passage is to the prior example. The only real difference is that this author endorses the specific alternative provided by the legal scholars, whereas the author of the previous passage simply demonstrated that the sociologists were wrong.

Once again, an example from the question set shows why the difference matters:

---

[4]PrepTest 22, Sec 1, Passage 2

9. Which one of the following best states the main idea of the passage?

(A)　Some legal scholars have sought to empower people historically excluded from traditional legal discourse by instructing them in the forms of discourse favored by legal insiders.

(B)　Some legal scholars have begun to realize the social harm caused by the adversarial atmosphere that has pervaded many legal systems for centuries.

(C)　Some legal scholars have proposed alleviating the harm caused by the prominence of objectivist principles within legal discourse by replacing that discourse with alternative forms of legal narrative.

(D)　Some legal scholars have contended that those who feel excluded from objectivist legal systems would be empowered by the construction of a new legal language that better reflected objectivist principles.

(E)　Some legal scholars have argued that the basic flaw inherent in objectivist theory can be remedied by recognizing that it is not possible to obtain a single neutral description of a particular event.[5]

All of the answer choices focus on the opinions of the legal scholars with whom the author sided. Your prediction should take this into account. The correct answer should indicate that the scholars reject objectivism and seek to replace it with personal stories. Only correct choice (C) matches this prediction.

These examples reinforce the importance of the author's point of view. When the author of an LSAT passage mentions outside opinions, be on the lookout for her reaction.

Provide a New Opinion

By now, you're very familiar with the author's tendency to support and refute third party opinions. Sometimes the author goes a step further and provides an entirely new opinion that doesn't necessarily flow directly from prior viewpoints. To illustrate, review the passage about the fiction of P. D. James, along with its Roadmap:

Critics: Praise James or attack her

Wherever the crime novels of P. D. James are discussed by critics, there is a tendency on the one hand to exaggerate her merits and on the other to castigate her as a genre writer who is getting above
(5)　herself. Perhaps underlying the debate is that familiar, false opposition set up between different kinds of fiction, according to which enjoyable novels are held to

---

be somehow slightly lowbrow, (and) a novel is not considered true literature unless it is a tiny bit dull.

Critics: who like James

(10) Those (commentators) who would (elevate) James's books to the status of high literature (point to) her painstakingly constructed characters, her elaborate settings, her sense of place, and her love of (abstractions:) notions about morality, duty, pain, and

(15) pleasure are never far from the lips of her police officers and murderers. (Others) find her pretentious and

Critics: who dislike James

tiresome; an inverted snobbery (accuses) her of abandoning the time-honored conventions of the detective genre (in favor) of a highbrow literary style.

(20) The (critic) Harriet Waugh wants P.D. James to get on with "the more taxing business of laying a tricky trail and then fooling the reader"; Philip Oakes in *The Literary Review* (groans,) "Could we please proceed with the business of clapping the handcuffs on the

(25) killer?"

Auth: James very descriptive

James is certainly capable of (strikingly) good writing. She takes (immense) trouble to provide her characters with convincing histories and passions. Her descriptive digressions are part of the pleasure of her

(30) books (and) give them dignity and weight. (But) it is equally true that they frequently interfere with the story; the patinas and aromas of a country kitchen receive more loving attention (than) does the plot itself. Her devices to advance the story can be (shameless) and

Sometimes bad for plot

(35) thin, (and) it is often impossible to see how her detective arrives at the truth; one is left to conclude that the detective solves crimes through intuition. At (this stage) in her career P. D. James seems to be (less) interested in the specifics of detection (than) in her characters'

(40) vulnerabilities and perplexities.

(However,) once the rules of a chosen genre cramp creative thought, there is (no reason) why an able and interesting writer should accept them. In her (latest)

James not limited by genre

book, there are signs that James is beginning to (feel)

(45) constrained by the crime-novel genre. Here her (determination) to leave areas of ambiguity in the solution of the crime (and) to distribute guilt among the murderer, victim, and bystanders (points to) a conscious (rebellion) against the (traditional) neatness of detective

(50) fiction. It is fashionable, (though reprehensible,) for one writer to prescribe to another. (But) perhaps the time has

James maybe go mainstr.

come for P. D. James to slide out of her handcuffs (and) stride into the territory of the mainstream novel.[6]

The author presents and agrees to some extent with two separate groups of critics as described in the first paragraph—those who "exaggerate her merits" and those consider her a genre writer "getting above herself." But pay close attention to lines 5–9, in which the author describes these conflicting opinions as a "false opposition."

---

[6]PrepTest 19, Sec 3, Passage 1

The author's true Purpose is revealed in the final paragraph, in which the author suggests that James should consider becoming a mainstream novelist. This time, the author isn't content to simply refute one side of an argument or agree with another. She ultimately defies both groups of critics and produces her own interpretation of James's work. In formulating the Purpose, you also know the Main Idea should reflect this new interpretation: P. D. James should consider moving beyond the detective novel genre. With this in mind, take another look at this question:

1. Which one of the following best states the author's main conclusion?

    (A) Because P. D. James's potential as a writer is stifled by her chosen genre, she should turn her talents toward writing mainstream novels.

    (B) Because the requirements of the popular novel are incompatible with true creative expression, P. D. James's promise as a serious author has been diminished.

    (C) The dichotomy between popular and sophisticated literature is well illustrated in the crime novels of P. D. James.

    (D) The critics who have condemned P. D. James's lack of attention to the specifics of detection fail to take into account her carefully constructed plots.

    (E) Although her plots are not always neatly resolved, the beauty of her descriptive passages justifies P. D. James's decision to write in the crime-novel genre.[7]

Correct choice (A) restates the author's opinion just as predicted. The other choices offer confused distortions of the various themes presented in the passage. Once again, a clear understanding of the author's Purpose guides you directly to the correct answer.

To reiterate, the key difference between this passage and the two previous examples is that the author of the James passage doesn't ultimately agree with the critics, but neither does she simply disagree with them and assume a clear opposite opinion. Instead she breaks away from the critics' arguments, using them as a launching point for her own separate Purpose.

Here's another example:

Star system of 20's

As one of the most pervasive and influential popular arts, the movies feed into and off of the rest of the culture in various ways. In the United States, the star system of the mid-1920s—in which actors were

(5) placed under exclusive contract to particular Hollywood film studios—was a consequence of studios' discovery that the public was interested in actors' private lives, and that information about actors could be used to promote their films. Public relations

---

[7]PrepTest 19, Sec 3, Q 1

Press benefits
from film

(10) agents fed the information to gossip columnists, whetting the public's appetite for the films—which, audiences usually discovered, had the additional virtue of being created by talented writers, directors, and producers devoted to the art of storytelling. The

(15) important feature of this relationship was not the benefit to Hollywood, but rather to the press; in what amounted to a form of cultural cross-fertilization, the press saw that they could profit from studios' promotion of new films.

Media
promotes
movies

(20) Today this arrangement has mushroomed into an intricately interdependent mass-media entertainment industry. The faith by which this industry sustains itself is the belief that there is always something worth promoting. A vast portion of the mass media—

(25) television and radio interviews, magazine articles, even product advertisements—now does most of the work for Hollywood studios attempting to promote their movies. It does so not out of altruism but because it makes for good business: If you produce a talk show

(30) or edit a newspaper, and other media are generating public curiosity about a studio's forthcoming film, it would be unwise for you not to broadcast or publish something about the film, too, because the audience for your story is already guaranteed.

Problem:
affects films

(35) The problem with this industry is that it has begun to affect the creation of films as well as their promotion. Choices of subject matter and actors are made more and more frequently by studio executives rather than by producers, writers, or directors. This

(40) problem is often referred to simply as an obsession with turning a profit, but Hollywood movies have almost always been produced to appeal to the largest possible audience. The new danger is that, increasingly, profit comes only from exciting an

Films are not
satisfying

(45) audience's curiosity about a movie instead of satisfying its desire to have an engaging experience watching the film. When movies can pull people into theaters instantly on the strength of media publicity rather than relying on the more gradual process of word of mouth

(50) among satisfied moviegoers, then the intimate relationship with the audience—on which the vitality of all popular art depends—is lost. But studios are making more money than ever by using this formula, and for this reason it appears that films whose appeal is

(55) due not merely to their publicity value but to their ability to affect audiences emotionally will become increasingly rare in the U.S. film industry.[8]

What is the author's Purpose? The author describes the developing relationship between film and the media in paragraphs 1 and 2. Then, in the final paragraph, the author describes the

---

[8]PrepTest 28, Sec 4, Passage 4

danger this relationship creates for the film industry. With this in mind, try to answer the following question:

25. Which one of the following most accurately describes the organization of the passage?

(A) description of the origins of a particular aspect of a popular art; discussion of the present state of this aspect; analysis of a problem associated with this aspect; introduction of a possible solution to the problem

(B) description of the origins of a particular aspect of a popular art; discussion of the present state of this aspect; analysis of a problem associated with this aspect; suggestion of a likely consequence of the problem

(C) description of the origins of a particular aspect of a popular art; analysis of a problem associated with this aspect; introduction of a possible solution to the problem; suggestion of a likely consequence of the solution

(D) summary of the history of a particular aspect of a popular art; discussion of a problem that accompanied the growth of this aspect; suggestion of a likely consequence of the problem; appraisal of the importance of avoiding this consequence

(E) summary of the history of a particular aspect of a popular art; analysis of factors that contributed to the growth of this aspect; discussion of a problem that accompanied the growth of this aspect; appeal for assistance in solving the problem[9]

The answer choices may seem abstract, and they're certainly repetitive, but don't worry. Apply the Kaplan Method and compare them to the author's Purpose. The only match is choice (B). The others all mention extraneous ideas; the author did mention a problem, but he never mentioned a solution to the problem or any way to avoid it.

How does the structure of this passage differ from that of the P. D. James passage? The author of the film industry passage never presents any opinion other than his own. The first two paragraphs are purely informational, and there isn't anyone for the author to agree or disagree with. But in spite of this difference, the two passages essentially follow the same pattern: In both cases, the author uses the bulk of the passage to provide context for the primary opinion delivered in the final paragraph.

That last LSAT question demonstrates why knowledge of these common patterns is worth points on test day. The test makers will often complicate a familiar question type by making

[9]PrepTest 28, Sec 4, Q 25

the answer choices wordy, abstract, and similar to one another. You absolutely must have a solid prediction to score the point efficiently, and that's much easier to do when you're able to identify a commonly recurring Purpose.

Remain Neutral

The final common passage pattern occurs when the author provides no opinion at all. Other opinions may be present, but the author simply describes them without evaluating them. Here's an example:

Phil. of Science like physics/ certainty

Philosophers of science have long been uneasy with biology, preferring instead to focus on physics. At the heart of this preference is a misstrust of uncertainty. Science is supposed to be the study of what is true (5) everywhere and for all times, and the phenomena of science are supposed to be repeatable, arising from universal laws, rather than historically contingent. After all if something pops up only on occasional Tuesdays or Thursdays, it is not classified as science (10) but as history. Philosophers of science have thus been fascinated with the fact that elephants and mice would fall at the same rate if dropped from the Tower of Pisa, but not much interested in how elephants and mice got to be such different sizes in the first place.

Biologists: bio is universal

(15)   Philosophers of science have not been alone in claiming that science must consist of universal laws. Some evolutionary biologists have also acceded to the general intellectual disdain for the merely particular and tried to emulate physicists, constructing their (20) science as a set of universal laws. In formulating the notion of a universal "struggle for existence that is the engine of biological history" or in asserting that virtually all DNA evolves at a constant clocklike rate, they have attempted to find their own versions of the

Other biologists: bio based on history

(25) law of gravity. Recently, however, some biologists have questioned whether biological history is really the necessary unfolding of universal laws of life, and they have raised the possibility that historical contingency is an integral factor in biology.

(30)   To illustrate the difference between biologists favoring universal, deterministic laws of evolutionary development and those leaving room for historical contingency, consider two favorite statements of philosophers (both of which appear, at first sight, to be (35) universal assertions): "All planets move in ellipses" and "All swans are white." The former is truly

Ex: planets are universal

universal because it applies not only to those planets that actually do exist, but also to those that could exist—for the shape of planetary orbits is a necessary (40) consequence of the laws governing the motion of objects in a gravitational field.

Bio determ.
say swans =
universal

(45)

Nondeterm.
say swans not
universal

(50)

(55)

Biological determinists (would say) that "All swans are white" is universal in the (same way,) (since,) if all swans were white, it would be (because) the laws of natural selection make it impossible for swans to be (otherwise;) natural selection favors those characteristics that increase the average rate of offspring production, (and so) traits that maximize flexibility and the ability to manipulate nature will eventually appear. Nondeterminist biologists would (deny this,) saying that "swans" is merely the name of a finite collection of historical object that (may happen) all to be white, (but not) of necessity. The history of evolutionary theory (has been) the history of the struggle between these two views of swans.[10]

Take a moment to review the various commentators in this passage: philosophers of science and physicists in the first paragraph, determinist biologists and nondeterminist biologists further in. Notably absent is the author of the passage. Does the author side with one group of biologists over the other? It's never stated. The author's primary Purpose should reflect this neutral tone: The author wrote to describe conflicting views of science. As always, the Main Idea follows from the Purpose, and it is similarly neutral: Biologists disagree about how certain their science is.

15. Which one of the following best summarizes the main idea of the passage?

   (A)   Just as philosophers of science have traditionally been reluctant to deal with scientific phenomena that are not capable of being explained by known physical laws, biologists have tended to shy away from confronting philosophical questions.

   (B)   While science is often considered to be concerned with universal laws, the degree to which certain biological phenomena can be understood as arising from such laws is currently in dispute.

   (C)   Although biologists have long believed that the nature of their field called for a theoretical approach different from that taken by physicists, some biologists have recently begun to emulate the methods of physicists.

   (D)   Whereas physicists have achieved a far greater degree of experimental precision than has been possible in the field of biology, the two fields employ similar theoretical approaches.

   (E)   Since many biologists are uncomfortable with the emphasis placed by philosophers of science on the need to construct universal laws, there has been little interaction between the two disciplines.[11]

---

[10]PrepTest 35, Sec 2, Passage 3

[11]PrepTest 35, Sec 2, Q 15

Choice (B) describes the unresolved nature of the dispute as predicted.

My students often express anxiety when working with a passage that, like this one, lacks a strong authorial viewpoint. Such passages tend to be somewhat abstract. They're also less common than passages with opinionated authors, and you may reach the end thinking to yourself, "Why didn't the author take sides? They *always* take sides!"

Let this exercise be a reminder: While the author usually is opinionated, there are exceptions. If the author remains neutral, don't be tempted to ascribe to her an opinion that she doesn't express. As always, read strategically and be sure to note any other viewpoints the passage provides. If the author was primarily concerned with describing the opinions of others, then those opinions are sure to show up in the questions:

17. Which one of the following statements about biology is most consistent with the view held by determinist biologists, as that view is presented in the passage?

18. It can be inferred from the passage that philosophers of science view the laws of physics as

19. It can be inferred from the passage that determinist biologists have tried to emulate physicists because these biologists believe that[12]

As long as you've applied the Kaplan Method, your Roadmap will guide you directly to the information you need to score these points.

---

[12]PrepTest 35, Sec 2, Qs 17–19

DRILL: RECOGNIZING THE PATTERNS

This Drill contains three LSAT passages, each with a question that requires knowledge of the author's Purpose. Remember, the author's primary Purpose is usually to support or refute an opinion, to provide an alternative opinion, or to remain neutral. Read each passage strategically, create a Roadmap, and answer its accompanying question. This is a longer exercise, so take your time. Explanations are provided after the Drill.

Three kinds of study have been performed on Byron. There is the biographical study—the very valuable examination of Byron's psychology and the events in his life; Escarpit's 1958 work is an example
(5) of this kind of study, and biographers to this day continue to speculate about Byron's life. Equally valuable is the study of Byron as a figure important in the history of ideas; Russell and Praz have written studies of this kind. Finally, there are
(10) studies that primarily consider Byron's poetry. Such literary studies are valuable, however, only when they avoid concentrating solely on analyzing the verbal shadings of Byron's poetry to the exclusion of any discussion of biographical considerations. A
(15) study with such a concentration would be of questionable value because Byron's poetry, for the most part, is simply not a poetry of subtle verbal meanings. Rather, on the whole, Byron's poems record the emotional pressure of certain moments
(20) in his life. I believe we cannot often read a poem of Byron's, as we often can one of Shakespeare's, without wondering what events or circumstances in his life prompted him to write it.

No doubt the fact that most of Byron's poems
(25) cannot be convincingly read as subtle verbal creations indicates that Byron is not a "great" poet. It must be admitted too that Byron's literary craftsmanship is irregular and often his temperament disrupts even his lax literary method
(30) (although the result, an absence of method, has a significant purpose: it functions as a rebuke to a cosmos that Byron feels he cannot understand). If Byron is not a "great" poet, his poetry is nonetheless of extraordinary interest to us because
(35) of the pleasure it gives us. Our main pleasure in reading Byron's poetry is the contact with a singular

personality. Reading his work gives us illumination—self-understanding—after we have seen our weaknesses and aspirations mirrored in
(40) the personality we usually find in the poems. Anyone who thinks that this kind of illumination is not a genuine reason for reading a poet should think carefully about why we read Donne's sonnets.

It is Byron and Byron's idea of himself that hold
(45) his work together (and that enthralled early-nineteenth-century Europe). Different characters speak in his poems, but finally it is usually he himself who is speaking: a far cry from the impersonal poet Keats. Byron's poetry alludes to
(50) Greek and Roman myth in the context of contemporary affairs, but his work remains generally of a piece because of his close presence in the poetry. In sum, the poetry is a shrewd personal performance, and to shut out Byron the man is to fabricate a work of pseudocriticism.

1. Which one of the following titles best expresses the main idea of the passage?

    (A) An Absence of Method: Why Byron Is Not a "Great" Poet

    (B) Byron: The Recurring Presence in Byron's Poetry

    (C) Personality and Poetry: The Biographical Dimension of Nineteenth-Century Poetry

    (D) Byron's Poetry: Its Influence on the Imagination of Early-Nineteenth-Century Europe

    (E) Verbal Shadings: The Fatal Flaw of Twentieth-Century Literary Criticism[13]

The United States Supreme Court has not always resolved legal issues of concern to Native Americans in a manner that has pleased the Indian nations. Many of the Court's decisions have been
(5) products of political compromise that looked more to the temper of the times than to enduring principles of law. But accommodation is part of the judicial system in the United States, and judicial decisions must be assessed with this fact in mind.

(10) Despite the "accommodating" nature of the judicial system, it is worth noting that the power of the Supreme Court has been exercised in a manner that has usually been beneficial to Native Americans, at least on minor issues, and has not
(15) been wholly detrimental on the larger, more important issues. Certainly there have been decisions that cast doubt on the validity of this assertion. Some critics point to the patronizing tone of many Court opinions and the apparent rejection
(20) of Native American values as important points to consider when reviewing a case. However, the validity of the assertion can be illustrated by reference to two important contributions that have resulted from the exercise of judicial power.

(25) First, the Court has created rules of judicial construction that, in general, favor the rights of Native American litigants. The Court's attitude has been conditioned by recognition of the distinct disadvantages Native Americans faced when
(30) dealing with settlers in the past. Treaties were inevitably written in English for the benefit of their authors, whereas tribal leaders were accustomed to making treaties without any written account, on the strength of mutual promises sealed by religious
(35) commitment and individual integrity. The written treaties were often broken, and Native Americans were confronted with fraud and political and

military aggression. The Court recognizes that past unfairness to Native Americans cannot be
(40) sanctioned by the force of law. Therefore, ambiguities in treaties are to be interpreted in favor of the Native American claimants, treaties are to be interpreted as the Native Americans would have understood them, and, under the reserved rights
(45) doctrine, treaties reserve to Native Americans all rights that have not been specifically granted away in other treaties.

A second achievement of the judicial system is the protection that has been provided against
(50) encroachment by the states into tribal affairs. Federal judges are not inclined to view favorably efforts to extend states' powers and jurisdictions because of the direct threat that such expansion poses to the exercise of federal powers. In the
(55) absence of a federal statute directly and clearly allocating a function to the states, federal judges are inclined to reserve for the federal government—and the tribal governments under its charge—all those powers and rights they can be said to have
(60) possessed historically.[14]

2. The author's attitude toward the United States Supreme Court's resolution of legal issues of concern to Native Americans can best be described as one of

(A) wholehearted endorsement
(B) restrained appreciation
(C) detached objectivity
(D) cautious opposition
(E) suppressed exasperation[15]

---

[14] PrepTest 16, Sec 4, Passage 2
[15] PrepTest 16, Sec 4, Q 12

When catastrophe strikes, analysts typically blame some combination of powerful mechanisms. An earthquake is traced to an immense instability along a fault line; a stock market crash is blamed on
(5) the destabilizing effect of computer trading. These explanations may well be correct. But systems as large and complicated as the Earth's crust or the stock market can break down not only under the force of a mighty blow but also at the drop of a pin.
(10) In a large interactive system, a minor event can start a chain reaction that leads to a catastrophe.

Traditionally, investigators have analyzed large interactive systems in the same way they analyze small orderly systems, mainly because the methods
(15) developed for small systems have proved so successful. They believed they could predict the behavior of a large interactive system by studying its elements separately and by analyzing its component mechanisms individually. For lack of a better
(20) theory, they assumed that in large interactive systems the response to a disturbance is proportional to that disturbance.

During the past few decades, however, it has become increasingly apparent that many large
(25) complicated systems do not yield to traditional analysis. Consequently, theorists have proposed a "theory of self-organized criticality": many large interactive systems evolve naturally to a critical state in which a minor event starts a chain reaction
(30) that can affect any number of elements in the system. Although such systems produce more minor events than catastrophes, the mechanism that leads to minor events is the same one that leads to major events.

(35) A deceptively simple system serves as a paradigm for self-organized criticality: a pile of sand. As sand is poured one grain at a time onto a flat disk, the grains at first stay close to the position where they land. Soon they rest on top of one
(40) another, creating a pile that has a gentle slope. Now and then, when the slope becomes too steep, the grains slide down, causing a small avalanche. The system reaches its critical state when the amount of sand added is balanced, on average, by the amount
(45) falling off the edge of the disk.

Now when a grain of sand is added, it can start an avalanche of any size, including a "catastrophic" event. Most of the time the grain will fall so that no avalanche occurs. By studying a specific area of the
(50) pile, one can even predict whether avalanches will occur there in the near future. To such a local observer, however, large avalanches would remain unpredictable because they are a consequence of the total history of the entire pile. No matter what
(55) the local dynamics are, catastrophic avalanches would persist at a relative frequency that cannot be altered. Criticality is a global property of the sandpile.[16]

3. In the passage, the author is primarily concerned with

(A) arguing against the abandonment of a traditional approach
(B) describing the evolution of a radical theory
(C) reconciling conflicting points of view
(D) illustrating the superiority of a new theoretical approach
(E) advocating the reconsideration of an unfashionable explanation[17]

---

[16]PrepTest 16, Sec 4, Passage 3
[17]PrepTest 16, Sec 4, Q 21

Explanations

1. **(B)**

Three kinds of study have been performed on Byron. There is the biographical study—the very valuable examination of Byron's psychology and the events in his life; Escarpit's 1958 work is an example

(5) of this kind of study, and biographers to this day continue to speculate about Byron's life. Equally valuable is the study of Byron as a figure important in the history of ideas; Russell and Praz have written studies of this kind. Finally, there are

(10) studies that primarily consider Byron's poetry. Such literary studies are valuable, however, only when they avoid concentrating solely on analyzing the verbal shadings of Byron's poetry to the exclusion of any discussion of biographical considerations. A

(15) study with such a concentration would be of questionable value because Byron's poetry, for the most part, is simply not a poetry of subtle verbal meaning. Rather, on the whole, Byron's poems record the emotional pressure of certain moments

(20) in his life. I believe we cannot often read a poem of Byron's, as we often can one of Shakespeare's, without wondering what events or circumstances in his life prompted him to write it.

No doubt the fact that most of Byron's poems

(25) cannot be convincingly read as subtle verbal creations indicates that Byron is not a "great" poet. It must be admitted too that Byron's literary craftsmanship is irregular and often his temperament disrupts even his lax literary method

(30) (although the result, an absence of method, has a significant purpose: it functions as a rebuke to a cosmos that Byron feels he cannot understand). If Byron is not a "great" poet, his poetry is nonetheless of extraordinary interest to us because

(35) of the pleasure it gives us. Our main pleasure in reading Byron's poetry is the contact with a singular personality. Reading his work gives us illumination—self-understanding—after we have seen our weaknesses and aspirations mirrored in

(40) the personality we usually find in the poems. Anyone who thinks that this kind of illumination is not a genuine reason for reading a poet should think carefully about why we read Donne's sonnets.

Margin notes:

Three studies on Byron

Auth: must examine Byron's life

Byron not great poet

Gives personal insights

It is Byron and Byron's idea of himself (that hold)

(45) his work together (and that enthralled early-nineteenth-century Europe). Different characters

Byron is in his poetry

speak in his poems, (but finally) it is usually he himself who is speaking: a (far cry from) the impersonal poet Keats. Byron's poetry alludes to

(50) Greek and Roman myth in the context of contemporary affairs, (but) his work remains generally of a piece because of his close presence in the poetry. (In sum,) the poetry is a shrewd personal performance, (and) to shut out Byron the man is to

(55) fabricate a work of pseudocriticism.[18]

1. Which one of the following titles best expresses the main idea of the passage?

    (A) An Absence of Method: Why Byron Is Not a "Great" Poet

    (B) Byron: The Recurring Presence in Byron's Poetry

    (C) Personality and Poetry: The Biographical Dimension of Nineteenth-Century Poetry

    (D) Byron's Poetry: Its Influence on the Imagination of Early-Nineteenth-Century Europe

    (E) Verbal Shadings: The Fatal Flaw of Twentieth-Century Literary Criticism[19]

This passage is an excellent illustration of the second common pattern I discussed in this chapter. The author describes three kinds of studies of Byron in the first paragraph and then promptly discards them in favor of her own interpretation in the subsequent paragraphs. The beginning of paragraph 3 provides a major clue—the author states that "Byron and Byron's idea of himself" constitute his work, going on to call his work a "shrewd personal performance" in lines 53–55. Don't worry about the odd wording of the question: You should look for an answer that refers to Byron's insertion of himself into his poetry. Choice (B) is the match.

2. **(B)**

The United States Supreme Court (has not)

Courts not always good for Native Americans

always resolved legal issues of concern to Native Americans in a manner that has (pleased) the Indian nations. (Many) of the Court's decisions have been

(5) (products of) political compromise that looked more to the temper of the times (than to) enduring principles of law. (But) accommodation is part of the

Auth: always accommodation

judicial system in the United States, (and) judicial decisions must be assessed with this fact in mind.

---

[18]PrepTest 16, Sec 4, Passage 1

[19]PrepTest 16, Sec 4, Q 1

(10)   Despite the "accommodating" nature of the
          judicial system, it is worth noting that the power of
          the Supreme Court has been exercised in a manner
          that has usually been beneficial to Native
          Americans, at least on minor issues, and has not

**Courts usually
beneficial**

(15)   been wholly detrimental on the larger, more
          important issues. Certainly there have been
          decisions that cast doubt on the validity of this
          assertion. Some critics point to the patronizing tone
          of many Court opinions and the apparent rejection

(20)   of Native American values as important points to

Counterexamples

          consider when reviewing a case. However, the
          validity of the assertion can be illustrated by

**Auth: two
contributions**

          reference to two important contributions that have
          resulted from the exercise of judicial power.

(25)   First, the Court has created rules of judicial
          construction that, in general, favor the rights of

**Laws favor
Native
Americans**

          Native American litigants. The court's attitude has
          been conditioned by recognition of the distinct
          disadvantages Native Americans faced when

(30)   dealing with settlers in the past. Treaties were
          inevitably written in English for the benefit of their
          authors, whereas tribal leaders were accustomed to
          making treaties without any written account, on the
          strength of mutual promises sealed by religious

(35)   commitment and individual integrity. The written
          treaties were often broken, and Native Americans
          were confronted with fraud and political and
          military aggression. The Court recognizes that past
          unfairness to Native Americans cannot be

(40)   sanctioned by the force of law. Therefore,
          ambiguities in treaties are to be interpreted in favor
          of the Native American claimants, treaties are to be
          interpreted as the Native Americans would have
          understood them, and under the reserved rights

(45)   doctrine, treaties reserve to Native Americans all
          rights that have not been specifically granted away
          in other treaties.

          A second achievement of the judicial system is

**Native
Americans
protected from
states**

          the protection that has been provided against
(50)   encroachment by the states into tribal affairs.
          Federal judges are not inclined to view favorably
          efforts to extend states' powers and jurisdictions
          because of the direct threat that such expansion
          poses to the exercise of federal powers. In the

(55)   absence of a federal statute directly and clearly
          allocating a function to the states, federal judges are
          inclined to reserve for the federal government—and
          the tribal governments under its charge—all those
          powers and rights they can be said to have

(60)   possessed historically.[20]

---

[20]PrepTest 16, Sec 4, Passage 2

2. The author's attitude toward the United States
   Supreme Court's resolution of legal issues of concern
   to Native Americans can best be described as one of

   (A) wholehearted endorsement
   (B) restrained appreciation
   (C) detached objectivity
   (D) cautious opposition
   (E) suppressed exasperation[21]

This passage exemplifies the first of the three common patterns. The author's primary Purpose in this passage is to rebut the Supreme Court's critics, primarily those mentioned in paragraph 2. In fact, paragraph 2 is where the author makes his primary assertions—that the Supreme Court's decisions have usually been beneficial and other times "not . . . wholly detrimental." Attention to tone is crucial when pinpointing the author's attitude, so be sure to note the qualifying language here. Words like "usually" in line 13 indicate the author may not *always* agree with the Supreme Court, but believes their judgments are generally sound. You should accordingly look for a choice that is positive but with some reservations. This should lead you to choice (B). Note the wrong answer trap, choice (A), which is too extreme and ignores the author's carefully qualified tone.

3. **(D)**

Catastrophes usually blamed on major causes

        When catastrophe strikes, analysts typically
        blame some combination of powerful mechanisms.
        An earthquake is traced to an immense instability
        along a fault line; a stock market crash is blamed on
    (5) the destabilizing effect of computer trading. These
        explanations may well be correct. But systems as
        large and complicated as the Earth's crust or the
        stock market can break down not only under the

Causes can be minor too

        force of a mighty blow but also at the drop of a pin.
    (10) In a large interactive system, a minor event can start
        a chain reaction that leads to a catastrophe.

Trad, treat big systems like small systems

        Traditionally, investigators have analyzed large
        interactive systems in the same way they analyze
        small orderly systems, mainly because the methods
    (15) developed for small systems have proved so
        successful. They believed they could predict the
        behavior of a large interactive system by studying its
        elements separately and by analyzing its component
        mechanisms individually. For lack of a better
    (20) theory, they assumed that in large interactive
        systems the response to a disturbance is
        proportional to that disturbance.

---

[21]PrepTest 16, Sec 4, Q 12

Now big systems
different/new (25)
theory

(During) the past few decades, (however,) it has become increasingly (apparent) that many large complicated systems (do not yield) to traditional analysis. (Consequently,) theorists have (proposed) a "theory of self-organized criticality": many large interactive systems evolve naturally to a (critical) state in which a minor event (starts) a chain reaction

(30) that (can affect) any number of elements in the system. (Although) such systems produce more minor events than catastrophes, the mechanism that leads to minor events (is the same) one that leads to major events.

Ex: sandpile

(35) A (deceptively simple) system serves as a paradigm for self-organized criticality: a pile of sand. (As) sand is poured one grain at a time onto a flat disk, the grains (at first) stay close to the position where they land. (Soon) they rest on top of one

(40) another, (creating) a pile that has a gentle slope. Now and then, when the slope becomes too steep, the grains slide down, (causing) a small avalanche. The system reaches its (critical state) when the amount of sand added is balanced, on average, by the amount

(45) falling off the edge of the disk.

Ex. continued

(Now) when a grain of sand is added, it (can start) an avalanche of any size, (including) a "catastrophic" event. (Most of the time) the grain will fall so that no avalanche occurs. (By studying) a specific area of the

(50) pile, one can even (predict) whether avalanches will occur there in the near future. To such a local observer, (however,) large avalanches would remain unpredictable (because) they are a consequence of the total history of the entire pile. (No matter) what

(55) the local dynamics are, catastrophic avalanches would (persist) at a relative frequency that cannot be altered. Criticality is a (global property) of the sandpile.[22]

3. In the passage, the author is primarily concerned with

(A) arguing against the abandonment of a traditional approach

(B) describing the evolution of a radical theory

(C) reconciling conflicting points of view

(D) illustrating the superiority of a new theoretical approach

(E) advocating the reconsideration of an unfashionable explanation[23]

This passage is neutral in tone. In the first two paragraphs, the author describes a traditional view of the causes of catastrophes. She then shifts gears, describing a new theory that has

---

been proposed to address the flaws in the older one. She never explicitly favors one theory over another, sticking to passive description. For example, she notes that complicated systems "do not yield" to traditional analysis in lines 23–26, but instead of critiquing the old theory, she simply goes on to state how investigators have compensated for this problem. This passage is purely descriptive, and while the author does acknowledge that the new theory is more robust, the balance of the passage is spent in detail-laden explanation. The author's Purpose is descriptive, which is noted in correct choice (D). Notice that choices (A), (C), and (E) all suggest a more vigorous tone than the author displays in this passage; she's doesn't argue, reconcile, or advocate anything. Choice (B) contains the properly neutral verb "describing," but then distorts the author's intent. She doesn't describe the evolution of a theory, but rather its replacement.

THE PURPOSE IS PREDICTABLE

I hope that in working through this chapter you've gained some further insight into the predictable nature of the LSAT. It's a subject that I'll return to often in this book. You may recall that in chapter 6 I mentioned that my students consistently cite the pressure of the clock as the primary reason that Reading Comprehension seems difficult. In order to lessen that pressure and increase your efficiency and confidence, you must gain a master's familiarity with the contents of the test. Learning to recognize common passage structures and the authorial Purposes that derive from them is part of that process. On test day, every passage should look familiar to you, not because you've actually seen them before (the test makers never reuse a passage) but because you've already applied the Kaplan Method to other passages that were structurally similar.

This same kind of thinking applies to questions as well, and I'll introduce that subject soon. But first, because it forms the foundation of Reading Comprehension success, a review of strategic reading as a whole is in order. That's coming up in chapter 8.

CHAPTER 8

STRATEGIC READING REVIEW

SUCCESS THROUGH STRATEGIC READING

When you began preparing for the LSAT, you might have thought it was impossible to read all four passages in a single Reading Comprehension section and complete every question in the allotted time period. I hope you can now see that, far from being a mysterious test of random knowledge, the LSAT is designed to reward skilled, confident test takers who understand how to read each passage efficiently and focus on the right information. Through the proper application of the Kaplan Method, you have learned to read passages not just quickly, but correctly, focusing on the information that will increase your score by noting the clues that the test makers provide. And remember, the clues are there in *every* LSAT passage, no matter how intimidating it may appear to a casual reader.

You still have plenty to learn about Reading Comprehension, and in Part II of this book I'll teach you about the different question types you'll see on test day and the most common types of wrong answers you're likely to see. But first I want you to review strategic reading as a whole, then put your understanding of the Kaplan Method to the test.

Locating and Understanding Keywords

When I first introduced strategic reading, I showed you how to stay focused on the big picture behind every passage, and how to avoid wasting time pondering details. I also pointed out that the test makers provide you with clues to aid you in this task: the Keywords located throughout the text. Because strategic reading depends so heavily upon the proper identification and usage of Keywords, I'll review the three core ideas you should remember on test day.

Keywords separate main ideas from supporting evidence.

The majority of the questions you'll see on test day will examine your knowledge of the author's primary opinions. It is therefore crucial that you always read with an eye for Keywords that indicate conclusion and emphasis. Review the following excerpt, keeping an eye out for Keywords:

> Although philanthropy—the volunteering of
> private resources for humanitarian purposes—reached
> its apex in England in the late nineteenth century,
> modern commentators have articulated two major
> (5)   criticisms of the philanthropy that was a mainstay of
> England's middle-class Victorian society.[1]

What was the author most interested in communicating here? The Keyword "although" at the beginning of the excerpt prepares you for a potentially important contrast to follow, and soon you learn that commentators have voiced two "major criticisms" of Victorian philanthropy. These Keywords separate less important background information (the definition of philanthropy and the century during which it reached its peak) from the line of inquiry the author plans to pursue further, the validity of the criticisms. This leads to another core idea:

When you find Keywords in a passage, circle them and think about what they mean.

It's never enough to simply acknowledge that Keywords are there; you must always take the second step of using them to guide your thinking about the passage. In the previous example, the Keyword "although" was the author's way of signaling that a contrasting idea was approaching, and that this idea was likely to be important. Hopefully this thought process is becoming second nature to you by now, but it doesn't hurt to remember just how important this two-step process is: Circle each Keyword you find, and then determine what it tells you about the structure of the passage.

---

[1]PrepTest 41, Sec 4, Passage 4

Keywords help you answer the questions.

It can't be overstated: No matter how difficult the passage may appear, Keywords always point the way to the answers you need. Review the following excerpt, again circling Keywords along the way:

> In addition, Marshall used sociological and
> (35) psychological statistics—presented in expert testimony,
> for example, about the psychological impact of
> enforced segregation—as a means of transforming
> constitutional law by persuading the courts that certain
> discriminatory laws produced public harms in violation
> (40) of constitutional principles. This tactic, while often
> effective, has been criticized by some legal scholars as
> a pragmatic attempt to give judges nonlegal material
> with which to fill gaps in their justifications for
> decisions where the purely legal principles appear
> (45) inconclusive.[2]

Now, consider the following question:

7. According to the passage, some legal scholars have criticized which one of the following?

   (A)   the ideology Marshall used to support his goals

   (B)   recent public interest campaigns

   (C)   the use of Marshall's techniques by politically conservative lawyers

   (D)   the use of psychological statistics in court cases

   (E)   the set of criteria for selecting public interest litigants[3]

The critics have disparaged one of Marshall's tactics. How can you quickly summarize what it was? The description of Marshall's tactic is denoted by the Keywords "in addition" and "for example" in the first sentence. A re-examination of the text shows you that it was the use of social and psychological statistics in the courtroom that irked the critics. With this summary in mind, choice (D) is the clear winner.

It is important to remember that, while most questions deal with the author's main ideas, sometimes you will need to reference supporting evidence, and important evidence is *always* surrounded by Keywords.

Creating and Using a Roadmap

Hopefully, you've reached the point in your practice at which you've become comfortable with Roadmapping passages. You may still be in the process of developing your own particular

---

[2]PrepTest 42, Sec 3, Passage 1

[3]PrepTest 42, Sec 3, Q 7

style of Roadmap, determining which information you should include, how to use shorthand effectively, and how much to write. That's perfectly fine. The most important thing is that you continue to practice and deepen your level of comfort on every passage you complete. Keep in mind the following points each time you construct a Roadmap.

Your Roadmap should be concise.

Perhaps you remember this example of a poorly Roadmapped paragraph from chapter 3:

James writes
strikingly

characters w/
stories give   (30)
dignity

Kitchen vs.
plot/story too
thin   (35)

crimes solved
by intuition /
char, more than
plot   (40)

>   James is certainly capable of strikingly good writing. She takes immense trouble to provide her characters with convincing histories and passions. Her descriptive digressions are part of the pleasure of her
> (30) books and give them dignity and weight. But it is equally true that they frequently interfere with the story; the patinas and aromas of a country kitchen receive more loving attention than does the plot itself. Her devices to advance the story can be shameless and
> (35) thin, and it is often impossible to see how her detective arrives at the truth; one is left to conclude that the detective solves crimes through intuition. At this stage in her career P. D. James seems to be less interested in the specifics of detection than in her characters'
> (40) vulnerabilities and perplexities.[4]

The margin notes are very thorough—so thorough that they no longer provide a quick and simple way to access information in the passage, which defeats the purpose of making notes. Once you've pinpointed that James writes "strikingly" according to the author, there's no need to reiterate all the evidence supplied. Remember that the information you need to answer the questions correctly is already in the passage, and sometimes you will have to return to the passage to find the text you need. The goal of the Roadmap is to help you do this quickly, not to restate everything the author says:

Auth: James is
striking writer

Sometimes bad
for plot   (35)

>   James is certainly capable of strikingly good writing. She takes immense trouble to provide her characters with convincing histories and passions. Her descriptive digressions are part of the pleasure of her
> (30) books and give them dignity and weight. But it is equally true that they frequently interfere with the story; the patinas and aromas of a country kitchen receive more loving attention than does the plot itself. Her devices to advance the story can be shameless and
> (35) thin, and it is often impossible to see how her detective arrives at the truth; one is left to conclude that the detective solves crimes through intuition. At this stage in her career P. D. James seems to be less interested in the specifics of detection than in her characters'
> (40) vulnerabilities and perplexities.[5]

---

[4]PrepTest 19, Sec 3, Passage 1

[5]PrepTest 19, Sec 3, Passage 1

This Roadmap simply reflects what the paragraph is about and provides you with a good point of reference. Your Roadmap should contain just as much information as is necessary to be useful and no more. My students usually require a fair amount of practice before they feel that they've struck the correct balance. Keep practicing, and always compare your own Roadmap to the answers and explanations in this book to help you refine your margin notes.

Your Roadmap makes passage structure easy to understand.

Students frequently tell me that, while they are diligently Roadmapping every passage they read, they don't often consult the notes that they've written once they actually get to the question set. So if they're not actually referencing it, why should they bother to create it?

It's true that different test takers will rely on the Roadmap as a reference tool to varying degrees. It's also true that some passages require more extensive research than others. But what some fail to realize is that, in constructing their Roadmaps, they're actively clarifying and committing to memory vital structural information about the passage. If they hadn't Roadmapped the passage, they wouldn't understand the passage as well as they do.

The implication of this is extremely important: No matter how often you reference your Roadmap, the very act of creating it helps you to clarify the structure of the passage. For this reason alone, you must stay in the habit of creating a Roadmap every time you practice LSAT Reading Comprehension, and you must Roadmap every passage you read on test day.

Your Roadmap helps you score points.

To reinforce the importance of understanding passage structure, revisit this passage and question from the previous chapter:

Star system of 20's

As one of the most pervasive and influential popular arts, the movies feed into and off of the rest of the culture in various ways. In the United States, the star system of the mid-1920s—in which actors were

(5) placed under exclusive contract to particular Hollywood film studios—was a consequence of studios' discovery that the public was interested in actors' private lives, and that information about actors could be used to promote their films. Public relations

(10) agents fed the information to gossip columnists, whetting the public's appetite for the films—which, audiences usually discovered, had the additional virtue of being created by talented writers, directors, and producers devoted to the art of storytelling. The

Press benefits from film

(15) important feature of this relationship was not the benefit to Hollywood, but rather to the press; in what amounted to a form of cultural cross-fertilization, the press saw that they could profit from studios' promotion of new films.

Media
promotes
movies

(20)   Today this arrangement has mushroomed into an
intricately interdependent mass-media entertainment
industry. The faith by which this industry sustains itself
is the belief that there is always something worth
promoting. A vast portion of the mass media—
(25)   television and radio interviews, magazine articles, even
product advertisements—now does most of the work
for Hollywood studios attempting to promote their
movies. It does so not out of altruism but because it
makes for good business: If you produce a talk show
(30)   or edit a newspaper, and other media are generating
public curiosity about a studio's forthcoming film, it
would be unwise for you not to broadcast or publish
something about the film, too, because the audience for
your story is already guaranteed.

Problem:
affects films

(35)   The problem with this industry is that it has begun
to affect the creation of films as well as their
promotion. Choices of subject matter and actors are
made more and more frequently by studio executives
rather than by producers, writers, or directors. This
(40)   problem is often referred to simply as an obsession
with turning a profit, but Hollywood movies have
almost always been produced to appeal to the largest
possible audience. The new danger is that,
increasingly, profit comes only from exciting an

Films are not
satisfying

(45)   audience's curiosity about a movie instead of satisfying
its desire to have an engaging experience watching the
film. When movies can pull people into theaters
instantly on the strength of media publicity rather than
relying on the more gradual process of word of mouth
(50)   among satisfied moviegoers, then the intimate
relationship with the audience—on which the vitality
of all popular art depends—is lost. But studios are
making more money than ever by using this formula,
and for this reason it appears that films whose appeal is
(55)   due not merely to their publicity value but to their
ability to affect audiences emotionally will become
increasingly rare in the U.S. film industry.[6]

25. Which one of the following most accurately describes the organization of the passage?

   (A) description of the origins of a particular aspect of a popular art; discussion of the present state of this aspect; analysis of a problem associated with this aspect; introduction of a possible solution to the problem

   (B) description of the origins of a particular aspect of a popular art; discussion of the present state of this aspect; analysis of a problem associated with this aspect; suggestion of a likely consequence of the problem

   (C) description of the origins of a particular aspect of a popular art; analysis of a problem associated with this aspect; introduction of a possible solution to the problem; suggestion of a likely consequence of the solution

   (D) summary of the history of a particular aspect of a popular art; discussion of a problem that accompanied the growth of this aspect; suggestion of a likely consequence of the problem; appraisal of the importance of avoiding this consequence

   (E) summary of the history of a particular aspect of a popular art; analysis of factors that contributed to the growth of this aspect; discussion of a problem that accompanied the growth of this aspect; appeal for assistance in solving the problem[7]

A question like this one is virtually impossible to answer quickly and accurately without a strong sense of passage structure. Note once more how correct choice (B) follows directly from the Roadmap, piece by piece. There's no denying that your ability to read for structure will be vital to your success in your first year of law school; that's why the test makers reward this skill so consistently. The more you practice thinking about the big picture of every passage, the easier it will become.

Identifying Topic, Scope, Purpose, and Main Idea

The good habits you form in identifying Keywords and creating solid Roadmaps will help you to identify Topic, Scope, Purpose, and Main Idea. To briefly review:

The Topic provides you with a broad sense of context.

Even though the Topic of the passage will not be directly tested, it's important that you establish a good sense of context from the moment you begin reading. At least some of the passages you encounter on test day will contain subject matter with which you are not familiar. Becoming acquainted with the Topic of the passage right away removes some of the mystery and abstraction from the passage and helps keeps you focused on the passage's content.

---

[7]PrepTest 28, Sec 4, Q 25

The Scope gives you insight into the author's goals.

Since the Scope specifies what narrower area within the Topic the author will address, you should pay close attention to it. If you know the author is writing on the Topic of dinosaurs, for example, it's to your advantage to determine what specifically about dinosaurs the author is interested in discussing so that you can deepen your sense of context. Staying focused on the Scope helps you avoid wrong answer choices, which are frequently outside the author's Scope.

The Purpose summarizes the structure of the passage.

Remember that a good Roadmap will allow you to describe the author's Purpose with ease. The number of Purposes that LSAT passages pursue is very limited; authors generally write to support or refute arguments, to explain phenomena, or to describe varying ideas. Questions that directly ask for the author's Purpose are common on the LSAT.

The Main Idea summarizes the author's opinions.

You've seen many examples of test questions that ask for the author's opinion. Having a solid description of the Main Idea makes these questions much easier to answer correctly and can significantly reduce the amount of time it takes you to conduct your research. As with Purpose, questions that directly ask for the author's Main Idea are common on the test.

Patterns and Predictions

Before you give your strategic reading skills some further practice, don't forget that predictive reading is one of the most powerful tools at your disposal. No matter how convoluted the passage may seem at first, if you stay in the habit of anticipating the author's direction as you read, you'll become a more confident and efficient reader. Far from being a totally distinct skill from those already discussed, prediction follows naturally from the habits you've already begun to form. Identifying and thinking about Keywords helps you anticipate where in the passage important ideas are likely to occur, and each time you Roadmap a paragraph, you've given yourself a sense of context with which to predict what is coming next.

Finally, if your practice thus far has shown you anything about LSAT Reading Comprehension, it should be that the passages just aren't terribly varied. The subjects change but the structures become familiar with practice. Even the types of questions that the test makers write are easily predictable and follow identifiable patterns. I'm not suggesting that Reading Comprehension is easy—if it was, you wouldn't have to practice—but it's good to reflect on the limited nature of the passages. They're predictable, and since they're predictable, you can prepare for them.

DRILL: COMPLETING A PASSAGE

Now it's time to apply everything that you've learned so far. In this Drill, your task is straightforward: Read and Roadmap the passage, circling Keywords as you go; identify Topic, Scope, Purpose, and Main Idea; and then answer each of the five questions that follow. Don't let the abstract nature of the passage disrupt the good habits you've established. Take your time, be patient, and stick to the Kaplan Method. Full answers and explanations follow, and, as always, review them carefully.

Scientists typically advocate the analytic method of studying complex systems: systems are divided into component parts that are investigated separately. But nineteenth-century critics of this method claimed that
(5) when a system's parts are isolated its complexity tends to be lost. To address the perceived weaknesses of the analytic method these critics put forward a concept called organicism, which posited that the whole determines the nature of its parts and that the parts of a
(10) whole are interdependent.

Organicism depended upon the theory of internal relations, which states that relations between entities are possible only within some whole that embraces them, and that entities are altered by the relationships
(15) into which they enter. If an entity stands in a relationship with another entity, it has some property as a consequence. Without this relationship, and hence without the property, the entity would be different— and so would be another entity. Thus, the property is
(20) one of the entity's defining characteristics. Each of an entity's relationships likewise determines a defining characteristic of the entity.

One problem with the theory of internal relations is that not all properties of an entity are defining
(25) characteristics: numerous properties are accompanying characteristics—even if they are always present, their presence does not influence the entity's identity. Thus, even if it is admitted that every relationship into which an entity enters determines some characteristic of the
(30) entity, it is not necessarily true that such characteristics will define the entity; it is possible for the entity to enter into a relationship yet remain essentially unchanged.

The ultimate difficulty with the theory of internal
(35) relations is that it renders the acquisition of knowledge impossible. To truly know an entity, we must know all of its relationships; but because the entity is related to everything in each whole of which it is a part, these wholes must be known completely before the entity
(40) can be known. This seems to be a prerequisite impossible to satisfy.

Organicists' criticism of the analytic method arose from their failure to fully comprehend the method. In rejecting the analytic method, organicists overlooked
(45) the fact that before the proponents of the method analyzed the component parts of a system, they first determined both the laws applicable to the whole system and the initial conditions of the system; proponents of the method thus did not study parts of a
(50) system in full isolation from the system as a whole. Since organicists failed to recognize this, they never advanced any argument to show that laws and initial conditions of complex systems cannot be discovered. Hence, organicists offered no valid reason for rejecting
(55) the analytic method or for adopting organicism as a replacement for it.[8]

1. Which one of the following most completely and accurately summarizes the argument of the passage?

   (A) By calling into question the possibility that complex systems can be studied in their entirety, organicists offered an alternative to the analytic method favored by nineteenth-century scientists.

   (B) Organicists did not offer a useful method of studying complex systems because they did not acknowledge that there are relationships into which an entity may enter that do not alter the entity's identity.

   (C) Organicism is flawed because it relies on a theory that both ignores the fact that not all characteristics of entities are defining and ultimately makes the acquisition of knowledge impossible.

   (D) Organicism does not offer a valid challenge to the analytic method both because it relies on faulty theory and because it is based on a misrepresentation of the analytic method.

   (E) In criticizing the analytic method, organicists neglected to disprove that scientists who employ the method are able to discover the laws and initial conditions of the systems they study.

---

[8]PrepTest 25, Sec 1, Passage 4

2. According to the passage, organicists' chief objection to the analytic method was that the method

   (A) oversimplified systems by isolating their components
   (B) assumed that a system can be divided into component parts
   (C) ignored the laws applicable to the system as a whole
   (D) claimed that the parts of a system are more important than the system as a whole
   (E) denied the claim that entities enter into relationships

3. The passage offers information to help answer each of the following questions EXCEPT:

   (A) Why does the theory of internal relations appear to make the acquisition of knowledge impossible?
   (B) Why did the organicists propose replacing the analytic method?
   (C) What is the difference between a defining characteristic and an accompanying characteristic?
   (D) What did organicists claim are the effects of an entity's entering into a relationship with another entity?
   (E) What are some of the advantages of separating out the parts of a system for study?

4. The passage most strongly supports the ascription of which one of the following views to scientists who use the analytic method?

   (A) A complex system is best understood by studying its component parts in full isolation from the system as a whole.
   (B) The parts of a system should be studied with an awareness of the laws and initial conditions that govern the system.
   (C) It is not possible to determine the laws governing a system until the system's parts are separated from one another.
   (D) Because the parts of a system are interdependent, they cannot be studied separately without destroying the system's complexity.
   (E) Studying the parts of a system individually eliminates the need to determine which characteristics of the parts are defining characteristics.

5. Which one of the following is a principle upon which the author bases an argument against the theory of internal relations?

   (A) An adequate theory of complex systems must define the entities of which the system is composed.
   (B) An acceptable theory cannot have consequences that contradict its basic purpose.
   (C) An adequate method of study of complex systems should reveal the actual complexity of the systems it studies.
   (D) An acceptable theory must describe the laws and initial conditions of a complex system.
   (E) An acceptable method of studying complex systems should not study parts of the system in isolation from the system as a whole.[9]

Answer Explanations follow on the next page.

Explanations

Scientist (typically) advocate the analytic method of studying complex systems: systems are divided into component parts that are investigated separately. (But) nineteenth-century (critics) of this method (claimed) that
(5) when a system's parts are isolated its complexity tends to be lost. (To address) the perceived (weaknesses) of the analytic method these (critics) put forward a concept called organicism, which (posited) that the whole determines the nature of its parts (and) that the parts of a
(10) whole are interdependent.

Organicism vs. analytic method

Organicism (depended) upon the theory of internal relations, which (states) that relations between entities are possible (only) within some whole that embraces them, (and) that entities are altered by the relationships
(15) into which they enter. (If) an entity stands in a relationship with another entity, it has some property as a (consequence.) Without this relationship, (and hence) without the property, the entity would be different—(and so) would be another entity. (Thus,) the property is
(20) one of the entity's defining characteristics. Each of an entity's relationships (likewise) determines a defining characteristic of the entity.

Organicism: depends on relations

(One problem) with the theory of internal relations is that (not all) properties of an entity are defining
(25) characteristics: numerous properties are accompanying characteristics—(even if) they are always present, their presence does not influence the entity's identity. (Thus,) (even if) it is admitted that every relationship into which an entity enters determines some characteristic of the
(30) entity, it is (not necessarily) true that such characteristics will define the entity; it is possible for the entity to enter into a relationship yet remain essentially unchanged.

Problem: not all relations define

The (ultimate difficulty) with the theory of internal
(35) relations is that it renders the acquisition of knowledge impossible. To truly know an entity, we must know all of its relationships, (but because) the entity is related to everything in each whole of which it is part, these wholes must be known completely (before) the entity
(40) can be known. This seems to be a prerequisite (impossible) to satisfy.

Big problem: impossible

(Organicists' criticism) of the analytic method arose (from) their (failure) to fully comprehend the method. In (rejecting) the analytic method, organicists overlooked
(45) the fact that (before) the proponents of the method analyzed the component parts of a system, they (first) determined both the laws applicable to the whole system (and) the initial conditions of the system;

Critics don't understand analytic method

(50) (proponents) of the method (thus) did not study parts of a
system in full isolation from the system as a whole.
(Since) organicists failed to recognize this, they (never)
advanced any argument to show that laws and initial
conditions of complex systems cannot be discovered.
(55) (Hence,) organicists offered (no valid reason) for rejecting
the analytic method or for adopting organicism as a
replacement for it.[10]

Paragraph Structure: Paragraph 1 sets up the central conflict that the author explores in the passage: The analytic method, currently in use by most scientists, and the theory of organicism proposed by 19th-century critics.

Paragraph 2 goes into more detail about the claims of the organicists. The author mentions the theory of internal relations, which underlies the organicists central ideas. This paragraph contains a lot of redundancy, which is typical of tougher LSAT science passages. Notice how keywords like "consequence," "thus," and "likewise" give some order to all this jargon.

Paragraphs 3 and 4 are very similar to one another structurally—both introduce an objection the author levels against the organicists. Paragraph three deals with the notion that relationships aren't always defining characteristics. Paragraph four begins with some very emphatic language, positing that the "ultimate difficulty" with the theory of internal relations is that it makes knowledge impossible to acquire (quite a handicap for any scientific theory).

Paragraph 5 closes the argument against the organicists and vindicates the analytic method. In lines 42–43 the author states that the organicists failed to comprehend the analytic method, thus leading to their objections to it. The author reinforces the importance of this idea in line 54 beginning with the keyword "hence."

Topic: competing scientific theories

Scope: organicism vs. analytic method

Purpose: to describe why organicism failed to successfully challenge the analytic method

Main Idea: The organicists failed to replace the analytic method because they misunderstood it, and because their own methods were fatally flawed.

---

[10]PrepTest 25, Sec 1, Passage 4

1. **(D)**

    Which one of the following most completely and
    accurately summarizes the argument of the passage?
    (A)   By calling into question the possibility that
           complex systems can be studied in their entirety,
           organicists offered an alternative to the analytic
           method favored by nineteenth-century scientists.
    (B)   Organicists did not offer a useful method of
           studying complex systems because they did not
           acknowledge that there are relationships into
           which an entity may enter that do not alter the
           entity's identity.
    (C)   Organicism is flawed because it relies on a theory
           that both ignores the fact that not all
           characteristics of entities are defining and
           ultimately makes the acquisition of knowledge
           impossible.
    (D)   Organicism does not offer a valid challenge to the
           analytic method both because it relies on faulty
           theory and because it is based on a
           misrepresentation of the analytic method.
    (E)   In criticizing the analytic method, organicists
           neglected to disprove that scientists who employ
           the method are able to discover the laws and
           initial conditions of the systems they study.[11]

The Main Idea question should be a familiar sight to you. Correct choice (D) perfectly matches
the author's thesis; it states that organicism failed, and it gives the author's primary reasons
for why it failed. Choices (A) and (E) both fail to explicitly state that organicism failed to successfully challenge the analytic method. Choice (B) is too narrowly focused; there were other
more important ideas given for the failure of organicism. Choice (C) may look good at first, as
it presents some of the author's objections to organicism, but it ultimately fails to capture the
author's biggest complaint, that the organicists misunderstood the method they were attacking.

2. **(A)**

    According to the passage, organicists' chief objection to
    the analytic method was that the method
    (A)   oversimplified systems by isolating their
           components
    (B)   assumed that a system can be divided into
           component parts
    (C)   ignored the laws applicable to the system as a
           whole
    (D)   claimed that the parts of a system are more
           important than the system as a whole
    (E)   denied the claim that entities enter into
           relationships[12]

---

[11]PrepTest 25, Sec 1, Q 22
[12]PrepTest 25, Sec 1, Q 23

Your Roadmap should have guided you directly to the first paragraph to research the answer to this question—this is the only place where the organicists' objections are explained. Beginning in line 4, the "claim" of the critics is spelled out: that complexity is lost when the pieces of a system are isolated. Correct choice (A) states this nearly word for word. Choice (B) doesn't describe a criticism made by the organicists, and choices (C) and (D) have no textual support, and are thus out of scope. Choice (E) is also out of scope—the practitioners of the analytic method never respond to the organicists' claims anywhere in the passage. When approaching this type of question, don't rely on your memory—use your Roadmap to research the correct answer.

3. **(E)**

The passage offers information to help answer each of the following questions EXCEPT:

(A) Why does the theory of internal relations appear to make the acquisition of knowledge impossible?

(B) Why did the organicists propose replacing the analytic method?

(C) What is the difference between a defining characteristic and an accompanying characteristic?

(D) What did organicists claim are the effects of an entity's entering into a relationship with another entity?

(E) What are some of the advantages of separating out the parts of a system for study?[13]

This kind of question can be a frustrating waste of time; the correct answer must be the only one that gets no support from the passage. Your Roadmap is essential in helping you eliminate wrong choices quickly. Choice (A) gets support in paragraph four; choice (B) in paragraph one (in fact, you just researched this very information); choice (C) is discussed in paragraph three; and choice (D) is covered in paragraph two. That leaves correct choice (E), which is not addressed in the passage.

---

[13]PrepTest 25, Sec 1, Q 24

4. **(B)**

    The passage most strongly supports the ascription of
    which one of the following views to scientists who use
    the analytic method?
    (A) A complex system is best understood by studying
         its component parts in full isolation from the
         system as a whole.
    (B) The parts of a system should be studied with an
         awareness of the laws and initial conditions that
         govern the system.
    (C) It is not possible to determine the laws governing
         a system until the system's parts are separated
         from one another.
    (D) Because the parts of a system are interdependent,
         they cannot be studied separately without
         destroying the system's complexity.
    (E) Studying the parts of a system individually
         eliminates the need to determine which
         characteristics of the parts are defining
         characteristics.[14]

Take your time when reading an oddly worded question like this one. Which view is held by
scientists who adhere to the analytic method? Since most of the passage is devoted to the view
of the organicists, your Roadmap should draw you to the final paragraph, in which the author
vindicates the analytic method. Lines 45–50 provide the Keywords you need: "First" practitioners
of the analytic method examine the entirety of the system, and "thus" do not examine parts
in isolation. Correct choice (B) describes this kind of thinking perfectly. Choices (A), (C), and (D)
are more in line with the organicists' view of the analytic method, not the author's. Choice (E)
is out of Scope, referencing ideas from paragraph three that are not applicable to this question
(and distorting them as well).

5. **(B)**

    Which one of the following is a principle upon which the
    author bases an argument against the theory of internal
    relations?
    (A) An adequate theory of complex systems must
         define the entities of which the system is
         composed.
    (B) An acceptable theory cannot have consequences
         that contradict its basic purpose.
    (C) An adequate method of study of complex systems
         should reveal the actual complexity of the
         systems it studies.
    (D) An acceptable theory must describe the laws and
         initial conditions of a complex system.
    (E) An acceptable method of studying complex
         systems should not study parts of the system in
         isolation from the system as a whole.[15]

---

[14]PrepTest 25, Sec 1, Q 25
[15]PrepTest 25, Sec 1, Q 26

This question requires you to recall the author's reasons for rejecting organicism. The emphatic Keywords "ultimate difficulty" in line 34 give you a good place to start; organicism seeks to explain systems, but it makes explanations impossible to achieve. Correct choice (B) echoes this sentiment, albeit using more general language. Choices (A), (C), and (E) are out of Scope, and choice (D) describes a principle underlying the author's acceptance of the analytic method, not his refutation of organicism.

PRACTICE, CONSISTENCY, AND CONFIDENCE

You undoubtedly still have many questions about LSAT Reading Comprehension at this point, and rest assured that I'll address them. But before you move on to Part II, I want you to take a moment to recommit yourself to strategic reading. It's not easy to change the way you've probably been reading all your life, which is why it is so very important to remain consistent when applying the Kaplan Method. Each time you work on a practice passage, remind yourself to read strategically, and review the core concepts laid out in this chapter. It is especially important for you to do this when you time yourself; I know from experience that many students revert to bad habits when the clock starts running. Stay focused and consistent, and be confident in your abilities.

It's worth stating one last time: *Anyone* can master LSAT Reading Comprehension, because the clues are *always* there. Now it's up to you to continue to take advantage of them!

PART II

PASSAGE AND QUESTION TYPES

CHAPTER 9

COMPARATIVE READING

COMPARATIVE READING BASICS

In the first section of this book you learned how, through dedicated practice and application of the Kaplan Method, you can increase your LSAT score. One of the primary reasons that the LSAT is so vulnerable to preparation is its predictability. Any LSAT administered in the last several years will be similar in all respects to the LSAT that you're preparing to take. Since the tests themselves are predictable, it follows that strategies that are effective on one test will be effective on all of them. In Part II of the book I'm going to introduce you to the common question types, challenging passages, trends the test has followed in recent years, and the Kaplan strategies that you need to prepare for them.

First, however, you should become familiar with one of the few major changes the test makers have made to the LSAT in recent years. Prior to this change, Reading Comprehension always consisted of four passages covering four broad subject areas: law, natural science, social science, and humanities. Each passage was accompanied by five to eight questions.

In the June 2007 administration of the LSAT, the test makers introduced a new exercise, called comparative reading. In comparative reading, instead of a single passage, you are presented with two separate, shorter passages, and a set of five to eight questions. It is important to note that the test makers announced this change months before they implemented it, and they provided examples and explanations on their website, www.lsac.org. I mention this because I don't want you to fear that the test makers will make sudden and unpredictable changes to the LSAT before you take it; they have historically announced when major changes were made and provided plenty of information well in advance.

Since its introduction in 2007, comparative reading has remained a consistent and predictable component of the Reading Comprehension section. In this chapter, I'll show you exactly what to expect from comparative reading and teach you the appropriate strategies to apply to it.

Comparative Passages vs. Single Passages

To begin, take a look at the first comparative reading passage set to appear on the LSAT. Don't read the passages carefully yet; just take a quick glance for now.

Passage A

Readers, like writers, need to search for answers. Part of the joy of reading is in being surprised, but academic historians leave little to the imagination. The perniciousness of the historiographic approach became
(5) fully evident to me when I started teaching. Historians require undergraduates to read scholarly monographs that sap the vitality of history; they visit on students what was visited on them in graduate school. They assign books with formulaic arguments that transform
(10) history into an abstract debate that would have been unfathomable to those who lived in the past. Aimed so squarely at the head, such books cannot stimulate students who yearn to connect to history emotionally as well as intellectually.

(15) In an effort to address this problem, some historians have begun to rediscover stories. It has even become something of a fad within the profession. This year, the American Historical Association chose as the theme for its annual conference some putative connection to
(20) storytelling: "Practices of Historical Narrative." Predictably, historians responded by adding the word "narrative" to their titles and presenting papers at sessions on "Oral History and the Narrative of Class Identity," and "Meaning and Time: The Problem of
(25) Historical Narrative." But it was still historiography, intended only for other academics. At meetings of historians, we still encounter very few historians telling stories or moving audiences to smiles, chills, or tears.

Passage B

Writing is at the heart of the lawyer's craft, and so,
(30) like it or not, we who teach the law inevitably teach aspiring lawyers how lawyers write. We do this in a few stand-alone courses and, to a greater extent, through the constraints that we impose on their writing throughout the curriculum. Legal writing, because of the purposes
(35) it serves, is necessarily ruled by linear logic, creating a path without diversions, surprises, or reversals. Conformity is a virtue, creativity suspect, humor forbidden, and voice mute.

Lawyers write as they see other lawyers write, and,
(40) influenced by education, profession, economic constraints, and perceived self-interest, they too often write badly. Perhaps the currently fashionable call for attention to narrative in legal education could have an effect on this. It is not yet exactly clear what role
(45) narrative should play in the law, but it is nonetheless true that every case has at its heart a story—of real events and people, of concerns, misfortunes, conflicts, feelings. But because legal analysis strips the human narrative content from the abstract, canonical legal
(50) form of the case, law students learn to act as if there is no such story.

It may well turn out that some of the terminology and public rhetoric of this potentially subversive movement toward attention to narrative will find its
(55) way into the law curriculum, but without producing corresponding changes in how legal writing is actually taught or in how our future colleagues will write. Still, even mere awareness of the value of narrative could perhaps serve as an important corrective.[1]

[1]PrepTest 52, Sec 4, Passage 2

This set is representative of what the comparative reading format always looks like: two passages written by two different authors, labeled "Passage A" and "Passage B." The combined length of the two passages amounts to the average length of a single, noncomparative passage. Comparative passages fall within the same general subject categories as other passages, and they are structurally similar as well. Every reading comprehension section contains exactly one set of comparative reading passages.

The comparative passages always share the same broad Topic and are similar in Scope, although their authors can vary markedly in tone. Be sure to note that, while the two passages will always represent two different viewpoints on a similar Topic, their authors never directly address one another—that is, the author of Passage B will not directly reference any part of Passage A, either in agreement or refutation. Instead, the authors will take approaches to the Topic that are similar in some ways and different in others.

The purpose of comparative reading is to test your ability to understand the nuances between different points of view, a skill you have developed throughout your study of strategic reading. Ultimately, comparative reading is not very different from the sort of reading you've already become familiar with, and you'll be able to apply the same Kaplan Method strategies you've been learning thus far.

READ PAIRED PASSAGES STRATEGICALLY

To maximize your score on comparative reading passages, stay methodical and read strategically. Apply the Kaplan Method to comparative reading just as you do to any other Reading Comprehension passage—identify and circle Keywords, construct a Roadmap, and identify the Topic, Scope, Purpose, and Main Idea. The only real difference is that you will have to perform this process twice before moving on to the questions.

Now, take a closer look at passage A from the previous example. Read and Roadmap it on your own before moving on.

Passage A

Readers, like writers, need to search for answers. Part of the joy of reading is in being surprised, but academic historians leave little to the imagination. The perniciousness of the historiographic approach became
(5) fully evident to me when I started teaching. Historians require undergraduates to read scholarly monographs that sap the vitality of history; they visit on students what was visited on them in graduate school. They assign books with formulaic arguments that transform
(10) history into an abstract debate that would have been unfathomable to those who lived in the past. Aimed so squarely at the head, such books cannot stimulate students who yearn to connect to history emotionally as well as intellectually.

(15)   In an effort to address this problem, some historians
have begun to rediscover stories. It has even become
something of a fad within the profession. This year, the
American Historical Association chose as the theme
for its annual conference some putative connection to
(20)   storytelling: "Practices of Historical Narrative."
Predictably, historians responded by adding the word
"narrative" to their titles and presenting papers at
sessions on "Oral History and the Narrative of Class
Identity," and "Meaning and Time: The Problem of
(25)   Historical Narrative." But it was still historiography,
intended only for other academics. At meetings of
historians, we still encounter very few historians telling
stories or moving audiences to smiles, chills, or tears.[2]

Paragraph Structure: This passage is not different in any way from the examples you've already seen in this book. The author begins by introducing the historiographic approach to scholarship, of which he seems to disapprove (in line 4, he describes the "perniciousness" of this approach). In the second paragraph, he describes the efforts of some historians to make their scholarship less dry, noting that narrative has become "something of a fad" (line 17) among them. Ultimately, however, the author notes that historical scholarship is still largely lacking in compelling stories.

Compare your reading of this passage to this sample Roadmap:

Passage A

Readers, (like writers) need to search for answers.
Part of the joy of reading is in being surprised, (but)
academic historians leave little to the imagination. The

*History
teaching
too dry*

(perniciousness) of the historiographic approach became
(5)   fully (evident to me) when I started teaching. Historians
(require) undergraduates to read scholarly monographs
that (sap the vitality) of history; they visit on students
what was visited on them in graduate school. They
assign books with (formulaic) arguments that (transform)
(10)   history into an abstract debate that would have been
unfathomable to those who lived in the past. Aimed so
squarely at the head, such books (cannot) stimulate
students who yearn to connect to history emotionally as
(well as) intellectually.

*Some efforts,
but historians
still not
interested in
stories*

(15)   In an (effort) to address this problem, (some historians)
have begun to rediscover stories. It has (even become)
something of a fad within the profession. This year, the
American Historical Association (chose) as the theme
for its annual conference some putative connection to
(20)   storytelling: "Practices of Historical Narrative."
(Predictably,) historians responded by adding the word
"narrative" to their titles and presenting papers at

---

[2]PrepTest 52, Sec 4, Passage 2

sessions on "Oral History and the Narrative of Class
Identity," and "Meaning and Time: The Problem of
(25) Historical Narrative." But it was still historiography,
intended only for other academics. At meetings of
historians, we still encounter very few historians telling
stories or moving audiences to smiles, chills, or tears.[3]

I'll stress once more just how similar this passage is to others you've already completed. Before moving on to Passage B, be sure to identify the Topic, Scope, Purpose, and Main Idea of this passage:

Topic: Historiography

Scope: Lack of narrative in historical scholarship

Purpose: To describe a problem with historiography

Main Idea: Although some efforts have been made to enliven history with compelling narrative, most historians prefer a drier form of scholarship

This is precisely how you should approach comparative reading on test day: Be sure not to begin reading Passage B until you've finished applying the Kaplan Method to Passage A.

Now move on to Passage B. Remember that, although there will be some similarities, this is a different passage with a different author, so be sure to read it as such. Try reading and Road-mapping this passage on your own.

Passage B

Writing is at the heart of the lawyer's craft, and so,
(30) like it or not, we who teach the law inevitably teach
aspiring lawyers how lawyers write. We do this in a few
stand-alone courses and, to a greater extent, through the
constraints that we impose on their writing throughout
the curriculum. Legal writing, because of the purposes
(35) it serves, is necessarily ruled by linear logic, creating a
path without diversions, surprises, or reversals.
Conformity is a virtue, creativity suspect, humor
forbidden, and voice mute.
Lawyers write as they see other lawyers write, and,
(40) influenced by education, profession, economic
constraints, and perceived self-interest, they too often
write badly. Perhaps the currently fashionable call for
attention to narrative in legal education could have an
effect on this. It is not yet exactly clear what role
(45) narrative should play in the law, but it is nonetheless
true that every case has at its heart a story—of real
events and people, of concerns, misfortunes, conflicts,

---

[3]PrepTest 52, Sec 4, Passage 2

feelings. But because legal analysis strips the human
narrative content from the abstract, canonical legal

(50) form of the case, law students learn to act as if there is
no such story.

It may well turn out that some of the terminology
and public rhetoric of this potentially subversive
movement toward attention to narrative will find its

(55) way into the law curriculum, but without producing
corresponding changes in how legal writing is actually
taught or in how our future colleagues will write. Still,
even mere awareness of the value of narrative could
perhaps serve as an important corrective.[4]

Paragraph Structure: In the first paragraph, the author introduces the Topic of legal writing, describing it as "necessarily ruled by linear logic" (line 35) and, consequently, humorless and unsurprising. In the second paragraph, he introduces the possibility of narrative playing a role in legal writing, but suggests that the role such narrative would play is "not yet exactly clear" (line 44). The author concludes in the final paragraph that, although it may not make any major changes to legal writing, the awareness of narrative might still form some sort of "corrective" (line 59) to current forms of discourse.

Once again, compare your Roadmap to this sample:

Passage B

Writing is at the heart of the lawyer's craft, and so,
(30) like it or not, we who teach the law inevitably teach
aspiring lawyers how lawyers write. We do this in a few

Legal
writing =
dry,
logical

stand-alone courses and, to a greater extent, through the
constraints that we impose on their writing throughout
the curriculum. Legal writing, because of the purposes

(35) it serves, is necessarily ruled by linear logic, creating a
path without diversions, surprises, or reversals.
Conformity is a virtue, creativity suspect, humor
forbidden, and voice mute.

Lawyers write as they see other lawyers write, and,

Narrative
left out
of legal
writing

(40) influenced by education, profession, economic
constraints, and perceived self-interest, they too often
write badly. Perhaps the currently fashionable call for
attention to narrative in legal education could have an
effect on this. It is not yet exactly clear what role

(45) narrative should play in the law, but it is nonetheless
true that every case has at its heart a story—of real
events and people, of concerns, misfortunes, conflicts,
feelings. But because legal analysis strips the human
narrative content from the abstract, canonical legal

(50) form of the case, law students learn to act as if there is
no such story.

---

[4]PrepTest 52, Sec 4, Passage 2

Awareness
of narrative
may help

It may well turn out that some of the terminology and public rhetoric of this potentially subversive movement toward attention to narrative will find its (55) way into the law curriculum, but without producing corresponding changes in how legal writing is actually taught or in how our future colleagues will write. Still, even mere awareness of the value of narrative could perhaps serve as an important corrective.[5]

Now think about the Topic, Scope, Purpose, and Main Idea of this passage:

Topic: Legal writing

Scope: The role of narrative in legal writing

Purpose: To describe a problem with legal writing and consider a possible partial solution

Main Idea: Although current interest in narrative is unlikely to greatly change the way legal writing is taught, it might have some beneficial effects.

Now that you've applied the Kaplan Method to both passages, take a few seconds to identify the key similarities and differences between them. Both authors express dissatisfaction with a specific field of scholarship: history in Passage A and legal writing in Passage B. Notice also that both authors seem personally invested in the problems they describe—the first author initially noticed them "when I started teaching" (line 5) and the second lays the issue at the feet of "we who teach the law" (line 30). Finally, you should definitely note that both authors describe a lack of compelling narrative as problematic in their respective fields.

Both authors reach similar conclusions, but there is an important and nuanced difference. The author of Passage A finishes rather pessimistically, noting that very few historians bother with interesting stories. The author of Passage B, in contrast, is slightly more hopeful that narrative may improve the dry discourse of legal writing.

Look for Similarities and Differences in Comparative Passages

The kind of similarities and differences you'll see in comparative reading will vary from example to example. In this exercise, the two authors observe similar problems in two different fields, and both think that more storytelling would help. But the relationship between the two passages won't always follow this template. Here are just a few of the possible ways in which the two authors might relate to one another:

- They examine similar evidence and reach contrary conclusions.
- One author describes a problem, and the other proposes a solution to that problem.
- Both authors agree that a policy is appropriate, but disagree on how it should be implemented.

[5]PrepTest 52, Sec 4, Passage 2

- One author takes a detached view of a subject, and the other a more partisan approach.
- The authors describe a phenomenon and propose different causes for it.

Regardless of exactly how the authors differ or coincide in their ideas, there are two things you can be certain of: There will always be similarities and differences, and you can always use the Kaplan Method to identify them. Thinking through the relationship between these passages is important to your LSAT score, because questions will directly test your understanding of it.

COMPARATIVE READING QUESTIONS

Since comparative reading is largely about comparison (hence the name), the time you spend thinking about the relationship between the two passages will be worth points in the question set:

7. Which one of the following does each of the passages display?[6]

Try to predict what the correct answer should say. Both authors were dissatisfied with bad writing within a given academic area, and both suggested that a lack of compelling narrative is the culprit.

Now identify the answer choice that matches this prediction:

7. Which one of the following does each of the passages display?

    (A) a concern with the question of what teaching methods are most effective in developing writing skills
    (B) a concern with how a particular discipline tends to represent points of view it does not typically deal with
    (C) a conviction that writing in specialized professional disciplines cannot be creatively crafted
    (D) a belief that the writing in a particular profession could benefit from more attention to storytelling
    (E) a desire to see writing in a particular field purged of elements from other disciplines

Choice (D) is the perfect match, since both authors advocate storytelling as a cure for dry writing. Neither of the passages support any of the other choices.

---

[6]PrepTest 52, Sec 4, Q 7

This is exactly the kind of question you should expect to see on test day, and it's a question that you can answer quickly and confidently if you've already thought through the primary similarities and differences between the two passages.

The following question shouldn't look very surprising:

10. In which one of the following ways are the passages NOT parallel?

   (A) Passage A presents and rejects arguments for an opposing position, whereas passage B does not.
   (B) Passage A makes evaluative claims, whereas passage B does not.
   (C) Passage A describes specific examples of a phenomenon it criticizes, whereas passage B does not.
   (D) Passage B offers criticism, whereas passage A does not.
   (E) Passage B outlines a theory, whereas passage A does not.[7]

This time you are asked to identify a key difference between the two passages. Since the passages were, overall, more similar than dissimilar, the correct answer may be tougher to predict. Note also that the answer choices employ structural language, suggesting that the Roadmap and Keywords of each passage are likely to be helpful.

Think about each choice in turn. Choice (A) is completely out of scope, since Passage A never presents and rejects any particular argument. Choice (B) is only partially correct, as both passages make evaluative claims (they both claim that scholarly writing is too dry, for example). Choice (C) is supported by the text, and is therefore the correct answer. Passage A does indeed cite specific examples of historians making use of the word "narrative" in a faddish way. Following the Keyword "predictably" in line 21 you'll find the names of specific presentations, such as "Oral History and the Narrative of Class Identity." In contrast, Passage B describes legal writing only in general terms. Choice (D) is wrong for the same reason as choice (B), since both passages offer criticism. Choice (E) is also completely out of scope. The authors describe problems, but neither outlines a theory.

Comparative reading questions are often designed to reward you for recognizing tone. Take a look at this example:

---

[7]PrepTest 52, Sec 4, Q 10

8. The passages most strongly support which one of the
    following inferences regarding the authors' relationships
    to the professions they discuss?

    (A) Neither author is an active member of the
         profession that he or she discusses.
    (B) Each author is an active member of the profession
         he or she discusses.
    (C) The author of passage A is a member of the
         profession discussed in that passage, but the
         author of passage B is not a member of either of
         the professions discussed in the passages.
    (D) Both authors are active members of the profession
         discussed in passage B.
    (E) The author of passage B, but not the author of
         passage A, is an active member of both of the
         professions discussed in the passages.[8]

Recall that you identified language in the passage that denotes each author's personal investment; each author self-identifies as a teacher. This prediction matches correct choice (B). Choice
(A) is the exact opposite of the correct choice, a common wrong answer trap that I'll refer to as
a 180. Choice (C) is wrong on both counts—the first author may or may not be a historian, and
the second author is definitely a legal scholar. Choice (D) incorrectly assumes that the author of
Passage A is a legal scholar, and choice (E) presumes without warrant that the second author
is a historian. Please notice how often the incorrect answer choices in comparative reading
describe a distorted view of the relationship between the passages—a trap you'll avoid with
ease as long as you keep reading strategically.

Take a look at one more example:

11. The phrase "scholarly monographs that sap the vitality of
    history" in passage A (lines 6–7) plays a role in that
    passage's overall argument that is most analogous to the
    role played in passage B by which one of the following
    phrases?

    (A) "Writing is at the heart of the lawyer's craft"
         (line 29)
    (B) "Conformity is a virtue, creativity suspect, humor
         forbidden, and voice mute" (lines 37–38)
    (C) "Lawyers write as they see other lawyers write"
         (line 39)
    (D) "every case has at its heart a story" (line 46)
    (E) "Still, even mere awareness of the value of
         narrative could perhaps serve as an important
         corrective" (lines 57–59)[9]

---

[8]PrepTest 52, Sec 4, Q 8
[9]PrepTest 52, Sec 4, Q 11

Don't be intimidated by the wordiness of the question stem—your firm grasp of the intentions of both authors will allow you to work through it. The question asks about the role played by the quoted text in lines 6–7. What is the author of Passage A talking about when he reaches this example? He's describing the dryness of historiography, claiming that its writing leaves "little to the imagination" (line 3). The reference to scholarly monographs mentioned in the question is an example of this sort of dryness. With this in mind, you must now find the answer choice that similarly describes ("is most analogous to") dull writing, but this time in Passage B.

Choice (A) does no such thing; it emphasizes the importance of writing, not its dullness. Choice (B), on the other hand, is a perfect match, describing the blandness of legal writing in great detail. Choices (C), (D), and (E) are just as far off as choice (A)—none of these quotes are used by the author to emphasize the dryness of legal writing.

Not every question in comparative reading will focus on the relationships between the passages, and you're likely to see a question or two on test day that focuses strictly on one passage or the other. You should approach these questions as you would any other, using the specific strategies I'll describe to you in the next few chapters. You should, however, expect most of the questions to test your ability to compare one passage to another as in each of the above examples.

DRILL: WORKING WITH COMPARATIVE PASSAGES

It's time to try a comparative passage on your own. Begin by reading each passage strategically, and don't forget to completely Roadmap Passage A and determine its Topic, Scope, Purpose, and Main Idea before proceeding to Passage B. When you've finished reading, take 10–20 seconds to think through the key similarities and differences between the two passages, then try to answer each question. Detailed explanations follow the Drill.

The passages discuss relationships between business interests and university research.

Passage A

As university researchers working in a "gift economy" dedicated to collegial sharing of ideas, we have long been insulated from market pressures. The recent tendency to treat research findings as
(5) commodities, tradable for cash, threatens this tradition and the role of research as a public good.

The nurseries for new ideas are traditionally universities, which provide an environment uniquely suited to the painstaking testing and revision of
(10) theories. Unfortunately, the market process and values governing commodity exchange are ill suited to the cultivation and management of new ideas. With their shareholders impatient for quick returns, businesses are averse to wide-ranging experimentation. And, what
(15) is even more important, few commercial enterprises contain the range of expertise needed to handle the replacement of shattered theoretical frameworks.

Further, since entrepreneurs usually have little affinity for adventure of the intellectual sort, they can
(20) buy research and bury its products, hiding knowledge useful to society or to their competitors. The growth of industrial biotechnology, for example, has been accompanied by a reduction in the free sharing of research methods and results—a high price to pay for
(25) the undoubted benefits of new drugs and therapies.

Important new experimental results once led university scientists to rush down the hall and share their excitement with colleagues. When instead the rush is to patent lawyers and venture capitalists, I
(30) worry about the long-term future of scientific discovery.

Passage B

The fruits of pure science were once considered primarily a public good, available for society as a whole. The argument for this view was that most of
(35) these benefits were produced through government support of universities, and thus no individual was entitled to restrict access to them.

Today, however, the critical role of science in the modern "information economy" means that what was
(40) previously seen as a public good is being transformed into a market commodity. For example, by exploiting the information that basic research has accumulated about the detailed structures of cells and genes, the biotechnology industry can derive profitable
(45) pharmaceuticals or medical screening technologies. In this context, assertion of legal claims to "intellectual property"—not just in commercial products but in the underlying scientific knowledge—becomes crucial.

Previously, the distinction between a scientific
(50) "discovery" (which could not be patented) and a technical "invention" (which could) defined the limits of industry's ability to patent something. Today, however, the speed with which scientific discoveries can be turned into products and the large profits
(55) resulting from this transformation have led to a blurring of both the legal distinction between discovery and invention and the moral distinction between what should and should not be patented.

Industry argues that if it has supported—either in
(60) its own laboratories or in a university—the makers of a scientific discovery, then it is entitled to seek a return on its investment, either by charging others for using the discovery or by keeping it for its own exclusive use.[10]

[10]PrepTest 53, Sec 4, Passage 3

1. Which one of the following is discussed in passage B but not in passage A?

   (A) the blurring of the legal distinction between discovery and invention
   (B) the general effects of the market on the exchange of scientific knowledge
   (C) the role of scientific research in supplying public goods
   (D) new pharmaceuticals that result from industrial research
   (E) industry's practice of restricting access to research findings

2. Both passages place in opposition the members of which one of the following pairs?

   (A) commercially successful research and commercially unsuccessful research
   (B) research methods and research results
   (C) a marketable commodity and a public good
   (D) a discovery and an invention
   (E) scientific research and other types of inquiry

3. Both passages refer to which one of the following?

   (A) theoretical frameworks
   (B) venture capitalists
   (C) physics and chemistry
   (D) industrial biotechnology
   (E) shareholders[11]

Explanations

The passages discuss relationships between business interests and university research.

Passage A

Commercial
research is bad

     As university researchers working in a "gift economy" (dedicated to) collegial sharing of ideas, we have (long been) insulated from market pressures. The (recent tendency) to treat research findings as
(5) commodities, tradable for cash, (threatens) this tradition and the role of research as a public good.

University
vs.
marketplace

     The nurseries for new ideas are (traditionally) universities, which provide an environment (uniquely) suited to the painstaking testing and revision of
(10) theories. (Unfortunately,) the market process and values governing commodity exchange are (ill suited) to the cultivation and management of new ideas. With their shareholders impatient for quick returns, businesses are (averse) to wide-ranging experimentation. And, what
(15) is even (more important,) few commercial enterprises contain the range of expertise needed to handle the replacement of shattered theoretical frameworks.

Market bad
for new
ideas

     (Further, since) entrepreneurs usually have little affinity for adventure of the intellectual sort, (they can)
(20) buy research and bury its products, hiding knowledge useful to society or to their competitors. The growth of industrial biotechnology, (for example) has been (accompanied by) a reduction in the free sharing of research methods and results—a high price to pay for
(25) the undoubted benefits of new drugs and therapies.

Market bad
for future

     (Important) new experimental results once led university scientists to rush down the hall and share their excitement with colleagues. When (instead) the rush is to patent lawyers and venture capitalists, I
(30) (worry) about the long-term future of scientific discovery.

Passage B

Science used
to be
a public good

     The fruits of pure science were (once considered) primarily a public good, available for society as a whole. The (argument) for this view was that most of
(35) these benefits were produced (through) government support of universities, and (thus) no individual was entitled to restrict access to them.

Science
is now a
commodity

     (Today, however,) the critical role of science in the modern "information economy" means that what was
(40) (previously) seen as a public good is being (transformed) into a market commodity. (For example,) by exploiting the information that basic research has accumulated about the detailed structures of cells and genes, the biotechnology industry (can derive) profitable
(45) pharmaceuticals or medical screening technologies. In this context, (assertion) of legal claims to "intellectual

property"—not just in commercial products but in the
underlying scientific knowledge—become crucial.
Previously, the distinction between a scientific
(50)   "discovery" (which could not be patented) and a
technical "invention" (which could) defined the limits
of industry's ability to patent something. Today,
however, the speed with which scientific discoveries
can be turned into products and the large profits

Patent rules (55)   resulting from this transformation have led to a
less clear   blurring of both the legal distinction between
discovery and invention and the moral distinction
between what should and should not be patented.
Industry argues that if it has supported—either in

Industry   (60)   its own laboratories or in a university—the makers of
argues for   a scientific discovery, then it is entitled to seek a return
profit earned   on its investment either by charging others for using
the discovery or by keeping it for its own exclusive
use.[12]

Paragraph Structure:

Passage A

The author begins by identifying a problem that "threatens" (line 5) the safety of collegiate research as a common good, namely the "recent tendency" (line 4) of some to view research as a commodity. The second paragraph expands on this idea, describing marketplace ideals as "ill suited" (line 11) to the goals of pure research. "Further" (line 18) at the beginning of the third paragraph signals more evidence from the author, this time describing the quashing of beneficial research by market pressures. In the final paragraph, the author summarizes a final "worry" (line 30) that commercial interests will be detrimental to research in the long run.

Topic: Academic research

Scope: The effect of the marketplace on research

Purpose: To give evidence for the detrimental effect of enterprise on research

Main Idea: The goals of the marketplace are incompatible with the goals of pure research, and the intrusion of commercial interests is detrimental to science.

Passage B

The author sets up a past/present dichotomy in the opening two paragraphs. Research was "once considered" (line 32) a public good, principally because of government support for universities. "Today, however" (line 38) the author indicates that science is being "transformed" (line 40) into a part of the marketplace. The third paragraph introduces a second, related dichotomy. "Previously" (line 49) there was a clear distinction between what was patentable and what

---

[12]PrepTest 53, Sec 4, Passage 3

wasn't, but "today" (line 52) the rapid pace of new discoveries has confused the issue. In the final paragraph, "industry argues" (line 59) that if it has contributed resources to institutions that conduct research, it has the right to expect a return on that investment.

Topic: Research

Scope: The role of industry in research

Purpose: To describe changes in industry's relationship to science over time

Main Idea: Through the privatization of research funding, scientific research is no longer seen as a public good, but as a commodity that industry supports and profits from.

Passage Comparison: Both authors address the intertwining of the marketplace with scientific research, and both agree that science has come to be seen less as a public good and more as a commodity. The author of Passage A is disheartened by this change, and worries that it will be damaging to science, providing evidence that this is the case. The author of Passage B doesn't render any such opinion, instead presenting the facts dispassionately and providing industry's point of view without necessarily endorsing it.

1. **(A)**
    Which one of the following is discussed in passage B but not in passage A?
    (A) the blurring of the legal distinction between discovery and invention
    (B) the general effects of the market on the exchange of scientific knowledge
    (C) the role of scientific research in supplying public goods
    (D) new pharmaceuticals that result from industrial research
    (E) industry's practice of restricting access to research findings[13]

Passage B explored the change from science as a public good to science as a commodity in greater detail than Passage A, and in doing so provided several examples of these changes. The Roadmap shows that the third paragraph of Passage B discusses an idea that is never raised in Passage A, that "previously" (line 49) the rules about what could and couldn't be patented (based on what was classified as a "discovery" or an "invention") were very clear but are now less so. This prediction leads to correct choice (A). Choices (B), (C), (D), and (E) are all touched on by both passages.

---

[13] PrepTest 53, Sec 4, Q 15

2. **(C)**

Both passages place in opposition the members
of which one of the following pairs?
(A)   commercially successful research and
       commercially unsuccessful research
(B)   research methods and research results
(C)   a marketable commodity and a
       public good
(D)   a discovery and an invention
(E)   scientific research and other types
       of inquiry[14]

If you take the time to think through the key relationships between the passages, you can answer this question quickly and easily. Both passages center on the opposition between science as a public good and science as a commodity. This prediction should lead directly to correct choice (C). Neither passage explores the relationship expressed in choices (A) and (B), placing them completely out of scope. The opposition between discovery and invention in choice (D) is only mentioned in Passage B, and the difference between scientific inquiry and market forces described in choice (E) is explored in Passage A but not in Passage B.

3. **(D)**

Both passages refer to which one of
the following?
(A)   theoretical frameworks
(B)   venture capitalists
(C)   physics and chemistry
(D)   industrial biotechnology
(E)   shareholders[15]

This question simply asks for an example common to both passages. Keywords help you answer this question swiftly, as biotechnology is highlighted by "for example" in line 22 of Passage A and line 41 of Passage B. This should lead you straight to correct choice (D), the only idea mentioned in both passages. Remember that while you shouldn't dwell on examples during your initial strategic reading, you should always take note of the Keywords that identify them in case you run into a question like this one.

THE KAPLAN METHOD STILL APPLIES

Although I began this chapter by introducing comparative reading as a major recent change to the LSAT, by now you've seen that you should approach these passages with the same strategies you've been perfecting since the beginning of your studies. Be certain to read each passage strategically, note the Topic, Scope, Purpose, and Main Idea of both, and identify their key points of similarity and difference. If you follow this approach carefully you'll be just as

[14]PrepTest 53, Sec 4, Q 16
[15]PrepTest 53, Sec 4, Q 17

prepared for comparative reading as the more familiar single passages you've worked with thus far. As with everything else in the LSAT, comparative reading is predictable and amenable to the Kaplan Method.

In the next five chapters, I'll show you how the same predictability applies to the questions as well as the passages.

CHAPTER 10

GLOBAL QUESTIONS

READING COMPREHENSION QUESTION TYPES

You've learned a lot about strategic reading, and you've had plenty of opportunities to practice. At this point you may still feel that you need a lot *more* practice, and that's no problem. The more proficient you become with the Kaplan Method, the more points you'll score on test day.

That said, it's now time to change focus. Reading the passages strategically is very important, but you score points by answering the questions correctly. You've seen plenty of questions in this book so far, and you've surely noticed that the same types of questions keep appearing repeatedly throughout. You may not have found a way to categorize the different types of questions, and I haven't been referring to them by specific names in the explanations. It might surprise you to discover that there are only five types of questions that commonly appear in the Reading Comprehension section. It's now time for you to learn what the five question types are, how to identify them, and, most importantly, what strategies you should apply to them to maximize your score.

Review of the Kaplan Method

Before I introduce Global questions, take a moment to review the Kaplan Method for Reading Comprehension in its entirety:

THE KAPLAN METHOD FOR READING COMPREHENSION

STEP 1 Read the Passage Strategically

STEP 2 Identify the Question Type

STEP 3 Research the Relevant Text

STEP 4 Make a Prediction

STEP 5 Evaluate the Answer Choices

Up until now, you've primarily focused on mastering the first step of the Method—identifying Keywords, creating a Roadmap, and identifying the Topic, Scope, Purpose, and Main Idea of every passage. Now I want you to pay particular attention to the remaining steps; this is the process you'll follow each time you encounter a question. I haven't presented this information to you since the first chapter, so take this opportunity to review these steps before moving on:

STEP 1: Read the Passage Strategically

As always, begin by reading the passage strategically, circling Keywords, creating a Roadmap, and identifying the Topic, Scope, Purpose, and Main Idea.

STEP 2: Identify the Question Type

To identify the question type, you simply need to read the question stem. Although it may seem obvious to begin by reading the question stem, remember that you're not reading it passively. Your goal in Step 2 is to actively identify the question type you're working on. Since there are only five types, it won't take you long to become familiar with them. It's very important to always identify the question type—that's how you know which Kaplan strategy to apply.

STEP 3: Research the Relevant Text

Once you know the question type, you'll probably need to return to the passage to review relevant information. The clues that help you find the right text will come from several sources: the question stem, your Roadmap, and Keywords you've circled. Of the five question types, only Global questions don't require you to look up specific text in the passage. *All of the others do.* This is extremely important. One of the most common mistakes I see students make is to over-rely on memory and intuition, selecting an answer choice that seems to match something they remember reading. But as you've seen in previous chapters, the wrong answer choices are frequently written to look similar to information in the passage, but with subtle distortions built in. Fortunately it's very easy to avoid this mistake—research the text and then move on to Step 4.

STEP 4: Make a Prediction

After you've done your research, but before you look at the answer choices, you should always try to predict what the correct answer will say. In the vast majority of Reading Comprehension questions, you will be able to predict the correct choice, and I will be sure to point out the rare exceptions as they come. Making a solid prediction serves two important purposes: It allows you to zero in on the correct answer quickly, and it makes it easier for you to avoid clever answer traps that might otherwise snare you. Remember that the top-scoring LSAT test takers are those who take the most control of the test day experience. It's much better to look at a choice and ask, "Does this match my prediction?" than to ask, "Does this seem right?" The former approach is confident and methodical, the latter uncertain and prone to error.

STEP 5: Evaluate the Answer Choices

As I just noted, most of the time Step 5 simply involves finding the choice that matches your prediction and selecting it. It's important to remember that you're looking for the choice that correctly matches the *concept* embodied in your prediction, not necessarily the specific wording of your prediction. Occasionally you may need to employ the process of elimination, either because you weren't able to make a prediction or because you aren't sure about the right match. In any case, remember that for every LSAT question there is precisely one—and only one—correct answer. The other four answers are completely incorrect. Further, the wrong answer choices also follow predictable patterns, and I'll explain those patterns as we go.

When taken in total, the Kaplan Method for Reading Comprehension provides you with a specific strategy to use in every situation the test makers present to you. You don't have time to spend on test day wondering what to do next; with diligent practice, you'll soon internalize the Method, and applying it will come naturally to you.

Now, with the Kaplan Method in mind, it's time to look at the five question types, beginning with one that will look very familiar to you: Global questions.

GLOBAL QUESTIONS
What Are Global Questions?

Global questions, as the name implies, ask about the big ideas of the passage. Any question that asks about the author's main point, the primary purpose of the passage, or the structure of the passage as a whole is classified as a Global question. Most passages come with one or more Global questions as part of their question set, and they're typically located at the beginning or the end of the set.

How Do You Identify Global Questions?

There aren't many variations on Global questions, and you've seen most of them already. Here are a few examples:

22. Which one of the following most completely and accurately summarizes the argument of the passage?[1]

21. Which one of the following best summarizes the main idea of the passage?[2]

26. Which one of the following best describes the organization of the passage?[3]

The highlighted words in each question provide you with clues that identify them as Global questions. Notice that in each case the question is asking for big-picture ideas. Presented in terms of the Kaplan Method, your thinking should go like this:

Step 2: Identify the Question Type: When the question asks for the Purpose, Main Idea, or organization of the passage as a whole, you know it's a Global question.

Global Question Strategy

Global questions require you to be fluent with the author's overarching themes and the passage structure. Fortunately, you've already gotten into the habit of identifying Topic, Scope, Purpose, and Main Idea—exactly what you need to answer this type of question correctly. For clarity, I'll present the strategy you should employ in each of Steps 3–5 of the Kaplan Method.

Step 3: Research the Relevant Text: Since you've already identified the author's big ideas by reading strategically, this is the one question type that doesn't require you to review specific text in the passage. Move on to Step 4 instead.

Step 4: Make a Prediction: In order to make a prediction, recall what the question is asking for, and then paraphrase the idea in your mind before going to the answer choices. Most Global questions will ask for either the Purpose or the Main Idea, and since you've already discovered them in Step 1, making a prediction won't take more than a few seconds. If the question asks for the organization of the passage, use your Roadmap to form your prediction—the notes you made next to each paragraph will give you structure at a glance.

Step 5: Evaluate the Answer Choices: Find the answer choice that matches your prediction.

Global Question Practice

To illustrate, try applying the Kaplan Method to a set of questions initially introduced in chapter 1. Don't worry if they look familiar to you—your goal is to get used to approaching each

---

[1]PrepTest 25, Sec 1, Q 22
[2]PrepTest 41, Sec 4, Q 21
[3]PrepTest 41, Sec 4, Q 26

question methodically, something you weren't thinking about the first time you saw them. Begin by rereading the passage, taking note of the sample Roadmap. Think about the Topic, Scope, Purpose, and Main Idea of the passage as you discover them.

Step 1:

Vict.
philanthropy
def.

Early crit.

Philanthropy
obsolete

Modern
crit.

Philanthropy
self serving

Author:
Modern
crit. Wrong

(5)

(10)

(15)

(20)

(25)

(30)

(35)

(40)

(45)

Although philanthropy—the volunteering of private resources for humanitarian purposes—reached its apex in England in the late nineteenth century, modern commentators have articulated two major criticisms of the philanthropy that was a mainstay of England's middle-class Victorian society. The earlier criticism is that such philanthropy was even by the later nineteenth century obsolete, since industrialism had already created social problems that were beyond the scope of small, private voluntary efforts. Indeed, these problems required substantial legislative action by the state. Unemployment, for example, was not the result of a failure of diligence on the part of workers or a failure of compassion on the part of employers, nor could it be solved by well-wishing philanthropists.

The more recent charge holds that Victorian philanthropy was by its very nature a self-serving exercise carried out by philanthropists at the expense of those whom they were ostensibly serving. In this view, philanthropy was a means of flaunting one's power and position in a society that placed great emphasis on status, or even a means of cultivating social connections that could lead to economic rewards. Further, if philanthropy is seen as serving the interests of individual philanthropists, so it may be seen as serving the interests of their class. According to this "social control" thesis, philanthropists, in professing to help the poor, were encouraging in them such values as prudence, thrift, and temperance, values perhaps worthy in themselves but also designed to create more productive members of the labor force. Philanthropy, in short, was a means of controlling the labor force and ensuring the continued dominance of the management class.

Modern critics of Victorian philanthropy often use the word's "amateurish" or "inadequate" to describe Victorian philanthropy, as though Victorian charity can only be understood as an antecedent to the era of state-sponsored, professionally administered charity. This assumption is typical of the "Whig fallacy": the tendency to read the past as an inferior prelude to an enlightened present. If most Victorians resisted state control and expended their resources on private, voluntary philanthropies, it could only be, the argument goes, because of their commitment to a vested interest, or because the administrative apparatus of the state was incapable of coping with the economic and social needs of the time.

Critics
incorrect

(50) This version of history (patronizes) the Victorians,
who were in fact well aware of their vulnerability to
charges of condescension and complacency, (but) were
equally well aware of the potential dangers of state-
managed charity. They were perhaps condescending to
the poor, (but)—to use an un-Victorian metaphor—they

(55) put their money where their mouths were, (and) gave of
their careers and lives as well.[4]

Paragraph Structure: The first paragraph introduces the Topic—Victorian philanthropy—and then introduces two criticisms beginning at line 4. The "earlier criticism" (line 6) is that Victorian philanthropy was obsolete even by the standards of its own time.

The second paragraph introduces a "more recent" criticism (line 16), something you were certainly prepared to see if you were reading predictively. This new criticism is that the Victorian philanthropists were ultimately self-serving, promoting values that may have helped the poor but that were also intended to create a more productive workforce.

The author responds to the critics in the final two paragraphs. He critiques the "assumption" (line 40) that underlies the two criticisms, that the behavior of the Victorians can "only be understood" (line 38) in the context of modern charity. He ultimately concludes that this assumption "patronizes" (line 49) the Victorians.

Topic: Victorian philanthropy

Scope: criticisms of Victorian philanthropists

Purpose: to examine criticisms of the Victorian philanthropists and refute them

Main Idea: Criticisms of Victorian philanthropy fail because they are based on flawed reasoning.

Now read the following question:

21. Which one of the following best summarizes the
    main idea of the passage?[5]

Work through this question using the Kaplan Method.

Step 2: The question asks you to summarize the main idea. This is definitely a Global question.

Step 3: Global questions don't require you to reference specific text, so move on to the next step.

Step 4: Base your prediction on your knowledge of the passage's Main Idea. The author's main point was that the critics of Victorian Philanthropy were incorrect because their arguments were based on bad logic.

---

[4]PrepTest 41, Sec 4, Passage 4
[5]PrepTest 41, Sec 4, Q 21

Step 5: Now examine the answer choices and identify the one that matches the prediction:

21. Which one of the following best summarizes the
    main idea of the passage?

    (A)   While the motives of individual practitioners
           have been questioned by modern
           commentators, Victorian philanthropy
           successfully dealt with the social ills of
           nineteenth-century England.
    (B)   Philanthropy, inadequate to deal with the
           massive social and economic problems of the
           twentieth century, has slowly been replaced
           by state-sponsored charity.
    (C)   The practice of reading the past as a prelude to
           an enlightened present has fostered
           revisionist views of many institutions, among
           them Victorian philanthropy.
    (D)   Although modern commentators have
           perceived Victorian philanthropy as either
           inadequate or self-serving, the theoretical bias
           behind these criticisms leads to an incorrect
           interpretation of history.
    (E)   Victorian philanthropists, aware of public
           resentment of their self-congratulatory
           attitude, used devious methods to camouflage
           their self-serving motives.[6]

Now evaluate each answer choice. Choice (A) mentions that the philanthropists were the
subject of criticism but it then goes astray by claiming that they successfully solved social
problems. Eliminate it. Choice (B) has nothing to do with the author's refutation of the critics,
so it's out as well. While choice (C) mentions an argument that the author made, it doesn't
capture the author's central argument as you predicted in Step 4. Move on to the next one.
Choice (D) is a perfect match: It nicely summarizes both the arguments of the critics and the
author's reason for rejecting them. This is the correct answer. For the record, choice (E), like
choice (B), fails to address the author's response to the critics, and likewise fails to match your
prediction. Using the Kaplan Method, you quickly spot correct choice (D), score this point, and
go on to the next question.

Try another question from the same passage. This time, execute Steps 2–5 on your own before
moving on to the explanation that follows.

---

[6]PrepTest 41, Sec 4, Q 21

24. Which one of the following best describes the primary purpose of the passage?

    (A) providing an extended definition of a key term
    (B) defending the work of an influential group of theorists
    (C) narrating the chronological development of a widespread practice
    (D) examining modern evaluations of a historical phenomenon
    (E) analyzing a specific dilemma faced by workers of the past[7]

Now compare your reasoning to this step-by-step explanation.

Step 2: The identifying phrase "primary purpose" tells you that this is a Global question.

Step 3: Once again, no specific research is necessary.

Step 4: Because you already identified it in Step 1, you know that the author's Purpose in this passage was to refute the critics of Victorian philanthropy.

Step 5: Finding a match for your prediction might have been a little more difficult in this case, but remember, you're looking for a *concept* that matches, not necessarily the exact wording of your prediction. Correct choice (D) is slightly more general than the wording of the prediction above, but it still perfectly describes the author's Purpose: to take on the critics' ideas (described in the choice as "modern evaluations"). None of the other choices refer to this central conflict of ideas at all and therefore are out of scope.

Try one more question from the same passage, once again applying the Kaplan Method:

26. Which one of the following best describes the organization of the passage?

    (A) Two related positions are discussed, then both are subjected to the same criticism.
    (B) Two opposing theories are outlined, then a synthesis between the two is proposed.
    (C) A position is stated, and two differing evaluations of it are given.
    (D) Three examples of the same logical inconsistency are given.
    (E) A theory is outlined, and two supporting examples are given.[8]

Now compare your reasoning with mine:

Step 2: This time the phrase "organization of the passage" is the clue that identifies this as a Global question. Questions that ask for the overall structure of a passage are considered Global.

[7]PrepTest 41, Sec 4, Q 24
[8]PrepTest 41, Sec 4, Q 26

Step 3: As with all Global questions, you don't need to do any specific textual research.

Step 4: Your best tool when tackling a question like this one is your Roadmap. The correct answer should indicate that criticisms were leveled at the philanthropists, and that the author then refuted them.

Step 5: With the strong prediction provided by a good Roadmap, correct choice (A) should be easy to spot. Notice how most of the incorrect answers use similar language but in a distorted way. Choice (B) mentions two theories, but suggests that they were opposed and ultimately synthesized, which never occurred in this passage. Choice (C) mentions the evaluation of a position, but there weren't two differing evaluations, just the one that the author provided. The three examples mentioned in choice (D) and the supporting examples in choice (E) are nowhere to be found in your prediction, making these choices incorrect.

This question illustrates just why prediction is such an important part of the Kaplan Method. If you attempt to answer this question without a review of the passage structure, you risk selecting a choice that contains familiar-looking language but that ultimately misses the mark.

I'd also like to remind you that all three of the practice questions you just examined came from the same LSAT passage. Since there are only six questions total, that means you scored half of the points available from this passage simply by understanding the big picture. Most passages will feature at least one global question, reinforcing the necessity of Strategic Reading—it pays off in points earned and time saved.

DRILL: ANSWERING GLOBAL QUESTIONS

Now practice applying the Kaplan Method to a new passage, beginning with Step 1. After you've read the passage strategically, answer each of the questions that follow by applying Steps 2–5 of the Method each time. Execute each step with care and focus on becoming comfortable with them. Explanations follow the Drill.

Most authoritarian rulers who undertake democratic reforms do so not out of any intrinsic commitment or conversion to democratic ideals, but rather because they foresee or recognize that certain changes and
(5) mobilizations in civil society make it impossible for them to hold on indefinitely to absolute power.

Three major types of changes can contribute to a society's no longer condoning the continuation of
(10) authoritarian rule. First, the values and norms in the society alter over time, reducing citizens' tolerance for repression and concentration of power and thus stimulating their demands for freedom. In some Latin American countries during the 1970s and 1980s, for
(15) example, this change in values came about partly as a result of the experience of repression, which brought in its wake a resurgence of democratic values. As people come to place more value on political freedom and civil liberties they also become more inclined to speak
(20) out, protest, and organize for democracy, frequently beginning with the denunciation of human rights abuses.

In addition to changing norms and values, the alignment of economic interests in a society can shift.
(25) As one scholar notes, an important turning point in the transition to democracy comes when privileged people in society—landowners, industrialists, merchants, bankers—who had been part of a regime's support base come to the conclusion that the authoritarian regime is
(30) dispensable and that its continuation might damage their long-term interests. Such a large-scale shift in the economic interests of these elites was crucial in bringing about the transition to democracy in the Philippines and has also begun occurring incrementally
(35) in other authoritarian nations.

A third change derives from the expanding resources, autonomy, and self-confidence of various segments of society and of newly formed organizations both formal and informal. Students march in the streets
(40) demanding change; workers paralyze key industries; lawyers refuse to cooperate any longer in legal

charades; alternative sources of information pierce and then shatter the veil of secrecy and disinformation; informal networks of production and exchange emerge
(45) that circumvent the state's resources and control. This profound development can radically alter the balance of power in a country, as an authoritarian regime that could once easily dominate and control its citizens is placed on the defensive.

(50) Authoritarian rule tends in the long run to generate all three types of changes. Ironically, all three types can be accelerated by the authoritarian regime's initial success at producing economic growth and maintaining social order—success that, by creating a period of
(55) stability, gives citizens the opportunity to reflect on the circumstances in which they live. The more astute or calculating of authoritarian rulers will recognize this and realize that their only hope of retaining some power in the future is to match these democratic social
(60) changes with democratic political changes.[9]

[9]PrepTest 34, Sec 1, Passage 1

1. Which one of the following most accurately expresses the main point of the passage?

   (A) Authoritarian rulers tend to undertake democratic reforms only after it becomes clear that the nation's economic and social power bases will slow economic growth and disrupt social order until such reforms are instituted.

   (B) Authoritarian regimes tend to ensure their own destruction by allowing opposition groups to build support among the wealthy whose economic interests are easily led away from support for the regime.

   (C) Authoritarian policies tend in the long run to alienate the economic power base in a nation once it becomes clear that the regime's initial success at generating economic growth and stability will be short lived.

   (D) Authoritarian principles tend in the long run to be untenable because they demand from the nation a degree of economic and social stability that is impossible to maintain in the absence of democratic institutions.

   (E) Authoritarian rulers who institute democratic reforms are compelled to do so because authoritarian rule tends to bring about various changes in society that eventually necessitate corresponding political changes.

2. Which one of the following titles most completely summarizes the content of the passage?

   (A) "Avenues for Change: The Case for Dissent in Authoritarian Regimes"

   (B) "Human Rights Abuses under Authoritarian Regimes: A Case Study"

   (C) "Democratic Coalitions under Authoritarian Regimes: Strategies and Solutions"

   (D) "Why Authoritarian Regimes Compromise: An Examination of Societal Forces"

   (E) "Growing Pains: Economic Instability in Countries on the Brink of Democracy"

3. Which one of the following most accurately describes the organization of the passage?

   (A) A political phenomenon is linked to a general set of causes; this set is divided into categories and the relative importance of each category is assessed; the possibility of alternate causes is considered and rejected.

   (B) A political phenomenon is linked to a general set of causes; this set is divided into categories and an explication of each category is presented; the causal relationship is elaborated upon and reaffirmed.

   (C) A political phenomenon is identified; the possible causes of the phenomenon are described and placed into categories; one possible cause is preferred over the others and reasons are given for the preference.

   (D) A political phenomenon is identified; similarities between this phenomenon and three similar phenomena are presented; the similarities among the phenomena are restated in general terms and argued for.

   (E) A political phenomenon is identified; differences between this phenomenon and three similar phenomena are presented; the differences among the phenomena are restated in general terms and argued for.[10]

---

[10]PrepTest 34, Sec 1, Qs 1, 3, 4

Explanations

Step 1:

Authoritarians
change
b/c they
have to

Most authoritarian rulers who undertake democratic reforms do so (not) out of any intrinsic commitment or conversion to democratic ideals, but (rather because) they foresee or recognize that certain
(5) changes and mobilizations in civil society make it impossible for them to hold on indefinitely to absolute power.

First
change:
values

(Three major types of) changes can contribute to a society's no longer condoning the continuation of
(10) authoritarian rule. (First,) the values and norms in the society alter over time, reducing citizens' tolerance for repression and concentration of power and (thus) stimulating their demands for freedom. In some Latin American countries during the 1970s and 1980s, for
(15) (example,) this change in values came about partly as a (result) of the experience of repression, which brought in its wake a resurgence of democratic values. As people come to place more value on political freedom and civil liberties they (also) become more inclined to speak
(20) out, protest, and organize for democracy, frequently beginning with the denunciation of human rights abuses.

Second
change:
economy

(In addition) to changing norms and values, the alignment of economic interests in a society can shift.
(25) As one (scholar notes,) an (important) turning point in the transition to democracy comes when privileged people in society—landowners, industrialists, merchants, bankers—who had been part of a regime's support base come to the (conclusion) that the authoritarian regime is
(30) dispensable (and) that its continuation might damage their long-term interests. Such a large-scale shift in the economic interests of these elites was (crucial) in bringing about the transition to democracy in the Philippines and has (also) begun occurring incrementally
(35) in other authoritarian nations.

Third change:
people more
confident

A (third) change derives from the expanding resources, autonomy, and self-confidence of various segments of society (and) of newly formed organizations both formal and informal. Students march in the streets
(40) demanding change; workers paralyze key industries; lawyers refuse to cooperate any longer in legal charades; alternative sources of information pierce and then shatter the veil of secrecy and disinformation; informal networks of production and exchange emerge
(45) that circumvent the state's resources and control. This (profound) development can (radically) alter the balance of power in a country, as an authoritarian regime that could (once) easily dominate and control its citizens is placed on the defensive.

Auth. regimes
cause own
problems

(50) Authoritarian rule (tends) in the long run to generate all three types of changes. (Ironically,) all three types can

be accelerated by the authoritarian regime's initial
success at producing economic growth and maintaining
social order—success that, (by) creating a period of
(55) stability, gives citizens the opportunity to reflect on the
circumstances in which they live. The more astute or
calculating of authoritarian rulers will recognize this
(and) realize that their (only hope) of retaining some
power in the future is to match these democratic social
(60) changes with democratic political changes.[11]

*Change to
retain power*

Paragraph Structure: The first paragraph contains a single sentence and sets the stage for the author's primary argument. Contrast Keywords "but rather because" in lines 3–4 point you toward the author's chief theme: authoritarian rulers generally adopt democratic principles because they require such principles to stay in power.

The next paragraph begins with an excellent group of Keywords: "Three major types of change" lead to trouble for authoritarian rulers. Unsurprisingly, paragraphs two through four go on to describe each of these changes. The author first mentions the alteration of values in a society, and then prepares to illustrate this idea with the keywords "for example" in lines 14–15. The second change, introduced in the third paragraph, is a shift in economic interests. Once again, the author illustrates this idea throughout the rest of the paragraph, citing evidence provided by the scholar mentioned in line 25. In the fourth paragraph, the author mentions the third change: the growing wealth and autonomy of society. As with the prior two paragraphs, the author goes on to describe this change in greater detail.

Hopefully you were prepared for the author to deliver some kind of final verdict about these changes in the final paragraph. She points out that, "ironically" (line 51), these changes typically come about by the regime's initial successes, and suggests that an authoritarian leader's "only hope" (line 58) of retaining power is to introduce democratic changes to society.

Topic: authoritarian regimes

Scope: why authoritarian leaders sometimes adopt democratic policies

Purpose: to illustrate the kinds of social changes that force authoritarian states to shift toward democratic policies

Main Idea: Authoritarian leaders who institute democratic changes in their regimes typically do so as a result of social changes that force them to.

---

[11]PrepTest 34, Sec 1, Passage 1

1. **(E)**

    Which one of the following most accurately expresses
    the main point of the passage?
    (A) Authoritarian rulers tend to undertake democratic
         reforms only after it becomes clear that the
         nation's economic and social power bases will
         slow economic growth and disrupt social order
         until such reforms are instituted.
    (B) Authoritarian regimes tend to ensure their own
         destruction by allowing opposition groups to
         build support among the wealthy whose
         economic interests are easily led away from
         support for the regime.
    (C) Authoritarian policies tend in the long run to
         alienate the economic power base in a nation
         once it becomes clear that the regime's initial
         success at generating economic growth and
         stability will be short lived.
    (D) Authoritarian principles tend in the long run to be
         untenable because they demand from the nation
         a degree of economic and social stability that is
         impossible to maintain in the absence of
         democratic institutions.
    (E) Authoritarian rulers who institute democratic
         reforms are compelled to do so because
         authoritarian rule tends to bring about various
         changes in society that eventually necessitate
         corresponding political changes.[12]

Step 2: Any question that asks for the "main point" of the passage is a Global question.

Step 3: No research is necessary.

Step 4: Reflecting on the Main Idea of the passage, you should predict that the correct answer
will mention that authoritarian regimes tend to become more democratic when changes in
society make it necessary.

Step 5: Correct choice (E) is the match—it describes the causal relationship between social
changes and democratic political changes. Choice (A) focuses too narrowly on two of the three
changes mentioned by the author, and the remaining choices all fail to address the reasons
why authoritarian rulers move toward democracy, placing them out of scope.

---

[12]PrepTest 34, Sec 1, Q 1

2. **(D)**

Which one of the following titles most completely summarizes the content of the passage?
- (A) "Avenues for Change: The Case for Dissent in Authoritarian Regimes"
- (B) "Human Rights Abuses under Authoritarian Regimes: A Case Study"
- (C) "Democratic Coalitions under Authoritarian Regimes: Strategies and Solutions"
- (D) "Why Authoritarian Regimes Compromise: An Examination of Societal Forces"
- (E) "Growing Pains: Economic Instability in Countries on the Brink of Democracy"[13]

Step 2: This is an unusual variant on the Global question stem that shows up on the LSAT from time to time. When the question asks you to provide the proper title for the piece, it's really asking you to summarize the author's thesis; once again, you're being asked for the big picture.

Step 3: No textual research is necessary.

Step 4: An exact prediction might be tricky to come up with on this question, but you should still remind yourself what the essential content of the correct answer will be: The correct title will reflect the idea that societal changes cause authoritarian regimes to become more democratic.

Step 5: Correct choice (D) matches the prediction: It encapsulates the author's Purpose by describing why authoritarian regimes change politically. The author never makes a case for dissent as described in choice (A), and choice (B) is far too narrowly focused. The strategies and solutions proposed in choice (C) never appeared in the passage, and choice (E) overly focuses on economic issues. It's also extreme—the author is talking about regimes that make democratic changes, not "countries on the brink of democracy."

---

[13]PrepTest 34, Sec 1, Q 3

3.   **(B)**

Which one of the following most accurately describes
the organization of the passage?

(A)   A political phenomenon is linked to a general set
of causes; this set is divided into categories and
the relative importance of each category is
assessed; the possibility of alternate causes is
considered and rejected.

(B)   A political phenomenon is linked to a general set
of causes; this set is divided into categories and
an explication of each category is presented; the
causal relationship is elaborated upon and reaffirmed.

(C)   A political phenomenon is identified; the possible
causes of the phenomenon are described and
placed into categories; one possible cause is
preferred over the others and reasons are given
for the preference.

(D)   A political phenomenon is identified; similarities
between this phenomenon and three similar
phenomena are presented; the similarities among
the phenomena are restated in general terms and
argued for.

(E)   A political phenomenon is identified; differences
between this phenomenon and three similar
phenomena are presented; the differences among
the phenomena are restated in general terms and
argued for.[14]

Step 2: Since the stem asks for the "organization of the passage," you know you're dealing with a Global question.

Step 3: No research is necessary.

Step 4: A review of the Roadmap gives you an excellent prediction about the organization of the passage: The author explains why authoritarian regimes move toward democracy, gives three examples, and finally restates her original assertion.

Step 5: The passage structure is described by correct choice (B). Choice (A) begins correctly, using the very same opening text as the correct answer but then veers off course by mentioning the "relative importance" of the various causes. Choice (C) makes a similar error in suggesting that the author prefers one explanation over another. Choice (D) gets the author's approach entirely wrong; she didn't present "similar phenomena" to the original but suggested causes for it. Choice (E) makes essentially the same mistake, this time suggesting that the author was concerned with the differences in phenomena.

---

[14]PrepTest 34, Sec 1, Q 4

COMMON WRONG ANSWER TYPES

Before moving on to the next Reading Comprehension question type, I'll point out some of the most common types of wrong answers you're likely to see when answering Global questions. Most of them appeared in the exercise above, so be on the lookout for them in your practice.

Overly Narrow Focus

Remember that the correct answer to a global question must stay high level—that is, it has to encapsulate the author's primary goals or conclusions. Beware of answer choices that dwell on a specific example presented in the passage.

> Which one of the following most accurately expresses the main point of the passage?
>
> (A) Authoritarian rulers tend to undertake democratic reforms only after it becomes clear that the nation's economic and social power bases will slow economic growth and disrupt social order until such reforms are instituted.
>
> (B) Authoritarian regimes tend to ensure their own destruction by allowing opposition groups to build support among the wealthy whose economic interests are easily led away from support for the regime.
>
> (C) Authoritarian policies tend in the long run to alienate the economic power base in a nation once it becomes clear that the regime's initial success at generating economic growth and stability will be short lived.
>
> (D) Authoritarian principles tend in the long run to be untenable because they demand from the nation a degree of economic and social stability that is impossible to maintain in the absence of democratic institutions.
>
> (E) Authoritarian rulers who institute democratic reforms are compelled to do so because authoritarian rule tends to bring about various changes in society that eventually necessitate corresponding political changes.[15]

Recall that the passage *did* mention the specific type of reform mentioned in choice (A), but this wasn't the author's main point. The author only mentioned this idea in service of the larger goal expressed in correct choice (E). This type of wrong answer can be tempting because it does identify concepts that the author mentioned, but don't confuse the Main Idea with supporting evidence.

---

[15]PrepTest 34, Sec 1, Q 1

Extreme

This answer trap is common on almost every type of Reading Comprehension question.

> Which one of the following titles most completely summarizes the content of the passage?
>
> (A) "Avenues for Change: The Case for Dissent in Authoritarian Regimes"
> (B) "Human Rights Abuses under Authoritarian Regimes: A Case Study"
> (C) "Democratic Coalitions under Authoritarian Regimes: Strategies and Solutions"
> (D) "Why Authoritarian Regimes Compromise: An Examination of Societal Forces"
> (E) "Growing Pains: Economic Instability in Countries on the Brink of Democracy"[16]

The author of the passage discussed reasons why authoritarian regimes sometimes make democratic changes, but at no point does he mention regimes that are actually becoming democracies, as choice (E) implies. Because this wrong answer type is so prevalent, you need to note the difference, and the test makers will reward you for taking notice of it.

Half Right/Half Wrong

This can be a dangerous wrong answer trap, particularly if you aren't carefully checking the answer choices against a strong prediction.

---

[16]PrepTest 34, Sec 1, Q 3

Which one of the following most accurately describes the organization of the passage?

(A)   A political phenomenon is linked to a general set of causes; this set is divided into categories and the relative importance of each category is assessed; the possibility of alternate causes is considered and rejected.

(B)   A political phenomenon is linked to a general set of causes; this set is divided into categories and an explication of each category is presented; the causal relationship is elaborated upon and reaffirmed.

(C)   A political phenomenon is identified; the possible causes of the phenomenon are described and placed into categories; one possible cause is preferred over the others and reasons are given for the preference.

(D)   A political phenomenon is identified; similarities between this phenomenon and three similar phenomena are presented; the similarities among the phenomena are restated in general terms and argued for.

(E)   A political phenomenon is identified; differences between this phenomenon and three similar phenomena are presented; the differences among the phenomena are restated in general terms and argued for.[17]

Note how choice (A) begins exactly like correct choice (B), but then goes out of scope by implying that the author evaluates the relative importance of his examples and posits alternative explanations. None of these things occur in the passage. You are likely to select this type of choice if you fail to identify the Purpose and Main Idea of the passage or if you read the choices carelessly; don't let the pressure of the clock lead you into this error.

TRUST IN THE KAPLAN METHOD

These aren't the only types of wrong answer that you'll see in Global questions, but they are among the most common. The best way to avoid them is to follow the Kaplan Method carefully and consistently so that you approach every question with a solid prediction. This holds true for other question types as well, as you'll see in the coming chapters.

---

[17]PrepTest 34, Sec 1, Q 4

CHAPTER 11

DETAIL QUESTIONS

ALL ABOUT DETAIL QUESTIONS

Now that you've reviewed the Kaplan Method and learned how to apply it to Global questions, it's time to examine another Reading Comprehension question type: Detail questions.

What Are Detail Questions?

Detail questions are, in a way, the direct opposites of Global questions. While Global questions ask about the overarching themes of a passage, Detail questions require you to review the text and identify specific information that the author cited in the passage, usually in the form of evidence provided to support central conclusions. This may seem like a pretty simple task—after all, the information you need is right there in the passage. Nevertheless, there are a couple of considerations I want you to keep in mind as you familiarize yourself with this common question type.

First, do not let the presence of Detail questions on the LSAT interfere with your commitment to strategic reading. You may find yourself thinking, "If some of the questions are going to ask me about particular examples in the text, shouldn't I read the examples more carefully?" This line of reasoning is understandable, but it isn't the best way to approach the test. Remember that no matter how carefully you dive into the details when you read, two things are certain to be true: Not all of the examples will be tested, and you won't be able to memorize the ones that *are* tested—there's simply too much information in the passage.

This brings me to the second point. Do *not* try to rely on your memory when answering Detail questions. As you will see in the examples in this chapter, the test makers are very good at distorting answer choices in subtle ways so that they resemble information in the passage while still being categorically wrong. Unlike the approach to Global questions you worked with in chapter 10, you absolutely must stay in the habit of researching the relevant text before predicting the correct answer to a Detail question.

You might be concerned about the time this takes, and I've certainly worked with many students who succumbed to the pressure of the clock and tried to answer these questions from memory. The results were predictable: They would become very good at getting the questions wrong in a short amount of time.

To avoid this problem, remember that by rigorously applying Step 1 of the Kaplan Method (Read the Passage Strategically) to every passage, you will save time that you can later spend researching the correct answers to the questions. Additionally, your careful attention to Keywords and a solid Roadmap will allow you to quickly and accurately find the information you need.

How Do You Identify Detail Questions?

Detail questions will always ask unambiguously for information specifically cited in the passage. Common identifying phrases include "the passage mentions which of the following" and "which of the following is an example cited by the author." Here are a few examples drawn from previous tests:

2. The author indicates that all politicians agree about the[1]

16. Which one of the following does the passage identify as being a result of a technological development?[2]

10. According to the passage, the term "legal principles" as used by Dworkin refers to[3]

Notice that there is no qualifying language in any of these examples. Detail questions don't ask what the passage "suggests" or what the author is "likely" to agree with (this kind of qualification indicates an Inference question, which I will introduce in the next chapter). They simply ask for what's explicitly stated. Detail questions often begin with the phrase "according to" as demonstrated in question 10 above, but other question types may feature this phrase as well. In terms of the Kaplan Method:

Step 2: Identify the Question Type

When the stem asks you to identify information that is explicitly stated in the passage, you know you're working with a Detail question.

---

[1]PrepTest 26, Sec 4, Q 2
[2]PrepTest 42, Sec 3, Q 16
[3]PrepTest 17, Sec 4, Q 10

Detail Question Strategy

There aren't many variations on Detail questions, and they all require the same essential strategy; use whatever clues the question provides in order to conduct your research as quickly as you can. In most cases your task is to simply paraphrase what you read in the passage and then identify the answer choice that expresses the same concept. In terms of the Kaplan Method:

Step 3: Research the Relevant Text
Find the relevant text in the passage. Use your Roadmap and circled Keywords in the passage to direct you to the information you need. Since Detail questions tend to ask about examples that you moved through quickly when first reading the passage, be prepared to take some time to understand what the example is saying now that you know it's worth points.

Step 4: Make a Prediction
Simplify the information you researched, and paraphrase it in your mind. The correct answer choice must embody the idea conveyed by the text, but it may not use the same words. Putting the example in your own words will help you stay flexible as you work through the answer choices.

Step 5: Evaluate the Answer Choices
Select the choice that best matches the information you paraphrased.

Detail Question Practice

Now for some examples. Read the following passage, noting the circled Keywords and the provided Roadmap. Determine the Topic, Scope, Purpose, and Main Idea of the passage before moving on to the questions.

Step 1:

Myth:
Native
pop's
didn't
burn
forests

The myth persists that in 1492 the Western Hemisphere was an untamed wilderness and that it was European settlers who harnessed and transformed its ecosystems. But scholarship shows that forests, in
(5) particular, had been altered to varying degrees well before the arrival of Europeans. Native populations had converted much of the forests to successfully cultivated stands, especially by means of burning. Nevertheless, some researchers have maintained that the extent,
(10) frequency, and impact of such burning was minimal. One geographer claims that climatic change could have accounted for some of the changes in forest composition; another argues that burning by native populations was done only sporadically, to augment the
(15) effects of natural fires.

Ev. for
burning
in U.S.

(However,) a large body of (evidence) for the routine
practice of burning exists in the geographical record.
One group of researchers found, (for example,) that
sedimentary charcoal accumulations in what is now the
(20)   northeastern United States are greatest where known
native American settlements were greatest. Other
(evidence) shows that, (while) the characteristics and
impact of fires set by native populations varied
regionally according to population size, extent of
(25)   resource management techniques, and environment, all
such fires had (markedly different) effects on vegetation
patterns than did natural fires. Controlled burning
created grassy openings such as meadows and glades.
Burning (also) promoted a mosaic quality to North and
(30)   South American ecosystems, creating forests in many
different stages of ecological development. Much of
the mature forestland was characterized by open,
herbaceous undergrowth, (another result) of the clearing
brought about by burning.

Ev. in
North
America

(35)   In North America, controlled burning created
conditions favorable to berries and other fire-tolerant
and sun-loving foods. Burning (also) converted mixed
stands of trees to homogeneous forest, (for example) the
longleaf, slash pine, and scrub oak forests of the
(40)   southeastern U.S. Natural fires do account for some of
this vegetation, (but) regular burning clearly extended
and maintained it. Burning (also) influenced forest
composition in the tropics, where natural fires are rare.
(An example) is the pine-dominant forests of Nicaragua,

Ev. in
tropics

(45)   where warm temperatures and heavy rainfall naturally
favor mixed tropical or rain forests. (While) there are
extensive pine forests in Guatemala and Mexico, these
(primarily) grow in cooler, drier, higher elevations,
regions where such vegetation is in large part natural
(50)   and even prehuman. (Today) the Nicaraguan pines
occur where there has been clearing (followed by)
regular burning (and) the same is likely to have occurred
in the past: such forests were present when Europeans
arrived and were found (only in) areas where native
(55)   settlements were substantial; when these settlements
were abandoned, the land returned to mixed
hardwoods. This succession is (also evident) elsewhere
in similar low tropical elevations in the Caribbean and
Mexico.[4]

Paragraph Structure: Structurally, this passage is quite simple. The author introduces the "myth" (line 1) of untamed wilderness in the Western Hemisphere prior to the arrival of European settlers, "but" (line 4) notes that scholarship indicates that native populations had been practicing controlled burning of forests. "Nevertheless" (line 8) some researchers still believe

---

the myth. The remainder of the paragraph presents the views of these researchers—"one geographer" in line 11 and "another" in line 13.

Given that the author identified the researchers' view as a myth in the first sentence, you hopefully weren't surprised when the second paragraph began with "however" (line 16), introducing the author's claim that there's an abundance of evidence for the burning of forests. The remainder of the passage consists entirely of examples to back up the author's claim. As always, you should resist the temptation to read these examples carefully, since you already understand their purpose (to bolster the author's claim). Instead, take careful note of Keywords that will help you locate them easily later, such as "for example" (line 18), "other evidence" (lines 21–22), "another result" (line 33), and "also" (line 42). Your Roadmap should reflect the general kind of evidence that each paragraph contains, perhaps noting that paragraph two shows evidence of burning in the United States and paragraph three describes examples in both North and South America. But note that the author doesn't state any opinions in these paragraphs—the author's sole claim, and the Main Idea of the passage, was stated in lines 16–17.

Topic: Controlled burning of forests

Scope: Burning by non-European natives in North and South America

Purpose: To demonstrate that a myth about the Western Hemisphere is untrue

Main Idea: Despite claims to the contrary, there is much evidence that the native people of North and South America cultivated forests by controlled burning.

3. Which one of the following is a type of forest identified by the author as a product of controlled burning in recent times?[5]

Before looking at the answer choices, apply the Kaplan Method.

Step 2: The stem asks for a type of forest "identified by the author." Since you're being asked to find a specific example, you know this is a Detail question.

Step 3: What clues appeared in the question stem to guide you to the proper text? The question asked about the product of burning in "recent times." Skim the Roadmap and circled Keywords to locate the proper place to research the answer.

Hopefully you clued in on the Keyword "today" (line 50) which shows where you'll find information about "recent times." The text indicates that Nicaraguan pines are found in places where burning has been applied, noting that the forests tend to return to "mixed hardwoods" when the burning stops. The author also mentions that this phenomenon occurs in other low tropical elevations. Since this is the only part of the text in which the author specifically mentions burning in recent times, this must be the information you're looking for.

---

[5]PrepTest 38, Sec 3, Q 3

Step 4: Before moving on to the choices, take a moment to paraphrase what you've just read, and make a prediction. The correct answer should mention pine trees growing in tropical areas of low elevation, as opposed to the mixed forests one would ordinarily expect to see.

Step 5: Now go to the choices and find the answer that matches your prediction.

3. Which one of the following is a type of forest identified
    by the author as a product of controlled burning in recent
    times?

    (A) scrub oak forests in the southeastern U.S.
    (B) slash pine forests in the southeastern U.S.
    (C) pine forests in Guatemala at high elevations
    (D) pine forests in Mexico at high elevations
    (E) pine forests in Nicaragua at low elevations[6]

The only answer choice that references the Nicaraguan pines of your prediction is correct choice (E). As expected, the correct answer is simply a paraphrase of information found in the passage.

I want to stress once more how very important it is to follow Steps 3 and 4 carefully. The incorrect answer choices represent a jumble of concepts that appeared in various places throughout the passage. Answering a question like this correctly from memory *might* be possible, but for most test takers it's highly unlikely. Do your research and make a prediction, and the right answer will clearly stand out from the others, allowing you to score the point with confidence.

Try the next question on your own, applying the Kaplan Method as always. When you have selected an answer choice, read on to the explanation.

4. Which one of the following is presented by the author as
    evidence of controlled burning in the tropics before the
    arrival of Europeans?

    (A) extensive homogeneous forests at high elevation
    (B) extensive homogeneous forests at low elevation
    (C) extensive heterogeneous forests at high elevation
    (D) extensive heterogeneous forests at low elevation
    (E) extensive sedimentary charcoal accumulations at
         high elevation[7]

Step 2: You are looking for information "presented by the author as evidence" for burning in the tropics. Such information will come directly from the passage, so you know this is a Detail question.

Step 3: The best clue offered by the question stem is the phrase "in the tropics." Your Roadmap directs you back to the third paragraph, and more specifically, to the example that begins

---

[6]PrepTest 38, Sec 3, Q 3
[7]PrepTest 38, Sec 3, Q 4

in line 44. This text should look very familiar; it's the same part of the passage you used to answer question 3.

Step 4: Take a moment to review the paraphrase you used in the previous question. As evidence of controlled burning in the tropics the author mentioned pine forests growing at low elevations, rather than mixed hardwoods that spring up when burning is absent. The correct answer will reflect this evidence.

Step 5: The terminology in the answer choices might be confusing, but you've got a strong prediction to aid you. Begin by determining which choices are potential matches and which can be eliminated. Choices (A) and (C) mention forests growing at high elevations rather than low, so they can be eliminated right away. Choice (E) is completely outside of the scope of your prediction and can also be discarded. That leaves choices (B) and (D). Are the pine forests of your prediction homogeneous or heterogeneous? If you aren't sure, try scanning the text prior to line 44 to see if these key terms are mentioned in context. Near the Keyword "also" in line 37 you'll see that burning was responsible for creating homogenous forests of various kinds, including pine. That's the final clue you need. Answer choice (B) is correct.

Detail EXCEPT Questions: A Slight Variation

I'll come back to the idea of researching for context again soon; it's a skill that has broad application in the Reading Comprehension section. Right now I want to introduce you to a common variant on the standard Detail question:

6. As evidence for the routine practice of forest burning by native populations before the arrival of Europeans, the author cites all of the following EXCEPT:[8]

Step 2: This is a Detail EXCEPT question. In this case, you are trying to find the one answer choice that *wasn't* explicitly stated in the passage as evidence of controlled burning.

This type of question will require a modified strategy, since it will be nearly impossible for you to predict something that didn't appear in the passage. This doesn't mean that you can't apply predictive thinking—it simply means you have to apply it in a slightly different way.

Step 3: This question stem isn't as generous with clues as the previous two. Evidence for controlled burning by native populations was provided throughout the entirety of the second and third paragraphs. The proper approach in this case is to use the answer choices to help guide your research and prediction.

---

[8]PrepTest 38, Sec 3, Q 6

(A)   the similar characteristics of fires in different
       regions
(B)   the simultaneous presence of forests at varying
       stages of maturity
(C)   the existence of herbaceous undergrowth in
       certain forests
(D)   the heavy accumulation of charcoal near populous
       settlements
(E)   the presence of meadows and glades in certain
       forests[9]

Based on the research you've performed so far, you know that the author's evidence has cen-tered around the characteristics of forests in the Western hemisphere as they appear today. A glance at the choices confirms that most of them mention such evidence, specifically choices (B), (C), and (E). That leaves choices (A) and (D) as most likely to be correct.

Your Roadmap indicates that the evidence for controlled burning was first introduced in the second paragraph, so you should return there to look for evidence that will help you eliminate answer choices. Use the Keywords to navigate the text efficiently. "For example" (line 18) leads you to evidence for charcoal accumulation, allowing you to eliminate choice (D). The "other evidence" presented in lines 21–27 refers to the differences in fires set across North America, which is the exact opposite of choice (A). Since you're trying to find an exception, choice (A) is almost certainly the correct answer.

Step 4: At this point you have a couple of options. You can either predict that choice (A) is correct and move on to Step 5, or you can continue to use the process of elimination to whittle down the choices until you're left with one. Since you've found a direct counterexample to choice (A) in the passage, you can be sure that it is correct.

Step 5: Based on your prediction, you should select correct choice (A) and move on. For the record, the examples cited in choices (B), (C), and (E) are from lines 27–34.

When working with a Detail EXCEPT question, remember that you won't always locate a specific counterexample as you did here; often the correct answer will simply contain information never mentioned in the passage. In such a situation, continue to use the process of elimination to get rid of wrong choices until you are left with the correct one. Don't forget that the choices themselves often contain clues that help you conduct your research. Just because this type of question doesn't lend itself to a straightforward prediction doesn't mean that you should simply reread the entire passage. Use all the clues that are available to you to make your research as efficient as possible. Above all, remember to stick to the Kaplan Method even in unusual situations. Although Detail EXCEPT questions are relatively rare, you'll probably see one or two of them on test day. Stay methodical and you'll score the point.

---

[9]PrepTest 38, Sec 3, Q 6

DRILL: ANSWERING DETAIL QUESTIONS

Now for some practice. Read the following passage strategically, applying Step 1 of the Kaplan Method. Then answer the three questions that follow, applying Steps 2–5 each time. Explanations follow the Drill.

Until recently, few historians were interested in analyzing the similarities and differences between serfdom in Russia and slavery in the United States. Even Alexis de Tocqueville, who recognized the
(5) significant comparability of the two nations, never compared their systems of servitude, despite his interest in United States slavery. Moreover, the almost simultaneous abolition of Russian serfdom and United States slavery in the 1860s—a riveting
(10) coincidence that should have drawn more modern scholars to a comparative study of the two systems of servitude—has failed to arouse the interest of scholars. Though some historians may have been put off by the forbidding political differences
(15) between nineteenth-century Russia and the United States—one an imperial monarchy, the other a federal democracy—a recent study by Peter Kolchin identifies differences that are illuminating, especially with regard to the different kinds of
(20) rebellion exhibited by slaves and serfs.

Kolchin points out that nobles owning serfs in Russia constituted only a tiny proportion of the population, while in the southern United States, about a quarter of all White people were members
(25) of slave-owning families. And although in the southern United States only 2 percent of slaves worked on plantations where more than a hundred slaves worked, in Russia almost 80 percent of the serfs worked for nobles who owned more than a
(30) hundred serfs. In Russia most serfs rarely saw their owners, who tended to rely on intermediaries to manage their estates, while most southern planters lived on their land and interacted with slaves on a regular basis.

(35) These differences in demographics partly explain differences in the kinds of resistance that slaves and serfs practiced in their respective countries. Both serfs and slaves engaged in a wide variety of rebellious activity, from silent sabotage, much of
(40) which has escaped the historical record, to organized armed rebellions, which were more common in Russia. The practice of absentee ownership, combined with the large numbers in which serfs were owned, probably contributed

(45) significantly to the four great rebellions that swept across Russia at roughly fifty-year intervals in the seventeenth and eighteenth centuries. The last of these, occurring between 1773 and 1774, enlisted more than a million serfs in a futile attempt to
(50) overthrow the Russian nobility. Russian serfs also participated in smaller acts of collective defiance called the *volnenie*, which typically started with a group of serfs who complained of grievances by petition and went out on strike. Confrontations
(55) between slaves and plantation authorities were also common, but they tended to be much less collective in nature than those that occurred in Russia, probably in part because the number of workers on each estate was smaller in the United States than
(60) was the case in Russia.[10]

1. According to the author, de Tocqueville was similar to many modern historians in his

    (A) interest in the demographic differences between Russia and the United States during the nineteenth century
    (B) failure to undertake a comparison of Russian serfdom and United States slavery
    (C) inability to explain why United States slavery and Russian serfdom were abolished during the same decade
    (D) overestimation of the significance of the political differences between Russia and the United States
    (E) recognition of the essential comparability of Russia and the United States

---

[10]PrepTest 14, Sec 3, Passage 4

2. The author cites which one of the following as a factor that might have discouraged historians from undertaking a comparative study of Russian serfdom and United States slavery?

(A) major differences in the political systems of the two counties

(B) major differences in the demographics of the two counties

(C) the failure of de Tocqueville to address the subject

(D) differences in the size of the estates on which slaves and serfs labored

(E) the comprehensiveness of Kolchin's own work

3. According to the passage, Kolchin's study asserts that which one of the following was true of Russian nobles during the nineteenth century?

(A) They agreed to the abolition of serfdom in the 1860s largely as a result of their having been influenced by the abolition of slavery in the United States.

(B) They became more directly involved in the management of their estates as a result of the rebellions that occurred in the previous century.

(C) They commonly agreed to at least some of the demands that arose out of the *volnenie*.

(D) They had relatively little direct contact with the serfs who worked on their estates.

(E) They hastened the abolition of serfdom by failing to devise an effective response to the collective nature of the serfs' rebellious activity.[11]

[11]PrepTest 14, Sec 3, Qs 22, 25, 26

Answer Explanations follow on the next page.

Explanations

Step 1:

Not many
studies
of
slave /
serf

(Until recently) few historians were interested in analyzing the similarities and differences (between) serfdom in Russia (and) slavery in the United States. (Even) Alexis de Tocqueville, who recognized the (5) significant comparability of the two nations, never compared their systems of servitude, (despite) his interest in United States slavery. (Moreover,) the almost simultaneous abolition of Russian serfdom and United States slavery in the 1860s—a (riveting) (10) coincidence that should have drawn more modern scholars to a comparative study of the two systems of servitude—has (failed) to arouse the interest of scholars. (Though) some historians may have been put off by the forbidding political differences (15) between nineteenth-century Russia and the United States—one an imperial monarchy, the other a federal democracy—a (recent study) by Peter

Kolchin's
study-
differences

Kolchin identifies differences that are illuminating, (especially) with regard to the different kinds of (20) rebellion exhibited by slaves and serfs.

(Kolchin points out) that nobles owning serfs in Russia constituted only a tiny proportion of the population, (while) in the southern United States, about a quarter of all White people were members (25) of slave-owning families. And (although) in the

Diff's
between
slaves
and
serfs

southern United States only 2 percent of slaves worked on plantations where more than a hundred slaves worked, in Russia almost 80 percent of the serfs worked for nobles who owned more than a (30) hundred serfs. In Russia most serfs rarely saw their owners, who tended to rely on intermediaries to manage their estates (while) most southern planters lived on their land and interacted with slaves on a regular basis.

(35)   These differences in demographics (partly explain) differences in the kinds of resistance that slaves and serfs practiced in their respective countries. (Both) serfs (and) slaves engaged in a wide variety of rebellious activity, from silent sabotage, much of (40) which has escaped the historical record, to organized armed rebellions, which were more common in Russia. The practice of absentee ownership, combined with the large numbers in

Diff.
types
of
rebellion

which serfs were owned, probably (contributed) (45) (significantly) to the four great rebellions that swept across Russia at roughly fifty-year intervals in the seventeenth and eighteenth centuries. The last of these, occurring between 1773 and 1774, enlisted more than a million serfs in a futile attempt to (50) overthrow the Russian nobility. Russian serfs (also)

participated in smaller acts of collective defiance
called the *volnenie*, which typically (started) with a
group of serfs who complained of grievances by
petition (and) went out on strike. Confrontations
(55) between slaves and plantation authorities were (also)
common, (but) they tended to be much less collective
in nature than those that occurred in Russia,
probably in part (because) the number of workers on
each estate was smaller in the United States than
(60) was the case in Russia.[12]

Paragraph Structure: The opening paragraph starts by asserting that "until recently" historians weren't interested in comparing serfdom in Russia to slavery in the United States. Although most of the paragraph describes these uninterested historians, the expected turnabout comes in line 16, when the author introduces Peter Kolchin, who was interested in exploring important differences between the two, with a particular focus on different forms of rebellion.

In the second paragraph, Kolchin points out several differences between serf-owning nobles in Russia and slave-owning families in the United States. The author stays focused on this comparison throughout the paragraph, using contrast Keywords like "although" (line 24) and "while" (line 30) to clearly illustrate these differences.

The third paragraph returns to rebellion as hinted at in the first paragraph. The author explains how the differences described in the second paragraph caused the varying forms of rebellion referenced in the third. Language of causality located throughout the paragraph (such as "contributed significantly" in line 42 and "in part because" in line 54) guides you through this relationship.

Topic: Serfdom and slavery

Scope: Differences between Russian serfdom and United States slavery

Purpose: To demonstrate important differences between two systems of bondage

Main Idea: Peter Kolchin points out that, because of key differences in demographics, the forms of rebellion enacted by Russian serfs were very different from those enacted by slaves in the United States.

---

[12]PrepTest 14, Sec 3, Passage 4

1.   **(B)**

According to the author, de Tocqueville was similar
to many modern historians in his
- (A)   interest in the demographic differences between
    Russia and the United States during the
    nineteenth century
- (B)   failure to undertake a comparison of Russian
    serfdom and United States slavery
- (C)   inability to explain why United States slavery
    and Russian serfdom were abolished during
    the same decade
- (D)   overestimation of the significance of the
    political differences between Russia and the
    United States
- (E)   recognition of the essential comparability of
    Russia and the United States[13]

Step 2: The phrase "according to the author" combined with a lack of qualified language
identifies this as a Detail question.

Step 3: How was de Tocqueville similar to modern historians? The only place he was referenced was in the first paragraph. Lines 5–6 indicate that "despite" his interest in slavery in the
United States, he never compared slavery to serfdom. This lack of interest is shared with other
historians, as indicated in the first sentence.

Step 4: To summarize: de Tocqueville was similar to other historians in that he wasn't interested
in comparing serfdom to slavery.

Step 5: Correct choice (B) is an exact match. Choices (A), (C), and (D) are completely outside
the scope of what little the passage says about de Tocqueville's views. Choice (E) does mention something that de Tocqueville was interested in, but not an interest he shared with the
other historians in the passage.

2.   **(A)**

The author cites which one of the following as a
factor that might have discouraged historians from
undertaking a comparative study of Russian serfdom
and United States slavery?
- (A)   major differences in the political systems of the
    two counties
- (B)   major differences in the demographics of the
    two counties
- (C)   the failure of de Tocqueville to address the
    subject
- (D)   differences in the size of the estates on which
    slaves and serfs labored
- (E)   the comprehensiveness of Kolchin's own work[14]

---

[13]PrepTest 14, Sec 3, Q 22

[14]PrepTest 14, Sec 3, Q 25

Step 2: The stem asks for a factor cited by the author. This is a Detail question.

Step 3: Why didn't historians compare serfdom to slavery? Your Roadmap should remind you that these historians are discussed in the first paragraph. Scanning for Keywords, you should quickly spot "though" in line 12, which introduces the contrast you're looking for. Historians were "put off" by political differences between the two countries.

Step 4: There isn't much to paraphrase here, since no other reasons are given for the historians' lack of enthusiasm, but stay in the habit. The correct answer should mention the political differences cited in the text.

Step 5: The only choice that mentions political differences is correct choice (A). The others are all completely outside the scope of this question.

3. **(D)**

According to the passage, Kolchin's study asserts that which one of the following was true of Russian nobles during the nineteenth century?

(A) They agreed to the abolition of serfdom in the 1860s largely as a result of their having been influenced by the abolition of slavery in the United States.

(B) They became more directly involved in the management of their estates as a result of the rebellions that occurred in the previous century.

(C) They commonly agreed to at least some of the demands that arose out of the *volnenie*.

(D) They had relatively little direct contact with the serfs who worked on their estates.

(E) They hastened the abolition of serfdom by failing to devise an effective response to the collective nature of the serfs' rebellious activity.[15]

Step 2: The phrase "according to the passage" combined with the word "asserts" helps you identify this as a Detail question.

Step 3: The stem references Russian nobles, who were mentioned in their relationships to their serfs. Your Roadmap should indicate that the second paragraph is the likeliest place to find this information, since it explores the essential differences between serfdom and slavery. The author reveals that serf-owning nobles were a tiny proportion of the population in lines 20–22, and that they rarely came into direct contact with their serfs in lines 28–30.

Step 4: To summarize, the correct answer should state that serf-owning nobles were a small part of the overall Russian population, or that they didn't directly deal with their serfs.

---

[15]PrepTest 14, Sec 3, Q 26

Step 5: Correct choice (D) is an exact match for the second part of your prediction. Choice (A) is completely out of scope; the author never reveals how nobles were connected to the abolition of serfdom. Choices (B), (C), and (E) all refer to possible responses of nobles to rebellion, another subject that the author never addresses.

COMMON WRONG ANSWER TYPES

Like Global questions, Detail questions are common and predictable. It follows that their wrong answer patterns are also predictable. Here are a few wrong answer types to look for:

Out of Scope

As you probably noticed, choices that are outside the scope of the question, or in some cases the passage as a whole, are very common in Detail questions. A strong prediction combined with a good sense of the Scope of the passage will allow you to dispose of these choices with confidence.

1. According to the author, de Tocqueville was similar many modern historians in his

   (A) interest in the demographic differences between Russia and the United States during the nineteenth century
   (B) failure to undertake a comparison of Russian serfdom and United States slavery
   (C) inability to explain why United States slavery and Russian serfdom were abolished during the same decade
   (D) overestimation of the significance of the political differences between Russia and the United States
   (E) recognition of the essential comparability of Russia and the United State[16]

In this question, three of the five answer choices refer to ideas that have no significance to the question at all, since the passage never relates them to de Tocqueville.

180

Occasionally, an answer choice will state the precise opposite of what you've predicted. I'll refer to this type of wrong answer as a 180. A 180 can be among the most dangerous wrong answer traps because it will often contain language very similar to what you would expect to see in the correct answer.

---

[16]PrepTest 14, Sec 3, Q 22

3. Which one of the following is a type of forest identified by the author as a product of controlled burning in recent times?

(A) scrub oak forests in the southeastern U.S.
(B) slash pine forests in the southeastern U.S.
(C) pine forests in Guatemala at high elevations
(D) pine forests in Mexico at high elevations
(E) pine forests in Nicaragua at low elevations[17]

Choice (E) is the correct answer, but notice how similar it looks to wrong answer traps (C) and (D), despite the fact that they describe opposing elevations. The easiest way to dodge this trap is to read the choices carefully when executing Step 5; don't become careless once you've made your prediction. You still have to find the right match.

Distortion

Similar to the 180, answer choices that refer to ideas mentioned in the passage while slightly skewing them are also quite common.

1. According to the author, de Tocqueville was similar to many modern historians in his

(A) interest in the demographic differences between Russia and the United States during the nineteenth century
(B) failure to undertake a comparison of Russian serfdom and United States slavery
(C) inability to explain why United States slavery and Russian serfdom were abolished during the same decade
(D) overestimation of the significance of the political differences between Russia and the United States
(E) recognition of the essential comparability of Russia and the United States[18]

Returning to this question, recall that the passage did refer to de Tocqueville's interest in the "significant comparability" of Russia to the United States. However, this was not something that he shared with other historians. If you attempt to rely on your memory when answering Detail questions you will become vulnerable to distortions in the answer choices. To avoid this trap, follow the Kaplan Method and always research the text as necessary.

I hope you're starting to feel very comfortable with the process of research and prediction. These skills will serve you well as you learn about Inference questions in the next chapter.

---

[17]PrepTest 38, Sec 3, Q 3
[18]PrepTest 14, Sec 3, Q 22

CHAPTER 12

INFERENCE QUESTIONS

ALL ABOUT INFERENCE QUESTIONS

I've shown you how to systematically employ the Kaplan Method when dealing with Global and Detail questions. Now I'll introduce you to Inference questions, which appear in both the Reading Comprehension and the Logical Reasoning sections. Similar to other question types, Inference questions are extremely predictable and appear in a limited number of variations. The skills you put into practice in chapter 11 will come in handy here—especially your growing mastery of research and prediction.

What Are Inference Questions?

Take a moment to think about the word "inference." What does it mean to you? How do you use it in everyday speech?

Now suppose I tell you that I'm a concert pianist. Assuming I'm telling you the truth, what might you infer from this statement? There are several conclusions that are very likely to come to your mind immediately. You'll probably infer that I've spent many hours practicing piano music, that I most likely received some kind of formal training in music, and that I'm familiar with the works of many composers. In real life, these would be reasonable inferences to make. They are all things that are very likely to be true of someone who is a concert pianist.

On the LSAT, *none* of the above inferences would be considered valid, and that's because the LSAT follows a very specific definition of the word "inference" that is quite different from the one you probably use in daily life. The definition is very simple: On the LSAT, an inference is something that *must be true*, using only those facts that are available to you in the passage.

In the above scenario I presented you with conclusions that are very likely to be true . . . but none of them *must be true*. It's certainly possible, though perhaps very unlikely, that you'll meet a concert pianist who rarely ever practiced, didn't receive any kind of training, and is familiar only with the works of a single composer.

In other words, if an LSAT passage informs you that Emily is a concert pianist, there isn't much you can infer about her other than that she plays the piano at concerts.

A few important principles follow from this extremely limited definition. First, when a question asks you to make an inference, it's simply asking you to take information from the passage and use it to draw a new conclusion that *must be true*. Second, an LSAT inference will never be a large leap of logic, but rather a small step from one fact to another. Third, inferences never require information outside of the passage, and you must be careful not to bring your own knowledge or ideas into an Inference question—use only what you read in the passage.

I'll illustrate all of these principles in a moment. In keeping with the Kaplan Method, however, I'll first show you how to identify the question type.

How Do You Identify Inference Questions?

Inference question stems tend to be a little more varied than Global or Detail stems. In general, any question that asks you to take the information from the passage and draw unstated conclusions from it is considered an Inference question. Here are a few common examples.

13. It can be inferred that the author of the passage regards Hart's theory of hard cases and the theory of standard law as[1]

11. Which one of the following expresses a view that the author of the passage would most probably hold concerning legal principles and legal rules?[2]

5. Based on the information in the passage, which one of the following would most likely be found objectionable by those who oppose compulsory national service?[3]

1. Which one of the following most accurately describes the author's attitude toward the relationship between citizenship and individual rights in a democracy?[4]

The first example is pretty straightforward, as it directly asks for an inference. But look closely at the second and third examples. The key language "most probably" and "most likely" is what

---

[1]PrepTest 17, Sec 4, Q 13
[2]PrepTest 17, Sec 4, Q 11
[3]PrepTest 26, Sec 4, Q 5
[4]PrepTest 26, Sec 4, Q 1

identifies both as Inference questions. In fact, qualified language is the most common identifying feature you should look for—unlike Detail questions, which ask for what is directly cited in the passage, Inference questions ask for what is *probably* true or what views the author (or any other speaker) is *likely* to agree or disagree with.

This might seem confusing at first. An Inference is something that *must be true*, and yet the question stem asks for something that is likely to be true. Don't let this contradiction throw you off; regardless of how the question is worded, the correct answer choice will be the only one that absolutely must follow from the text.

The final example above asks for the author's attitude about a particular idea. This is a somewhat less-common variety of Inference question, but one that you've seen before in this book. In order to pinpoint the author's attitude, you must research the text for Keywords indicating tone and opinion, then use this information to create a general description that isn't explicitly expressed at any point in the passage. Putting it all together:

Step 2: Identify the Question Type

When the stem asks you to draw a new conclusion from the passage, to identify the author's attitude, or to indicate what is likely to be true, you know you're working with an Inference question.

Inference Question Strategy

The proper strategic approach to Inference questions is very similar to that used in Detail questions. Here it is, step by step.

Step 3: Research the Relevant Text

Find the relevant text in the passage. The question stem contains clues that help you determine what you need to know and where you can find it, although some Inference questions provide more clues than others. Use your Roadmap and circled Keywords in the passage to find the information you need.

Step 4: Make a Prediction

Think about what facts *must be true*, remembering that the correct answer can't stray very far from the text.

Step 5: Evaluate the Answer Choices

Find the answer choice that best matches your prediction. If there is no obvious match, use your research to determine which answer choice must be true.

Inference Question Practice

It's time to look at some examples. First, read the following passage and its sample Roadmap. Then try to identify the Topic, Scope, Purpose, and Main Idea of the passage before reading on.

Step 1:

Chinese cult. rev. affected art

The Cultural Revolution of 1966 to 1976, (initiated) by Communist Party Chairman Mao Zedong in an attempt to reduce the influence of China's intellectual elite on the country's institutions, has had
(5) (lasting repercussions) on Chinese art. It (intensified) the absolutist mind-set of Maoist Revolutionary Realism, which had dictated the content and style of Chinese art even before 1966 by (requiring) that artists ("truthfully") depict the realities of socialist life in

Art had to be political, approved by party

(10) China. Interest in nonsocial, nonpolitical subjects was strictly (forbidden) and, during the Cultural Revolution, what constituted truth was entirely for revolutionary forces to decide—the (only) reality artists could portray was one that had been thoroughly
(15) colored and distorted by political ideology.

Led to opposite kinds of art

(Ironically) the same set of requirments that constricted artistic expression during the Cultural Revolution has had the (opposite effect) since; many artistic movements have flourished in reaction to the
(20) monotony of Revolutionary Realism. (One of these), the Scar Art movement of the 1980s, was spearheaded by a group of intellectual painters who had been trained in Maoist art schools and then exiled to rural areas during the Cultural Revolution.

Scar art: exposed rural poverty

(25) In exile, these painters were for perhaps the (first time) confronted with the (harsh realities) of rural poverty and misery—aspects of life in China that their Maoist mentors would probably have preferred they ignore, As a (result) of these experiences, they developed a
(30) radically new approach to realism. (Instead) of depicting the version of reality sanctioned by the government, the Scar Art painters (chose to) represent the "scarred reality" they had seen during their exile. Their version of realist painting (emphasized) the day-

Scar art opposed to Rev. Realism

(35) to-day hardship or rural life. (While) the principles of Revolutionary Realism had insisted that artists choose public, monumental, and universal subjects, the Scar artists chose (instead) to focus on the private, the mundane, and the particular; where the principles of
(40) Revolutionary Realism had demanded that they depict contemporary Chines society as outstanding or perfect, the Scar artists chose (instead) to portray the bleak realities of modernization.

As the 1980s progressed, the Scar artists' radical
(45) approach to realism became (increasingly) co-opted for
political purposes, and as this political cast became
stronger and more obvious, many artists abandoned
the movement. (Yet) a preoccupation with rural life
persisted, (giving rise) to a related development known
(50) as the Native Soil movement, which (focused on) the
native landscape and embodied a growing nostalgia
for the charms of peasant society in the face of
modernization. (Where) the Scar artists had reacted to
the ideological rigidity of the Cultural Revolution by
(55) emphasizing the damage inflicted by modernization,
the Native Soil painters reacted (instead) by idealizing
traditional peasant life. (Unfortunately) in the end
Native Soil painting was (trivialized) by a tendency to
romanticize certain qualities of rural Chinese society
(60) in order to appeal Western galleries and collectors.[5]

*Gov co-opted
scar art*

*Native Soil:
focused on rural
settings*

*Trivialized
by subject
matter*

Paragraph Structure: The author begins by providing historical context for the Topic, explaining that the Cultural Revolution has had "lasting repercussions" (line 5) on Chinese art. Artists were required by the government to "truthfully" (line 9) depict life in socialist china. I hope you noticed the quotation marks around the word "truthfully," a clue that the author believes that these artists were *not* truthful in their work. In fact, the "only reality" (line 13) that artists could portray was one described by politicians.

The second, lengthier paragraph makes the author's Scope clearer – beginning with "ironically" in line 16, the author describes the unintended effect the government's policies had on subsequent artistic movements. She then focuses specifically on the Scar Art movement, describing its creators as exiled intellectuals who became aware of the "harsh realities" (line 26) of rural life. "As a result" (line 29), the Scar Artists depicted reality as they observed it rather than as described by politicians. The author highlights this dichotomy with Keywords of contrast throughout the remainder of the paragraph, specifically "while (line 35), and "instead" in lines 38 and 42. This kind of repetition simplifies the paragraph considerably.

In the third paragraph the author notes that Scar Art became "increasingly co-opted" (line 45) by the government, leading to a weakening of the movement. "Yet" (line 48) there remained an interest in rural life, which was subsequently explored by the Native Soil movement. But "where" (line 53) the Scar Artists portrayed the misery of impoverishment, the Native Soil artists "instead" (line 56) idealized rural life, and "unfortunately" (line 57) this led to the trivialization of the movement.

Topic: Chinese art

Scope: Effects of the Cultural Revolution on Chinese art

---

[5]PrepTest 47, Sec 2, Passage 2

Purpose: To describe artistic movements that came into being as a result of the Cultural Revolution

Main Idea: Artistic movements such as Scar Art and Native Soil came about as an unintended consequence of the state-sanctioned art of the Cultural Revolution.

The strong grasp of authorial opinion that strategic reading provides you gives you a great advantage when you encounter Inference questions. Look at this example:

> 8. Which one of the following statements about realism in Chinese art can most reasonably be inferred from the passage?[6]

Step 2: The stem provides you with very clear identifying language. "Most reasonably inferred" indicates that this is an Inference question. You need to determine what must be true about realism in Chinese art.

Step 3: Where in the passage should you go for information about realism? Because the question mentioned Chinese art in general, not a specific artistic movement, you should prepare to look in several places. Using your Roadmap as a guide, you'll see that the first paragraph described Revolutionary Realist art as "colored and distorted" (line 15) by the government. Scar Art, as described in paragraph 2, opposed Revolutionary Realism, instead describing a harsher reality. By paying close attention to these contrasts in the passage you can clearly see that realism in Chinese art has changed from movement to movement, and that the reality depicted hasn't always been accurate.

Step 4: Make your prediction, remembering that the correct answer must be true. The author has demonstrated that realism in Chinese art has changed from movement to movement, and hasn't always reflected the truth of Chinese life. The correct answer should describe this ambivalence.

Step 5: Now examine the choices and find the one that matches your prediction:

---

[6]PrepTest 47, Sec 2, Passage 2, Q 8

8. Which one of the following statements about realism in Chinese art can most reasonably be inferred from the passage?

   (A)   The artists who became leaders of the Native Soil movement practiced a modified form of realism in reaction against the styles and techniques of Scar Art.

   (B)   Chinese art has encompassed conflicting conceptions of realism derived from contrasting political and artistic purposes.

   (C)   The goals of realism in Chinese art have been effectively furthered by both the Scar Art movement and the Native Soil movement.

   (D)   Until the development of the Scar Art movement, interest in rural life had been absent from the types of art that prevailed among Chinese realist painters.

   (E)   Unlike the art that was predominant during the Cultural Revolution, Scar Art was not a type of realist art.[7]

The correct answer, choice (B), matches your prediction and must be true. Choice (A) brings in ideas that are out of Scope, since the author never described Native Soil as a reaction against Scar Art. Choice (C) describes the goals of realism, something that was never clarified in the passage, so you can't know whether or not particular movements advanced those goals. Similarly, choice (D) is incorrect because there is no way to know whether or not an interest in rural life was or wasn't absent from Chinese art prior to the Scar Art movement. Choice (E) is in opposition to the passage, which says that the Scar Artists developed a new approach to realism, not that they didn't produce realist art.

I'd like to emphasize once more that LSAT inferences are small leaps of logic. In the last example, the correct answer was simply a broad restatement of ideas that the passage presented explicitly. Most of the other choices described ideas that were possible, but not definitely true.

With this in mind, try the following question on your own before reading the explanations that follow.

---

[7]PrepTest 47, Sec 2, Passage 2, Q 8

11. It can be inferred from the passage that the author
     would be most likely to agree with which one of the
     following views of the Native Soil movement?

     (A)   Its development was the inevitable
           consequence of the Scar Art movement's
           increasing politicization.
     (B)   It failed to earn the wide recognition that Scar
           Art had achieved.
     (C)   The rural scenes it depicted were appealing to
           most people in China.
     (D)   Ironically, it had several key elements in
           common with Revolutionary Realism, in
           opposition to which it originally developed.
     (E)   Its nostalgic representation of rural life was the
           means by which it stood in opposition to
           Revolutionary Realism.[8]

Step 2: Once again, the word "inferred" identifies this as an Inference question. You must determine what the author believes must be true about the Native Soil movement.

Step 3: The Roadmap indicates that the Native Soil movement was discussed in the final paragraph. The author contrasts this movement with its predecessor, Scar Art, explaining that the Native Soil painters reacted to the Cultural Revolution by idealizing rural life, and that this eventually led to their art becoming trivialized.

Step 4: The relatively brief discussion of the Native Soil painters means that a good prediction should be easy to formulate. Since the correct answer must be true, it must conform to one of the handful of ideas you found in your research. It will likely focus on the primary contrast between Native Soil and Scar Art, so you should expect an answer that describes a tendency to romanticize rural life.

Step 5: Correct choice (E) must be true. It essentially paraphrases the description of the Native Soil movement found in lines 53–57. Choice (A) goes too far in describing Native Soil as an inevitable consequence of Scar Art. Choice (C) is similarly extreme. The passage does describe a preoccupation with rural life, but never suggests that rural scenes appealed to most people in China. Choice (B) describes a comparison that is never made in the passage, and choice (D) distorts the author's ideas—Native Soil was a reaction to the Cultural Revolution, but the passage never says it was developed in opposition to Revolutionary Realism.

These examples are typical of the kinds of Inference questions you should expect to see on test day. Now take a look at a slight variation:

9.   It can be inferred from the passage that the author
     would be LEAST likely to agree with which one of
     the following statements regarding the Cultural
     Revolution?[9]

[8]PrepTest 47, Sec 2, Passage 2, Q 11
[9]PrepTest 47, Sec 2, Passage 2, Q 9

You've seen EXCEPT questions in previous chapters, so this example shouldn't look too unusual. As always, apply the Kaplan Method, but be prepared to think carefully about how to characterize the right and wrong answer choices. Here's how:

Step 2: The stem asks which idea regarding the Cultural Revolution the author would be LEAST likely to agree with. This is an Inference question, but this time, the correct answer will be something that *isn't* a proper inference. There are a couple of possibilities—the right answer might contradict the author's opinion, or it might simply be out-of-scope (an out-of-scope choice can't be proved or disproved by the text, so by definition it doesn't have to be true.) By contrast, the four wrong answer choices will all be proper inferences.

If you encounter this type of question on test day, make sure you take a moment to think about what characteristics the right and wrong choices will display. Because out-of-scope choices are usually incorrect, you're probably in the habit of discarding them on sight, and in this case you would miss the question as a result. You can't afford to lose points to a careless reading of the question stem, so always apply Step 2 carefully!

Step 3: The stem refers to the Cultural Revolution. Since the scope of the question is somewhat broad, let your Roadmap be your guide. According to the first paragraph, the Cultural Revolution led to a type of art that was strictly controlled by the government, required to reflect dominating political ideas. The second paragraph begins the author's discussion of artistic movements that "ironically" (line 16) came into being later, and which contrasted in many ways with Revolutionary Realism.

Step 4: Since the right answer can be anything that the author doesn't explicitly agree with, trying to make a specific prediction is a waste of time. Instead, keep the author's broad ideas in mind and prepare to use the process of elimination to get rid of incorrect choices.

Step 5:

9. It can be inferred from the passage that the author would be LEAST likely to agree with which one of the following statements regarding the Cultural Revolution?

(A) It had the ironic effect of catalyzing art movements at odds with its policies.

(B) The art that was endorsed by its policies was less varied and interesting than Chinese art since the Cultural Revolution.

(C) Much of the art that it endorsed did not accurately depict the realities of life in China but rather a politically motivated idealization.

(D) Its effects demonstrate that restrictive policies generally foster artistic growth more than liberal policies do.

(E) Its impact has continued to be felt in the Chinese art world years after it ended.[10]

---

[10]PrepTest 47, Sec 2, Passage 2, Q 9

Choice (A) is definitely true, summarizing much of the content of the second and third paragraphs, so you should eliminate it. Choice (B) can also be inferred—the author describes later artistic movements as a contrast to the "monotony" (line 20) of Revolutionary Realism. Choice (C) paraphrases the latter half of the first paragraph and can likewise be eliminated. But correct choice (D) must be *false*. The author goes to great lengths to contrast the flourishing of artistic movements after the Revolution with the restrictive political art it fostered. Finally, the truth of choice (E) is confirmed by the very first sentence of the passage, so it too must be incorrect.

Questions like this one can be intimidating, and can potentially be time-consuming, so it's especially important that you approach them with care. Read the question stem carefully and make sure you don't confuse a *true* answer with the *correct* one. Also note that, because the stem didn't provide highly specific research clues, the Roadmap became indispensable in allowing you to find useful information in the text quickly. Inference EXCEPT questions are much less common on the LSAT than straightforward Inference, but you should still expect to see one or two questions of this type on test day. As I've demonstrated, they're just as vulnerable to the Kaplan Method as any other.

I'll come back to the subject of challenging Inference questions later in this book. For now, it's time to put your Inference skills to the test.

DRILL: TACKLING INFERENCE QUESTIONS

Read the following passage strategically, applying Step 1 of the Kaplan Method. Then answer the three questions, applying Steps 2–5 each time. Explanations follow the Drill.

Faced with the problems of insufficient evidence, of conflicting evidence, and of evidence relayed through the flawed perceptual, retentive, and narrative abilities of witnesses, a jury is forced to
(5) draw inferences in its attempt to ascertain the truth. By applying the same cognitive tools they have developed and used over a lifetime, jurors engage in the inferential exercise that lawyers call fact-finding. In certain decision-making contexts that are
(10) relevant to the trial of lawsuits, however, these normally reliable cognitive tools may cause jurors to commit inferential errors that distort rather than reveal the truth.

Although juries can make a variety of inferential
(15) errors, most of these mistakes in judgment involve the drawing of an unwarranted conclusion from the evidence, that is, deciding that the evidence proves something that, in reality, it does not prove. For example, evidence that the defendant in a criminal
(20) prosecution has a prior conviction may encourage jurors to presume the defendant's guilt, because of their preconception that a person previously convicted of a crime must be inclined toward repeated criminal behavior. That commonly held
(25) belief is at least a partial distortion of reality; not all former convicts engage in repeated criminal behavior. Also, a jury may give more probative weight than objective analysis would allow to vivid photographic evidence depicting a shooting victim's
(30) wounds, or may underestimate the weight of defense testimony that is not delivered in a sufficiently forceful or persuasive manner. Finally, complex or voluminous evidence might be so confusing to a jury that its members would draw
(35) totally unwarranted conclusions or even ignore the evidence entirely.

Recent empirical research in cognitive psychology suggests that people tend to commit inferential errors like these under certain
(40) predictable circumstances. By examining the available information, the situation, and the type of decision being made, cognitive psychologists can describe the kinds of inferential errors a person or group is likely to make. These patterns of human
(45) decision-making may provide the courts with a guide to evaluating the effect of evidence on the reliability of the jury's inferential processes in certain situations.

The notion that juries can commit inferential
(50) errors that jeopardize the accuracy of the fact-finding process is not unknown to the courts. In fact, one of a presiding judge's duties is to minimize jury inferential error through explanation and clarification. Nonetheless, most judges now employ
(55) only a limited and primitive concept of jury inferential error: limited because it fails to recognize the potential for error outside certain traditional situations, primitive because it ignores the research and conclusions of psychologists in
(60) favor of notions about human cognition held by lawyers."[11]

1. Which one of the following best describes the author's attitude toward the majority of judges today?

   (A) apprehensive about whether they are consistent in their instruction of juries
   (B) doubtful of their ability to draw consistently correct conclusions based on the evidence
   (C) critical of their failure to take into account potentially helpful research
   (D) pessimistic about their willingness to make significant changes in trial procedure
   (E) concerned about their allowing the presentation of complex and voluminous evidence in the courtroom

---

[11]PrepTest 13, Sec 3, Passage 4

2. It can be inferred from the passage that the author would be most likely to agree with which one of the following generalizations about lawyers?

   (A) They have a less sophisticated understanding of human cognition than do psychologists.
   (B) They often present complex or voluminous information merely in order to confuse a jury.
   (C) They are no better at making logical inferences from the testimony at a trial than are most judges.
   (D) They have worked to help judges minimize jury inferential error.
   (E) They are unrealistic about the ability of jurors to ascertain the truth.

3. The author would be most likely to agree with which one of the following generalizations about a jury's decision-making process?

   (A) The more evidence that a jury has, the more likely it is that the jury will reach a reliable verdict.
   (B) Juries usually overestimate the value of visual evidence such as photographs.
   (C) Jurors have preconceptions about the behavior of defendants that prevent them from making an objective analysis of the evidence in a criminal trial.
   (D) Most of the jurors who make inferential errors during a trial do so because they are unaccustomed to having to make difficult decisions based on inferences.
   (E) The manner in which evidence is presented to a jury may influence the jury either to overestimate or to underestimate the value of that evidence.[12]

Answer Explanations follow on the next page.

Explanations

Step 1:

Juries make
inferences

They can be
mistaken

Juries draw bad
conclusions

Research:
how errors
are made

Faced with the (problems) of insufficient evidence, of conflicting evidence, and of evidence relayed through the flawed perceptual, retentive, and narrative abilities of witnesses, a jury (is forced) to
(5) draw inferences in its attempt to ascertain the truth. By applying the same cognitive tools they have developed and used over a lifetime, jurors (engage in) the inferential exercise that lawyers call fact-finding. In certain decision-making contexts that are
(10) relevant to the trial of lawsuits, (however,) these (normally) reliable cognitive tools may (cause) jurors to commit inferential errors that distort (rather than) reveal the truth.

(Although) juries can make a variety of inferential
(15) errors, most of these mistakes in judgment (involve) the drawing of an unwarranted conclusion from the evidence, (that is,) deciding that the evidence proves something that, in reality, it does not prove. For (example,) evidence that the defendant in a criminal
(20) prosecution has a prior conviction may encourage jurors to (presume) the defendant's guilt (because) of their preconception that a person previously convicted of a crime must be inclined toward repeated criminal behavior. That commonly held
(25) belief is at least a partial (distortion) of reality; not all former convicts engage in repeated criminal behavior. (Also) a jury may give more probative weight than objective analysis would allow to vivid photographic evidence depicting a shooting victim's
(30) wounds, (or) may underestimate the weight of defense testimony that is not delivered in a sufficiently forceful or persuasive manner. (Finally,) complex or voluminous evidence might be (so) (confusing) to a jury that its members would draw
(35) totally unwarranted conclusions (or even) ignore the evidence entirely.

(Recent) empirical research in cognitive psychology (suggests) that people tend to commit inferential errors like these under certain
(40) predictable circumstances. (By examining) the available information, the situation, and the type of decision being made, cognitive psychologists can (describe) the kinds of inferential errors a person or group is likely to make. These patterns of human
(45) decision-making (may provide) the courts with a guide to evaluating the effect of evidence on the reliability of the jury's inferential processes in certain situations.

The notion that juries can commit inferential
(50) errors that jeopardize the accuracy of the fact-
finding process is not unknown to the courts. (In
fact,) one of a presiding judge's duties is to minimize
jury inferential error (through) explanation and
clarification. (Nonetheless,) most judges now employ
(55) only a limited primitive concept of jury
inferential error: limited (because) it fails to
recognize the potential for error outside certain
traditional situations, primitive (because) it ignores
the research and conclusions of psychologists in
(60) (favor of) notions about human cognition held by
lawyers.[13]

Judges don't fully understand problem

Paragraph Structure: The author opens the passage by discussing the methods by which jurors reach conclusions. His true scope is signaled by the Keyword "however" in line 10; he thinks these methods are flawed and can cause jurors to distort the truth.

The second paragraph is somewhat longer, but it is mostly composed of details. The author states that "although" (line 14) juries can make many different errors, most of the time they draw unwarranted conclusions. This is immediately followed by "for example" (lines 18–19), signaling the first of many supporting ideas. The chain of evidence continues with "also" in line 27 and concludes with "finally" in line 32. Be sure to circle these important Keywords, but don't get lost in the details; they'll still be there if you need to research them later.

The third paragraph is somewhat technical, but "suggests" in line 38 points to the gist of the research. Psychologists believe that the circumstances under which people are likely to make errors are predictable. The author believes this research "may provide" (line 45) courts with a means of determining how reliable juries really are in certain situations. Again, be careful not to get bogged down in a dense paragraph like this one; read for the basic idea behind the research and move on.

The final paragraph reveals that judges are aware of the cognitive problems that jurors exhibit, but opines that they "nonetheless" (line 54) employ a "limited and primitive" understanding of them. Take heed when the author voices strong opinions; they're likely to be tested.

Topic: Fact-finding in juries

Scope: Inferential errors

Purpose: To describe the errors jurors are likely to make as well as judges' current understanding of research into such errors

Main Idea: Although cognitive science has revealed how jurors might make inferential errors, judges currently rely on a more primitive view of the problem.

---

[13]PrepTest 13, Sec 3, Passage 4

1. **(C)**

    Which one of the following best describes the
    author's attitude toward the majority of judges
    today?
    (A)   apprehensive about whether they are
          consistent in their instruction of juries
    (B)   doubtful of their ability to draw consistently
          correct conclusions based on the evidence
    (C)   critical of their failure to take into account
          potentially helpful research
    (D)   pessimistic about their willingness to make
          significant changes in trial procedure
    (E)   concerned about their allowing the
          presentation of complex and voluminous
          evidence in the courtroom[14]

Step 2: This is an Inference question—it asks for the author's attitude.

Step 3: Specifically, the question stem asks for the author's attitude about judges. Your Roadmap should lead you straight to the final paragraph, and to the opinionated language therein.
The author describes the judges' understanding of inferential error as "limited and primitive"
because it ignores recent advances in cognitive psychology.

Step 4: The correct answer must reflect disapproval of the judges' failure to understand current science.

Step 5: The match for your prediction is correct choice (C). The only other choice that comes
near the concepts described in the final paragraph is choice (A), but the author never expresses
any apprehension about judges' ability to instruct juries. The remaining choices are completely
out of scope.

2. **(A)**

    It can be inferred from the passage that the author
    would be most likely to agree with which one of the
    following generalizations about lawyers?
    (A)   They have a less sophisticated understanding
          of human cognition than do psychologists.
    (B)   They often present complex or voluminous
          information merely in order to confuse a jury.
    (C)   They are no better at making logical inferences
          from the testimony at a trial than are most
          judges.
    (D)   They have worked to help judges minimize jury
          inferential error.
    (E)   They are unrealistic about the ability of jurors
          to ascertain the truth.[15]

---

[14]PrepTest 13, Sec 3, Q 24
[15]PrepTest 13, Sec 3, Q 26

Step 2: The identifying phrase in this stem is "most likely to agree." This is an Inference question.

Step 3: You need to research the author's opinion about lawyers. Since most of this passage is concerned with the inferential errors of jurors, lawyers are only mentioned in a couple of places specifically. The only time the author offers any strong opinion language is, once again, at the end of the final paragraph. The author considers judges' understanding of inferential error to be primitive because they ignore current science in "favor of" (line 60) views held by lawyers.

Step 4: Based on this research, you can make a solid prediction. If judges are wrong to favor the views of lawyers over the views of scientists, that must mean the author considers the lawyers' views to be inferior.

Step 5: Choice (A) is correct, matching your prediction. Choice (B) is a distortion of information in the second paragraph. The author does state that information is sometimes overwhelming and confusing to a jury, but never claims that lawyers do this intentionally. The comparison made in choice (C) is irrelevant and never appears in the passage. Choices (D) and (E) are also completely out of scope.

3. **(E)**

    The author would be most likely to agree with which one of the following generalizations about a jury's decision-making process?
    (A) The more evidence that a jury has, the more likely it is that the jury will reach a reliable verdict.
    (B) Juries usually overestimate the value of visual evidence such as photographs.
    (C) Jurors have preconceptions about the behavior of defendants that prevent them from making an objective analysis of the evidence in a criminal trial.
    (D) Most of the jurors who make inferential errors during a trial do so because they are unaccustomed to having to make difficult decisions based on inferences.
    (E) The manner in which evidence is presented to a jury may influence the jury either to overestimate or to underestimate the value of that evidence.[16]

Step 2: The phrase "most likely to agree" in the stem tells you that this is an Inference question.

Step 3: Your only real clue in the stem is the reference to a jury's decision-making process. Since most of the text in the passage describes this process (and the errors in it) it may not immediately be clear where you should begin to conduct your research. It's likely that you can find the information you need somewhere in the second paragraph; recall the extensive list of examples demarcated by Keywords in lines 19 (because), 27 (also), and 32 (finally). Rather than attempting to summarize the entire paragraph, you should proceed to Step 4 and think about the big picture.

---

[16]PrepTest 13, Sec 3, Q 27

Step 4: Review your Roadmap and the author's Main Idea, recalling the author's principal ideas regarding how juries make decisions. His primary focus was on the flaws inherent in the process, and the fact that juries are likely to follow the evidence presented to false conclusions. With this general prediction in mind, move on to the choices and prepare to employ the process of elimination.

Step 5: Choice (A) is in direct conflict with lines 32–36, wherein the author says that too much evidence can actually overwhelm and confuse a jury. Choices (B) and (C) are both too extreme. Remember to keep the author's tone in mind at all times—he never claims that juries "usually" overestimate the value of photographs or that they definitely have preconceptions that prevent them from staying objective. He does say that these things *can* happen in certain circumstances, an important difference. Choice (D) is false; the author states in the first paragraph that jurors use cognitive skills that have been developed "over a lifetime" (lines 6–8). The only choice remaining is (E), the correct answer. Unlike choices (B) and (C), this one gets the author's tone just right: the way in which evidence is presented "may influence" the jury to make inferential errors.

Don't be discouraged if you found this question to be tricky; careful research will always get you to the correct answer, and the information you require is always in the passage. With practice, you'll be able to research efficiently and accurately on test day.

COMMON WRONG ANSWER TYPES

Inference questions share many common wrong answer types with Global and Detail questions. In addition, there are two types you should be especially wary of.

Distorted POV

Since LSAT passages frequently describe multiple viewpoints, sometimes the test makers will ask for one party's opinion and present an opposing opinion in the answer choices. Other times distortion of viewpoint may be more subtle.

8. Which one of the following statements about realism
    in Chinese art can most reasonably be inferred from
    the passage?

    (A)   The artists who became leaders of the Native
          Soil movement practiced a modified form of
          realism in reaction against the styles and
          techniques of Scar Art.
    (B)   Chinese art has encompassed conflicting
          conceptions of realism derived from
          contrasting political and artistic purposes.
    (C)   The goals of realism in Chinese art have been
          effectively furthered by both the Scar Art
          movement and the Native Soil movement.
    (D)   Until the development of the Scar Art
          movement, interest in rural life had been
          absent from the types of art that prevailed
          among Chinese realist painters.
    (E)   Unlike the art that was predominant during
          the Cultural Revolution, Scar Art was not a
          type of realist art.[17]

Recall that the author did say that the Scar Artists were realists, but they defined realism
differently than the state-controlled art that preceded them. Choice (E) therefore sounds more
like an opinion that the Revolutionary Realists in the first paragraph of the passage might have
endorsed. As always, be mindful of the different opinions presented in the text, and use your
Roadmap to avoid confusing one for another.

Extreme

Answer choices that take the opinions expressed in the passage too far are among the most
common wrong answers you'll encounter when tackling Inference questions.

27. The author would be most likely to agree with which
    one of the following generalizations about a jury's
    decision-making process?

    (A)   The more evidence that a jury has, the more
          likely it is that the jury will reach a reliable
          verdict.
    (B)   Juries usually overestimate the value of visual
          evidence such as photographs.
    (C)   Jurors have preconceptions about the behavior
          of defendants that prevent them from making
          an objective analysis of the evidence in a
          criminal trial.
    (D)   Most of the jurors who make inferential errors
          during a trial do so because they are
          unaccustomed to having to make difficult
          decisions based on inferences.
    (E)   The manner in which evidence is presented to
          a jury may influence the jury either to
          overestimate or to underestimate the value of
          that evidence.[18]

---

[17]PrepTest 47, Sec 2, Passage 2, Q 8
[18] PrepTest 13, Sec 3, Q 27

Be very careful to note any qualifying language you come across in the passage; if the author says that certain evidence "may encourage" a juror to reach a certain conclusion, don't mistake this for the claim that the jurors will *usually* be compelled by that evidence. The test makers reward those who pay attention to these vitally important distinctions, so be on the lookout for them in your practice.

Inference questions are among the most common to appear on the LSAT, and they can sometimes be among the most nuanced. As always, practice and adherence to the Kaplan Method are the keys to scoring these points. In the next two chapters, I'll walk you through the final two Reading Comprehension question types.

CHAPTER 13

LOGIC QUESTIONS: REASONING

ALL ABOUT LOGIC: REASONING QUESTIONS

The final two question types left to examine—Logical Reasoning and Logic Function—are two variations of the same general category, called Logic questions. I'll begin by introducing you to questions of Logical Reasoning (which I'll hereafter refer to as "Reasoning questions").

What Are Reasoning Questions?

While the focus of this book has been exclusively on the Reading Comprehension section of the LSAT, you are no doubt also preparing for the Logical Reasoning section of the test as well. Reasoning questions in Reading Comprehension simply mimic similar questions in the Logical Reasoning section of the test. Fortunately, there are only a small number of commonly occurring Reasoning questions, and the strategies you'll use to tackle each of them are similar. Before moving on, I'll describe each of these common types in a little more detail.

Strengthen/Weaken

One common Reasoning question is called Strengthen/Weaken. As the name suggests, these questions ask you to examine an argument made in the passage and select the answer choice that either strengthens or weakens it. It's important to remember that on the LSAT, you don't have to *prove* an argument in order to strengthen it, and you don't have to *disprove* it to weaken it. Strengthening and weakening simply means to make an argument more or less likely to be true.

Principle

A second common reasoning question is the Principle question. Principle questions usually ask you to identify a general principle, policy or guiding rule that governs the thinking in the passage. Here's an example:

> Most of what has been written about Thurgood Marshall, a former United States Supreme Court justice who served from 1967 to 1991, has just focused on his judicial record and on the ideological content of his
> (5) earlier achievements as a lawyer pursuing civil rights issues in the courts. But when Marshall's career is viewed from a technical perspective, his work with the NAACP (National Association for the Advancement of Colored People) reveals a strategic and methodological
> (10) legacy to the field of public interest law.[1]

In the excerpt above, a specific claim is being made about the body of scholarship on Thurgood Marshall. In LSAT terms, a principle is a more general rule that can be drawn from such a claim. In this case, you might say that a principle that guides the author's thinking is that "some scholarship on Supreme Court justices excludes important aspects of their work." Note that this principle doesn't stray far from what the text already says, but merely expands the scope of the claim from Thurgood Marshall in particular to justices in general. I'll come back to this concept a little later, but for now just think of a principle as a general rule that can be extrapolated from specific examples.

Parallel Reasoning

A third reasoning question you might encounter is called Parallel Reasoning, a question that cites a situation or example in the passage and asks you to identify an analogous example in the answer choices. Parallel Reasoning questions are slightly more rare than Strengthen/Weaken and Principle questions, but they are susceptible to the same strategies.

If you already have some experience with these types of questions from your work with the Logical Reasoning section of the LSAT, that's great. If not, don't worry—the Kaplan Method provides a solution in each case, and you'll soon become as familiar with this question type as with all the others.

How Do You Identify Reasoning Questions?

There are a variety of Reasoning question types, so it's important that you learn to differentiate them. As with all other question types, the question stem will always contain the clues you need.

---

[1]PrepTest 42, Sec 3, Passage 1

3. Which one of the following pairs of tactics used by an environmental-advocacy public interest law firm is most closely analogous to the strategies that Marshall utilized during his work with the NAACP?[2]

13. Which one of the following principles most likely underlies the author's characterization of literary interpretation?[3]

20. Which one of the following, if true, would most weaken Papi's theory regarding homing pigeons' homing ability?[4]

All of the above are Reasoning questions, but each is a different type. In the first example, the key phrase "analogous to" identifies the question as Parallel Reasoning. In the second, you are asked to find an underlying principle in the author's argument, making this a Principle question. The third question requires you to weaken an argument. These examples are typical of Reasoning questions in general; their identifying language is usually easy to spot. As always, I'll summarize in terms of Step 2 of the Kaplan Method:

Step 2: Identify the Question Type

When the question stem asks you to perform a task similar to one in the Logical Reasoning section, such as strengthening an argument or identifying a principle, you know you are working with a Reasoning question.

Reasoning Question Strategy

The strategies you should employ when working with Reasoning questions vary from type to type, but they all fit within the structure of the Kaplan Method.

Step 3: Research the Relevant Text

As always, you'll find clues in the question stem that will guide you to the relevant portion of the text. Reasoning questions tend to focus on a single specific argument or example from the passage, such as a hypothesis. They may provide you with line references, but if not, your Roadmap will help you locate the required information.

Step 4: Make a Prediction

Reasoning questions are almost always amenable to prediction. Your prediction will sometimes have to be a relatively general one (as you'll see in Parallel Reasoning questions) but even a broad prediction will help you accurately locate the correct answer.

---

[2]PrepTest 42, Sec 3, Q 3
[3]PrepTest 39, Sec 3, Q 13
[4]PrepTest 27, Sec 3, Q 20

Step 5: Evaluate the Answer Choices

Locate a match for your prediction. In rare cases you may need to proceed by elimination, but overall a strong prediction is the best approach.

Reasoning Question Practice

Now for some examples. Read the following passage, noting the circled Keywords in the provided Roadmap. Determine the Topic, Scope, Purpose, and Main Idea of the passage before moving on to the questions.

Step 1:

Trad. communities decline

(Traditionally,) members of a community such as a town or neighborhood share a common location and a sense of (necessary) interdependence that includes, for (example,) mutual respect and emotional support. (But) as
(5) modern societies grow more technological and sometimes more alienating, people (tend) to spend less time in the kinds of interactions that their communities, require in order to thrive. (Meanwhile) technology has made it possible for individuals to interact via personal
(10) computer with others who are geographically distant.

comp. conf. become communities

(Advocates claim) that these computer conferences, in which large numbers of participants communicate by typing comments that are immediately read by other participants and responding immediately to those
(15) comments they read, (function) as communities that can substitute for traditional interactions with neighbors.

Char. of comp conf. communities

What are the characteristics that advocates claim allow computer conferences to function as communities? (For one) participants often share
(20) common interests or concerns; conferences are frequently organized around specific topics such as music or parenting. (Second,) because these conferences are conversations, participants have adopted certain conventions in recognition of the importance of
(25) respecting each others' sensibilities. Abbreviations are used to convey commonly expressed sentiments of

Conventions show respect

courtesy (such as) "pardon me for cutting in" ("pmfci") or "in my humble opinion" ("imho"). (Because) a humorous tone can be difficult to communicate in
(30) writing, participants will often end an intentionally humorous comment with a set of characters that, when looked at sideways, resembles a smiling or winking face. Typing messages entirely in capital letters is avoided, (because) its tendency to demand the attention
(35) of a reader's eye is considered the computer equivalent of shouting. These conventions, (advocates claim,)

Form genuine relationships

constitute a form of etiquette, and with this etiquette as a foundation, people often form genuine, trusting relationships, even offering advice and support during
(40) personal crises (such as) illness or the loss of a loved one.

(But while) it is true that conferences can be both respectful and supportive, they (nonetheless) fall short of communities. (For example,) conferences discriminate
(45) along educational and economic lines (because) participation requires a basic knowledge of computers and the ability to afford access to conferences. (Further,) while advocates claim that a shared interest makes computer conferences similar to traditional
(50) communities—insofar as the shared interest is analogous to a traditional community's shared location—this analogy simply does not work. Conference participants are a (self-selecting) group; they are drawn together by their shared interest in the topic
(55) of the conference. (Actual) communities, (on the other) hand, are "nonintentional": the people who inhabit towns or neighborhoods are thus more likely to exhibit genuine diversity—of age, career, or personal interests—(than) are conference participants. It might be
(60) easier to find common ground in a computer conference than in today's communities, (but) in so doing it would be (unfortunate) if conference participants cut themselves off further from valuable interactions in their own towns or neighborhoods.[5]

Auth: Comp. conf. not community

Actual communities nonintentional

[5]PrepTest 36, Sec 2, Passage 1

Paragraph Structure: This passage follows a fairly straightforward progression as indicated by its abundant keywords. In the opening paragraph, the author describes what "traditionally" (line 1) defines a community, specifically an interdependent group of individuals in a single location. "But" (line 4) modernization has weakened the traditional community. "Meanwhile" (line 8) technology has led to the development of computer conferences, which "advocates claim" (line 11) can function as substitute communities.

The second paragraph begins with a rhetorical question: "What are the characteristics that allow computer conferences to function as communities?" The answers are indicated by Keywords of sequence. "For one" (line 19) conferences tend to center around common interests. "Second" (line 22) the members demonstrate respect for one another through conventions of communication. The "advocates claim" (line 36) that such conventions form the basis of genuinely caring relationships.

"But" (line 42) in spite of these claims, the author declares, computer conferences aren't actually communities. "For example" (line 44) they cater only to certain groups of individuals, and "further" (line 47) their members self-select on the basis of shared interests, unlike "actual communities" (line 55) which are comprised of more diverse groups of individuals. Because of this, the author would consider it "unfortunate" (line 62) if participants in computer conferences neglect their own neighborhoods.

Topic: The characteristics of communities

Scope: Computer conferences as substitute communities

Purpose: To argue against the advocates' claim that computer conferences can function as surrogate communites

Main Idea: Computer conferences aren't truly communities because they are self-selecting and therefore lack the diversity of traditional communities.

Now apply the Kaplan Method to the following question:

6. Which one of the following, if true, would most weaken one of the author's arguments in the last paragraph?

(A) Participants in computer conferences are generally more accepting of diversity than is the population at large.

(B) Computer technology is rapidly becoming more affordable and accessible to people from a variety of backgrounds.

(C) Participants in computer conferences often apply the same degree of respect and support they receive from one another to interactions in their own actual communities.

(D) Participants in computer conferences often feel more comfortable interacting on the computer because they are free to interact without revealing their identities.

(E) The conventions used to facilitate communication in computer conferences are generally more successful than those used in actual communities.[6]

Step 2: The Reasoning question language is fairly clear: you're being asked to weaken an argument made by the author.

Step 3: The question stem specifically guides you to arguments presented by the author in the final paragraph. Keywords highlight the author's primary claims, all of which describe reasons why computer conferences shouldn't be considered true communities. "For example" in line 44 introduces the idea that conferences discriminate against those who lack the money or education to use a home computer, and "further" in line 47 leads to the author's complaint about their self-selecting nature.

Step 4: The correct answer will provide data that runs contrary to one or both of these arguments. A highly specific prediction might be difficult to make, but that doesn't mean you should read the choices idly. Actively search for the answer suggesting that computer conferences aren't discriminatory, or that they don't self-select.

Step 5: The match for your prediction is choice (B). If computers are becoming more available to those who traditionally can't afford them, the author's claim of discrimination is weakened considerably. Choice (A) contains a distortion: the author's argument wasn't that computer conferences fail to accept diversity, but that they lack diversity. Choices (C), (D), and (E) fail to address either of the author's arguments, and are therefore out of Scope.

Sometimes Logic Reasoning questions combine elements of more than one common question type. Here's an example from the same passage:

---

[6]PrepTest 36, Sec 2, Passage 1, Q 6

4. Given the information in the passage, the author can most reasonably be said to use which one of the following principles to refute the advocates' claim that computer conferences can function as communities (line 15)?

(A) A group is a community only if its members are mutually respectful and supportive of one another.

(B) A group is a community only if its members adopt conventions intended to help them respect each other's sensibilities.

(C) A group is a community only if its members inhabit the same geographic location.

(D) A group is a community only if its members come from the same educational or economic background.

(E) A group is a community only if its members feel a sense of interdependence despite different economic and educational backgrounds.[7]

Step 2: This question stem is somewhat more complex. You are being asked to identify a principle that refutes the claim that computer conferences can be considered communities. This is a Reasoning question of Principle, but it also requires you to weaken an argument.

Step 3: The stem provides a specific line reference, so begin your research there. The claim referenced actually begins at line 11, and describes the position of the advocates: computer conferences are communities. This doesn't provide any useful new information, so use your Roadmap to determine where the author's primary arguments against this claim are located. This should take you right back to the third paragraph and the objections of discrimination and self-selection that the author raises there.

Step 4: Recall the definition of a Principle on the LSAT. You need to determine a general rule that the author follows in declaring that computer conferences aren't communities. The author describes such a rule when he defines "actual communities" (line 55) as groups of individuals who are interdependent despite the fact that they're grouped together by chance rather than intention. The correct answer should describe this relationship.

Step 5: The correct answer, choice (E), encapsulates the author's argument against the advocates perfectly. You might have been drawn to choice (C), but the author never claims that geographic closeness is in and of itself a requirement for community, but rather the diversity that tends to spring from such closeness. Choices (A) and (B) both describe characteristics that computer conferences display, and therefore strengthen the advocates' claim. Choice (D) states the complete opposite of what the author claims: a group whose members come from similar backgrounds are likely *not* to be a community.

---

[7]PrepTest 36, Sec 2, Passage 1, Q 4

Notice that while questions 4 and 6 both required you to weaken an argument, they asked you to weaken different, opposing arguments—the author's in one case, the advocates' in the other. This should remind you just how important it is to execute Step 2 of the Kaplan Method with care. Be sure you understand whose point of view the question is asking for!

Before moving on, I'll present one more example. First read the following passage excerpt, noting the sample Roadmap provided:

The blues =
not just sadness

The term "blues" is conventionally used to refer to a state of sadness or melancholy, but to conclude from this that the musical genre of the same name is merely an expression of unrelieved sorrow is to miss its deeper
(5) meaning. Despite its frequent focus on such themes as suffering and self-pity, and despite the censure that it has sometimes received from church communities, the blues, understood more fully, actually has much in

Blues similar
to spirituals

common with the traditional religious music known as
(10) spirituals. Each genre, in its own way, aims to bring about what could be called a spiritual transformation: spirituals produce a religious experience and the blues elicits an analogous response. In fact the blues has even been characterized as a form of "secular spiritual." The
(15) implication of this apparently contradictory terminology is clear: the blues shares an essential

Blues + spirituals
from same
experience

aspect of spirituals. Indeed the blues and spirituals may well arise from a common reservoir of experience, tapping into an aesthetic that underlies many aspects of
(20) African American culture.

Afr. Amer.
folk traditions

Critics have noted that African American folk tradition, in its earliest manifestations, does not sharply differentiate reality into sacred and secular strains or into irreconcilable dichotomies between good and evil,
(25) misery and joy. This is consistent with the apparently dual aspect of the blues and spirituals. Spirituals, like the blues, often express longing or sorrow, but these

Similar to
blues + spirituals

plaintive tones are indicative of neither genre's full scope: both aim at transforming their participants'
(30) spirits to elation and exaltation. In this regard, both musical forms may be linked to traditional African American culture in North America and to its ancestral cultures in West Africa, in whose traditional religions worshippers play an active role in invoking the

Rooted in
W. Afr.
religion

(35) divine—in creating the psychological conditions that are conducive to religious experience. These conditions are often referred to as "ecstasy," which is to be understood here with its etymological connotation of standing out from oneself, or rather from one's
(40) background psychological state and from one's centered concept of self.[8]

---

[8]PrepTest 34, Sec 1, Passage 2

Now take a look at this question:

12. Which one of the following is most closely analogous to the author's account of the connections among the blues, spirituals, and certain West African religious practices?

   (A) Two species of cacti, which are largely dissimilar, have very similar flowers; this has been proven to be due to the one's evolution from a third species, whose flowers are nonetheless quite different from theirs.

   (B) Two species of ferns, which are closely similar in most respects, have a subtly different arrangement of stem structures; nevertheless, they may well be related to a third, older species, which has yet a different arrangement of stem structures.

   (C) Two types of trees, which botanists have long believed to be unrelated, should be reclassified in light of the essential similarities of their flower structures and their recently discovered relationship to another species, from which they both evolved.

   (D) Two species of grass, which may have some subtle similarities, are both very similar to a third species, and thus it can be inferred that the third species evolved from one of the two species.

   (E) Two species of shrubs, which seem superficially unalike, have a significantly similar leaf structure; this may be due to their relation to a third, older species, which is similar to both of them.[9]

Step 2: The stem asks for something that is analogous to the relationships among the blues, spirituals, and certain religious practices. Since you must describe a new situation that follows the same pattern as one described in the text, this is a Parallel Reasoning question.

Step 3: The scope of this question is quite wide, since the connections referenced in the stem are described throughout two paragraphs. For this reason, the Roadmap will be indispensable in helping you make a prediction quickly. Review it carefully. The first paragraph describes an essential similarity between spirituals and the blues. The second paragraph suggests that both art forms can be linked to West African religious practices, with which they share some characteristics.

Step 4: Remember that the answer choices in Parallel Reasoning questions can encompass virtually any subject matter, and may therefore appear unrelated to the question at hand. It's therefore especially important that you approach them with a strong prediction. Stay focused on a general description of the passage content. Two types of music were described as similar

---

[9]PrepTest 34, Sec 1, Passage 2, Q 12

to one another, and then both were shown to be similar to a third, related set of practices. Keep this pattern in mind as you examine the answer choices.

Step 5: Examine each choice and compare it to your prediction. Choice (A) describes two species that are largely dissimilar. That's the opposite of what you predicted. Choice (B) also focuses on differences among different items, so eliminate it as well. Choice (C) is a little trickier, but is goes wrong in suggesting that two types of trees should be reclassified. No such reclassification is part of your prediction. Choice (D) distorts the relationship described in your prediction, as the similarities between music and religious practices weren't used to infer that one evolved from the other. That only leaves correct choice (E), which matches your prediction note for note. It describes two things that are alike in specific way, and then traces their connection to a predecessor.

I want to stress again just how vitally important a strong prediction is to answering a question like this one correctly and efficiently. The similarities in the answer choices can easily lead to error and frustration. Before you begin to work with them, determine what you're looking for and be prepared to stick with it. Parallel Reasoning questions are traditionally among the toughest the LSAT will throw at you, so you must approach them methodically and with confidence.

Now that you've seen a few of the most common types of Logic Reasoning questions, it's time for some practice.

DRILL: ANSWERING REASONING QUESTIONS

Read the following passage strategically, applying Step 1 of the Kaplan Method. Then answer the two questions, applying Steps 2–5 each time. Explanations follow the Drill.

In a recent court case, a copy-shop owner was accused of violating copyright law when, in the preparation of "course packs"—materials photocopied from books and journals and packaged as readings for
(5) particular university courses—he copied materials without obtaining permission from or paying sufficient fees to the publishers. As the owner of five small copy shops serving several educational institutions in the area, he argued, as have others in the photocopy
(10) business, that the current process for obtaining permissions is time-consuming, cumbersome, and expensive. He also maintained that course packs, which are ubiquitous in higher education, allow professors to assign important readings in books and journals too
(15) costly for students to be expected to purchase individually. While the use of copyrighted material for teaching purposes is typically protected by certain provisions of copyright law, this case was unique in that the copying of course packs was done by a copy
(20) shop and at a profit.
Copyright law outlines several factors involved in determining whether the use of copyrighted material is protected, including: whether it is for commercial or nonprofit purposes; the nature of the copyrighted work;
(25) the length and importance of the excerpt used in relation to the entire work; and the effect of its use on the work's potential market value. In bringing suit, the publishers held that other copy-shop owners would cease paying permission fees, causing the potential
(30) value of the copyrighted works of scholarship to diminish. Nonetheless, the court decided that this reasoning did not demonstrate that course packs would have a sufficiently adverse effect on the current or potential market of the copyrighted works or on the
(35) value of the copyrighted works themselves. The court instead ruled that since the copies were for educational purposes, the fact that the copy-shop owner had profited from making the course packs did not prevent him from receiving protection under the law.
(40) According to the court, the owner had not exploited copyrighted material because his fee was not based on the content of the works he copied; he charged by the page, regardless of whether the content was copyrighted.
(45) In the court's view, the business of producing and selling course packs is more properly seen as the exploitation of professional copying technologies and a result of the inability of academic parties to reproduce printed materials efficiently, not the exploitation of
(50) these copyrighted materials themselves. The court held that copyright laws do not prohibit professors and students, who may make copies for themselves, from using the photo reproduction services of a third party in order to obtain those same copies at lesser cost.

1. Which one of the following describes a role most similar to that of professors in the passage who use copy shops to produce course packs?

(A) An artisan generates a legible copy of an old headstone engraving by using charcoal on newsprint and frames and sells high-quality photocopies of it at a crafts market.
(B) A choir director tapes a selection of another well-known choir's best pieces and sends it to a recording studio to be reproduced in a sellable package for use by members of her choir.
(C) A grocer makes several kinds of sandwiches that sell for less than similar sandwiches from a nearby upscale café.
(D) A professional graphic artist prints reproductions of several well-known paintings at an exhibit to sell at the museum's gift shop.
(E) A souvenir store in the center of a city sells miniature bronze renditions of a famous bronze sculpture that the city is noted for displaying.

2. Which one of the following, if true, would have most strengthened the publishers' position in this case?

    (A) Course packs for courses that usually have large enrollments had produced a larger profit for the copy-shop owner.

    (B) The copy-shop owner had actively solicited professors' orders for course packs.

    (C) The revenue generated by the copy shop's sale of course packs had risen significantly within the past few years.

    (D) Many area bookstores had reported a marked decrease in the sales of books used for producing course packs.

    (E) The publishers had enlisted the support of the authors to verify their claims that the copy-shop owner had not obtained permission.[10]

---

[10]PrepTest 41, Sec 4, Qs 5–6

Explanations

Step 1:

Suit over
course packs

In a (recent) court case, a copy-shop owner was (accused) of violating copyright law (when,) in the preparation of "course packs"—materials photocopied from books and journals and packaged as readings for

(5) particular university courses—he copied materials (without) obtaining permission from (or) paying sufficient fees to the publishers. As the owner of five small copy shops serving several educational institutions in the area, (he argued,) as have others in the photocopy

(10) business, that the (current process) for obtaining permissions is time-consuming, cumbersome, and expensive. He (also) maintained that course packs, which are ubiquitous in higher education, (allow) professors to assign important readings in books and journals too

(15) costly for students to be expected to purchase individually. (While) the use of copyrighted material for teaching purposes is (typically) protected by certain provisions of copyright law, this case was (unique) in that the copying of course packs was done by a copy

(20) shop and at a profit.

Unique:
profit

Copyright law outlines (several factors) involved in determining whether the use of copyrighted material is protected, (including) whether it is for commercial or nonprofit purposes; the nature of the copyrighted work;

(25) the length and importance of the excerpt used in relation to the entire work; and the effect of its use on the work's potential market value. In bringing suit, the publishers (held) that other copy-shop owners would cease paying permission fees, (causing) the potential

Court: copies
didn't hurt
copyright

(30) value of the copyrighted works of scholarship to diminish. (Nonetheless,) the court decided that this reasoning (did not demonstrate) that course packs would have a sufficiently adverse effect on the current or potential market of the copyrighted works (or) on the

(35) value of the copyrighted works themselves. The court (instead) ruled that since the copies were for educational purposes, (the fact) that the copy-shop owner had profited from making the course packs did not prevent him from receiving protection under the law.

(40) (According to) the court, the owner had not exploited copyrighted material (because) his fee was not based on the content of the works he copied; he charged by the page, (regardless) of whether the content was copyrighted.

Court:

packs not

exploitative

(45)   In the court's view, the business of producing and
selling course packs is more properly seen as the
exploitation of professional copying technologies and a
result of the inability of academic parties to reproduce
printed materials efficiently, not the exploitation of

(50)   these copyrighted materials themselves. The court held
that copyright laws do not prohibit professors and
students, who may make copies for themselves, from
using the photoreproduction services of a third party in
order to obtain those same copies at lesser cost.[11]

Paragraph Structure: The opening paragraph introduces a court case. A copy-shop owner was accused of copyright violations by reproducing course packs for students. The author spends most of this paragraph describing the owner's arguments, but the contrast word "while" in line 16 points to what made this particular case noteworthy (or "unique" as the author puts it in line 18): There was profit involved.

The second paragraph moves on to the arguments made by the copyright holders, who "held" (line 28) that the shop owner was setting a bad precedent. "Nonetheless" (line 31), the court ruled that the owner was not in violation of copyright since the course packs were for educational purposes and were priced without reference to content.

"In the court's view" (line 45), the reproduction of course packs is not exploitative of copyright holders.

Topic: Copyright law

Scope: A case involving course packs

Purpose: To explain the reasoning behind the verdict in a specific court case

Main Idea: The court ruled that, since the copy-shop owner didn't charge for content, he didn't violate copyright laws in reproducing course packs.

---

[11]PrepTest 41, Sec 4, Passage 1

1. **(B)**

Which one of the following describes a role most
similar to that of professors in the passage who use
copy shops to produce course packs?

(A) An artisan generates a legible copy of an old
headstone engraving by using charcoal on
newsprint and frames and sells high-quality
photocopies of it at a crafts market.

(B) A choir director tapes a selection of another
well-known choir's best pieces and sends it to
a recording studio to be reproduced in a
sellable package for use by members of her
choir.

(C) A grocer makes several kinds of sandwiches
that sell for less than similar sandwiches from
a nearby upscale café.

(D) A professional graphic artist prints
reproductions of several well-known
paintings at an exhibit to sell at the museum's
gift shop.

(E) A souvenir store in the center of a city sells
miniature bronze renditions of a famous
bronze sculpture that the city is noted for
displaying.[12]

Step 2: The phrase "a role most similar" is your main clue here. When the stem asks you to
find a situation that is analogous to one mentioned in the passage, you know it's a Parallel
Reasoning question.

Step 3: The description of professors formed part of the copy-shop owner's defense, which
was given in the first paragraph. Course packs "allow" (line 13) professors to provide students
with vital reading that they wouldn't otherwise be able to afford.

Step 4: A specific prediction would be impossible to make in this case; the analogous situation could be almost anything. Instead, you should take the specific situation described in
the passage and think about it in general terms (much like with questions of principle): The
professors hired a vendor to make copies of protected material for the purposes of education.
The correct answer will follow this same general structure, regardless of subject matter.

Step 5: Choice (A) goes wrong in several directions, as the artisan is both making copies himself
and then turning his own profit. Choice (B), however, is spot-on. The choir director, like the
professors, hires a vendor to provide copies for educational purposes. It matches the structure
of the prediction and is the correct answer. Choice (C) has nothing to do with reproduction,
choice (D) focuses incorrectly on profit, and choice (E) doesn't necessarily have anything to
do with copyrighted material. Remember that, while a *specific* prediction is hard to make on

---

[12]PrepTest 41, Sec 4, Q 5

a Parallel Reasoning question, a general prediction based on structure makes a question like this very manageable.

2. **(D)**

Which one of the following, if true, would have most strengthened the publishers' position in this case?

   (A)   Course packs for courses that usually have large enrollments had produced a larger profit for the copy-shop owner.

   (B)   The copy-shop owner had actively solicited professors' orders for course packs.

   (C)   The revenue generated by the copy shop's sale of course packs had risen significantly within the past few years.

   (D)   Many area bookstores had reported a marked decrease in the sales of books used for producing course packs.

   (E)   The publishers had enlisted the support of the authors to verify their claims that the copy-shop owner had not obtained permission.[13]

Step 2: This Reasoning question asks you to strengthen an argument.

Step 3: The publishers' side of the story was located in the second paragraph. In lines 27–31, the publishers "held" that the copy-shop owner's sale of course packs diminished the value of their intellectual property, a claim that the court says they "did not demonstrate" (line 32).

Step 4: If the publishers failed to demonstrate a loss of value, then new evidence showing that the creation of course packs *does* diminish the worth of the publishers' property would strengthen their claim. The correct answer should reflect this loss of value.

Step 5: Correct choice (D) describes just the sort of scenario predicted. A decrease in sales of books certainly represents a loss of value. Choice (A) introduces the irrelevant idea of large enrollments, and choice (B) has nothing to do with the value of the published material. Choices (C) and (E) similarly fall totally out of scope; they have nothing to do with the claim of purported loss of value, and hence cannot strengthen the publishers' argument.

COMMON WRONG ANSWER TYPES

Hopefully you noticed two wrong answer traps in particular that are common to all kinds of reasoning questions:

Out of Scope

This type of wrong answer should be very familiar to you by now.

---

[13]PrepTest 41, Sec 4, Q 6

6. Which one of the following, if true, would most weaken one of the author's arguments in the last paragraph?

    (A) Participants in computer conferences are generally more accepting of diversity than is the population at large.

    (B) Computer technology is rapidly becoming more affordable and accessible to people from a variety of backgrounds.

    (C) Participants in computer conferences often apply the same degree of respect and support they receive from one another to interactions in their own actual communities.

    (D) Participants in computer conferences often feel more comfortable interacting on the computer because they are free to interact without revealing their identities.

    (E) The conventions used to facilitate communication in computer conferences are generally more successful than those used in actual communities.[14]

Recall that this question asked you to argue against the author's claim that computer conferences shouldn't be considered true communities because they are self-selecting. The ideas referenced in choices (D) and (E) have nothing to do with this argument and therefore fall outside the Scope of the question. If you stay in the habit of making strong predictions you'll have little trouble avoiding answers like these.

180

Prediction is equally vital in avoiding answer choices that reflect the opposite of the correct answer.

4. Given the information in the passage, the author can most reasonably be said to use which one of the following principles to refute the advocates' claim that computer conferences can function as communities (line 15)?

    (A) A group is a community only if its members are mutually respectful and supportive of one another.

    (B) A group is a community only if its members adopt conventions intended to help them respect each other's sensibilities.

    (C) A group is a community only if its members inhabit the same geographic location.

    (D) A group is a community only if its members come from the same educational or economic background.

    (E) A group is a community only if its members feel a sense of interdependence despite different economic and educational backgrounds.[15]

---

[14]PrepTest 36, Sec 2, Passage 1, Q 6

[15]PrepTest 36, Sec 2, Passage 1, Q 4

In this case, choice (D) reverses the author's claim that groups of individuals that gather on the basis of a shared background are not likely to be a true community. This type of wrong answer trap is most dangerous to the test taker who becomes careless and reads the choices too quickly. Stay methodical on test day and keep focused on your prediction to avoid 180s.

There are a few rarer variations on Reasoning questions that I'll address in chapter 16. For now, it's time to move on to the final common Reading Comprehension question type: Logic Function.

CHAPTER 14

LOGIC QUESTIONS: FUNCTION

ALL ABOUT LOGIC: FUNCTION QUESTIONS

Now that you've learned about Reasoning questions, it's time to turn to the final Reading Comprehension question type: Function questions. Function questions are less varied than Reasoning questions, and they all provide you with the same essential task in slightly differing formats. Since they've been appearing with increased frequency on more recent tests, it's imperative that you become comfortable with them in order to maximize your LSAT score.

What Are Function Questions?

In general, Function questions ask about structure. Specifically, they ask why the author used a specific word, phrase, or example. The typical Function question will point you directly to a relevant portion of the text, often with an accompanying line number, and ask you to explain what the author's purpose was in presenting the example cited.

Students are sometimes initially confused about the difference between Detail questions and Function questions, since both make reference to specific details in the passage and may use similar language. The difference is simple. Detail questions ask you to simply identify the example and paraphrase it. Function questions ask *why* the example was there to begin with.

For this reason, Function questions demand a thorough understanding of overall passage structure, and reward you for respecting the importance of context in a passage. I'll explain this concept in greater detail a little later on, but for the moment, it's important that you know how to spot a function question so that you can apply the appropriate strategy.

How Do You Identify Function Questions?

You can identify the most common function questions by one of two key phrases: "in order to" and "for which of the following reasons." Examine a few sample Function question stems:

12. In the passage, the author uses the example of the
    word "vehicle" to[1]

2. The author refers to the "patinas and aromas of a country
   kitchen" (line 32) most probably in order to[2]

17. The primary function of the third paragraph is to[3]

17. As used in the passage, the word "democratizing"
    (line 9) most nearly means equalizing which one of the
    following?[4]

The first stem asks you to identify why the author chose to use a particular example. The second stem is very similar, asking for the author's purpose in mentioning the quoted phrase. The third stem asks you to identify the purpose of an entire paragraph in the context of the passage as a whole, while the fourth asks for the approximate meaning of a specific word as used by the author. I'll refer to this final type of Function question as a Vocab-in-Context question.

Though the examples may seem varied at first, notice that they all center around the question *why*. Why did the author mention the example, or write a particular paragraph, or choose a particular word or phrase? To summarize in terms of Step 2 of the Kaplan Method:

Step 2: Identify the Question Type
When the stem asks you to identify the reason why a particular word, phrase, or example was used in the passage, you know you are working with a Function question.

Function Question Strategy

The proper strategy for dealing with Function questions always comes down to understanding context, either of a specific part of the passage or the passage as a whole. I'll show you what I mean. Read the following question stem and think about how you might answer it:

---

[1]PrepTest 17, Sec 4, Q 12
[2]PrepTest 19, Sec 3, Q 2
[3]PrepTest 25, Sec 1, Q 17
[4]PrepTest 42, Sec 3, Q 17

15.   The author most likely states that "cultural borrowing is, of course, old news" (lines 47–48) primarily to[5]

How would you determine why the author made this statement? You might start by going back to the line references, but what do you expect to see there? Probably the text that's already been quoted in the stem. That isn't likely to be very helpful. Without understanding how the phrase fits contextually into the author's larger argument, there's no way to determine why it's there.

Instead we should approach this question the Kaplan way. You've seen this passage before, but re-read it carefully, thinking about its Topic, Scope, Purpose, and Main Idea.

Soc: gatherings mean tribal decline

(Even) in the midst of its (resurgence) as a vital tradition, many (sociologists) have viewed the current form of the powwow, a ceremonial gathering of native Americans, (as a sign) that tribal culture is in decline.
(5)   (Focusing) on the dances and rituals that have (recently) come to be shared by most tribes, they (suggest) that an intertribal movement is now in ascension and (claim) the (inevitable) outcome of this tendency is the eventual dissolution of tribes (and) the complete assimilation of
(10)   native Americans into Euroamerican society.

Pan-Indian theory, evidence

(Proponents) of this "Pan-Indian" theory (point to) the greater frequency of travel and communication between reservations, the greater urbanization of native Americans, (and,) most (recently,) their increasing
(15)   politicization in (response) to common grievances as the chief causes of the shift toward intertribalism.

Intertribalism on rise

(Indeed) the rapid diffusion of dance styles, outfits, and songs from one reservation to another offers (compelling evidence) that intertribalism has been

Unique traditions rising too

(20)   increasing. (However,) these (sociologists) have (failed) to note the concurrent revitalization of many traditions unique to individual tribes. (Among) the Lakota, for (instance,) the Sun Dance was revived, after a forty-year hiatus, during the 1950's. (Similarly,) the Black Legging
(25)   Society of the Kiowa and the Hethuska Society of the Ponca—(both) traditional groups within their respective tribes—have gained (new popularity.) (Obviously,) a more

P.I.T doesn't explain

complex societal shift is taking place(than) the theory of Pan-Indianism can account for.

(30)   An (examination) of the theory's underpinnings may

Auth: must examine theory

be (critical) at this point, (especially) given that native Americans themselves (chafe most) against the Pan-Indian classification. (Like) other assimilationist theories with which it is associated, the Pan-Indian view is
(35)   (predicated upon) an a priori assumption about the nature or cultural contact: that (upon) contact minority

Theory based on wrong assump.

societies (immediately) begin to succumb in every respect—biologically, linguistically, and culturally—to the majority society. (However,) there is (no evidence)
(40)   that this is happening to native American groups.

---

[5]PrepTest 25, Sec 1, Q 15

Intertribal act.
still important

(45)

Tribal and
intertribal
distinct

(50)

Auth: Both
are important

(55)

Yet the fact remains that intertribal activities are a major facet of native American culture today. Certain dances at powwows, for instance, are announced as intertribal, others as traditional. Likewise, speeches given at the beginnings of powwows are often delivered in English, while the prayer that follows is usually spoken in a native language. Cultural borrowing is, of course, old news. What is important to note is the conscious distinction native Americans make between tribal and intertribal tendencies.

Tribalism, although greatly altered by modern history, remains a potent force among native Americans: It forms a basis for tribal identity, and aligns music and dance with other social and cultural activities important to individual tribes. Intertribal activities, on the other hand, reinforce native American identity along a broader front, where this identity is directly threatened by outside influences.[6]

Topic: Native American culture

Scope: The effects of intertribalism

Purpose: To argue against the proponents of the Pan-Indian theory

Main Idea: Despite the claims of proponents of the Pan-Indian theory, intertribalism indicates a strengthening of tribal life rather than a decline.

15. The author most likely states that "cultural borrowing is, of course, old news" (lines 47–48) primarily to[7]

Step 2: Identify the Question Type

The author mentioned a specific idea "primarily to" do what? The stem asks why the specified text was mentioned, and is therefore a Function question.

Step 3: Research the Relevant Text

It's time to read for context. Instead of going directly to the text quoted in the stem, examine the Roadmap and recall the purpose of the paragraph as a whole. The author is demonstrating the distinctiveness of tribal and intertribal activities. Now scan the text surrounding lines 47–48, looking for helpful Keywords. Line 48 says that what "is important" is that Native Americans view different activities in different ways.

Step 4: Make a Prediction

Now to put it all together. If the author's goal in the latter half of this paragraph is to emphasize the distinction Native Americans make between certain activities, why did he mention that

---

[6]PrepTest 25, Sec 1, Passage 3
[7]PrepTest 25, Sec 1, Q 15

cultural borrowing is "old news?" The Keywords indicate that cultural borrowing isn't really all that important to the author, so that must be the reason he mentioned it: To indicate what is *less* important before moving on to discuss what is *more* important.

Step 5: Evaluate the Answer Choices

15. The author most likely states that "cultural borrowing is, of course, old news" (lines 47–48) primarily to

    (A) acknowledge that in itself the existence of intertribal tendencies at powwows is unsurprising
    (B) suggest that native Americans' use of English in powwows should be accepted as unavoidable
    (C) argue that the deliberate distinction of intertribal and traditional dances is not a recent development
    (D) suggest that the recent increase in intertribal activity is the result of native Americans borrowing from non-native American cultures
    (E) indicate that the powwow itself could have originated by combining practices drawn from both native and non-native American cultures[8]

The only choice that matches the contextual reading is (A), the correct answer. Choices (B), (D), and (E) are all completely out of scope for this question. Choice (C) contains a distortion—the text quoted in the stem demonstrates that cultural borrowing is old news, not the distinction between tribal and intertribal dances. This answer choice might look good if you hadn't conducted your research and paid careful attention to context, but because you did, you avoided it and earned the point.

Function Question Practice

I'll say it again: Context is key. Function questions reward your ability to understand the role of a specific bit of text when set against the purpose of the whole paragraph or passage. To hone your skills further, read the following passage. Note the sample Roadmap, and identify the Topic, Scope, Purpose, and Main Idea.

Step 1:

> Women's participation in the revolutionary events in France between 1789 and 1795 has (only recently) been given nuanced treatment. (Early) twentieth-century historians of the French Revolution are
> (5) (typified) by Jaures, who, (though) sympathetic to the woman's movement of his own time, (never even) mentions its antecedents in revolutionary France.

---

[8]PrepTest 25, Sec 1, Q 15

New
research:

women in
rev. France

(10)

3 phases
of partic.

(15)

(20)

(25)

(30)

(35)

Studies
look
at
end of
movement

(40)

(45)

(50)

(55)

Studies
differ but
all are
good

(60)

Even today most general histories treat only cursorily
a few individual women, like Marie Antoinette. The
recent studies by Landes, Badinter, Godineau, and
Roudinesco, however, should signal a much-needed
reassessment of women's participation.

Godineau and Roudinesco point to three
significant phases in that participation. The first, up
to mid-1792, involved those women who wrote
political tracts. Typical of their orientation to
theoretical issues—in Godineau's view, without
practical effect—is Marie Gouze's *Declaration of the
Rights of Women*. The emergence of vocal middle-
class women's political clubs marks the second phase.
Formed in 1791 as adjuncts of middle-class male
political clubs, and originally philanthropic in
function, by late 1792 independent clubs of women
began to advocate military participation for women.
In the final phase, the famine of 1795 occasioned a
mass women's movement: women seized food
supplies, held officials hostage, and argued for the
implementation of democratic politics. This phase
ended in May of 1795 with the military suppression
of this multiclass movement. In all three phases
women's participation in politics contrasted
markedly with their participation before 1789.
Before that date some noblewomen participated
indirectly in elections, but such participation by more
than a narrow range of the population—women or
men—came only with the Revolution.

What makes the recent studies particularly
compelling, however, is not so much their
organization of chronology as their unflinching
willingness to confront the reasons for the collapse of
the woman's movement. For Landes and Badinter,
the necessity of women's having to speak in the
established vocabularies of certain intellectual and
political traditions diminished the ability of the
women's movement to resist suppression. Many
women, and many men, they argue, located their
vision within the confining tradition of Jean-Jacques
Rousseau, who linked male and female roles with
public and private spheres respectively. But when
women went on to make political alliances with
radical Jacobin men, Badinter asserts, they adopted a
vocabulary and a violently extremist viewpoint that
unfortunately was even more damaging to their
political interests.

Each of these scholars has a different political
agenda and takes a different approach—Godineau,
for example, works with police archives while
Roudinesco uses explanatory schema from modern
psychology. Yet, admirably, each gives center stage
to a group that previously has been marginalized, or

at best undifferentiated by historians. And (in the) (case) of Landes and Badinter, the reader is left with a sobering awareness of the cost to the women of the Revolution of speaking in borrowed voices.[9]

Paragraph Structure: The author begins by emphasizing that "only recently" (line 2) have historians closely examined the role of women in the French Revolution. He substantiates this assertion by contrasting the new scholarship with that of "early" (line 3) historians, noting that one prominent scholar "never even mentions" (line 6-7) the subject. The recent studies, "however" (line 11), supply a "much needed' (line 11) analysis.

As you probably predicted, the second paragraph goes on to examine the recent scholarship in detail. The author notes that scholars "point to three significant phases" (lines 13–14) in the participation of women in the revolution. Each phase is described, marked by the Keywords "first" (line 14), "second" (line 20), and "final" (line 25). The author ties the three phases together by noting that they "contrasted" (line 30) with the role women played in earlier years.

The third and fourth paragraphs provide the author's opinions of these studies in greater detail. What makes the studies compelling is "not" (line 38) their chronology "so much . . . as" (lines 38–39) their treatment of the end of the women's movement. Some of the scholars trace this collapse back to the "necessity" (line 42) of women's use of a particular vocabulary. The author describes this phenomenon in greater detail, then presents a final conclusion in the fourth paragraph. Each scholar has a "different" (line 55) political agenda, "yet admirably" (line 59) they all provided necessary examination of a neglected area of history—something the author approves of.

Topic: Women in the French Revolution

Scope: Recent studies of the participation of women in rebellion

Purpose: To describe several recent studies of a historical phenomenon

Main Idea: Though they emerge from different political and social agendas, all of the recent studies are valuable.

17. The primary function of the first paragraph of the passage is to[10]

Step 2: The key phrase "primary function" tells you that this is a Function question.

Step 3: The question stem asks for the function of the first paragraph, and you have just the tool to help you identify it—your Roadmap. The first paragraph describes the lack of scholarship regarding the revolutionary activities of French women. The author mentions "recent studies" (line 10) that mark the turning point, signaling a "much needed" reexamination of history. The importance of this new scholarship appears in the Roadmap as the central idea of the paragraph.

Step 4: To summarize: The first paragraph introduced the new scholarship, contrasting it with the lack of scholarship that preceded it. The correct answer should reflect this idea.

Step 5:

17. The primary function of the first paragraph of the passage is to

   (A) outline the author's argument about women's roles in France between 1789 and 1795
   (B) anticipate possible challenges to the findings of the recent studies of women in France between 1789 and 1795
   (C) summarize some long-standing explanations of the role of individual women in France between 1789 and 1795
   (D) present a context for the discussion of recent studies of women in France between 1789 and 1795
   (E) characterize various eighteenth-century studies of women in France[11]

Choice (A) is completely off track; the author doesn't outline any arguments in the first paragraph. Choices (B) and (C) are similarly out of scope. Choice (D) is the match you're looking for. The first paragraph creates context for the discussion to follow by pointing out why the new scholarship is relevant. Choice (E) represents a faulty use of detail; the passage does mention (briefly) studies from the 20th century, but nothing from the 18th century. In any case, the purpose of the paragraph wasn't to mention individual studies, but to demonstrate why the new ones are important.

19. In the context of the passage, the word "cost" in line 63 refers to the[12]

Step 2: The stem asks you to define a key term in the context in which it was used. This is a Function question, specifically a Vocabulary-in-Context question.

Step 3: The word "cost" refers to the penalty paid by women who spoke in "borrowed voices." This information alone doesn't really define what that cost was, so you'll need to conduct additional research. Back up a bit and look for context earlier in the passage. A scan of Keywords should bring you to line 42, wherein the author describes the necessity of women having to use established vocabularies when speaking out. This paragraph is ultimately about the col-

---

[11]PrepTest 4, Sec 2, Q 17
[12]PrepTest 4, Sec 2, Q 19

lapse of the women's movement, as indicated by the Roadmap, and if you scan further through the text, the author asserts that the language used by the women "diminished" (line 44) their ability to resist suppression.

Remember that, when searching for the context that will allow you to answer the question, you may need to conduct research outside of the paragraph in which the text cited in the question stem appears. When the need arises, use Keywords and the Roadmap to guide you.

Step 4: It's time to make a prediction. According to the third paragraph, the ultimate result of the rhetorical devices used by women led to the demise of their movement. This is the "cost" referred to in the final paragraph.

Step 5:

19. In the context of the passage, the word "cost" in line 63 refers to the

    (A) dichotomy of private roles for women and public roles for men
    (B) almost nonexistent political participation of women before 1789
    (C) historians' lack of differentiation among various groups of women
    (D) political alliances women made with radical Jacobin men
    (E) collapse of the women's movement in the 1790s[13]

The proper match is choice (E), which unequivocally refers to the end of the movement. Note that, with a good prediction in hand, none of the other answer choices even remotely reflect what your research revealed. These choices make reference to various small details found in the latter paragraphs of the passage but none of them define the "cost" paid by the women mentioned in the stem.

You've now seen the three most common varieties of function questions—those that ask for the function of an example, the function of a paragraph, or the definition of a key term. All of them rely on your ability to read for context. To solve Function questions efficiently, you should be prepared to use your Roadmap to understand that context.

---

[13]PrepTest 4, Sec 2, Q 19

DRILL: ANSWERING FUNCTION QUESTIONS

Now for some additional practice. Read the following passage strategically, applying Step 1 of the Kaplan Method. Then answer the two questions, applying Steps 2–5 each time. Explanations follow the Drill.

Social scientists have traditionally defined multipolar international systems as consisting of three or more nations, each of roughly equal military and economic strength. Theoretically, the members of such (5) systems create shifting, temporary alliances in response to changing circumstances in the international environment. Such systems are, thus, fluid and flexible. Frequent, small confrontations are one attribute of multipolar systems and are usually the result of less (10) powerful members grouping together to counter threats from larger, more aggressive members seeking hegemony. Yet the constant and inevitable counterbalancing typical of such systems usually results in stability. The best-known example of a (15) multipolar system is the Concert of Europe, which coincided with general peace on that continent lasting roughly 100 years beginning around 1815.

Bipolar systems, on the other hand, involve two major members of roughly equal military and (20) economic strength vying for power and advantage. Other members of lesser strength tend to coalesce around one or the other pole. Such systems tend to be rigid and fixed, in part due to the existence of only one axis of power. Zero-sum political and military (25) maneuverings, in which a gain for one side results in an equivalent loss for the other, are a salient feature of bipolar systems. Overall superiority is sought by both major members, which can lead to frequent confrontations, debilitating armed conflict, and, (30) eventually, to the capitulation of one or the other side. Athens and Sparta of ancient Greece had a bipolar relationship, as did the United States and the USSR during the Cold War.

However, the shift in the geopolitical landscape (35) following the end of the Cold War calls for a reassessment of the assumptions underlying these two theoretical concepts. The emerging but still vague multipolar system in Europe today brings with it the unsettling prospect of new conflicts and shifting

(40) alliances that may lead to a diminution, rather than an enhancement, of security. The frequent, small confrontations that are thought to have kept the Concert of Europe in a state of equilibrium would today, as nations arm themselves with modern (45) weapons, create instability that could destroy the system. And the larger number of members and shifting alliance patterns peculiar to multipolar systems would create a bewildering tangle of conflicts.

This reassessment may also lead us to look at the (50) Cold War in a new light. In 1914 smaller members of the multipolar system in Europe brought the larger members into a war that engulfed the continent. The aftermath—a crippled system in which certain members were dismantled, punished, or voluntarily (55) withdrew—created the conditions that led to World War II. In contrast, the principal attributes of bipolar systems—two major members with only one possible axis of conflict locked in a rigid yet usually stable struggle for power—may have created the necessary (60) parameters for general peace in the second half of the twentieth century.[14]

1. Which one of the following statements most accurately describes the function of the final paragraph?

   (A) The weaknesses of both types of systems are discussed in the context of twentieth-century European history.
   (B) A prediction is made regarding European security based on the attributes of both types of systems.
   (C) A new argument is introduced in favor of European countries embracing a new bipolar system.
   (D) Twentieth-century European history is used to expand on the argument in the previous paragraph.
   (E) The typical characteristics of the major members of a bipolar system are reviewed.

[14]PrepTest 40, Sec 4, Passage 1

2. The author's reference to the possibility that
    confrontations may lead to capitulation (lines 27–30)
    serves primarily to

    (A) indicate that bipolar systems can have certain
         unstable characteristics
    (B) illustrate how multipolar systems can transform
         themselves into bipolar systems
    (C) contrast the aggressive nature of bipolar members
         with the more rational behavior of their
         multipolar counterparts
    (D) indicate the anarchic nature of international
         relations
    (E) suggest that military and economic strength shifts
         in bipolar as frequently as in multipolar systems[15]

---

[15]PrepTest 40, Sec 4, Qs 2–3

Explanations

Step 1:

Multipolar
systems

Social scientists have (traditionally) defined multipolar international systems as (consisting of) three or more nations, each of roughly equal military and economic strength. (Theoretically,) the members of such
(5) systems create shifting, temporary alliances (in response) to changing circumstances in the international environment. Such systems are, (thus,) fluid and flexible. Frequent, small confrontations are one (attribute) of multipolar systems and are usually the (result) of less
(10) powerful members grouping together to (counter) threats from larger, more aggressive members seeking hegemony. (Yet) the constant and (inevitable) counterbalancing typical of such systems usually (results) in stability. The best-known (example) of a
(15) multipolar system is the Concert of Europe, which coincided with general peace on that continent lasting roughly 100 years beginning around 1815.

Bipolar
systems

Bipolar systems, (on the other hand,) involve two major members of roughly equal military and
(20) economic strength vying for power and advantage. (Other) members of lesser strength (tend to) coalesce around one or the other pole. Such systems (tend to) be rigid and fixed, in part (due to) the existence of only one axis of power. Zero-sum political and military
(25) maneuverings, (in which) a gain for one side results in an equivalent loss for the other, are a (salient feature) of bipolar systems. (Overall) superiority is sought by (both) major members, which can (lead to) frequent confrontations, debilitating armed conflict, and,
(30) (eventually,) to the capitulation of one or the other side. Athens and Sparta of ancient Greece had a bipolar relationship, (as did) the United States and the USSR during the Cold war.

New
landscape=
changes
in systems

(However,) the shift in the geopolitical landscape
(35) (following) the end of the Cold War calls for a reassessment of the (assumptions) underlying these two theoretical concepts. The emerging (but still) vague multipolar system in Europe (today) brings with it the unsettling prospect of new conflicts and shifting
(40) alliances that may (lead to) a diminution, rather (than an) enhancement, of security. The frequent, small confrontations that are thought to have kept the Concert of Europe in a state of equilibrium would (today,) as nations arm themselves with modern
(45) weapons, create instability that could destroy the system. (And) the larger number of members and shifting alliance patterns peculiar to multipolar systems would create a bewildering tangle of conflicts.

This reassessment may (also lead) us to look at the
(50) Cold War in a new light. In 1914 smaller members of
the multipolar system in Europe (brought) the larger
members into a war that engulfed the continent. The
(aftermath)—a crippled system in which certain
members were dismantled, punished, or voluntarily
(55) withdrew—created the conditions that (led to) World
War II. In (contrast,) the principal attributes of bipolar
systems—two major members with only one possible
axis of conflict locked in a rigid yet usually stable
struggle for power—may have (created) the necessary
(60) parameters for general peace in the second half of the
twentieth century.[16]

*Review of
past
systems*

Paragraph Structure: The author sets the stage by describing multipolar systems in the first paragraph and bipolar systems in the second. Note that these two paragraphs have very similar structures; the first begins by describing how multipolar systems are "traditionally" defined, goes on to describe their essential flexibility, and then gives the "best-known" example of such a system in lines 14–17. The second paragraph follows the same pattern: bipolar systems, "on the other hand" (line 18), tend to be more stable. The author gives examples at the conclusion of the paragraph.

"However," as the author begins the third paragraph, a reexamination of these ideas is in order. Changes in politics and technology may "lead to" (line 40) a lessening of security in multipolar systems. In the final paragraph, the author suggests that we "may also" (line 49) need to rethink current assumptions about the Cold War, suggesting that the existence of a bipolar system, "in contrast" (line 56) to the conflicts brought about by multipolar systems in previous years, may have led to a stable peace.

Topic: International relations

Scope: Bipolar and multipolar systems

Purpose: To describe how geopolitical changes may affect the functioning of certain international systems

Main Idea: Major geopolitical changes in the 20th century should lead us to reassess the functions of multipolar and bipolar systems in the past and present.

---

[16]PrepTest 40, Sec 4, Passage 1

1. **(D)**

    Which one of the following statements most accurately describes the function of the final paragraph?
    (A) The weaknesses of both types of systems are discussed in the context of twentieth-century European history.
    (B) A prediction is made regarding European security based on the attributes of both types of systems.
    (C) A new argument is introduced in favor of European countries embracing a new bipolar system.
    (D) Twentieth-century European history is used to expand on the argument in the previous paragraph.
    (E) The typical characteristics of the major members of a bipolar system are reviewed.[17]

Step 2: Because the stem asks for the function of a paragraph, this is a Function question.

Step 3: The final paragraph begins by saying the reasoning described previously "may also lead" us to reexamine the Cold War. The rest of the paragraph goes on to describe this new interpretation of history.

Step 4: The continuation language that begins the final paragraph is an excellent clue. The purpose of this paragraph is to further the logic of the previous one, providing examples from recent history.

Step 5: Choice (D) describes the continuation perfectly and is the correct answer. Choice (A) distorts the facts, since the weaknesses of one system are discussed, not both. Choices (B) and (C) are out of scope; the author makes no predictions or arguments for political change. Choice (E) misuses detail. The final paragraph does mention an important bipolar system, but that isn't its primary purpose. The example is only there as part of a larger confirmation of the author's argument.

2. **(A)**

    The author's reference to the possibility that confrontations may lead to capitulation (lines 27–30) serves primarily to
    (A) indicate that bipolar systems can have certain unstable characteristics
    (B) illustrate how multipolar systems can transform themselves into bipolar systems
    (C) contrast the aggressive nature of bipolar members with the more rational behavior of their multipolar counterparts
    (D) indicate the anarchic nature of international relations
    (E) suggest that military and economic strength shifts in bipolar as frequently as in multipolar systems[18]

---

[17]PrepTest 40, Sec 4, Q 2
[18]PrepTest 40, Sec 4, Q 3

Step 2: The key phrase "serves primarily to" alerts you that this is a Function question.

Step 3: According to the Roadmap, this paragraph is descriptive of bipolar systems. Indeed, Keywords spread throughout ("tend to" in line 22, "salient feature" in line 26) point to the various attributes that define such a system.

Step 4: Since the author uses this paragraph to describe bipolar systems, the reference to catastrophic conflicts must be considered a part of that description.

Step 5: Choice (A), the correct answer, fulfills the prediction right away. The reference did indeed describe bipolar systems, specifically describing one of their unstable attributes. Choices (B) and (C) veer out of scope, as the author never mentions the transformation of one system to another, nor does he use this paragraph to make a direct comparison between the two. Choice (D), a gross generalization, is also well out of scope. Choice (E) once again introduces a comparison that doesn't apply to the reference in question.

COMMON WRONG ANSWER TYPES

Most of the wrong answer traps you've seen in previous question types will show up in Function questions as well. I'll point out two of note from the previous exercise.

Distortion

Always be on the lookout for answer choices that are similar to your prediction but not quite right.

1. Which one of the following statements most accurately describes the function of the final paragraph?

    (A) The weaknesses of both types of systems are discussed in the context of twentieth-century European history.
    (B) A prediction is made regarding European security based on the attributes of both types of systems.
    (C) A new argument is introduced in favor of European countries embracing a new bipolar system.
    (D) Twentieth-century European history is used to expand on the argument in the previous paragraph.
    (E) The typical characteristics of the major members of a bipolar system are reviewed.[19]

The final paragraph did mention the major members of a bipolar system (the US and the USSR), but the purpose of the paragraph was not to "review" their characteristics, but rather to mention them as support of a standing argument. When thinking about the function of a paragraph, stick to your Roadmap and keep the big picture in mind.

---

[19]PrepTest 40, Sec 4, Q 2

Irrelevant comparison

The test makers will occasionally write answer choices that take advantage of the tendency to focus on comparisons and contrasts in the passage.

2. The author's reference to the possibility that confrontations may lead to capitulation (lines 27–30) serves primarily to

    (A) indicate that bipolar systems can have certain unstable characteristics
    (B) illustrate how multipolar systems can transform themselves into bipolar systems
    (C) contrast the aggressive nature of bipolar members with the more rational behavior of their multipolar counterparts
    (D) indicate the anarchic nature of international relations
    (E) suggest that military and economic strength shifts in bipolar as frequently as in multipolar systems[20]

The second paragraph of the passage was solely focused on describing bipolar systems, and this question asked about a detail in service of that goal. It's not uncommon in Function questions for wrong answer traps to leave the context of the stem behind and focus instead on larger issues that are out of scope. This passage *does* eventually comment on the interrelations between bipolar and multipolar systems, but not in the paragraph that's relevant to this question. Remember not to lose sight of what the question is asking for.

YOU KNOW THE QUESTION TYPES

Take a deep breath, then congratulate yourself on reaching an important milestone: You've now learned how to identify and apply the proper strategies to every type of question that appears in LSAT Reading Comprehension. I'll revisit rare variations on these question types a little later, but first it's time to challenge yourself. In the next chapter you'll bring everything you've learned to bear as you learn how to score the toughest points on the test.

---

[20]PrepTest 40, Sec 4, Q 3

CHAPTER 15

CHALLENGING PASSAGES

SOME PASSAGES ARE HARDER THAN OTHERS

Now that you've had time to practice and apply the Kaplan Method, I hope you're feeling an increased confidence with every Reading Comprehension passage you take on. You've learned that the passages and questions follow predictable patterns, and you're well on your way to mastering the strategies that will help you to maximize your score. For the most part, each time you practice, the passages should become a little more familiar, the questions a little easier, and the correct answers simpler to spot.

Nonetheless, you'll still encounter the occasional bump in the road. Perhaps you've read a natural science passage that you just couldn't wrap your head around, and found the questions consequently bewildering. Maybe you've come across law passages that seemed too abstract to understand, or passages so steeped in jargon that it seemed only an expert in the field could possibly understand them. Perhaps you've encountered questions that seem impossible to answer quickly.

If you're like most of my students, you've had all of these experiences at one time or another, and I understand the frustration these situations cause. The fact is that some passages are designed by the test makers to be more challenging than others, and on average every LSAT Reading Comprehension section contains one such passage. Certainly there is some subjectivity here—what's challenging for one test taker might seem quite straightforward for another—but like everything else on the LSAT, the attributes of challenging passages are pattern-oriented and predictable. Here are some of the ways in which the test makers craft a high-difficulty passage.

Abstraction

The passage may deal with concepts that aren't easily imagined, such as philosophical ideas or schools of legal thought. Abstract passages are often made more challenging by a lack of concrete examples to illustrate its ideas.

> Organicism depended upon the theory of internal relations, which states that relations between entities are possible only within some whole that embraces them, and that entities are altered by the relationships
> (15) into which they enter. If an entity stands in a relationship with another entity, it has some property as a consequence. Without this relationship, and hence without the property, the entity would be different— and so would be another entity. Thus, the property is
> (20) one of the entity's defining characteristics. Each of an entity's relationships likewise determines a defining characteristic of the entity.[1]

This paragraph is a perfect illustration of abstraction in a passage. The theory of internal relations is described in some detail, but the language is vague throughout. The highlighted sentence, describing the relationship of "entities" to one another and acquiring "some property" as a result isn't by itself easy to imagine. It is vital that, when reading such a passage, you adhere scrupulously to Step 1 of the Kaplan Method and read strategically, using Keywords to help you navigate the vague language.

> *Organicism: depends on relations*
>
> Organicism depended upon the theory of internal relations, which states that relations between entities are possible only within some whole that embraces them, and that entities are altered by the relationships
> (15) into which they enter. If an entity stands in a relationship with another entity, it has some property as a consequence. Without this relationship, and hence without the property, the entity would be different— and so would be another entity. Thus, the property is
> (20) one of the entity's defining characteristics. Each of an entity's relationships likewise determines a defining characteristic of the entity.[2]

Recall from the sample Roadmap what really matters—the main point that the author is trying to convey. The Keywords "depended upon" tell you that, regardless of what else the paragraph may say, there is an important relationship between organicism and the theory of internal relations. Once you understand that much and get it into your Roadmap, the esoteric ideas can wait until it's time to research them for a question.

---

[1]PrepTest 25, Sec 1, Passage 4

[2]PrepTest 25, Sec 1, Passage 4

Jargon

If you've been working through this book carefully, you're very familiar with passages that rely on field-specific jargon to communicate their ideas. Unfamiliar language can make a passage seem intimidating and may give you the false impression that it cannot be understood without specialized knowledge of the subject matter.

(10) H. L. A. Hart's *The Concept of Law* is still the clearest and most persuasive statement of both the standard theory of hard cases and the standard theory of law on which it rests. For Hart, the law consists of legal rules formulated in general terms; these terms he calls "open textured," which means that they contain a "core" of settled meaning and a "penumbra" or "periphery" where their meaning is not determinate.[3]

This excerpt is full of jargon. Many of its key terms are in quotes, and while they are all defined, it still might not be entirely clear what the core, penumbra, and periphery of legal rules really are.

(15) For example, suppose an ordinance prohibits the use of vehicles in a park. "Vehicle" has a core of meaning which includes cars and motorcycles. But, Hart claims, other vehicles, such as bicycles, fall within the peripheral meaning of "vehicle," so that the law does not establish whether they are prohibited.[4]

As the paragraph continues, an example is provided that clarifies the jargon somewhat. Keep in mind that while you should generally skim through examples, in a more challenging passage they can provide the context you need to decipher key ideas. As always, Keywords will help you parse this information efficiently. In this case, the Keyword "but" allows you to quickly identify the key distinction—peripheral meanings are unclear, so it must follow that core meanings are well-established.

It is important to remember that *every* passage, no matter how difficult its language, will contain sufficient Keywords and other context clues to allow you to understand its main ideas. Law schools don't expect you to begin your first year already understanding the law; similarly, the LSAT test makers don't expect you to approach Reading Comprehension with full knowledge of the passages' content (in fact, they're counting on the opposite).

Structure

Sometimes the structure of a passage can make it more difficult to comprehend. Don't reread the following passage in depth, but rather glance quickly at the beginning of each paragraph.

---

[3]PrepTest 17, Sec 4, Passage 2
[4]PrepTest 17, Sec 4, Passage 2

Traditionally, members of a community such as a town or neighborhood share a common location and a sense of necessary interdependence that includes, for example, mutual respect and emotional support. But as
(5) modern societies grow more technological and sometimes more alienating, people tend to spend less time in the kinds of interactions that their communities require in order to thrive. Meanwhile, technology has made it possible for individuals to interact via personal
(10) computer with others who are geographically distant. Advocates claim that these computer conferences, in which large numbers of participants communicate by typing comments that are immediately read by other participants and responding immediately to those
(15) comments they read, function as communities that can substitute for traditional interactions with neighbors.

What are the characteristics that advocates claim allow computer conferences to function as communities? For one, participants often share
(20) common interests or concerns; conferences are frequently organized around specific topics such as music or parenting. Second, because these conferences are conversations, participants have adopted certain conventions in recognition of the importance of
(25) respecting each others' sensibilities. Abbreviations are used to convey commonly expressed sentiments of courtesy such as "pardon me for cutting in" ("pmfci") or "in my humble opinion" ("imho"). Because a humorous tone can be difficult to communicate in
(30) writing, participants will often end an intentionally humorous comment with a set of characters that, when looked at sideways, resembles a smiling or winking face. Typing messages entirely in capital letters is avoided, because its tendency to demand the attention
(35) of a reader's eye is considered the computer equivalent of shouting. These conventions, advocates claim, constitute a form of etiquette, and with this etiquette as a foundation, people often form genuine, trusting relationships, even offering advice and support during
(40) personal crises such as illness or the loss of a loved one.

But while it is true that conferences can be both respectful and supportive, they nonetheless fall short of communities. For example, conferences discriminate
(45) along educational and economic lines because participation requires a basic knowledge of computers and the ability to afford access to conferences. Further, while advocates claim that a shared interest makes computer conferences similar to traditional
(50) communities—insofar as the shared interest is analogous to a traditional community's shared location—this analogy simply does not work. Conference participants are a self-selecting group; they are drawn together by their shared interest in the topic
(55) of the conference. Actual communities, on the other hand, are "nonintentional": the people who inhabit towns or neighborhoods are thus more likely to exhibit genuine diversity—of age, career, or personal interests—than are conference participants. It might be
(60) easier to find common ground in a computer conference than in today's communities, but in so doing it would be unfortunate if conference participants cut themselves off further from valuable interactions in their own towns or neighborhoods.[5]

---

[5]PrepTest 36, Sec 2, Passage 1

Even if you hadn't already worked with this passage, the simplicity of its structure should be obvious. It is neatly divided into several paragraphs, each of which signals its primary purpose immediately with familiar Keywords. You get a good approximation of the author's goals without even reading the rest of the text.

Compare it with this passage. Again, skim the text, paying attention primarily to the highlighted text at the beginning of each paragraph.

Because the market system enables entrepreneurs and investors who develop new technology to reap financial rewards from their risk of capital, it may seem that the primary result of this activity is that some
(5) people who have spare capital accumulate more. But in spite of the fact that the profits derived from various technological developments have accrued to relatively few people, the developments themselves have served overall as a remarkable democratizing force. In fact,
(10) under the regime of the market, the gap in benefits accruing to different groups of people has been narrowed in the long term.

This tendency can be seen in various well-known technological developments. For example, before the
(15) printing press was introduced centuries ago, few people had access to written materials, much less to scribes and private secretaries to produce and transcribe documents. Since printed materials have become widely available, however, people without special
(20) position or resources—and in numbers once thought impossible—can take literacy and the use of printed texts for granted. With the distribution of books and periodicals in public libraries, this process has been extended to the point where people in general can have
(25) essentially equal access to a vast range of texts that would once have been available only to a very few. A more recent technological development extends this process beyond printed documents. A child in school with access to a personal computer and modem—
(30) which is becoming fairly common in technologically

advanced societies—has computing power and database access equal to that of the best-connected scientists and engineers at top-level labs of just fifteen years ago, a time when relatively few people had
(35) personal access to any computing power. Or consider the uses of technology for leisure. In previous centuries only a few people with abundant resources had the ability and time to hire professional entertainment, and to have contact through travel and written
(40) communication—both of which were prohibitively expensive—with distant people. But now broadcast technology is widely available, and so almost anyone can have an entertainment cornucopia unimagined in earlier times. Similarly, the development of
(45) inexpensive mail distribution and telephone connections and, more recently, the establishment of the even more efficient medium of electronic mail have greatly extended the power of distant communication.

This kind of gradual diffusion of benefits across
(50) society is not an accident of these particular technological developments, but rather the result of a general tendency of the market system. Entrepreneurs and investors often are unable to maximize financial success without expanding their market, and this
(55) involves structuring their prices to the consumers so as to make their technologies genuinely accessible to an ever-larger share of the population. In other words, because market competition drives prices down, it tends to diffuse access to new technology across
(60) society as a result.[6]

_____

[6]PrepTest 42, Sec 3, Passage 3

The structure of this passage is less simple than in the previous example. There are longer paragraphs, making the author's Purpose more challenging to map out. The second paragraph is particularly long and laden with details. The paragraphs begin with longer sentences containing more complex ideas. You're not likely to skim this passage and come away with a firm grasp of its ideas.

But once again, I'll remind you that the Keywords are still there. No matter how complex the passage structure may seem, you still have all the clues you need to make sense of it.

> Because the market system enables entrepreneurs and investors who develop new technology to reap financial rewards from their risk of capital, it may seem that the primary result of this activity is that some
> (5)   people who have spare capital accumulate more. But in spite of the fact that the profits derived from various technological developments have accrued to relatively few people, the developments themselves have served overall as a remarkable democratizing force. In fact,
> (10) under the regime of the market, the gap in benefits accruing to different groups of people has been narrowed in the long term.[7]

"Because" of certain features of the market system, you might expect the "primary" result to be that people with spare cash earn more.

Predictive reading allows you to guess what comes next: "But" market forces have "overall" been democratizing. If this term is unfamiliar to you, use the Keywords to help you approximate its meaning. Since the author is describing a contrast to the expected result (those with extra money make even more), a democratizing force must be one that *doesn't* simply allow the rich to become richer. "In fact," the gap between different groups has narrowed.

Strategic reading always allows you to take an unwieldy block of text and reduce it to a handful of simpler ideas, no matter how challenging the structure may look initially.

YOU CAN NAVIGATE ANY PASSAGE

Challenging passages are a reality of the LSAT, but the test makers aren't in the business of crafting impossible tasks; the test will always be fair, if not always simple. In all of the above cases, I demonstrated ways in which you can navigate difficult text by properly applying the Kaplan Method. The solutions should have looked very familiar to you: reliance on context, Keywords, and predictive reading, tools you've been using throughout this book.

Perhaps most importantly, you must approach challenging passages with confidence and a dedication to methodical thinking. It's very easy to become intimidated by a tough passage when

[7]PrepTest 42, Sec 3, Passage 3

the clock is ticking, and it's just as easy to let method fall by the wayside. Don't let this happen. Remember that you always have control over the way you approach the passage—maintain this control and you can handle any challenge the Reading Comprehension section throws at you.

Challenging Passage Practice

Put these ideas to the test on a tough passage, one paragraph at a time.

> Many legal theorists have argued that the only
> morally legitimate goal in imposing criminal penalties
> against certain behaviors is to prevent people from
> harming others. Clearly, such theorists would oppose
> (5) laws that force people to act purely for their own
> good or to refrain from certain harmless acts purely
> to ensure conformity to some social norm. But the
> goal of preventing harm to others would also justify
> legal sanctions against some forms of nonconforming
> (10) behavior to which this goal might at first seem not to
> apply.[8]

The first paragraph indicates an abstract topic, so careful attention to Keywords will be vital as you apply Step 1 of the Kaplan Method. The theorists in line 1 "have argued" that the only good reason to impose criminal penalties is to prevent people from harming each other. So far so good; keep this definition in mind as you proceed.

"Clearly" (line 4) you would expect theorists to oppose laws that prevent harmless acts. Predictive reading should prepare you for what comes next, since LSAT passages rarely focus on the expected. The author will likely introduce a contrary opinion soon. "But" (line 7) it turns out there are some forms of behavior that should be illegal even though they might at first seem harmless.

> Only reason for | Many (legal theorists) have (argued) that the only
> law = prevent | morally legitimate goal in imposing criminal penalties
> harm | against certain behaviors is to prevent people from
> | harming others. (Clearly,) such theorists would (oppose)
> (5) | laws that force people to act purely for their own
> | good (or to) refrain from certain harmless acts purely
> | to ensure conformity to some social norm. (But) the
> | goal of preventing harm to others would also justify
> Unexpected | legal sanctions against some forms of nonconforming
> cases | (10) behavior to which this goal might at first seem not to
> | apply.[9]

When faced with an abstract passage, it's especially important that you remember to read predictively. The author has asserted that there are certain kinds of "nonconforming behavior" that cause harm even though they appear not to. The following paragraphs are likely to

---

[8]PrepTest 46, Sec 1, Passage 4

[9]PrepTest 46, Sec 1, Passage 4

provide examples of these behaviors. Keep this in mind as you read the next paragraph. This time, circle Keywords as you come to them and create a Roadmap as you go.

> In many situations it is in the interest of each member of a group to agree to behave in a certain way on the condition that the others similarly agree.
> (15) In the simplest cases, a mere coordination of activities is itself the good that results. For example, it is in no one's interest to lack a convention about which side of the road to drive on, and each person can agree to drive on one side assuming the others do
> (20) too. Any fair rule, then, would be better than no rule at all. On the assumption that all people would voluntarily agree to be subject to a coordination rule backed by criminal sanctions, if people could be assured that others would also agree, it is argued to
> (25) be legitimate for a legislature to impose such a rule. This is because prevention of harm underlies the rationale for the rule, though it applies to the problem of coordination less directly than to other problems, for the act that is forbidden (driving on the other side
> (30) of the road) is not inherently harm-producing, as are burglary and assault; instead, it is the lack of a coordinating rule that would be harmful.[10]

This lengthy, detail-filled paragraph is much easier to work with if you keep the context of the first paragraph in mind as you read it. There are "many situations" (line 12) in which people should agree to behave the same way. This is presumably because doing so will prevent harm. "For example" in line 16 marks the beginning of a dense example—one that is very easy to get lost in. Remember your sense of context, and stay active as you read; think about why the author would use the example. According to your prediction, it should describe a situation where conformity serves to prevent harm. The example makes perfect sense in this context; people should agree to drive on the same side of the road, because failing to do so would be dangerous. The paragraph makes this simple idea seem more complex than it really is, but take note of the repetitive nature of the language. It is ultimately "argued" (line 24) that a rule requiring people to drive on the same side of the road is legitimate, "because" (line 26) it is designed to prevent harm. The paragraph becomes rather long-winded toward line 27, but don't fall into the trap of trying to parse every word of this detailed language—stay focused on useful Keywords. The author's gist is signaled by a contrast in line 31: The text following "instead" ties the paragraph up by centering once again on the idea that it would be harmful not to have a conformity rule for drivers.

At this point, you may be nervous about what appears to be a cursory treatment of the text. Wouldn't it be better to dive into this paragraph and really understand everything that it's saying? By now I hope your answer to this question is a resounding "No!" On test day, you absolutely do not have time to work through the minutiae of this paragraph. Trust the clues, and use the repetitious ideas to your advantage. All this paragraph really does is point out that

[10]PrepTest 46, Sec 1, Passage 4

a rule requiring conformity (such as making everyone drive on the same side of the road) can achieve the goal of preventing harm. Your Roadmap should reflect this.

Ex:
coordination:
can be good

In (many situations) it is in the interest of each member of a group to agree to behave in a certain way on the condition that the others similarly agree.
(15) In the simplest (cases,) a mere coordination of activities is itself the good that results. (For example) it is in no one's interest to lack a convention about which side of the road to drive on, and each person can agree to drive on one side (assuming) the others do
(20) too. Any fair rule, (then,) would be better than no rule at all. On the (assumption) that all people would voluntarily agree to be subject to a coordination rule backed by criminal sanctions, (if) people could be assured that others would also agree, it (is argued) to
(25) be legitimate for a legislature to impose such a rule. This is (because) prevention of harm underlies the rationale for the rule, (though) it applies to the problem of coordination less directly than to other problems, (for) the act that is forbidden (driving on the other side
(30) of the road) is not inherently harm-producing, (as are) burglary and assault; (instead,) it is the lack of a coordinating rule that would be harmful.[11]

Take a moment to predict what is likely to come next. Then read the final paragraph strategically, circling Keywords and creating a Roadmap. Use the Keywords to stay focused on the main idea.

In some other situations involving a need for legally enforced coordination, the harm to be averted
(35) goes beyond the simple lack of coordination itself. This can be illustrated by an example of a coordination rule—instituted by a private athletic organization—which has analogies in criminal law. At issue is whether the use of anabolic steroids, which
(40) build muscular strength but have serious negative side effects, should be prohibited. Each athlete has at stake both an interest in having a fair opportunity to win and an interest in good health. If some competitors use steroids, others have the option of either
(45) endangering their health or losing their fair opportunity to win. Thus they would be harmed either way. A compulsory rule could prevent that harm and thus would be in the interest of all competitors. If they understand its function and trust the techniques
(50) for its enforcement, they will gladly consent to it. So while it might appear that such a rule merely forces people to act for their own good, the deeper rationale for coercion here—as in the above example—is a somewhat complex appeal to the legitimacy of
(55) enforcing a rule with the goal of preventing harm.[12]

---

[11] PrepTest 46, Sec 1, Passage 4

[12] PrepTest 46, Sec 1, Passage 4

You probably predicted that the author would continue to provide examples of conformity rules that can be legally justified. This prediction is important, since the opening of the paragraph doesn't clearly spell out what it's going to describe; it merely asserts that sometimes the need to prevent harm goes beyond a "simple lack of coordination" (line 35). If this doesn't make sense, read on for more concrete text. The example of anabolic steroids given in lines 38–50 provides the clarity you need.

The problem described once again comes down to harm. "If" (line 43) some athletes use steroids, others have to choose between taking harmful drugs themselves or becoming less competitive. Either way, harm is done (line 46). Lines 50–55 simply summarize the author's logic. "While" (line 51) it might seem as though the steroid rule doesn't prevent people from harming others, it contains a "deeper rationale" (line 52) that causes it to do so.

Ex: beyond coordination

This can be illustrated by an example of a coordination rule—instituted by a private athletic organization—which has analogies in criminal law. At issue is whether the use of anabolic steroids, which
(40) build muscular strength but have serious negative side effects, should be prohibited. Each athlete has at stake both an interest in having a fair opportunity to win and an interest in good health. If some competitors use steroids, others have the option of either
(45) endangering their health or losing their fair opportunity to win. Thus they would be harmed either way. A compulsory rule could prevent that harm and thus would be in the interest of all competitors. If they understand its function and trust the techniques
(50) for its enforcement, they will gladly consent to it. So while it might appear that such a rule merely forces

Rule = not causing harm

people to act for their own good, the deeper rationale for coercion here—as in the above example—is a somewhat complex appeal to the legitimacy of
(55) enforcing a rule with the goal of preventing harm.[13]

In summary, this abstract passage really only proposes a single idea in the first paragraph and then provides two very detailed examples of that idea.

Only reason for law = prevent harm

Many legal theorists have argued that the only morally legitimate goal in imposing criminal penalties against certain behaviors is to prevent people from harming others. Clearly, such theorists would oppose
(5) laws that force people to act purely for their own good or to refrain from certain harmless acts purely to ensure conformity to some social norm. But the goal of preventing harm to others would also justify legal sanctions against some forms of nonconforming

Unexpected cases

(10) behavior to which this goal might at first seem not to apply.

---

[13] PrepTest 46, Sec 1, Passage 4

Ex: coordination can be good

In (many situations) it is in the interest of each member of a group to agree to behave in a certain way on the condition that the others similarly agree.
(15) In the simplest (cases,) a mere coordination of activities is itself the good that results. (For example,) it is in no one's interest to lack a convention about which side of the road to drive on, and each person can agree to drive on one side (assuming) the others do
(20) too. Any fair rule, (then,) would be better than no rule at all. On the (assumption) that all people would voluntarily agree to be subject to a coordination rule backed by criminal sanction, (if) people could be assured that others would also agree, it (is argued) to
(25) be legitimate for a legislature to impose such rule. This is (because) prevention of harm underlies the rationale for the rule, (though) it applies to the problem of coordination less directly than to other problems, (for) the act that is forbidden (driving on the other side
(30) of the road) is not inherently harm-producing, (as are) burglary and assault; (instead,) it is the lack of a coordinating rule that would be harmful.

Ex: beyond coordination

In some (other situations) involving a need for legally enforced coordination, the harm to be averted
(35) goes beyond the simple lack of coordination itself. This can be (illustrated by) an example of a coordination rule—instituted by a private athletic organization—which has analogies in criminal law. At (issue) is whether the use of anabolic steroids, which
(40) build muscular strength but have serious negative side effects, should be prohibited. Each athlete has at stake (both) an interest in having a fair opportunity to win (and) an interest in good health. (If) some competitors use steroids, others have the option of either
(45) endangering their health or losing their fair opportunity to win. (Thus) they would be harmed either way. A compulsory rule could prevent that harm and (thus) would be in the interest of all competitors. (If) they understand its function and trust the techniques

Rule = not causing harm

(50) for its enforcement, they will gladly consent to it. (So) while it might appear that such a rule merely forces people to act for their own good, the (deeper rationale) for coercion here—as in the above example—is a somewhat complex appeal to the legitimacy of
(55) enforcing a rule with the goal of preventing harm.[14]

Topic: Legal rules

Scope: Rules that prevent harm

Purpose: To provide examples of a particular legal principle

Main Idea: Although certain coordinating rules might not at first seem to prevent people from harming each other, they actually do.

---

[14]PrepTest 46, Sec 1, Passage 4

Take a moment to appreciate how basic the Main Idea of this passage is, and just how much text the author used to communicate it. Abstract passages put your understanding of Strategic Reading to the test; over-thinking this passage is a dangerous waste of time. You understand the big picture, and that's all you need to confidently approach the questions.

22. Which one of the following most accurately states the main point of the passage?

   (A) In order to be morally justifiable, laws prohibiting activities that are not inherently harm-producing must apply equitably to everyone.

   (B) It is justifiable to require social conformity where noncompliance would be harmful to either the nonconforming individual or the larger group.

   (C) Achieving coordination can be argued to be a morally legitimate justification for rules that prevent directly harmful actions and others that prevent indirectly harmful actions.

   (D) It is reasonable to hold that restricting individual liberty is always justified on the basis of mutually agreed-upon community standards.

   (E) The principle of preventing harm to others can be used to justify laws that do not at first glance appear to be designed to prevent such harm.[15]

Approach this question using the Kaplan Method.

Step 2: Identify the Question Type
Stems that ask for the "main point" indicate Global questions.

Step 3: Research the Relevant Text
You've already identified the Main Idea, so you can proceed directly to Step 4.

Step 4: Make a Prediction
To summarize: Rules that prevent people from harming one another may not always appear to do so at first.

Step 5: : Evaluate the Answer Choices
Choices (A) and (B) are too narrow in their focus, focusing on specific evidence rather than the author's larger argument. Choice (C) brings in the out-of-scope idea of indirectly harmful actions, and choice (D) is both too narrow and too extreme (the author never claims that restricting individual liberties is "always" justified in cases if community agreement). Choice (E), however, matches the prediction and is the correct answer.

---

[15]PrepTest 46, Sec 1, Passage 4, Q 22

Try the next question:

23. It can be most reasonably inferred from the passage
     that the author considers which one of the following
     factors to be generally necessary for the justification of
     rules compelling coordination of people's activities?

     (A) evidence that such rules do not force
          individuals to act for their own good
     (B) enactment of such rules by a duly elected or
          appointed government lawmaking
          organization
     (C) the assurance that criminal penalties are
          provided as a means of securing compliance
          with such rules
     (D) some form of consent on the part of rational
          people who are subject to such rules
     (E) a sense of community and cultural uniformity
          among those who are required to abide by
          such rules[16]

Step 2: The key phrase "most reasonably inferred" marks this as an Inference question.

Step 3: The stem asks what the author considers "generally necessary" for the justification of
coordinating rules. Since the second and third paragraphs lay out the author's reasoning for
the acceptance of rules, either one might contain the information you need. A glance through
the Keywords reveals that a rule is "argued" to be legitimate (lines 24–25) on the assumption
(line 21) that people agree to follow the rule. Similar reasoning can be found in the second
paragraph, lines 48–50, where the author notes that "if" people understand the rule "they will
gladly consent to it."

Step 4: The author's primary concern regarding the legitimacy of rules seems to center around
the agreement of people to follow those rules. The correct answer should reflect this idea.

Step 5: Choice (A) is a distortion; the author never specifically decries rules that prevent self-
harm. Choice (B) is completely out of scope. Choice (C) mentions criminal penalties, which the
author does cite in paragraph two, but not as a required feature of a coordination rule. Choice
(D), consent of the governed, matches your prediction and is the correct answer. For the record,
choice (E) brings in the out-of-scope concept of cultural uniformity.

As you can see, the questions that accompany a tough passage are just as amenable to the
Kaplan Method as those that follow a simpler one. It's also worth noting that, just because
the passage may be challenging, it doesn't mean that all of the questions will be as well. Most
tough passages come with a mix of simpler and harder questions, and I'll discuss the importance of managing questions of differing difficulty a bit later.

---

[16]PrepTest 46, Sec 1, Passage 4, Q 23

DRILL: WORKING WITH CHALLENGING PASSAGES

Now I want you to attempt a challenging passage on your own. Read the passage strategically, applying Step 1 of the Kaplan Method. Circle Keywords, create a Roadmap, and identify the Topic, Scope, Purpose, and Main Idea. This passage is among the toughest to have ever appeared on the LSAT, so be sure to apply the strategies covered in this chapter. Then try the four questions that follow. Be sure to review the explanations carefully when you've finished.

In explaining the foundations of the discipline known as historical sociology—the examination of history using the methods of sociology—historical sociologist Philip Abrams argues that, while people are
(5) made by society as much as society is made by people, sociologists' approach to the subject is usually to focus on only one of these forms of influence to the exclusion of the other. Abrams insists on the necessity for sociologists to move beyond these one-sided
(10) approaches to understand society as an entity constructed by individuals who are at the same time constructed by their society. Abrams refers to this continuous process as "structuring."

Abrams also sees history as the result of
(15) structuring. People, both individually and as members of collectives, make history. But our making of history is itself formed and informed not only by the historical conditions we inherit from the past, but also by the prior formation of our own identities and capacities,
(20) which are shaped by what Abrams calls "contingencies"—social phenomena over which we have varying degrees of control. Contingencies include such things as the social conditions under which we come of age, the condition of our household's
(25) economy, the ideologies available to help us make sense of our situation, and accidental circumstances. The ways in which contingencies affect our individual or group identities create a structure of forces within which we are able to act, and that partially determines
(30) the sorts of actions we are able to perform.

In Abrams's analysis, historical structuring, like social structuring, is manifold and unremitting. To understand it, historical sociologists must extract from it certain significant episodes, or events, that their
(35) methodology can then analyze and interpret. According to Abrams, these events are points at which action and contingency meet, points that represent a cross section of the specific social and individual forces in play at a given time. At such moments, individuals stand forth
(40) as agents of history not simply because they possess a

unique ability to act, but also because in them we see the force of the specific social conditions that allowed their actions to come forth. Individuals can "make their mark" on history, yet in individuals one also finds the
(45) convergence of wider social forces. In order to capture the various facets of this mutual interaction, Abrams recommends a fourfold structure to which he believes the investigations of historical sociologists should conform: first, description of the event itself; second,
(50) discussion of the social context that helped bring the event about and gave it significance; third, summary of the life history of the individual agent in the event; and fourth, analysis of the consequences of the event both for history and for the individual.

1. Which one of the following most accurately states the central idea of the passage?

    (A) Abrams argues that historical sociology rejects the claims of sociologists who assert that the sociological concept of structuring cannot be applied to the interactions between individuals and history.

    (B) Abrams argues that historical sociology assumes that, despite the views of sociologists to the contrary, history influences the social contingencies that affect individuals.

    (C) Abrams argues that historical sociology demonstrates that, despite the views of sociologists to the contrary, social structures both influence and are influenced by the events of history.

    (D) Abrams describes historical sociology as a discipline that unites two approaches taken by sociologists to studying the formation of societies and applies the resulting combined approach to the study of history.

    (E) Abrams describes historical sociology as an attempt to compensate for the shortcomings of traditional historical methods by applying the methods established in sociology.

2. Given the passage's argument, which one of the following sentences most logically completes the last paragraph?

   (A) Only if they adhere to this structure, Abrams believes, can historical sociologists conclude with any certainty that the events that constitute the historical record are influenced by the actions of individuals.

   (B) Only if they adhere to this structure, Abrams believes, will historical sociologists be able to counter the standard sociological assumption that there is very little connection between history and individual agency.

   (C) Unless they can agree to adhere to this structure, Abrams believes, historical sociologists risk having their discipline treated as little more than an interesting but ultimately indefensible adjunct to history and sociology.

   (D) By adhering to this structure, Abrams believes, historical sociologists can shed light on issues that traditional sociologists have chosen to ignore in their one-sided approaches to the formation of societies.

   (E) By adhering to this structure, Abrams believes, historical sociologists will be able to better portray the complex connections between human agency and history.

3. The passage states that a contingency could be each of the following EXCEPT:

   (A) a social phenomenon
   (B) a form of historical structuring
   (C) an accidental circumstance
   (D) a condition controllable to some extent by an individual
   (E) a partial determinant of an individual's actions

4. Which one of the following is most analogous to the ideal work of a historical sociologist as outlined by Abrams?

   (A) In a report on the enactment of a bill into law, a journalist explains why the need for the bill arose, sketches the biography of the principal legislator who wrote the bill, and ponders the effect that the bill's enactment will have both on society and on the legislator's career.

   (B) In a consultation with a patient, a doctor reviews the patient's medical history, suggests possible reasons for the patient's current condition, and recommends steps that the patient should take in the future to ensure that the condition improves or at least does not get any worse.

   (C) In an analysis of a historical novel, a critic provides information to support the claim that details of the work's setting are accurate, explains why the subject of the novel was of particular interest to the author, and compares the novel with some of the author's other books set in the same period.

   (D) In a presentation to stockholders, a corporation's chief executive officer describes the corporation's most profitable activities during the past year, introduces the vice president largely responsible for those activities, and discusses new projects the vice president will initiate in the coming year.

   (E) In developing a film based on a historical event, a filmmaker conducts interviews with participants in the event, bases part of the film's screenplay on the interviews, and concludes the screenplay with a sequence of scenes speculating on the outcome of the event had certain details been different.[17]

---

[17]PrepTest 38, Sec 3, Passage 3, Qs 15–18

Explanations

Step 1:

In (explaining) the foundations of the discipline

*Soc: focus
on people or
society only*

known as historical sociology—the examination of
history using the methods of sociology—historical
sociologist Philip (Abrams argues) that, (while) people are

(5) made by society (as much) as society is made by people,
sociologists' (approach) to the subject is (usually) to focus
on only one of these forms of influence to the
(exclusion) of the other. (Abrams insists) on the necessity
for sociologists to move beyond these one-sided

*Abrams: people
and society
affect one
another*

(10) approaches to understand society as an entity
constructed by individuals who are (at the same time)
constructed by their society. Abrams (refers) to this
continuous process as "structuring."

Abram (also) sees history as the (result) of

(15) structuring. People, both individually and as members
of collectives, make history. (But) our making of history
is itself formed and informed (not only) by the historical

*History =
structuring*

conditions we inherit from the past, (but also) by the
(prior) formation of our own identities and capacities,

(20) which are shaped by what Abrams calls
("contingencies")—social phenomena over which we
have varying degrees of control. Contingencies (include)

Contingencies

such things as the social conditions under which we
come of age, the condition of our household's

(25) economy, the ideologies available to help us make
sense of our situation, and accidental circumstances.
The ways in which contingencies (affect) our individual
or group identities create a structure of forces within
which we are able to act, and that partially (determines)

(30) the sorts of actions we are able to perform.

In Abrams's (analysis,) historical structuring, (like)
social structuring, is manifold and unremitting. To
understand it, historical sociologists (must extract) from
it certain significant episodes, or events, that their

*Need to
examine*

(35) methodology can then analyze and interpret. (According)

specific events

to Abrams, these events are points at which action and
contingency meet, points at (represent) a cross section
of the specific social and individual forces in play at a
given time. At such moments, individuals stand forth

(40) as agents of history (not simply) because they possess a
unique ability to act, (but also) because in them we see
the force of the specific social conditions that allowed
their actions to come forth. Individuals can "make their
mark" on history, (yet) in individuals one (also) finds the

(45) convergence of wider social forces. (In order) to capture

Structure for
examination

the various facets of this mutual interaction, Abrams
(recommends) a fourfold structure to which he believes
the investigations of historical sociologists should
conform: (first,) description of the event itself; (second,)

(50) discussion of the social context that helped bring the
event about and gave it significance; (third,) summary of
the life history of the individual agent in the event; and
(fourth,) analysis of the consequences of the event both
for history and for the individual.[18]

Paragraph Structure: The opening paragraph introduces historical sociology and, more importantly, the views of Philip Abrams. He "argues" (line 4) that society is made by people and vice versa. This view contrasts with the view held by sociologists, who "usually" (line 6) focus only on one influence or the other. Note the emphatic language in line 8: Abrams "insists" that sociologists embrace a model that is less one-sided, coming again to the notion of society affecting people as people affect society. This is the second time in one short paragraph that this two-way influence has been mentioned, so it definitely belongs in your Roadmap.

The second paragraph describes Abrams's views in greater detail. The long, jargon-filled sentence beginning at line 16 is easier to understand by putting it into context. Abrams believes that people affect history, and history affects people; the author is now restating that idea in slightly different terms, saying that our making of history is informed "not only" (line 17) by our own history, "but also" (line 18) by our identities as shaped by "contingencies." The rest of the paragraph describes what contingencies are and how they affect us. While you shouldn't delve too deeply into these details now, be sure to take note of their location; they'll almost certainly be the focus of at least one question.

The third paragraph delves more deeply into historical structuring, describing it as "manifold and unremitting" in line 32. If this is confusing, move on and look for Keywords that will help clear things up. "According to Abrams" in lines 35 to 45, the passage returns to a familiar dichotomy: Individuals can make history at crucial moments "not simply" (line 40) because they can act, "but also" (line 41) because specific social conditions have made their actions possible. Abrams concludes by providing a specific structure in which to understand these relationships beginning in line 45. Like the contingencies of the second paragraph, be ready to return to this information when the questions call for it, but don't waste your time memorizing it now.

This abrupt ending to the passage may seem surprising, but ultimately all the author seemed interested in was explaining Abrams's views on historical sociology. As always, stay focused on the big picture in a passage like this; don't succumb to the details, and be on the lookout for repetitious ideas.

---

[18]PrepTest 38, Sec 3, Passage 3

Topic: Historical sociology

Scope: Abrams's approach to historical sociology

Purpose: To describe Abrams's views on historical sociology

Main Idea: Abrams suggests that history is best understood by examining the relationships between individuals that make history and the history that affects those individuals.

1. **(D)**
    Which one of the following most accurately states the central idea of the passage?
    (A) Abrams argues that historical sociology rejects the claims of sociologists who assert that the sociological concept of structuring cannot be applied to the interactions between individuals and history.
    (B) Abrams argues that historical sociology assumes that, despite the views of sociologists to the contrary, history influences the social contingencies that affect individuals.
    (C) Abrams argues that historical sociology demonstrates that, despite the views of sociologists to the contrary, social structures both influence and are influenced by the events of history.
    (D) Abrams describes historical sociology as a discipline that unites two approaches taken by sociologists to studying the formation of societies and applies the resulting combined approach to the study of history.
    (E) Abrams describes historical sociology as an attempt to compensate for the shortcomings of traditional historical methods by applying the methods established in sociology.[19]

Step 2: This is a Global question, as identified by the stem's request for a "central idea."

Step 3: No research is necessary.

Step 4: In summary: Abrams's view of historical sociology was that we should study the influence of people on history as well as history on people.

Step 5: Correct choice (D) describes Abrams's approach accurately. He does seek to unite the two approaches taken by sociologists (people make history, history makes people). Choice (A) contains a major distortion; the sociologists in the passage never make any claims about the

---

[19]PrepTest 38, Sec 3, Q 15

applicability of structuring. Choice (B) again gives a view to the sociologists that they don't express and distorts Abrams views to boot. Choice (C) is a bit more tricky, but it too distorts the views of the sociologists, who make no claims about "social structures" in this passage. Choice (E) is out of scope; Abrams is never described as compensating for history.

2. **(E)**

    Given the passage's argument, which one of the following sentences most logically completes the last paragraph?

    (A)   Only if they adhere to this structure, Abrams believes, can historical sociologists conclude with any certainty that the events that constitute the historical record are influenced by the actions of individuals.

    (B)   Only if they adhere to this structure, Abrams believes, will historical sociologists be able to counter the standard sociological assumption that there is very little connection between history and individual agency.

    (C)   Unless they can agree to adhere to this structure, Abrams believes, historical sociologists risk having their discipline treated as little more than an interesting but ultimately indefensible adjunct to history and sociology.

    (D)   By adhering to this structure, Abrams believes, historical sociologists can shed light on issues that traditional sociologists have chosen to ignore in their one-sided approaches to the formation of societies.

    (E)   By adhering to this structure, Abrams believes, historical sociologists will be able to better portray the complex connections between human agency and history.[20]

Step 2: This odd question type is a rare variety of Inference, since you are being asked to suggest a new idea that the author must agree with in order to complete the passage.

Step 3: Research this question on a Global-question scale; take notice that the author's primary goal was to describe Abrams's approach to his field, and the fourth paragraph begins by describing the relationships between human action and history before moving on to the fourfold approach Abrams offers to help sociologists understand these "mutual interactions" (line 46).

---

[20]PrepTest 38, Sec 3, Q 16

Step 4: The correct answer should provide a logical addendum to Abrams's thoughts. It is likely to mention the mutual interactions described in line 46, reaffirming that Abrams's approach to historical sociology will help sociologists understand them.

Step 5: Choice (E) correctly completes the author's thoughts, just as predicted. Choices (A), (B), and (C) are extreme; the author never portrays Abrams's approach as mandatory, and Abrams himself "recommends" (line 47) his approach rather than demanding it. Choice (D) distorts the views of the sociologists, suggesting that they've "chosen" to ignore issues. Once again, this harshness of tone does not fit with the author's neutral voice.

3. **(B)**

The passage states that a contingency could be each of the following EXCEPT:
(A) a social phenomenon
(B) a form of historical structuring
(C) an accidental circumstance
(D) a condition controllable to some extent by an individual
(E) a partial determinant of an individual's actions[21]

Step 2: The question asks about what the passage "states." Such unequivocal language indicates a Detail question, or in this case, a Detail EXCEPT question.

Step 3: The stem asks which choice would not be considered a contingency. This leads you straight to the end of the third paragraph, starting at line 21, wherein the author defines a "contingency" as a social phenomenon over which we have varying degrees of control, then goes on to give a number of examples.

Step 4: Since the correct answer will not conform to the definition you just researched, you should proceed by process of elimination, expecting a correct answer choice that is out of scope.

Step 5: Choice (B) is the correct answer; contingencies are not defined as a form of historical structuring, a concept that was discussed earlier in the paragraph. All of the other choices are supported by the text; contingencies are defined as social phenomena that are both controlling and controlled by a person's actions and may include accidental circumstances.

---

[21]PrepTest 38, Sec 3, Passage 3, Q 17

4. **(A)**

Which one of the following is most analogous to the ideal work of a historical sociologist as outlined by Abrams?

(A)   In a report on the enactment of a bill into law, a journalist explains why the need for the bill arose, sketches the biography of the principal legislator who wrote the bill, and ponders the effect that the bill's enactment will have both on society and on the legislator's career.

(B)   In a consultation with a patient, a doctor reviews the patient's medical history, suggests possible reasons for the patient's current condition, and recommends steps that the patient should take in the future to ensure that the condition improves or at least does not get any worse.

(C)   In an analysis of a historical novel, a critic provides information to support the claim that details of the work's setting are accurate, explains why the subject of the novel was of particular interest to the author, and compares the novel with some of the author's other books set in the same period.

(D)   In a presentation to stockholders, a corporation's chief executive officer describes the corporation's most profitable activities during the past year, introduces the vice president largely responsible for those activities, and discusses new projects the vice president will initiate in the coming year.

(E)   In developing a film based on a historical event, a filmmaker conducts interviews with participants in the event, bases part of the film's screenplay on the interviews, and concludes the screenplay with a sequence of scenes speculating on the outcome of the event had certain details been different.[22]

Step 2: The word "analogous" is your clue; this is a Parallel Reasoning question.

Step 3: The "ideal work" most likely refers to Abrams's recommended four-step approach at the end of the passage. Abrams believes, starting at line 49 with the Keyword "first," that a historical sociologist should describe an event, discuss its context in history, summarize the historical figure involved, and finally examine consequences for the individual and history.

---

[22]PrepTest 38, Sec 3, Passage 3, Q 18

Step 4: The correct answer will adhere to the general format of Abrams's approach without referencing the same specific subject matter. Evaluate the choices with this in mind.

Step 5: Choice (A) is a perfect match. In it, the journalist describes events that prompted the bill, the author of the bill, and the bill's likely effect on both history and the author. Choice (B) doesn't reflect this two-way relationship, describing the strictly one-way dictates of the doctor to the patient. Choice (C) brings in an out-of-scope comparison between the author's novel and other books. Choices (D) and (E) are similarly out of scope, failing to describe events that fall within the context of an event and the human agent that affects and is affected by the event.

CHALLENGING PASSAGES ARE VULNERABLE TO STRATEGY

Take a deep breath. You've just worked through a couple of very challenging examples, and you should be proud of your diligence. A lot of ideas were presented in this chapter; most of them were review, but I want to summarize the main points so that you have them at hand as you practice.

Read Predictively

Challenging passages often present excellent contextual information in the first paragraph. Read predictively, building a sense of structure as you go. This will help you understand the more abstract ideas in the passage.

> Many legal theorists have argued that the only morally legitimate goal in imposing criminal penalties against certain behaviors is to prevent people from harming others. Clearly, such theorists would oppose
> (5) laws that force people to act purely for their own good or to refrain from certain harmless acts purely to ensure conformity to some social norm. But the goal of preventing harm to others would also justify legal sanctions against some forms of nonconforming
> (10) behavior to which this goal might at first seem not to apply.[23]

Recall that the two complicated paragraphs following this one served no other purpose than to illustrate the concept described in the highlighted sentence. It's much easier to understand the author's potentially confusing examples if you know that they *must* provide support for this much more simply stated idea.

[23]PrepTest 46, Sec 1, Passage 4

Look for Repetition

Many tough passages are extremely repetitive. Learn to recognize when the author is using different terms to repeat the same idea.

> In many situations it is in the interest of each member of a group to agree to behave in a certain way on the condition that the others similarly agree.
>
> (15) In the simplest cases, a mere coordination of activities is itself the good that results. For example, it is in no one's interest to lack a convention about which side of the road to drive on, and each person can agree to drive on one side assuming the others do
> (20) too. Any fair rule, then, would be better than no rule at all. On the assumption that all people would voluntarily agree to be subject to a coordination rule backed by criminal sanctions, if people could be assured that others would also agree, it is argued to
> (25) be legitimate for a legislature to impose such a rule. This is because prevention of harm underlies the rationale for the rule, though it applies to the problem of coordination less directly than to other problems, for the act that is forbidden (driving on the other side
> (30) of the road) is not inherently harm-producing, as are burglary and assault; instead, it is the lack of a coordinating rule that would be harmful.[24]

While each of these sentences serves a slightly different purpose in the paragraph, they all center around the same idea: Sometimes it's a good idea to make everyone do the same thing.

Use Examples to Clarify

Resist the urge to pore over every detail, but at the same time, recognize that an abstractly worded idea may be clarified by more concrete examples provided by the author. Be prepared to use such examples to help you understand the author's Main Idea if necessary.

> In some other situations involving a need for legally enforced coordination, the harm to be averted
> (35) goes beyond the simple lack of coordination itself. This can be illustrated by an example of a coordination rule—instituted by a private athletic organization—which has analogies in criminal law. At issue is whether the use of anabolic steroids, which
> (40) build muscular strength but have serious negative side effects, should be prohibited.[25]

---

[24]PrepTest 46, Sec 1, Passage 4
[25]PrepTest 46, Sec 1, Passage 4

Even the most well-prepared test taker could be forgiven for finding the first sentence of this paragraph confusing. But if it "can be illustrated by an example," and the example is a straightforward one (most readers will be familiar with the steroid ban in sports), use the example to help you clarify the issue.

Keep Moving

The most common mistake that my students make when faced with a difficult passage is to slow to a crawl and attempt to understand every word, when the author's principle conclusion can be summed up in a short sentence. If the text you're reading is hopelessly unclear, review your Roadmap and move forward to find a better sense of context.

> In some other situations involving a need for
> legally enforced coordination, the harm to be averted
> (35) goes beyond the simple lack of coordination itself.
> This can be illustrated by an example of a
> coordination rule—instituted by a private athletic
> organization—which has analogies in criminal law. At
> issue is whether the use of anabolic steroids, which
> (40) build muscular strength but have serious negative side
> effects, should be prohibited. Each athlete has at stake
> both an interest in having a fair opportunity to win
> and an interest in good health. If some competitors
> use steroids, others have the option of either
> (45) endangering their health or losing their fair
> opportunity to win. Thus they would be harmed either
> way. A compulsory rule could prevent that harm and
> thus would be in the interest of all competitors. If
> they understand its function and trust the techniques
> (50) for its enforcement, they will gladly consent to it. So
> while it might appear that such a rule merely forces
> people to act for their own good, the deeper rationale
> for coercion here—as in the above example—is a
> somewhat complex appeal to the legitimacy of
> (55) enforcing a rule with the goal of preventing harm.[26]

Note how the final sentence neatly sums up the entire paragraph. If the steroid-ban example didn't clarify the author's goals for you, this brief conclusion certainly will, particularly because it references the concept of "preventing harm." This idea should look familiar—it's part of the author's Main Idea and should already be in your Roadmap by the time you reach this paragraph.

---

[26]PrepTest 46, Sec 1, Passage 4

Stay Confident

Finally, and most importantly, don't let the pressure of a challenging passage lead you to abandon the Kaplan Method. Stay in control of the passage and approach it the right way; remember that confidence leads to a higher score.

REVIEW, REVIEW, REVIEW

I would strongly encourage you to review all of the examples in this chapter. Dealing with tough passages efficiently takes practice and often will require you to more thoroughly review your work. When you're ready, move on to the next chapter, where I'll be leading you through some examples of odd variations on familiar question types.

CHAPTER 16

Unusual Questions

RARE VARIATIONS ON COMMON QUESTIONS

Now that you've become familiar with the common Reading Comprehension question types that you'll see on test day, I hope their predictability has boosted your confidence. With only five common question types and proven Kaplan strategies to counter each one, Reading Comprehension is revealed to be very limited, and therefore very manageable.

That said, the test makers will occasionally write questions that at first glance don't appear to fit neatly into a single category or that present a common task in an unusual way. These unusual questions can be worrisome. My students frequently ask me about such questions in a state of near-panic, concerned that the predictability of the test has become suspect, and fearful that their LSAT will be full of strange tasks they've never seen before and that they are completely unprepared to deal with.

I tell them the same thing I'll tell you—that unusual questions are nothing to fear. First of all, by definition they don't appear often on the test (otherwise they wouldn't be unusual questions). Second, while these questions may look bizarre initially, they can always be reduced to variations on common types with which you're already familiar. And this means that, like all LSAT questions, they are amenable to the Kaplan Method.

My students eventually learn to stay calm and methodical when they encounter strange-looking questions, once they understand that such questions aren't very different from questions they've already mastered. That's the primary lesson I want you to take away from this chapter: Although the occasional odd question will appear on the test, if you confidently apply the

Kaplan Method, you will score the point. Every question has an answer, and all the information you need is *always* in the passage.

Before I present some specific examples, I want to point out that in this chapter I'll be focusing more on specific question variations than on strategic reading. For this reason, you'll see shorter excerpts from passages rather than complete Roadmaps. Please remember that in your practice you should *always* create a Roadmap for every passage you read just as you will on test day.

Common Questions in Disguise

An exhaustive list of every unusual question to appear on the LSAT would be very hard to compile, and rather subjective as well. A better way to prepare for such questions is to learn how to properly apply the Kaplan Method to any unusual situation. In fact, you've already seen examples of such questions in previous chapters of this book.

3. Which one of the following titles most completely summarizes the content of the passage?

    (A) "Avenues for Change: The Case for Dissent in Authoritarian Regimes"
    (B) "Human Rights Abuses under Authoritarian Regimes: A Case Study"
    (C) "Democratic Coalitions under Authoritarian Regimes: Strategies and Solutions"
    (D) "Why Authoritarian Regimes Compromise: An Examination of Societal Forces"
    (E) "Growing Pains: Economic Instability in Countries on the Brink of Democracy"[1]

The question stem asks you to select an appropriate title for the passage. What function does the title of a work serve? Ideally, it should briefly encapsulate the author's thesis. In LSAT terms, it should reflect the author's Main Idea. So, this question is just a Global question in disguise, which you may recall first seeing in chapter 10.

You might have been surprised by the wording of this question when you initially encountered it, but it probably didn't take you very long to understand what it was really asking for. Here's another example, this time from chapter 15:

16. Given the passage's argument, which one of the following sentences most logically completes the last paragraph?[2]

---

[1]PrepTest 34, Sec 1, Q 3
[2]PrepTest 38, Sec 3, Q 16

The stem asks you to select an appropriate ending for the final paragraph of a passage. Once again, take a moment to think through the task. The last sentence should logically complete the author's thoughts, bringing the paragraph to a tidy conclusion. Since the stem asks you to infer what new information could appropriately be added to the passage, this is simply a rare form of Inference question.

In order to determine what would logically follow, you should go back to the text and think about what the author's goals were in the final paragraph. Review the paragraph and note any Keywords, as always:

> In Abrams's analysis, historical structuring, like
> social structuring, is manifold and unremitting. To
> understand it, historical sociologists must extract from
> it certain significant episodes, or events, that their
> (35) methodology can then analyze and interpret. According
> to Abrams, these events are points at which action and
> contingency meet, points that represent a cross section
> of the specific social and individual forces in play at a
> given time. At such moments, individuals stand forth
> (40) as agents of history not simply because they possess a
> unique ability to act, but also because in them we see
> the force of the specific social conditions that allowed
> their actions to come forth. Individuals can "make their
> mark" on history, yet in individuals one also finds the
> (45) convergence of wider social forces. In order to capture
> the various facets of this mutual interaction, Abrams
> recommends a fourfold structure to which he believes
> the investigations of historical sociologists should
> conform: first, description of the event itself; second,
> (50) discussion of the social context that helped bring the
> event about and gave it significance; third, summary of
> the life history of the individual agent in the event; and
> fourth, analysis of the consequences of the event both
> for history and for the individual.[3]

Abrams emphatically states that historical sociologists "must extract" significant episodes from history and then elaborates on why this is the case, focusing on the importance of the relationship between events and individuals. He then "recommends a fourfold structure" that he believes others should adhere to. This paragraph is all about Abrams's recommendations. The correct answer should reflect this, reemphasizing the importance of the structured approach Abrams lays out.

---

[3]PrepTest 38, Sec 3, Passage 3

16. Given the passage's argument, which one of the following sentences most logically completes the last paragraph?

(A) Only if they adhere to this structure, Abrams believes, can historical sociologists conclude with any certainty that the events that constitute the historical record are influenced by the actions of individuals.

(B) Only if they adhere to this structure, Abrams believes, will historical sociologists be able to counter the standard sociological assumption that there is very little connection between history and individual agency.

(C) Unless they can agree to adhere to this structure, Abrams believes, historical sociologists risk having their discipline treated as little more than an interesting but ultimately indefensible adjunct to history and sociology.

(D) By adhering to this structure, Abrams believes, historical sociologists can shed light on issues that traditional sociologists have chosen to ignore in their one-sided approaches to the formation of societies.

(E) By adhering to this structure, Abrams believes, historical sociologists will be able to better portray the complex connections between human agency and history.[4]

The only answer choice that connects Abrams's recommendations back to a better understanding of history is correct choice (E).

The examples you've seen so far may be somewhat unusual, but you could ultimately identify each one as belonging to one of the five common question types. However, other questions might seem to defy such simple categorization. In any case, every question you see on the LSAT will present tasks that you've seen before. As long as you read each question carefully and think about what clues will lead you to the correct answer, the familiar process of research and prediction will allow you to score the point.

Here's another example, this time in terms of the Kaplan Method:

15. Which one of the following persons displays an approach that most strongly suggests sympathy with the principles of reader-response theory?[5]

Step 2: Identify the Question Type

You're asked to identify a person who behaves in accordance with the principles of reader-response theory. Hopefully you recognized this as a variant of Parallel Reasoning, since the correct answer should be in some way analogous to the theory as it's presented in the passage.

---

[4]PrepTest 38, Sec 3Q16
[5]PrepTest 43, Sec 1, Passage 3

Step 3: Research the Relevant Text

Review the following text:

> Reader-response theory, a type of literary theory
> that arose in reaction to formalist literary criticism,
> has endeavored to shift the emphasis in the
> interpretation of literature from the text itself to the
> (5) contributions of readers to the meaning of a text.
> According to literary critics who endorse reader-
> response theory, the literary text alone renders no
> meaning; it acquires meaning only when encountered
> by individual readers, who always bring varying
> (10) presuppositions and ways of reading to bear on the
> text, giving rise to the possibility—even probability—
> of varying interpretations.[6]

Reader-response theory suggests that the meaning of a text is derived not from the author, but from the reader. In fact, it claims that the text alone "renders no meaning" (lines 7–8) and that a work will likely give rise to varying interpretations based on the assumptions supplied by readers.

Step 4: Make a Prediction

What kind of person would sympathize with reader response theory? Simply put, someone who believes that his or her interpretation of a work is valuable, possible more valuable than the original work itself. The correct answer should reflect this idea in some way.

Step 5: Evaluate the Answer Choices

15. Which one of the following persons displays an
    approach that most strongly suggests sympathy with the
    principles of reader-response theory?

    (A) a translator who translates a poem from Spanish
         to English word for word so that its original
         meaning is not distorted
    (B) a music critic who insists that early music can
         be truly appreciated only when it is played on
         original instruments of the period
    (C) a reviewer who finds in the works of a novelist
         certain unifying themes that reveal the
         novelist's personal concerns and preoccupations
    (D) a folk artist who uses conventional cultural
         symbols and motifs as a way of conveying
         commonly understood meanings
    (E) a director who sets a play by Shakespeare in
         nineteenth-century Japan to give a new
         perspective on the work[7]

---

[6]PrepTest 43, Sec 1, Passage 3
[7]PrepTest 43, Sec 1, Passage 3, Q 15

Correct choice (E) is the match. The director takes the work of another author and reinterprets it, which is very much in line with reader-response theory. Choices (A) and (B) run contrary to your prediction—they insist on conformity to aspects of an original work. Choice (C) is similarly off the mark, as it is concerned with divining the ideas of a work's author. Choice (D) goes out of Scope in describing a process of writing rather than a method of interpretation.

Once again, an unusual question proves to be vulnerable to critical thinking and the Kaplan Method.

Convoluted Question Stems

Sometimes a question stem may seem too complicated or wordy to deal with efficiently. Here is an example:

> 23. Suppose that pesticide X drastically slows the reproductive rate of cyclamen mites and has no other direct effect on cyclamen mites or *Typhlodromus*. Based on the information in the passage, which one of the following would most likely have occurred if, in the experiments mentioned in the passage, pesticide X had been used instead of parathion, with all other conditions affecting the experiments remaining the same?[8]

I want to stress once more how important it is not to be intimidated by a question like this one. Read the stem carefully, think about what you're being asked, and proceed through the Kaplan Method.

Step 2: This is an Inference question, since the stem asks what "would most likely have occurred" in a given situation. You are given some additional hypothetical information to consider: A pesticide slows the reproduction of cyclamen mites. What would have to be true if, in an experiment, this new pesticide had been used instead of parathion?

Step 3: Read the following excerpt from the passage, which details the experiment referenced in the question:

> Greenhouse experiments have verified the importance of *Typhlodromus* predation for keeping
> (40) cyclamen mites in check. One group of strawberry plants was stocked with both predator and prey mites; a second group was kept predator-free by regular application of parathion, an insecticide that kills the predatory species but does not affect the cyclamen
> (45) mite. Throughout the study, populations of cyclamen mites remained low in plots shared with *Typhlodromus*, but their infestation attained significantly damaging proportions on predator-free plants.[9]

---

[8]PrepTest 53, Sec 4, Q 23
[9]PrepTest 53, Sec 4, Passage 4

The experiment demonstrates that a certain kind of predator mite, *Typhlodromus,* is useful in controlling the population of cyclamen mites. When parathion was used to control the predators, cyclamen mites reproduced to damaging levels.

Step 4: Now think through the hypothetical provided by the question stem and make a prediction. What if the experimenters used pesticide X, which slows the reproductive rate of cyclamen mites, instead of parathion? You would expect to see a drop in the number of cyclamen mites on the plants treated with pesticide X. There is evidence that the cyclamen mites will also be subject to control by predation, since the new pesticide doesn't negatively affect the *Typhlodromus* mites. In sum, you should predict that the use of pesticide X would result in control of the cyclamen mite population.

Step 5:

23. Suppose that pesticide X drastically slows the reproductive rate of cyclamen mites and has no other direct effect on cyclamen mites or *Typhlodromus.* Based on the information in the passage, which one of the following would most likely have occurred if, in the experiments mentioned in the passage, pesticide X had been used instead of parathion, with all other conditions affecting the experiments remaining the same?

    (A) In both treated and untreated plots inhabited by both *Typhlodromus* and cyclamen mites, the latter would have been effectively controlled.
    (B) Cyclamen mite populations in all treated plots from which *Typhlodromus* was absent would have been substantially lower than in untreated plots inhabited by both kinds of mites.
    (C) In the treated plots, slowed reproduction in cyclamen mites would have led to a loss of reproductive synchrony between *Typhlodromus* and cyclamen mites.
    (D) In the treated plots, *Typhlodromus* populations would have decreased temporarily and would have eventually increased.
    (E) In the treated plots, cyclamen mite populations would have reached significantly damaging levels more slowly, but would have remained at those levels longer, than in untreated plots.[10]

The prediction should lead you directly to correct choice (A). Since the new pesticide controls cyclamen mites while leaving its predators unharmed, cyclamen mites should be controlled in all cases. Choice (B) is extreme, suggesting without warrant that the new pesticide would be more effective in controlling cyclamen mites than natural predation—which might be true, but

---

[10]PrepTest 53, Sec 4, Q 23

doesn't necessarily have to be. Choices (D) and (E) similarly cannot be inferred with available information, and choice (C) is completely out of scope.

No matter how complicated the question stem may seem at first glance, the task is always there for you to discover, provided that you approach every question methodically. Here's one more example of a complicated-looking question:

> 20. Suppose a study is conducted that measures the amount of airtime allotted to imported television programming in the daily broadcasting schedules of several developing nations. Given the information in the passage, the results of that study would be most directly relevant to answering which one of the following questions?[11]

Step 2: A hypothetical study is presented, and you are asked to determine what question this study might best help to answer. The question type may seem unclear, but the correct answer must be the one that falls within the scope of the proposed study; you're looking for what the study would be "most directly relevant" in answering. Since the answer choices will present a series of hypothetical questions that were never mentioned in the passage, you're essentially being asked to identify new information that is compatible with the text. You can therefore think of this as an Inference question. Use these clues to guide you as you apply Step 3 of the Kaplan Method.

Step 3: The first paragraph is helpful in finding the answer to this question:

> Specialists in international communications almost unanimously assert that the broadcasting in developing nations of television programs produced by industrialized countries amounts to cultural
> (5) imperialism: the phenomenon of one culture's productions overwhelming another's, to the detriment of the flourishing of the latter. This assertion assumes the automatic dominance of the imported productions and their negative effect on the domestic culture. But
> (10) the assertion is polemical and abstract, based on little or no research into the place held by imported programs in the economies of importing countries or in the lives of viewers.[12]

Whether the author agrees with these specialists, the passage presents the view that the broadcasting of foreign programs into developing nations presents that nation with new cultural productions (which may or may not be a form of cultural imperialism).

---

[11]PrepTest 51, Sec 2, Q 20
[12]PrepTest 51, Sec 2, Passage 3

Step 4: Since all you know for sure is that the nations in question are receiving new cultural products, a study that examines how much outside broadcasting is allowed in a particular nation would be useful in determining, in part, how much exposure that nation gets to such cultural products.

Step 5:

20. Suppose a study is conducted that measures the amount of airtime allotted to imported television programming in the daily broadcasting schedules of several developing nations. Given the information in the passage, the results of that study would be most directly relevant to answering which one of the following questions?

    (A) How does the access to imported cultural productions differ among these nations?
    (B) What are the individual viewing habits of citizens in these nations?
    (C) How influential are the domestic television industries in these nations?
    (D) Do imported programs attract larger audiences than domestic ones in these nations?
    (E) What model best describes the relationship between imported cultural influences and domestic culture in these nations?[13]

The correct answer, choice (A), matches the prediction. Choices (B) and (C) fall out of scope by introducing individual viewing habits and domestic television industries, neither of which are relevant to the experiment described in the question stem. Choices (D) and (E) present irrelevant comparisons—the information in the passage doesn't provide the sort of detailed information about imported vs. domestic culture that would be required to make either of these choices correct.

When faced with a wordy question stem, particularly one that presents you with hypothetical information, it is crucial that you take your time when executing Step 2 of the Kaplan Method. As always, all the information you need to answer the question is provided, but the more complex the stem, the more opportunities there are to misunderstand what the question is asking or to overlook a key piece of information. Don't let the pressure of the clock interfere with your thinking when you approach this type of question—be sure you've understood what the question asks you, and carefully follow each step of the method.

---

[13]PrepTest 51, Sec 2, Q 20

Challenging Research

You know that some questions provide more precise research clues than others. Compare these questions:

4. Which one of the following is presented by the author as evidence of controlled burning in the tropics before the arrival of Europeans?[14]

6. As evidence for the routine practice of forest burning by native populations before the arrival of Europeans, the author cites all of the following EXCEPT:[15]

These two Detail questions give you the same essential task, but question 6 presents a potentially greater research challenge—since detail EXCEPT questions require you to identify the single piece of information that *doesn't* appear in the passage, you may have to reexamine several portions of the text to eliminate incorrect answers. Because EXCEPT questions are not as amenable to simple prediction, they can also be time-consuming.

The challenge of complex research can also present itself in other types of questions. Here's one example:

22. The logical relationship of lines 8–13 of the passage to lines 23–25 and 49–53 of the passage is most accurately described as[16]

By itself, this question may look so abstract as to defy solution. As always, you'll find the solution by applying the Kaplan Method.

Step 2: The question asks for a "logical relationship" between various sections of the passage. This question is likely asking about structure, and it resembles a Logic Function question since it requires you to identify what role specific parts of the text play.

Step 3: Take a look at the quoted portions of the text. Start with lines 8–13:

But the
(10) practical benefits of such automated reasoning systems have fallen short of optimistic early predictions and have not resulted in computer systems that can independently provide expert advice about substantive law.[17]

---

[14]PrepTest 38, Sec 3, Q 4

[15]PrepTest 38, Sec 3, Q 6

[16]PrepTest 51, Sec 2, Q 22

[17]PrepTest 51, Sec 2, Passage 4

This portion of the text describes the shortcomings of certain kinds of computer systems despite predictions to the contrary. Now examine lines 23–25:

> Such systems underestimated the
> problems of interpretation that can arise at every
> (25) stage of a legal argument.[18]

This appears to be supporting evidence for the shortcomings described earlier. Similar evidence appears in lines 49–53:

> Unfortunately, in the case-based systems
> (50) currently in development, the criteria for similarity
> among cases are system dependent and fixed by the
> designer, so that similarity is found only by testing
> for the presence or absence of predefined factors.[19]

Even if you don't understand all the jargon, the Keyword "unfortunately" at the beginning would indicate that the case-based systems are disappointing in some respect.

Step 4: Although a fair amount of research was required, you're now in a good place to make a prediction. The first quoted sentence described a problem with certain computer systems, and the following two quotes provided illustrations of the problem.

Step 5:

22. The logical relationship of lines 8–13 of the passage to lines 23–25 and 49–53 of the passage is most accurately described as

    (A) a general assertion supported by two specific observations
    (B) a general assertion followed by two arguments, one of which supports and one of which refutes the general assertion
    (C) a general assertion that entails two more specific assertions
    (D) a theoretical assumption refuted by two specific observations
    (E) a specific observation that suggests two incompatible generalizations[20]

Choice (A), the correct answer, gives an excellent general description that matches the prediction. Choice (B) incorrectly identifies the supporting evidence as arguments, and choice (C) suggests that that the two pieces of evidence follow from the assertion—a 180, since the evidence supports the claim, not vice versa. The refutation mentioned in choice (D) never occurred, and neither do the two incompatible generalizations mentioned in choice (E).

---

[18]PrepTest 51, Sec 2, Passage 4
[19]PrepTest 51, Sec 2, Passage 4
[20]PrepTest 51, Sec 2, Q 22

Take a moment to appreciate how quickly the Kaplan Method allowed you to transform this very abstract-looking question into a simple, familiar task. Once you identified the language of a Logic Function question in Step 2 and conducted proper research in Step 3, a prediction was not far behind.

Now for one final example. In the previous example, your research was spread out over the passage, but specific line references made the task much easier. Sometimes the question won't provide such straightforward clues:

> 6. Which one of the following aspects of Mphahlele's work does the author of the passage appear to value most highly?[21]

Step 2: This is an Inference question, albeit an oddly worded one. The stem asks for the author's attitude, specifically the aspect of Mphahlele's work that the author is most interested in.

Step 3: A scan for Keywords of emphasis across the passage will tell you where the author's primary interest lies. Examine the following excerpts:

> Critics have variously
> decried the former as too fictionalized and the latter
> as too autobiographical, (but) those who focus on
> (15) traditional labels inevitably (miss the fact) that
> Mphahlele manipulates different prose forms (purely)
> (in the service) of the social message he
> advances.

> But his (greater concern) is the social vision
> that pervades his work, though it too is prone to
> (35) misunderstandings and underappreciation.

> As
> he claims, the whole point of the exercise of writing
> has nothing to do with classification; (in all forms)
> writing is the transmission of ideas, and (important)
> (55) (ideas) at that: "Whenever you write prose or poetry or
> drama you are writing a social criticism of one kind
> or another. If you don't, you are completely
> irrelevant—you don't count."[22]

Step 4: In each of the above quotes, the author emphasizes Mphahlele's devotion to social commentary in his work.

---

[21]PrepTest 51, Sec 2, Q 6

[22]PrepTest 51, Sec 2, Passage 1

Step 5:

6. Which one of the following aspects of Mphahlele's work does the author of the passage appear to value most highly?

    (A) his commitment to communicating social messages
    (B) his blending of the categories of fiction and autobiography
    (C) his ability to redefine established literary categories
    (D) his emphasis on the importance of details
    (E) his plan for bringing about the future he envisions[23]

Only correct choice (A) mentions the importance of social commentary. Choice (B) is a distortion; the author does mention Mphahlele's blending of categories, but only because they don't impede his ability to communicate social messages. Choice (C) also distorts the author's ideas, since the redefining of categories is not mentioned. Choice (D) presents the out of Scope idea of the importance of details, and choice (E) is extreme—Mphahlele is described as having a "social vision," but there is no mention of any plan to fulfill such a vision.

This question represents only a slight variation on author's-attitude questions you've seen before. As always, the author's primary concerns will be identified by plenty of Keywords. Methodical attention to these Keywords will make short work of what might at first appear to be a time-consuming research task.

THE KAPLAN METHOD ALWAYS APPLIES

It isn't within anyone's power to predict exactly how the test makers will phrase the questions on the LSAT. You should expect the majority of the Reading Comprehension questions you see on your test to look very familiar to the ones you most commonly see in your practice. Nonetheless, you must also be prepared for the occasional oddly worded stem. As you've learned, most of these questions are variations of familiar types, and all of them—without exception—are amenable to the Kaplan Method. If you encounter an unfamiliar-looking question on test day, don't panic—read the stem carefully, use the clues the test makers provide you, and apply the Kaplan Method with care. Every question has a correct answer, and the information you need is *always* there.

---

[23]PrepTest 51, Sec 2, Q 6

CHAPTER 17

RECENT TRENDS

READING COMPREHENSION REMAINS PREDICTABLE

You've now learned everything you need to know about Kaplan's Method for Reading Comprehension, and you've applied what you've learned to a variety of LSAT passages and questions. A major theme throughout this book has been the predictability of the LSAT in general and the Reading Comprehension section in particular. Before you move on to Part III, I'd like to share a little information with you about the composition of recent tests and what this means for your test day experience.

The great news is that very little has changed in LSAT Reading Comprehension over the last few years, and a passage randomly selected from a test administered ten years ago is very much like a passage from the last few years. The essential composition of the section—that is, four exercises representing humanities, social sciences, natural sciences, and law—has remained the same. There have been a few observable changes of note, and the most obvious one is the recent addition of comparative reading.

Comparative Reading

As you learned in chapter 9, comparative reading was first introduced in the June 2007 administration of the LSAT. Since then, exactly one set of paired passages has appeared in each Reading Comprehension section. This came as no surprise, as the LSAC formally announced this change months in advance of its occurrence, providing a sample passage and question set on their official website immediately following the February 2007 test.

Among the LSATs released as of the time of this writing there are examples of the comparative passages appearing first, second, third, and fourth within the section. However, of the released pairs (eighteen through the end of 2012), fourteen have been in either the second or third position. Given the small sample size, it's difficult to say how the distribution of the paired passages will trend in the coming years.

Another trend that has emerged relates to the subject area of the set of paired passages. Of the eighteen passage pairs available at the time of writing, eight have been written about the natural sciences, four about the social sciences, four about law, and just two about humanities. Thus, natural science comparative passages account for just under half of the paired passages disclosed through the December 2012 administration of the LSAT. However, three of the last four released tests have had law as the subject matter of the comparative passages. While these statistics by no means guarantee that the comparative reading on your LSAT will deal with natural science or law, it may indicate a preference on the part of the test makers. What is most important for you to note is that there have been passage pairs representing each of the four subject areas, so be prepared to see any one of them on test day.

It's also worth noting that comparative passages tend to feature a relatively high proportion of Logic Reasoning questions. Because these question types are generally considered more challenging than some other question types, comparative passages are likewise considered more difficult than an average single passage. This is useful to know when you consider how to best manage an entire Reading Comprehension section. I'll go into greater detail about section management in the next chapter.

Section Difficulty

As Kaplan continues to collect data from students taking practice sections and previously released LSATs, trends also emerge regarding the difficulty (both real and perceived) of the Reading Comprehension section as a whole.

It is interesting (and hopefully reassuring) to note that our students rarely report that they considered the Reading Comprehension sections of their tests to be the most difficult section of the test. In fact, the percentage who did consider Reading Comprehension the most difficult has declined significantly since 2007, a year which saw a significant spike in the perceived difficulty of Reading Comprehension. For example, in December of 2007 47% of students—nearly half of those reporting—identified this section as the most challenging of their exam. Occasionally other tests have also seen some high numbers—on the June 2011 exam, for example, 50% of test takers reported Reading Comprehension as the most challenging section—but overall the number has decreased since 2007. In 2012, of Kaplan students taking any of the four administration dates, a range of just 26% to 34% reported that they considered Reading Comprehension to be the most challenging section.

There are two interesting facts that, once again, suggest that Reading Comprehension hasn't actually changed very much in difficulty over the years. One is that as our students take previously released LSATs under timed conditions, the overall difficulty level of Reading Comprehension sections as a whole (as determined by percentage of questions answered correctly vs. incorrectly) has remained very consistent over the last five years. The other thing to note is that the spike in perceived difficulty of the test began with the June 2007 administration of the LSAT—the first time that comparative reading appeared. By December of 2008 a significantly smaller percentage of our students (only 30% for the December 2008 test) reported that they considered Reading Comprehension to be the most difficult LSAT section. It's therefore a definite possibility that students perceived the section to be more difficult in 2007–2008 because of the relative newness of comparative reading.

Taken all together, this data suggests a disparity between how our students *perceive* the difficulty of the section and how difficult it actually is. This should serve to remind you just how important confidence is to your LSAT score. No matter how challenging a section or passage may seem to you, it isn't likely to deviate in a significant way from what you've already seen in your practice. The familiarity you gain through practice is one of your most powerful advantages on test day—remember to trust in what you've learned.

Question Trends

Once again, the composition of question types from test to test is extremely predictable, and there haven't been many notable shifts in either the overall difficulty of the questions or the types of questions appearing. At the time of this writing, every released practice test in the last three years has contained 27 Reading Comprehension questions. Averaged out, each passage will come with about seven questions (although the actual range will always be between five to eight questions).

From 2008 to the present, an average Reading Comprehension section comprised approximately five Global questions, five Detail questions, three Logic Function questions, three Logic Reasoning questions, and eleven Inference questions. These numbers are fairly representative of older LSATs as well, although there has been a very slight increase in the number of Inference and Reasoning questions over the last ten years. More than anything, this should remind you that the test makers seek to reward your ability to think critically about the information in the passage much more than your ability to repeat details. This makes strategic reading that much more crucial to the overall health of your LSAT score.

It's also important to note that, of the questions most often missed by our students in their reported practice on recent tests, the majority are Inference questions. This is probably partially due to the larger number of such questions appearing on a given test, and because they tend to be more challenging than Global and Detail questions; in any case, a thorough review of Inference questions is advisable for any LSAT student. Keep this in mind as you review the full-length practice sections coming up a bit later in this book.

Stick to the Kaplan Method

On the whole the Reading Comprehension section of today is very, very similar to the section of 2005, with the addition of comparative reading as the one big difference. The Kaplan Method has been an effective approach to the Reading Comprehension regardless of small changes in the composition of the section, and careful research has allowed us to adapt it to fit the larger ones. The questions and passages that you've seen in this book are representative of the ones you'll see on test day, and the full-length practice sections you'll complete in Part III of this book are from recently administered tests. Reading Comprehension is not likely to hold any big surprises for you when you take your LSAT. Keep this in mind as you continue to practice, and let it motivate you to stick to the strategies that have proven to be effective.

PART III

FULL-LENGTH SECTION PRACTICE

CHAPTER 18

TIMING AND SECTION MANAGEMENT IN A NUTSHELL

TAKE CONTROL OF THE SECTION

If you've made it this far, you've learned everything you need to know about Reading Comprehension passages, the kinds of questions you'll encounter on test day, and how to apply the Kaplan Method to all of them. You've learned a whole new way of reading and you've internalized the strategies you require to score the points. This is a fantastic accomplishment, and I congratulate you for your perseverance and dedication.

Now it's time to start thinking about the bigger picture and learn how to effectively approach an entire Reading Comprehension section. Just as you might think about the LSAT as a series of five individual mini-tests (six if you include the Writing Sample), you can also think of a single Reading Comprehension section as a set of four distinct challenges. In this chapter, I'll give you some general guidelines to follow as you take on these challenges.

When you first began to learn the Kaplan Method, you may have thought it impossible to read the passages in the time allotted. As you became more familiar with the predictable nature of the passages, you learned that by reading in an active, purposeful way, you can efficiently focus on the right information. You learned how to take control of the passages.

Similarly, you might have found the questions confusing and the answer choices abstract and difficult to deal with. If you're like the majority of my students, you were almost certainly answering most questions by a laborious process of elimination, evaluating the answer choices without a clear idea of what you were looking for. Now you understand the tasks that the questions present you, and you know how to approach them actively, answering the questions efficiently and accurately. In this way, you take control of the questions.

Now you must take everything you've learned and use it to take control of the entire section. Without this sense of control, the pressure of the clock will always work against you in unpredictable ways. To help you begin countering this problem, I'll introduce you to some basic principles, then move on to specific strategies that deal with passage and question selection.

GENERAL TIMING PRINCIPLES
Efficiency vs. Speed

I've been very careful throughout this book to use the word "efficient" when describing the merits of a time-saving strategy, and I've used this word for a very specific reason. To score your best on the LSAT, you must accomplish the tasks it presents you with efficiently, but this is very different from simply doing things quickly.

Efficiency is all about saving time while still doing everything you need to do in order to score points. For example, Step 1 of the Kaplan Method is focused on efficiency. By staying focused on the big picture as you read and by focusing on the author's main ideas (and refusing to dwell on details), you ultimately read more efficiently. At the same time, you circle and think about Keywords, write a solid Roadmap, and ask predictive questions of the passage as you move from paragraph to paragraph.

You might think that you can save even more time by skipping the Roadmap or making a mental note of Keywords instead of actually circling them, but this is a classic example of favoring speed over efficiency. If you ignore the crucial elements of the Kaplan Method, it is certainly possible that you'll spend less time reading the passage, but the consequences would outweigh any time gained. You're much less likely to have a sound understanding of the author's Purpose and Main Idea, making Global questions cumbersome and difficult to answer. Without a Roadmap to guide you, you'll find it harder to research relevant text, and may be tempted to rely on your memory too much when answering questions (a very risky thing to do). Not only will you have sacrificed accuracy in the question set, but any time you gained by careless reading will likely be lost as you struggle to answer the questions without a solid grasp of the passage.

The same principles apply to individual questions. Taking the time to correctly identify the question type allows you to instantly recall the proper strategy to use, rather than wasting time trying to figure out how to proceed. Skillful research (aided by Keywords and your Roadmap) allows you to predict and match your answer with confidence rather than fumbling with each answer choice (and thereby letting the test guide your thinking rather than you taking control of the test . . . another risky practice). Any time you gain by cutting corners is likely to be lost again when you struggle with the questions, and if you rely upon your intuition rather than a proven, methodical approach, your accuracy will suffer.

This is what I mean when I tell you to be efficient. Be patient, adhere to the Kaplan Method, and save time by doing the right things, not by skipping steps.

Divide and Conquer

On any given passage (or set of paired passages) there are optimal timing guidelines you should follow. Since you have four passages to complete in 35 minutes, you have an average of eight minutes and 45 seconds for each one. Since you will begin every timed section with a brief overview of the section (discussed later in this chapter), that average is actually closer to eight minutes and 30 seconds. With patience and practice, your goal should be to strategically read any given passage in 3–4 minutes, leaving the remaining time (about five minutes) to work with the questions.

If at first you struggle to hit these timing guidelines, take a look at your work and try to get a sense for where you're investing too much time. Be sure that you're not merely circling Keywords, but actively using them to guide your thinking. If you circle the words "for example" but then go right on to pore over the example in exacting detail, you're not using the Keywords to your maximum advantage. Remember to always read predictively; anticipate where the author is going from paragraph to paragraph, and use the understanding of structure this provides you to find the author's key ideas more easily. Look critically at your Roadmap and be sure you're not over-annotating. While the Roadmap must be thorough enough to guide your research, it shouldn't amount to a summary of every detail presented in the text.

Be similarly critical of your approach to individual questions. Are you able to easily identify the five common question types? Can you confidently recall the strategies that are associated with each one? If not, some review is in order. One of the big advantages of the Kaplan Method is the time you save by never having to wonder what to do next. Make sure you're reaping the full benefits of this advantage.

If in the last section I encouraged you to be patient in your practice, I'm now urging you to be confident. Far too many of my students begin their LSAT journeys with the entirely mistaken notion that scoring more points will lead to a feeling of confidence, when the relationship is actually the complete opposite. Approach every passage and every question with a confident knowledge of the strategies that work, and your timing will improve, as well as your score. Build that confidence by continuing to improve your application of the Kaplan Method.

Know When to Guess Strategically

One of the most useful things to know about great timing is that there is no penalty for guessing on the LSAT. That means that, unlike the SAT, you aren't penalized for bubbling in an incorrect answer. You should therefore answer every question and be prepared to guess when time is tight. If you must guess on multiple questions in a section, you are statistically more likely to score additional points if you guess a consistent choice each time (that is, fill in every unanswered question with (A), (B), or whichever choice you prefer, rather than choosing a different choice each time).

Another crucial lesson, one that my students sometimes find difficult to learn, is that you absolutely must be prepared to skip a time-consuming question if it's in your best interest to do so. This is innately challenging for most students—you probably don't want to feel like you're giving up, and you certainly don't want to let go of a valuable point. Nevertheless, the best test takers also understand that your only goal on the LSAT is to score as many points as possible in every section. If you read a question stem and realize you aren't sure how to proceed with your research, or that the research required is likely to take a lot of time, skip the question and move on to others that you can answer more quickly. In your test booklet, circle each question you skip (and be sure to circle the entire question, not just the question number—this will make it much easier to find if you return to it later). A skipped question will still be there for you to come back to once you've scored the easier points in the section. And if you have to guess, it's much better to guess on a difficult question than an easy one. Remember, each question is worth a single point, regardless of difficulty. If you have to sacrifice one tough question in order to answer two or three easier ones, the trade is worth it.

Remember also that a question that seems difficult when you first approach it may become easier after you've completed other questions in the section, usually because of the research you've conducted. Take a look at three questions, presented in their original order from an actual LSAT passage, and think about the order in which you should answer them:

21. The passage provides information that answers each of the following questions EXCEPT:[1]

22. The primary function of the first two paragraphs of the passage is to[2]

23. The passage is primarily concerned with[3]

Question 21 will almost certainly require some careful research to answer accurately and is not amenable to easy prediction. If you're savvy, you'll skip this question and move on to question 23, a straightforward Global question, and then proceed to question 22, which you

---

[1]PrepTest 39, Sec 3, Q 21
[2]PrepTest 39, Sec 3, Q 22
[3]PrepTest 39, Sec 3, Q 23

can answer in seconds with a glance at your Roadmap. Return to question 21 if you can, but don't waste valuable time on tough questions when there are still easy ones left in the section.

PASSAGE TRIAGE

Another important timing fundamental to remember is that you don't have to complete the passages in the order in which they're presented. An average LSAT Reading Comprehension section will consist of one easy passage, two of medium difficulty, and one that is more difficult than the others. Always begin a section by taking one minute to look over the passages and scan them for clues that help you determine which are easier and which are more challenging.

To demonstrate, try an experiment. Read the following paragraphs. Each is the opening paragraph of a different LSAT passage from the same 35-minute section. Take no more than 30 seconds to glance at these two paragraphs and try to determine which passage is likely to be more challenging.

With the approach of the twentieth century, the classical wave theory of radiation—a widely accepted theory in physics—began to encounter obstacles. This theory held that all electromagnetic radiation—the
(5) entire spectrum from gamma and X rays to radio frequencies, including heat and light—exists in the form of waves. One fundamental assumption of wave theory was that as the length of a wave of radiation shortens, its energy increases smoothly—like a volume
(10) dial on a radio that adjusts smoothly to any setting— and that any conceivable energy value could thus occur in nature.[4]

Users of the Internet—the worldwide network of interconnected computer systems—envision it as a way for people to have free access to information via their personal computers. Most Internet communication
(5) consists of sending electronic mail or exchanging ideas on electronic bulletin boards; however, a growing number of transmissions are of copyrighted works— books, photographs, videos and films, and sound recordings. In Canada, as elsewhere, the goals of
(10) Internet users have begun to conflict with reality as copyright holders look for ways to protect their material from unauthorized and uncompensated distribution.[5]

Both paragraphs are roughly the same length. At a glance, you probably noticed that the first paragraph is somewhat abstract and filled with scientific jargon, whereas the second deals with the familiar topic of the Internet and is written in simpler language. I want you to note

---

[4]PrepTest 39, Sec 3, Passage 3

[5]PrepTest 39, Sec 3, Passage 4

that these examples are presented in order, excerpted from the third and fourth passages, respectively, from the same section.

Since you have the option of completing the passages in any order, you'd be wiser to start with the second passage and then move back to the first. This isn't to say that tougher passages always come with tougher questions, but more challenging passages usually take longer to read and Roadmap, and therefore present added time pressure when you reach the question set. The general rule is that you should always score easy points before going after hard ones. If you are having a difficult time choosing between two passages that seem to be of equivalent difficulty, start with the passage that has more questions—this way you get a larger return on the reading you invest. If both passages have an equivalent number of questions, simply take them in order.

Passage triage is a skill and takes practice to develop. (It might be helpful to review chapter 15, in which you worked with abstract passages.) I would also encourage you to take note of which content areas you feel most comfortable with. Your LSAT will include one comparative reading exercise and three single passages. Because comparative passages tend to feature challenging question types, it's generally a good idea to tackle them after you've finished one or two simpler passages, or to save them for the end. Ultimately, passage order is not an exact science, since what is challenging is subjective to a degree. Take note of what *you* find challenging in the passages, and when you practice a 35-minute section, complete those more challenging passages after you've finished the ones that are more comfortable.

QUESTION TRIAGE

I've already mentioned how important it is to know when to skip a question. To help you do this, there are some guidelines to follow when deciding whether to answer a question immediately or leave it for later. Generally speaking, here is how you should prioritize the different question types:

- Global Questions: You should always answer Global questions first, since they require little or no research and are based on Purpose and Main Idea, concepts you've already thought through. Global questions are usually located at the very beginning and very end of question sets, so look for them in these locations and complete them immediately. Even if you are running out of time on a passage, you can still score Global points if you've read the passage strategically.
- Detail Questions: Tackle these next, remembering that they can often be identified by the opening phrase "according to the passage/author." Most Detail questions will provide you with enough information to conduct research easily in conjunction with your Roadmap, and since they ask you to paraphrase information that is already present in the passage, they're usually easy to predict.

- Logic Questions: Function and Reasoning questions should typically come next. Logic Function stems often provide you with specific line or paragraph references, making research more efficient. Reasoning questions are somewhat more varied, but you've become familiar with the most common types.

- Inference Questions: Inference questions tend to be more challenging than other types of questions. This is because they usually require thorough research and often force you to make a more general prediction than other types, which may lead to more time spent working with the answer choices. Be particularly alert for Inference questions that provide few clues in the stem to help guide your research. These tend to be among the most time-consuming on the test, so work with them after you've scored the easier points.

- EXCEPT Questions: Regardless of type, be wary of questions that contain the word EXCEPT. Sometimes these questions have answers that are hard to predict, and so they may force you to proceed by process of elimination. This doesn't necessarily mean that they're harder to answer correctly, but they can be more time consuming, and therefore should be given lower priority.

- Unusual Questions: As you saw in chapter 16, you may occasionally run into questions that are oddly worded and challenging to understand. If you can't immediately work out what the question stem is asking you to do, consider skipping it and coming back to it after you've completed questions that are more familiar.

I want to stress that these guidelines, while useful, are by no means mandatory. In your practice, you may find that a different priority works better for you. In any case, as with passages, your ultimate goal is to complete easier, less time-consuming questions first, leaving tougher questions for later. If you have to guess, make sure you're guessing on a question that might have taken three minutes to complete instead of thirty seconds.

As a final note, try to avoid random guessing, as an educated guess is always preferable. Keep track in your test booklet of which answer choices you've eliminated, and remember that your knowledge of the author's Scope can make it easier for you to get rid of wrong answer choices at a quick glance (but to be clear, this is the kind of strategy you should use *only* when you're short of time; in general, you should read answer choices carefully to avoid careless mistakes). In other words, if you have to guess, guess as strategically as possible.

KEEP MOVING, STAY METHODICAL

There is a common theme running through all of the advice that I've given you in this chapter, and I'll summarize it here: When you take on a 35-minute section, you must not get bogged down. You can only score points if you keep moving forward. If a question is holding you up, don't be afraid to skip it and come back to it. If a passage looks challenging during your initial overview of the section, save it for the end. Just as you shouldn't let yourself become mired in the details of any one passage, you must never get caught up in a time-wasting battle with a single question.

Remember that time management is always your responsibility. Keep track of time as you work on each passage; if you're nearing the 8.5-minute mark, you must prepare to move on to the next passage. This may require you to leave a point or two behind, but that's better than having to leave an entire *passage* behind.

Similarly, use your knowledge of the test to make good timing decisions, but never simply speed up and neglect the proper application of the Kaplan Method. All of the strategies you've worked so hard to master are designed to make you efficient without sacrificing accuracy, and it won't do your LSAT score any favors if you complete the Reading Comprehension section in 30 minutes but miss all the questions. Your goal is to score as many points as possible. Stay focused on the strategies that will allow you to be successful, and remember that you *can* take control of the section. Keep this in mind as you work with the 35-minute sections coming up in the next two chapters.

CHAPTER 19

FULL-LENGTH SECTION PRACTICE

In the following two chapters, you'll have the opportunity to take two full Reading Comprehension sections, just as they appeared on the original exams. When you take them, make sure that you'll have 35 uninterrupted minutes in a quiet place. Time yourself carefully using an analog watch (the only kind of timepiece you'll be allowed to bring to your LSAT), and be sure to complete an entire section before referring to its answers and explanations.

WHEN AND HOW TO USE SECTION PRACTICE

First and foremost, do *not* complete either timed section before you have completed all of the preceding chapters in this book. You may be eager to apply the strategies you've learned to a whole section, and I certainly understand if you're curious to tabulate how many questions you're getting correct or incorrect on average. This kind of information is certainly important, but if you rush into full sections before you've gained a thorough understanding of the Kaplan Method, you're likely to find the experience frustrating rather than enlightening.

Before you begin working on a timed section, please take a few minutes to review Kaplan's Method for Reading Comprehension and remind yourself to stay methodical. A phenomenon I've observed in my students is that, no matter how well they've understood the proper approach to individual passages and questions, they sometimes throw everything they've learned out the window as soon as they begin doing timed work, completing the section by intuition instead (and losing points that they would have otherwise scored). The remarkable thing is that these students are rarely aware that they're doing this. The pressure of the clock can easily cause even a well-prepared student to revert to bad habits. I want you to avoid this problem, so review the method before you begin working, and you'll be sure to apply it properly.

When your 35 minutes have expired, stop working immediately. You won't be able to sneak in a few extra answers on your actual LSAT, so don't do so in your practice either. After you've completed the first section, be sure to review the provided answers and explanations thoroughly before completing the second one. This is *very* important; the only way to get maximum benefit from both sections is to learn everything you can from the first, then apply what you've learned to the second. Remember that there is no guess penalty on the LSAT, so try to answer every question before your time runs out. Don't be afraid to make the best guess you can when necessary. Any guess—whether it's based on partial elimination of wrong choices or it's completely random—is better than leaving a question blank.

Finally, don't forget what you've learned about section management. Review the ideas I presented to you in chapter 18 carefully before moving on, and don't forget to triage passages and questions. The test makers reward those who make good decisions, so stay alert and don't be afraid to skip a time-consuming question if it makes sense to do so. Remember that your goal is to score as many points as possible, not to complete every question in a given passage.

HOW TO CALCULATE YOUR SCORE

Once you've completed the section, score your responses against the provided answer key. Mark each of the answers you got right or wrong, but review every passage and question using the Explanations following the section. There's no way to determine your overall LSAT score from any single section. Test scores are produced based on the overall number of correct answers. Figure 19.1 shows a couple of score conversion tables from recently-released LSATs. There are almost always 101 scored questions per LSAT, of which 26–28 come from the Reading Comprehension section.

CONVERSION CHART

For converting Raw Score to the 120–180 LSAT Scaled Score
LSAT Prep Test 47

REPORTED SCORE	LOWEST RAW SCORE	HIGHEST RAW SCORE
180	99	100
179	98	98
178	97	97
177	96	96
176	--*	--*
175	95	95
174	94	94
173	93	93
172	92	92
171	91	91
170	90	90
169	89	89
168	88	88
167	87	87
166	85	86
165	84	84
164	83	83
163	81	82
162	80	80
161	78	79
160	77	77
159	75	76
158	73	74
157	72	72
156	70	71
155	68	69
154	66	67
153	65	65
152	63	64
151	61	63
150	59	60
149	57	58
148	55	56
147	54	54
146	52	53
145	50	51
144	48	49
143	46	47
142	45	45
141	43	44
140	41	42
139	40	40
138	38	39
137	36	37
136	35	35
135	33	34
134	32	32
133	30	31
132	29	29
131	27	28
130	26	26
129	25	25
128	24	24
127	22	23
126	21	21
125	20	20
124	19	19
123	18	18
122	17	17
121	16	16
120	0	15

*There is no raw score that will produce this scaled score for the test.

CONVERSION CHART

For converting Raw Score to the 120–180 LSAT Scaled Score
LSAT Prep Test 50

REPORTED SCORE	LOWEST RAW SCORE	HIGHEST RAW SCORE
180	98	100
179	97	97
178	--*	--*
177	96	96
176	95	95
175	94	94
174	--*	--*
173	93	93
172	92	92
171	91	91
170	90	90
169	89	89
168	88	88
167	86	87
166	85	85
165	84	84
164	83	83
163	81	82
162	80	80
161	78	79
160	77	77
159	75	76
158	73	74
157	72	72
156	70	71
155	68	69
154	66	67
153	64	65
152	63	63
151	61	62
150	59	60
149	57	58
148	55	56
147	53	54
146	52	52
145	50	51
144	48	49
143	46	47
142	45	45
141	43	44
140	41	42
139	40	40
138	38	39
137	36	37
136	35	35
135	33	34
134	32	32
133	30	31
132	29	29
131	27	28
130	26	26
129	25	25
128	23	24
127	22	22
126	21	21
125	20	20
124	18	19
123	17	17
122	16	16
121	15	15
120	0	14

*There is no raw score that will produce this scaled score for the test.

Figure 19.1   Score Conversion Tables

```
┌─────────────────────────────────────────────────────┐
│                  SCORING WORKSHEET                    │
│                                                       │
│   1.  Enter the number of questions you answered      │
│       correctly in each section                       │
│                              NUMBER                   │
│                              CORRECT                  │
│          SECTION I . . . . . . . . . .  _____        │
│                                                       │
│          SECTION II . . . . . . . . .  _____         │
│                                                       │
│          SECTION III. . . . . . . .  _____           │
│                                                       │
│          SECTION IV . . . . . . . .  _____           │
│                                                       │
│   2.  Enter the sum here:    _____   THIS IS YOUR    │
│                                       RAW SCORE.      │
│                                                       │
└─────────────────────────────────────────────────────┘
```

Figure 19.2

By estimating the number of points you'd score from the remaining sections of the test, you can gain an idea of the impact that your Reading Comprehension performance will have on your score. To improve your performance on the other sections of the test, study this book's companion volumes, *LSAT Logic Games: Strategies and Tactics* and *LSAT Logical Reasoning: Strategies and Tactics*.

One final thought: No matter how important section practice is, remember that it's still practice, and still an opportunity to learn and improve. Approach each section with confidence and do the best you can.

CHAPTER 20

FULL-LENGTH SECTION 1[1]

Time—35 minutes

27 Questions

<u>Directions:</u> Each set of questions in this section is based on a single passage or a pair of passages. The questions are to be answered on the basis of what is <u>stated</u> or <u>implied</u> in the passage or pair of passages. For some of the questions, more than one of the choices could conceivably answer the question. However, you are to choose the <u>best</u> answer, that is, the response that most accurately and completely answers the question, and blacken the corresponding space on your answer sheet.

---

[1]PrepTest 54, Section 1

This passage was adapted from an article published in 1996.

The Internet is a system of computer networks that allows individuals and organizations to communicate freely with other Internet users throughout the world. As a result, an astonishing
(5) variety of information is able to flow unimpeded across national and other political borders, presenting serious difficulties for traditional approaches to legislation and law enforcement, to which such borders are crucial.
(10) Control over physical space and the objects located in it is a defining attribute of sovereignty. Lawmaking presupposes some mechanism for enforcement, i.e., the ability to control violations. But jurisdictions cannot control the information and
(15) transactions flowing across their borders via the Internet. For example, a government might seek to intercept transmissions that propagate the kinds of consumer fraud that it regulates within its jurisdiction. But the volume of electronic communications
(20) crossing its territorial boundaries is too great to allow for effective control over individual transmissions. In order to deny its citizens access to specific materials, a government would thus have to prevent them from using the Internet altogether. Such a draconian
(25) measure would almost certainly be extremely unpopular, since most affected citizens would probably feel that the benefits of using the Internet decidedly outweigh the risks.
One legal domain that is especially sensitive to
(30) geographical considerations is that governing trademarks. There is no global registration of trademarks; international protection requires registration in each country. Moreover, within a country, the same name can sometimes be used
(35) proprietarily by businesses of different kinds in the same locality, or by businesses of the same kind in different localities, on the grounds that use of the trademark by one such business does not affect the others. But with the advent of the Internet, a business
(40) name can be displayed in such a way as to be accessible from any computer connected to the Internet anywhere in the world. Should such a display advertising a restaurant in Norway be deemed to infringe a trademark in Brazil just because it can be
(45) accessed freely from Brazil? It is not clear that any particular country's trademark authorities possess, or

should possess, jurisdiction over such displays. Otherwise, any use of a trademark on the Internet could be subject to the jurisdiction of every country
(50) simultaneously.
The Internet also gives rise to situations in which regulation is needed but cannot be provided within the existing framework. For example, electronic communications, which may pass through many
(55) different territorial jurisdictions, pose perplexing new questions about the nature and adequacy of privacy protections. Should French officials have lawful access to messages traveling via the Internet from Canada to Japan? This is just one among many
(60) questions that collectively challenge the notion that the Internet can be effectively controlled by the existing system of territorial jurisdictions.

1. Which one of the following most accurately expresses the main point of the passage?

   (A) The high-volume, global nature of activity on the Internet undermines the feasibility of controlling it through legal frameworks that presuppose geographic boundaries.

   (B) The system of Internet communications simultaneously promotes and weakens the power of national governments to control their citizens' speech and financial transactions.

   (C) People value the benefits of their participation on the Internet so highly that they would strongly oppose any government efforts to regulate their Internet activity.

   (D) Internet communications are responsible for a substantial increase in the volume and severity of global crime.

   (E) Current Internet usage and its future expansion pose a clear threat to the internal political stability of many nations.

2. The author mentions French officials in connection with messages traveling between Canada and Japan (lines 57–59) primarily to

   (A) emphasize that the Internet allows data to be made available to users worldwide
   (B) illustrate the range of languages that might be used on the Internet
   (C) provide an example of a regulatory problem arising when an electronic communication intended for a particular destination passes through intermediate jurisdictions
   (D) show why any use of a trademark on the Internet could be subject to the jurisdiction of every country simultaneously
   (E) highlight the kind of international cooperation that made the Internet possible

3. According to the passage, which one of the following is an essential property of political sovereignty?

   (A) control over business enterprises operating across territorial boundaries
   (B) authority over communicative exchanges occurring within a specified jurisdiction
   (C) power to regulate trademarks throughout a circumscribed geographic region
   (D) control over the entities included within a designated physical space
   (E) authority over all commercial transactions involving any of its citizens

4. Which one of the following words employed by the author in the second paragraph is most indicative of the author's attitude toward any hypothetical measure a government might enact to deny its citizens access to the Internet?

   (A) benefits
   (B) decidedly
   (C) unpopular
   (D) draconian
   (E) risks

5. What is the main purpose of the fourth paragraph?

   (A) to call into question the relevance of the argument provided in the second paragraph
   (B) to provide a practical illustration that questions the general claim made in the first paragraph
   (C) to summarize the arguments provided in the second and third paragraphs
   (D) to continue the argument that begins in the third paragraph
   (E) to provide an additional argument in support of the general claim made in the first paragraph

Passage A

Drilling fluids, including the various mixtures known as drilling muds, play essential roles in oil-well drilling. As they are circulated down through the drill pipe and back up the well itself, they lubricate the
(5) drill bit, bearings, and drill pipe; clean and cool the drill bit as it cuts into the rock; lift rock chips (cuttings) to the surface; provide information about what is happening downhole, allowing the drillers to monitor the behavior, flow rate, pressure, and
(10) composition of the drilling fluid; and maintain well pressure to control cave-ins.

Drilling muds are made of bentonite and other clays and polymers, mixed with a fluid to the desired viscosity. By far the largest ingredient of drilling
(15) muds, by weight, is barite, a very heavy mineral of density 4.3 to 4.6. It is also used as an inert filler in some foods and is more familiar in its medical use as the "barium meal" administered before X-raying the digestive tract.
(20) Over the years individual drilling companies and their expert drillers have devised proprietary formulations, or mud "recipes," to deal with specific types of drilling jobs. One problem in studying the effects of drilling waste discharges is that the drilling
(25) fluids are made from a range of over 1,000, sometimes toxic, ingredients—many of them known, confusingly, by different trade names, generic descriptions, chemical formulae, and regional or industry slang words, and many of them kept secret by companies or individual
(30) formulators.

Passage B

Drilling mud, cuttings, and associated chemicals are normally released only during the drilling phase of a well's existence. These discharges are the main environmental concern in offshore oil production, and
(35) their use is tightly regulated. The discharges are closely monitored by the offshore operator, and releases are controlled as a condition of the operating permit.

One type of mud—water-based mud (WBM)—is a mixture of water, bentonite clay, and chemical
(40) additives, and is used to drill shallow parts of wells. It is not particularly toxic to marine organisms and disperses readily. Under current regulations, it can be dumped directly overboard. Companies typically recycle WBMs until their properties are no longer
(45) suitable and then, over a period of hours, dump the entire batch into the sea.

For drilling deeper wells, oil-based mud (OBM) is normally used. The typical difference from WBM is the high content of mineral oil (typically 30 percent).
(50) OBMs also contain greater concentrations of barite, a powdered heavy mineral, and a number of additives. OBMs have a greater potential for negative environmental impact, partly because they do not disperse as readily. Barite may impact some
(55) organisms, particularly scallops, and the mineral oil may have toxic effects. Currently only the residues of OBMs adhering to cuttings that remain after the cuttings are sieved from the drilling fluids may be discharged overboard, and then only mixtures up to a
(60) specified maximum oil content.

6. A primary purpose of each of the passages is to

(A) provide causal explanations for a type of environmental pollution
(B) describe the general composition and properties of drilling muds
(C) point out possible environmental impacts associated with oil drilling
(D) explain why oil-well drilling requires the use of drilling muds
(E) identify difficulties inherent in the regulation of oil-well drilling operations

7. Which one of the following is a characteristic of barite that is mentioned in both of the passages?

(A) It does not disperse readily in seawater.
(B) It is not found in drilling muds containing bentonite.
(C) Its use in drilling muds is tightly regulated.
(D) It is the most commonly used ingredient in drilling muds.
(E) It is a heavy mineral.

8. Each of the following is supported by one or both of the passages EXCEPT:

(A) Clay is an important constituent of many, if not all, drilling muds.
(B) At least one type of drilling mud is not significantly toxic to marine life.
(C) There has been some study of the environmental effects of drilling-mud discharges.
(D) Government regulations allow drilling muds to contain 30 percent mineral oil.
(E) During the drilling of an oil well, drilling mud is continuously discharged into the sea.

9. Which one of the following can be most reasonably inferred from the two passages taken together, but not from either one individually?

(A) Barite is the largest ingredient of drilling muds, by weight, and also the most environmentally damaging.

(B) Although barite can be harmful to marine organisms, it can be consumed safely by humans.

(C) Offshore drilling is more damaging to the environment than is land-based drilling.

(D) The use of drilling muds needs to be more tightly controlled by government.

(E) If offshore drilling did not generate cuttings, it would be less harmful to the environment.

10. Each of the following is supported by one or both of the passages EXCEPT:

(A) Drillers monitor the suitability of the mud they are using.

(B) The government requires drilling companies to disclose all ingredients used in their drilling muds.

(C) In certain quantities, barite is not toxic to humans.

(D) Oil reserves can be found within or beneath layers of rock.

(E) Drilling deep oil wells requires the use of different mud recipes than does drilling shallow oil wells.

11. Based on information in the passages, which one of the following, if true, provides the strongest support for a prediction that the proportion of oil-well drilling using OBMs will increase in the future?

(A) The cost of certain ingredients in WBMs is expected to increase steadily over the next several decades.

(B) The deeper an offshore oil well, the greater the concentration of barite that must be used in the drilling mud.

(C) Oil reserves at shallow depths have mostly been tapped, leaving primarily much deeper reserves for future drilling.

(D) It is unlikely that oil drillers will develop more efficient ways of removing OBM residues from cuttings that remain after being sieved from drilling fluids.

(E) Barite is a common mineral, the availability of which is virtually limitless.

12. According to passage B, one reason OBMs are potentially more environmentally damaging than WBMs is that OBMs

(A) are slower to disperse

(B) contain greater concentrations of bentonite

(C) contain a greater number of additives

(D) are used for drilling deeper wells

(E) cannot be recycled

Aida Overton Walker (1880–1914), one of the most widely acclaimed African American performers of the early twentieth century, was known largely for popularizing a dance form known as the cakewalk
(5) through her choreographing, performance, and teaching of the dance. The cakewalk was originally developed prior to the United States Civil War by African Americans, for whom dance was a means of maintaining cultural links within a slave society. It
(10) was based on traditional West African ceremonial dances, and like many other African American dances, it retained features characteristic of African dance forms, such as gliding steps and an emphasis on improvisation.

(15) To this African-derived foundation, the cakewalk added certain elements from European dances: where African dances feature flexible body postures, large groups and separate-sex dancing, the cakewalk developed into a high-kicking walk performed by a
(20) procession of couples. Ironically, while these modifications later enabled the cakewalk to appeal to European Americans and become one of the first cultural forms to cross the racial divide in North America, they were originally introduced with satiric
(25) intent. Slaves performed the grandiloquent walks in order to parody the processional dances performed at slave owners' balls and, in general, the self-important manners of slave owners. To add a further irony, by the end of the nineteenth century, the cakewalk was
(30) itself being parodied by European American stage performers, and these parodies in turn helped shape subsequent versions of the cakewalk.

While this complex evolution meant that the cakewalk was not a simple cultural phenomenon—
(35) one scholar has characterized this layering of parody upon parody with the phrase "mimetic vertigo"—it is in fact what enabled the dance to attract its wide audience. In the cultural and socioeconomic flux of the turn-of-the-century United States, where
(40) industrialization, urbanization, mass immigration, and rapid social mobility all reshaped the cultural landscape, an art form had to be capable of being many things to many people in order to appeal to a large audience.

(45) Walker's remarkable success at popularizing the cakewalk across otherwise relatively rigid racial boundaries rested on her ability to address within her interpretation of it the varying and sometimes conflicting demands placed on the dance. Middle-
(50) class African Americans, for example, often denounced the cakewalk as disreputable, a complaint reinforced by the parodies circulating at the time. Walker won over this audience by refining the cakewalk and emphasizing its fundamental grace.
(55) Meanwhile, because middle- and upper-class European Americans often felt threatened by the tremendous cultural flux around them, they prized what they regarded as authentic art forms as bastions of stability; much of Walker's success with this

audience derived from her distillation of what was widely acclaimed as the most authentic cakewalk. Finally, Walker was able to gain the admiration of many newly rich industrialists and financiers, who found in the grand flourishes of her version of the
(65) cakewalk a fitting vehicle for celebrating their newfound social rank.

13. Which one of the following most accurately expresses the main point of the passage?

(A) Walker, who was especially well known for her success in choreographing, performing, and teaching the cakewalk, was one of the most widely recognized African American performers of the early twentieth century.

(B) In spite of the disparate influences that shaped the cakewalk, Walker was able to give the dance broad appeal because she distilled what was regarded as the most authentic version in an era that valued authenticity highly.

(C) Walker popularized the cakewalk by capitalizing on the complex cultural mix that had developed from the dance's original blend of satire and cultural preservation, together with the effects of later parodies.

(D) Whereas other versions of the cakewalk circulating at the beginning of the twentieth century were primarily parodic in nature, the version popularized by Walker combined both satire and cultural preservation.

(E) Because Walker was able to recognize and preserve the characteristics of the cakewalk as African Americans originally performed it, it became the first popular art form to cross the racial divide in the United States.

14. The author describes the socioeconomic flux of the turn-of-the-century United States in the third paragraph primarily in order to

(A) argue that the cakewalk could have become popular only in such complex social circumstances

(B) detail the social context that prompted performers of the cakewalk to fuse African and European dance forms

(C) identify the target of the overlapping parodic layers that characterized the cakewalk

(D) indicate why a particular cultural environment was especially favorable for the success of the cakewalk

(E) explain why European American parodies of the cakewalk were able to reach wide audiences

15. Which one of the following is most analogous to the author's account in the second paragraph of how the cakewalk came to appeal to European Americans?

    (A) Satirical versions of popular music songs are frequently more popular than the songs they parody.

    (B) A style of popular music grows in popularity among young listeners because it parodies the musical styles admired by older listeners.

    (C) A style of music becomes admired among popular music's audience in part because of elements that were introduced in order to parody popular music.

    (D) A once popular style of music wins back its audience by incorporating elements of the style of music that is currently most popular.

    (E) After popular music begins to appropriate elements of a traditional style of music, interest in that traditional music increases.

16. The passage asserts which one of the following about the cakewalk?

    (A) It was largely unknown outside African American culture until Walker popularized it.

    (B) It was mainly a folk dance, and Walker became one of only a handful of people to perform it professionally.

    (C) Its performance as parody became uncommon as a result of Walker's popularization of its authentic form.

    (D) Its West African origins became commonly known as a result of Walker's work.

    (E) It was one of the first cultural forms to cross racial lines in the United States.

17. It can be inferred from the passage that the author would be most likely to agree with which one of the following statements?

    (A) Because of the broad appeal of humor, satiric art forms are often among the first to cross racial or cultural divisions.

    (B) The interactions between African American and European American cultural forms often result in what is appropriately characterized as "mimetic vertigo."

    (C) Middle-class European Americans who valued the cakewalk's authenticity subsequently came to admire other African American dances for the same reason.

    (D) Because of the influence of African dance forms, some popular dances that later emerged in the United States featured separate-sex dancing.

    (E) Some of Walker's admirers were attracted to her version of the cakewalk as a means for bolstering their social identities.

18. The passage most strongly suggests that the author would be likely to agree with which one of the following statements about Walker's significance in the history of the cakewalk?

    (A) Walker broadened the cakewalk's appeal by highlighting elements that were already present in the dance.

    (B) Walker's version of the cakewalk appealed to larger audiences than previous versions did because she accentuated its satiric dimension.

    (C) Walker popularized the cakewalk by choreographing various alternative interpretations of it, each tailored to the interests of a different cultural group.

    (D) Walker added a "mimetic vertigo" to the cakewalk by inserting imitations of other performers' cakewalking into her dance routines.

    (E) Walker revitalized the cakewalk by disentangling its complex admixture of African and European elements.

19. The passage provides sufficient information to answer which one of the following questions?

    (A) What were some of the attributes of African dance forms that were preserved in the cakewalk?

    (B) Who was the first performer to dance the cakewalk professionally?

    (C) What is an aspect of the cakewalk that was preserved in other North American dance forms?

    (D) What features were added to the original cakewalk by the stage parodies circulating at the end of the nineteenth century?

    (E) For about how many years into the twentieth century did the cakewalk remain widely popular?

In principle, a cohesive group—one whose members generally agree with one another and support one another's judgments—can do a much better job at decision making than it could if it were
(5) noncohesive. When cohesiveness is low or lacking entirely, compliance out of fear of recrimination is likely to be strongest. To overcome this fear, participants in the group's deliberations need to be confident that they are members in good standing and
(10) that the others will continue to value their role in the group, whether or not they agree about a particular issue under discussion. As members of a group feel more accepted by the others, they acquire greater freedom to say what they really think, becoming less
(15) likely to use deceitful arguments or to play it safe by dancing around the issues with vapid or conventional comments. Typically, then, the more cohesive a group becomes, the less its members will deliberately censor what they say out of fear of being punished socially
(20) for antagonizing their fellow members.

But group cohesiveness can have pitfalls as well: while the members of a highly cohesive group can feel much freer to deviate from the majority, their desire for genuine concurrence on every important
(25) issue often inclines them not to use this freedom. In a highly cohesive group of decision makers, the danger is not that individuals will conceal objections they harbor regarding a proposal favored by the majority, but that they will think the proposal is a good one
(30) without attempting to carry out a critical scrutiny that could reveal grounds for strong objections. Members may then decide that any misgivings they feel are not worth pursuing—that the benefit of any doubt should be given to the group consensus. In this way, they
(35) may fall victim to a syndrome known as "groupthink," which one psychologist concerned with collective decision making has defined as "a deterioration of mental efficiency, reality testing, and moral judgment that results from in-group pressures."
(40) Based on analyses of major fiascoes of international diplomacy and military decision making, researchers have identified groupthink behavior as a recurring pattern that involves several factors: overestimation of the group's power and morality,
(45) manifested, for example, in an illusion of invulnerability, which creates excessive optimism;

closed-mindedness to warnings of problems and to alternative viewpoints; and unwarranted pressures toward uniformity, including self-censorship with
50 respect to doubts about the group's reasoning and a concomitant shared illusion of unanimity concerning group decisions. Cohesiveness of the decision-making group is an essential antecedent condition for this syndrome but not a sufficient one, so it is important
(55) to work toward identifying the additional factors that determine whether group cohesiveness will deteriorate into groupthink or allow for effective decision making.

20. Which one of the following most accurately expresses the main point of the passage?

(A) Despite its value in encouraging frank discussion, high cohesion can lead to a debilitating type of group decision making called groupthink.

(B) Group members can guard against groupthink if they have a good understanding of the critical role played by cohesion.

(C) Groupthink is a dysfunctional collective decision-making pattern that can occur in diplomacy and military affairs.

(D) Low cohesion in groups is sometimes desirable when higher cohesion involves a risk of groupthink behavior.

(E) Future efforts to guard against groupthink will depend on the results of ongoing research into the psychology of collective decision making.

21. A group of closely associated colleagues has made a disastrous diplomatic decision after a series of meetings marked by disagreement over conflicting alternatives. It can be inferred from the passage that the author would be most likely to say that this scenario

    (A) provides evidence of chronic indecision, thus indicating a weak level of cohesion in general
    (B) indicates that the group's cohesiveness was coupled with some other factor to produce a groupthink fiasco
    (C) provides no evidence that groupthink played a role in the group's decision
    (D) provides evidence that groupthink can develop even in some groups that do not demonstrate an "illusion of unanimity"
    (E) indicates that the group probably could have made its decision-making procedure more efficient by studying the information more thoroughly

22. Which one of the following, if true, would most support the author's contentions concerning the conditions under which groupthink takes place?

    (A) A study of several groups, each made up of members of various professions, found that most fell victim to groupthink.
    (B) There is strong evidence that respectful dissent is more likely to occur in cohesive groups than in groups in which there is little internal support.
    (C) Extensive analyses of decisions made by a large number of groups found no cases of groupthink in groups whose members generally distrust one another's judgments.
    (D) There is substantial evidence that groupthink is especially likely to take place when members of a group develop factions whose intransigence prolongs the group's deliberations.
    (E) Ample research demonstrates that voluntary deference to group opinion is not a necessary factor for the formation of groupthink behavior.

23. The passage mentions which one of the following as a component of groupthink?

    (A) unjustified suspicions among group members regarding an adversary's intentions
    (B) strong belief that the group's decisions are right
    (C) group members working under unusually high stress, leading to illusions of invulnerability
    (D) the deliberate use of vapid, clichéd arguments
    (E) careful consideration of objections to majority positions

24. It can be inferred from the passage that both the author of the passage and the researchers mentioned in the passage would be most likely to agree with which one of the following statements about groupthink?

    (A) Groupthink occurs in all strongly cohesive groups, but its contribution to collective decision making is not fully understood.
    (B) The causal factors that transform group cohesion into groupthink are unique to each case.
    (C) The continued study of cohesiveness of groups is probably fruitless for determining what factors elicit groupthink.
    (D) Outside information cannot influence group decisions once they have become determined by groupthink.
    (E) On balance, groupthink cannot be expected to have a beneficial effect in a group's decision making.

25. In the passage, the author says which one of the following about conformity in decision-making groups?

   (A) Enforced conformity may be appropriate in some group decision situations.
   (B) A high degree of conformity is often expected of military decision-making group members.
   (C) Inappropriate group conformity can result from inadequate information.
   (D) Voluntary conformity occurs much less frequently than enforced conformity.
   (E) Members of noncohesive groups may experience psychological pressure to conform.

26. In line 5, the author mentions low group cohesiveness primarily in order to

   (A) contribute to a claim that cohesiveness can be conducive to a freer exchange of views in groups
   (B) establish a comparison between groupthink symptoms and the attributes of low-cohesion groups
   (C) suggest that there may be ways to make both cohesive and noncohesive groups more open to dissent
   (D) indicate that both cohesive and noncohesive groups may be susceptible to groupthink dynamics
   (E) lay the groundwork for a subsequent proposal for overcoming the debilitating effects of low cohesion

27. Based on the passage, it can be inferred that the author would be most likely to agree with which one of the following?

   (A) Highly cohesive groups are more likely to engage in confrontational negotiating styles with adversaries than are those with low cohesion.
   (B) It is difficult for a group to examine all relevant options critically in reaching decisions unless it has a fairly high degree of cohesiveness.
   (C) A group with varied viewpoints on a given issue is less likely to reach a sound decision regarding that issue than is a group whose members are unified in their outlook.
   (D) Intense stress and high expectations are the key factors in the formation of groupthink.
   (E) Noncohesive groups can, under certain circumstances, develop all of the symptoms of groupthink.

Answer Explanations follow on the next page.

ANSWER KEY

1.	A	15.	C
2.	C	16.	E
3.	D	17.	E
4.	D	18.	A
5.	E	19.	A
6.	B	20.	A
7.	E	21.	C
8.	E	22.	C
9.	B	23.	B
10.	B	24.	E
11.	C	25.	E
12.	A	26.	A
13.	C	27.	B
14.	D		

TRIAGE REVIEW

The first passage is probably the best place to begin this section. The Topic deals with the Internet, a subject you're probably familiar with to some degree, and the four medium-length paragraphs present few obvious structural challenges. You might be dismayed by the lack of questions—only five—but remember that your goal is to grab the easiest points right away, and these questions are short and straightforward.

The third passage should also take high priority. Five brief paragraphs suggest a simple structure, and the language is nontechnical. Because this passage is worth seven points, you might prefer to tackle it first. Either order is fine; as long as you identify the simpler passages and score their points before moving on to the more challenging passages, you've made the right decision.

You would be wise to complete passages two and four later in the section. Passage two is comparative reading and appears to address a more technical subject. Additionally, you may have noticed two EXCEPT questions (these are easy to spot out during your question triage because the word EXCEPT will always be in all caps) and a large number of Inference questions. All of these clues suggest that this passage is likely to be more time-consuming.

Passage four appears abstract even at a quick glance (although it clearly has something to do with "cohesiveness"), and the three long, dense paragraphs will require some time to work through. Although there are eight questions, the stems and choices are lengthy, and a glance at the beginning and end of the question set will confirm that there's only one global question—most of the remaining questions are Logic and Inference. You should tackle this one either third or fourth, depending on whether you prefer to complete it before or after the comparative passages.

Explanations

Passage One: "Internet Regulations"
Step 1:

This passage was adapted from an article published in 1996.

Internet raises
internat. legal
problems

(5)

The Internet is a system of computer networks that (allows) individuals and organizations to communicate freely with other Internet users throughout the world. (As a result,) an (astonishing) variety of information is able to flow unimpeded across national and other political borders, presenting (serious difficulties) for (traditional) approaches to legislation and law enforcement, to which such borders are (crucial.)

(10)

Net info can't
be controlled

Control over physical space and the objects located in it is a (defining) attribute of sovereignty. Lawmaking (presupposes) some mechanism for enforcement, i.e., the ability to control violations. (But) jurisdictions (cannot control) the information and

(15)

transactions flowing across their borders via the Internet. (For example,) a government might seek to intercept transmissions that propagate the kinds of consumer fraud that it regulates within its jurisdiction. (But) the volume of electronic communications

(20)

crossing its territorial boundaries is too great to allow for effective control over individual transmissions. (In order) to deny its citizens access to specific materials, a government would (thus) have to prevent them from using the Internet altogether. Such a (draconian)

Tough laws
would be
unpopular

(25)

measure would almost certainly be extremely unpopular, (since) most affected citizens would probably feel that the benefits of using the Internet decidedly (outweigh) the risks.

(30)

TMs

One legal domain that is (especially) sensitive to geographical considerations is that governing trademarks. There is no global registration of trademarks; international protection (requires) registration in each country. (Moreover,) within a country, the same name can sometimes be used

(35)

proprietarily by businesses of different kinds in the same locality, (or by) businesses of the same kind in different localities, (on the grounds) that use of the trademark by one such business does not affect the others. (But) with the advent of the Internet, a business

Net makes TM
law difficult

(40)

name can be displayed in such a way as to be accessible from any computer connected to the Internet anywhere in the world. (Should) such a display advertising a restaurant in Norway be deemed to infringe a trademark in Brazil just (because) it can be

(45) accessed freely from Brazil? It is not clear that any
particular country's trademark authorities possess, or
should possess, jurisdiction over such displays.
Otherwise, any use of a trademark on the Internet
could be subject to the jurisdiction of every country
(50) simultaneously.

Needed regulations can't be provided

    The Internet also gives rise to situations in which
regulation is needed but cannot be provided within
the existing framework. For example, electronic
communications, which may pass through many
(55) different territorial jurisdictions, pose perplexing new
questions about the nature and adequacy of privacy
protections. Should French officials have lawful
access to messages traveling via the Internet from
Canada to Japan? This is just one among many
(60) questions that collectively challenge the notion that
the Internet can be effectively controlled by the
existing system of territorial jurisdictions.

Paragraph Structure: This explanatory passage follows a straightforward structure that likely didn't provide any unusual challenges to your strategic reading skills. The first paragraph introduces the **Topic** of the passage immediately: Internet regulations. The author's **Scope** involves the "serious difficulties" (line 7) that arise when attempting to regulate the Internet across international borders.

The second paragraph explores this problem in a bit more detail. Since physical space is a "defining" (line 11) characteristic of state sovereignty, the Internet necessarily introduces unforeseen problems since nations cannot control the flow of information across their borders. This is complicated by the fact that any "draconian" (line 24) measures such as banning Internet access altogether would likely be unpopular.

The final two paragraphs consist primarily of supporting details—the enforcement of trademarks is complicated by the Internet, and certain regulations that might be necessary to control the flow of information can't be provided within the "existing framework" (line 53), primarily because of issues of privacy.

Taken all together, you should note the author's neutral tone as you consider the **Purpose** of the passage: to describe legal problems associated with the Internet. Note that the author doesn't propose solutions to these problems, but merely explains them. The **Main Idea** of the passage, then, is that the Internet has introduced new legal challenges to the international community that defy easy solution.

Question Triage: Look for the Global questions first, as always. Question 1 should be a quick point, so score it right away. Questions 3 and 5 are good ones to consider next—a Detail question and a Function question that can be answered with a quick glance at your Roadmap. That leaves question 2, a Function question, and question 4, an author's attitude Inference question, which you should take in order.

1.   **(A)**

Which one of the following most accurately expresses the main point of the passage?

(A)   The high-volume, global nature of activity on the Internet undermines the feasibility of controlling it through legal frameworks that presuppose geographic boundaries.

(B)   The system of Internet communications simultaneously promotes and weakens the power of national governments to control their citizens' speech and financial transactions.

(C)   People value the benefits of their participation on the Internet so highly that they would strongly oppose any government efforts to regulate their Internet activity.

(D)   Internet communications are responsible for a substantial increase in the volume and severity of global crime.

(E)   Current Internet usage and its future expansion pose a clear threat to the internal political stability of many nations.[2]

Step 2: The clue "main point" identifies this as a Global question.

Step 3: Instead of researching the text, think about the Main Idea of the passage.

Step 4: The Main Idea was that the Internet has raised legal challenges that aren't easily solved.

Step 5: Correct choice (A) properly reflects the prediction. Choice (B) addresses issues that are completely out of scope of the Main Idea, choice (C) focuses too narrowly on a specific detail, and choices (D) and (E) propose ideas that were never mentioned in the passage and are therefore outside the scope.

2.   **(C)**

The author mentions French officials in connection with messages traveling between Canada and Japan (lines 57–59) primarily to

(A)   emphasize that the Internet allows data to be made available to users worldwide

(B)   illustrate the range of languages that might be used on the Internet

(C)   provide an example of a regulatory problem arising when an electronic communication intended for a particular destination passes through intermediate jurisdictions

(D)   show why any use of a trademark on the Internet could be subject to the jurisdiction of every country simultaneously

(E)   highlight the kind of international cooperation that made the Internet possible[3]

[2]PrepTest 54, Sec 1, Q 1

[3]PrepTest 54, Sec 1, Q 2

Step 2: The question asks for the primary reason why the passage mentions an example, making this a Logic Function question.

Step 3: Although you are provided with a specific line reference, you should start reading at the beginning of the paragraph to get a good sense of context. The paragraph describes "perplexing" (line 55) questions that arise when communications pass through several jurisdictions; this seems to be what the author is chiefly interested in describing here.

Step 4: So why did the author mention the French officials? The Keywords "for example" (line 53) tell you that this is an illustration of the point the author just made: That communications crossing jurisdictions are problematic for lawmakers.

Step 5: The match for your prediction is choice (C). Note that none of the wrong answer choices even come close to mentioning the context you researched in Step 3. It's true that choice (D) mentions the term "jurisdiction" (line 62), but then goes out of scope by bringing up the issue of trademarks, which was dealt with in an earlier paragraph (line 32). Be careful not to fall for the half right/half wrong answer trap. This is why application of the Kaplan Method and careful attention to context is so important when dealing with a Logic Function question.

3. **(D)**

    According to the passage, which one of the following
    is an essential property of political sovereignty?
    (A) control over business enterprises operating
         across territorial boundaries
    (B) authority over communicative exchanges
         occurring within a specified jurisdiction
    (C) power to regulate trademarks throughout a
         circumscribed geographic region
    (D) control over the entities included within a
         designated physical space
    (E) authority over all commercial transactions
         involving any of its citizens[4]

Step 2: When the question asks for a specific fact, or "property" in this case, you know you're working with a Detail question. Also note "according to the passage," another common Detail question identifier.

Step 3: The Keywords in the second paragraph help you discover the "defining" (line 11) attributes of sovereignty.

Step 4: The passage simply describes "control over physical space" (line 10) as defining sovereignty. The correct answer must reflect this.

Step 5: A quick scan of the choices should bring you to correct choice (D). None of the other choices mentions the idea of physical space, making them all out of scope.

---

[4]PrepTest 54, Sec 1, Q 3

4. **(D)**

Which one of the following words employed by the author in the second paragraph is most indicative of the author's attitude toward any hypothetical measure a government might enact to deny its citizens access to the Internet?

(A) benefits
(B) decidedly
(C) unpopular
(D) draconian
(E) risks[5]

Step 2: Questions that ask for the "author's attitude" are Inference questions. Research the text carefully to determine what must be true.

Step 3: The question stem directs you to the second paragraph, where you discover that the author refers to Internet bans as "draconian" (line 24) and certain to be "unpopular" (line 26) with citizens.

Step 4: The research you've already conducted gives you the prediction you need: The author used the word "draconian" to describe these hypothetical laws. Even if you're not sure about the meaning of this word, it forms the basis of a strong prediction.

Step 5: Correct choice (D) contains the term you were looking for. Choice (B) isn't quoted in the relevant portion of the second paragraph. The remaining choices refer to words that the author used to describe *citizens'* views of such laws, but not necessarily the author's. Always pay close attention to whose point of view a question is asking for.

5. **(E)**

What is the main purpose of the fourth paragraph?

(A) to call into question the relevance of the argument provided in the second paragraph
(B) to provide a practical illustration that questions the general claim made in the first paragraph
(C) to summarize the arguments provided in the second and third paragraphs
(D) to continue the argument that begins in the third paragraph
(E) to provide an additional argument in support of the general claim made in the first paragraph[6]

Step 2: The phrase "main purpose" might suggest a Global question at first glance, but since the stem focuses on a single paragraph, you're instead working with a Logic Function question. You must determine why the author included the fourth paragraph in the overall structure.

---

[5]PrepTest 54, Sec 1, Q 4
[6]PrepTest 54, Sec 1, Q 5

Step 3: You can't ask for a better research source than your Roadmap. Use it to review the passage structure as a whole.

Step 4: The author's Main Idea was laid out in the first paragraph: The Internet has created new legal challenges. Each of the remaining paragraphs supports this idea; according to the Roadmap, the final paragraph specifically mentions that needed regulations become hard to provide across multiple jurisdictions.

Step 5: The correct answer, choice (E), identifies the final paragraph as evidence for the author's Main Idea. Choice (A) describes a relationship that doesn't exist—paragraph four in no way refutes paragraph two. Choice (B) is a classic 180—paragraph four *supports* the first paragraph. It doesn't question it. Choice (C) is irrelevant, as there is no summary of paragraphs two and three here. Choice (D) suggests that paragraph four is a continuation of paragraph three, also incorrect. Strategic Reading is *crucial* when you face this type of question. Trust in your Roadmap and your understanding of the big picture in order to score this point easily and efficiently.

Passage Two: "Comparative Passages on Drilling Muds"
Step 1:

Passage A

Drilling fluids, including the various mixtures known as drilling muds, play essential roles in oil-well drilling. As they are circulated down through the drill pipe and back up the well itself, they lubricate the
(5) drill bit, bearings, and drill pipe; clean and cool the drill bit as it cuts into the rock; lift rock chips (cuttings) to the surface; provide information about what is happening downhole, allowing the drillers to monitor the behavior, flow rate, pressure, and
(10) composition of the drilling fluid; and maintain well pressure to control cave-ins.

Drilling muds are made of bentonite and other clays and polymers, mixed with a fluid to the desired viscosity. By far the largest ingredient of drilling
(15) muds, by weight, is barite, a very heavy mineral of density 4.3 to 4.6. It is also used as an inert filler in some foods and is more familiar in its medical use as the "barium meal" administered before X-raying the digestive tract.
(20)   Over the years individual drilling companies and their expert drillers have devised proprietary formulations, or mud "recipes," to deal with specific types of drilling jobs. One problem in studying the effects of drilling waste discharges is that the drilling
(25) fluids are made from a range of over 1,000, sometimes toxic, ingredients—many of them known, confusingly, by different trade names, generic descriptions, chemical formulae, and regional or industry slang words, and many of them kept secret by companies or individual
(30) formulators.

Drilling muds defined

How they're made

Prob. with studies: too many fluids

Passage B

Drilling
discharges
carefully
controlled

            Drilling mud, cuttings, and associated chemicals
        are normally released only during the drilling phase of
        a well's existence. These discharges are the main
        environmental concern in offshore oil production, and
(35)   their use is tightly regulated. The discharges are closely
        monitored by the offshore operator, and releases are
        controlled as a condition of the operating permit.
            One type of mud—water-based mud (WBM)—is
        a mixture of water, bentonite clay, and chemical
(40)   additives, and is used to drill shallow parts of wells. It
        is not particularly toxic to marine organisms and

WBM not as
bad

        disperses readily. Under current regulations, it can be
        dumped directly overboard. Companies typically
        recycle WBM until their properties are no longer
(45)   suitable and then, over a period of hours, dump the
        entire batch into the sea.
            For drilling deeper wells, oil-based mud (OBM) is

OBM more
dangerous

        normally used. The typical difference from WBM is the
        high content of mineral oil (typically 30 percent).
(50)   OBMs also contain greater concentrations of barite, a
        powdered heavy mineral and a number of additives.
        OBMs have a greater potential for negative
        environmental impact, partly because they do not
        disperse as readily. Barite may impact some
(55)   organisms, particularly scallops, and the mineral oil
        may have toxic effects. Currently only the residues of
        OBMs adhering to cuttings that remain after the
        cuttings are sieved from the drilling fluids may be
        discharged overboard, and then only mixtures up to a
(60)   specified maximum oil content.

Paragraph Structure: As always, with comparative reading passages you should read and Roadmap each passage independently. Be sure to determine the **Topic, Scope, Purpose,** and **Main Idea** for Passage A before moving on to Passage B.

Passage A: The opening paragraph is purely descriptive, presenting the author's **Topic** (drilling muds) and the "essential roles" (line 2) they play in offshore oil production (the author's **Scope**). The second paragraph is similarly concerned with detail, describing the creation and composition of drilling muds. The author does note that barite is "by far" (line 14) the largest ingredient in most muds, an emphasis that you should definitely take note of. The final paragraph switches direction slightly, describing "one problem" (line 23) with the study of the environmental effects of the discharge of drilling muds and other fluids from drilling operations—there is a large profusion of different fluids currently in use, and their varying compositions and trade names make them difficult to examine closely. The **Purpose** of this passage is to describe drilling muds and some problems associated with them, and the **Main Idea** encapsulates all of this: Drilling muds have many uses, they are composed largely of barite, and their environmental ramifications are hard to study.

Passage B: This passage begins by addressing the "main environmental concern" (lines 33–34) with offshore drilling (the **Topic**), the discharge of muds and other fluids. The author's **Scope** becomes clear in the second and third paragraphs: a discussion of WBMs as compared to OBMs. The primary difference lies in the threat to the environment and resultant levels of regulation. The second paragraph describes WBMs as less environmentally dangerous, and therefore subject to fewer regulations. The "difference" (line 48) with OBMs, as described in the third paragraph, is that the composition of OBMs makes them more dangerous to the environment, and thus more tightly regulated. Once again, the author's **Purpose** was descriptive: to explain differences between different types of drilling muds. The **Main Idea** should define this difference: Drilling muds can pose environmental threats, although OBMs are more hazardous on the whole than WBMs.

By quickly comparing and contrasting the passages, you can see many similarities. Both passages discuss drilling muds, and both touch on some of the environmental problems associated with their use. Passage A is more concerned with the manufacture and composition of muds generally, only raising environmental issues in the final paragraph, while Passage B leads with environmental concerns and centers the discussion around them, although it too addresses drilling mud composition. Both authors maintain a neutral, scholarly tone throughout their respective passages, preferring to remain descriptive without offering suggestions or judgments.

Question Triage: There's a single Global point to be scored—question 6—so grab it right away. Avoiding the EXCEPT questions for now, questions 7 and 12 ask for specific details in the passages, so tackle them next. Question 11, a Strengthen question with plenty of clues in the stem, is a better choice than question 9, a vaguely worded Inference question. Questions 8 and 10 are identically worded and will probably require more challenging research. Save them for last, and skip one or both of them for now if necessary.

6. **(B)**
   A primary purpose of each of the passages is to
   (A) provide causal explanations for a type of environmental pollution
   (B) describe the general composition and properties of drilling muds
   (C) point out possible environmental impacts associated with oil drilling
   (D) explain why oil-well drilling requires the use of drilling muds
   (E) identify difficulties inherent in the regulation of oil-well drilling operations[7]

Step 2: "Primary purpose" in the stem identifies this as a Global question.

[7]PrepTest 54, Sec 1, Q 6

Step 3: Recall the Main Ideas of both passages and prepare to base your prediction in the next step on them

Step 4: Passage A was primarily concerned with describing drilling muds generally. In distinguishing between the threat to the environment posed by two different types of muds, Passage B also described some of their chemical properties. This is the similarity you're looking for in the choices.

Step 5: Correct choice (B) is a direct match for the prediction. Choice (A) is completely out of the scope of Passage A, which mentions pollution only in passing, as is choice (C). (Passage A never mentions specific environmental impacts.) Passage B never addresses why muds are required, eliminating choice (D), and choice (E) is touched upon briefly in Passage A but not in Passage B.

7. **(E)**

Which one of the following is a characteristic of barite that is mentioned in both of the passages?
(A)   It does not disperse readily in seawater.
(B)   It is not found in drilling muds containing bentonite.
(C)   Its use in drilling muds is tightly regulated.
(D)   It is the most commonly used ingredient in drilling muds.
(E)   It is a heavy mineral.[8]

Step 2: The question asks for a specific characteristic mentioned in both passages. This is a Detail question.

Step 3: Your Roadmap should lead you back to the second paragraph of Passage A, which describes the composition of muds. In Passage B, barite is only specifically mentioned in the third paragraph dealing with OBMs.

Step 4: What do both passages explicitly mention about barite? Only that it is a heavy mineral. The correct answer must reflect this.

Step 5: With a strong prediction, correct choice (E) is the clear winner. Choice (A) is only referenced in Passage B, and choice (B) isn't mentioned in either passage. Choice (C) contains a distortion—the discharge of certain muds is regulated, not necessarily their barite content. Choice (D) is only mentioned in Passage A.

---

[8]PrepTest 54, Sec 1, Q 7

8. **(E)**

    Each of the following is supported by one or both of the passages EXCEPT:
    (A)   Clay is an important constituent of many, if not all, drilling muds.
    (B)   At least one type of drilling mud is not significantly toxic to marine life.
    (C)   There has been some study of the environmental effects of drilling-mud discharges.
    (D)   Government regulations allow drilling muds to contain 30 percent mineral oil.
    (E)   During the drilling of an oil well, drilling mud is continuously discharged into the sea.[9]

Step 2: This Inference EXCEPT question might be a bit tricky—you are looking for something that is *not* supported in either passage.

Step 3: The stem doesn't give you any concrete clues to guide your research, so process of elimination is likely to be the appropriate strategy. First, think through the Main Idea of each passage in order to make elimination easier.

Step 4: Passage A describes the composition and usage of muds, and Passage B compares two specific types. Keep this in mind as you work through the choices to maximize your research efficiency.

Step 5: You can eliminate choice (A) with a quick glance back at Passage A, paragraph two. Choice (B) is supported by paragraph two of Passage B. Both passages support choice (C). You can find the specific information in choice (D) in Passage B, paragraph two, which mentions specific regulations. The only remaining choice, (E), is never mentioned in either passage and is therefore the correct answer.

A question like this one can be time consuming, but you can eliminate choices more easily by skillfully using your Roadmap. When dealing with an EXCEPT question, read the question stem carefully and make sure you've completely understood the task at hand. Finally, remember that Inference EXCEPT questions are definitely low-priority, so don't be afraid to skip this one and come back to it if time permits.

---

[9]PrepTest 54, Sec 1, Q 8

9. **(B)**

    Which one of the following can be most reasonably
    inferred from the two passages taken together, but
    not from either one individually?
    (A)   Barite is the largest ingredient of drilling
          muds, by weight, and also the most
          environmentally damaging.
    (B)   Although barite can be harmful to marine
          organisms, it can be consumed safely by
          humans.
    (C)   Offshore drilling is more damaging to the
          environment than is land-based drilling.
    (D)   The use of drilling muds needs to be more
          tightly controlled by government.
    (E)   If offshore drilling did not generate cuttings, it
          would be less harmful to the environment.[10]

Step 2: The obvious clue in the stem is the word "inferred." This is an Inference question. It is,
however, an unusual type of Inference question—you must find the choice that can only be
inferred by combining information from both passages.

Step 3: Once again, this stem doesn't provide specific research clues. You should think about
the big picture instead.

Step 4: What concepts did both passages mention? Both described properties of drilling muds
and their composition (you may recall thinking through this when you tackled question 6). The
correct answer is likely to fall within this general scope, but a more specific prediction might
be hard to make. Use your general prediction to make the answer choices easier to evaluate.

Step 5: Choice (A) describes barite, which does appear in both passages, but includes a fatal distortion—neither passage describes barite as the "most damaging" component of drilling muds (note the
extreme language). Choice (B), by contrast, *is* supported by both passages and is the correct answer.
Passage A indicates that barite can be safely ingested by humans, and Passage B describes some
of barite's harmful effects on sea life. Choices (C), (D), and (E) are not supported by either passage.

10. **(B)**

    Each of the following is supported by one or both of
    the passages EXCEPT:
    (A)   Drillers monitor the suitability of the mud
          they are using.
    (B)   The government requires drilling companies to
          disclose all ingredients used in their drilling
          muds.
    (C)   In certain quantities, barite is not toxic to
          humans.
    (D)   Oil reserves can be found within or beneath
          layers of rock.
    (E)   Drilling deep oil wells requires the use of
          different mud recipes than does drilling
          shallow oil wells.[11]

---

[10]PrepTest 54, Sec 1, Q 9
[11]PrepTest 54, Sec 1, Q 10

Step 2: This question is identical to question 8. Once again, you must find the Inference that *can't* be made from either passage.

Step 3: Little is provided in the way of specific research clues. Not to worry—all the information you need is in the passage.

Step 4: As with the previous two questions, stay focused on the big picture and prepare to employ the process of elimination.

Step 5: You're likely to find support for choice (A) in Passage A, which discussed muds in a more general sense. The third paragraph mentions that drillers devise better muds to suit their purposes; this allows you to eliminate choice (A). The same paragraph mentions that many mud formulae are kept secret, which directly contradicts answer choice (B). Since choice (B) is false, it must be the correct answer. Choices (C) and (D) can be inferred from Passage A, and choice (E) is mentioned in Passage B.

11. **(C)**

Based on information in the passages, which one of the following, if true, provides the strongest support for a prediction that the proportion of oil-well drilling using OBMs will increase in the future?

(A)   The cost of certain ingredients in WBMs is expected to increase steadily over the next several decades.

(B)   The deeper an offshore oil well, the greater the concentration of barite that must be used in the drilling mud.

(C)   Oil reserves at shallow depths have mostly been tapped, leaving primarily much deeper reserves for future drilling.

(D)   It is unlikely that oil drillers will develop more efficient ways of removing OBM residues from cuttings that remain after being sieved from drilling fluids.

(E)   Barite is a common mineral, the availability of which is virtually limitless.[12]

Step 2: The question asks you which choice provides "support" for the prediction that OBM use will increase. This is a Logic Reasoning question, one that requires you to strengthen a prediction.

Step 3: A glance at your Roadmap should direct you straight to Passage B, paragraph three.

Step 4: What might cause an increase in the use of OBMs? The information you need is at the very beginning of the paragraph. OBMs are typically used in deeper wells. The correct answer choice should indicate an increased proportion of deep wells—this would require a greater proportion of OBMs.

[12]PrepTest 54, Sec 1, Q 11

Step 5: The correct choice is (C)—if most future wells will be much deeper, you should expect to see a resultant increase in the use of OBMs. Choice (A) may have looked tempting, but even if the cost of WBM ingredients goes up, this doesn't necessarily imply that more OBMs will be used as a consequence (recall that the passages specify different usages for the different types of muds). Choices (B), (D), and (E) are irrelevant to the issue at hand; none of them gives a compelling reason why the proportion of OBMs would rise in the future.

12. **(A)**

According to passage B, one reason OBMs are potentially more environmentally damaging than WBMs is that OBMs
- (A) are slower to disperse
- (B) contain greater concentrations of bentonite
- (C) contain a greater number of additives
- (D) are used for drilling deeper wells
- (E) cannot be recycled[13]

Step 2: The stem asks for an explicitly stated reason why OBMs may be more damaging than WBMs. This is a Detail question.

Step 3: The stem directs you to Passage B, and your Roadmap indicates that the dangers of OBMs are discussed in paragraph three.

Step 4: The passage indicates that there is a "greater potential" (line 52) for harm because the hazardous components of OBMs do not disperse as quickly as those in WBMs.

Step 5: With so many excellent clues available, choice (A) is the clear match. Choice (B) contains a distortion—OBMs contain a greater concentration of barite, not necessarily bentonite. Choice (C) is not cited as a specific reason for the increased danger of OBMs, and neither is choice (E). While choice (D) does describe a property of OBMs, it's not a property that is tied to environmental damage.

Passage Three: "Overton Walker's 'Cakewalk'"
Step 1:

Walker popularized cakewalk

Aida Overton Walker (1880–1914), one of the most widely acclaimed African American performers of the early twentieth century, was known largely for popularizing a dance form known as the cakewalk
(5) through her choreographing, performance, and teaching of the dance. The cakewalk was originally developed prior to the United States Civil War by African Americans, for whom dance was a means of maintaining cultural links within a slave society. It
(10) was based on traditional West African ceremonial dances, and like many other African American dances, it retained features characteristic of African dance forms, such as gliding steps and an emphasis on improvisation.

---

[13]PrepTest 54, Sec 1, Q 12

(15)   To this African-derived foundation, the cakewalk
(added) certain elements from European dances: (where)

Cakewalk mix African dances feature flexible body postures, large
of African and groups and separate-sex dancing, the cakewalk
European (developed) into a high-kicking walk performed by a

(20)   procession of couples. (Ironically,) (while) these
modifications later enabled the cakewalk to appeal to
European Americans (and) become one of the first
cultural forms to cross the racial divide in North
America, they were (originally,) introduced with satiric

(25)   intent. Slaves performed the grandiloquent walks in
Different levels (order to) parody the processional dances performed at
of parody slave owners' balls and, (in general,) the self-important
manners of slave owners. To add a (further irony,) by
the end of the nineteenth century, the cakewalk was

(30)   itself being (parodied) by European American stage
performers, (and) these parodies (in turn) helped shape
subsequent versions of the cakewalk

        (While) this complex evolution meant that the
cakewalk was not a simple cultural phenomenon—

(35)   (one scholar) has characterized this layering of parody
upon parody with the phrase "mimetic vertigo"—it is
(in fact) what enabled the dance to attract its wide
Complex audience. In the cultural and socioeconomic flux of
roots led to the turn-of-the-century United States, (where)
popularity (40)   industrialization, urbanization, mass immigration, and
rapid social mobility all reshaped the cultural
landscape, an art form (had to be) capable of being
many things to many people (in order to) appeal to a
large audience.

(45)   Walker's (remarkable) success at popularizing the
cakewalk across otherwise relatively rigid racial
Walker's boundaries (rested on) her ability to address within her
interpr. was interpretation of it the varying and sometimes
diversify conflicting demands placed on the dance. Middle-

(50)   class African Americans, (for example,) often
(denounced) the cakewalk as disreputable, a complaint
reinforced by the parodies circulating at the time.
Won over Walker (won over) this audience (by) refining the
different social cakewalk and emphasizing its fundamental grace.
groups (55)   Meanwhile, (because) middle- and upper-class
European American often felt (threatened) by the
tremendous cultural flux around them, they (prized)
what they regarded as authentic art forms as bastions
of stability; much of Walker's success with this

(60)   audience (derived from) her distillation of what was
widely (acclaimed) as the most authentic cakewalk.
(Finally,) Walker was able to gain the admiration of
many newly rich industrialists and financiers, who
(found) in the grand flourishes of her version of the

(65)   cakewalk a fitting vehicle for celebrating their
newfound social rank.

Paragraph Structure: The passage introduces the **Topic** right out of the gate (the cakewalk) and the **Scope**, specifically Walker's popularization of it. The first paragraph establishes that Walker was known "largely" (line 3) for her performance of the cakewalk, then goes on to describe some defining features of the dance itself, noting that it was "based on" (line 10) traditional West African styles of dance.

The second paragraph expands on the cakewalk's background. It "added" (line 16) to its West African roots influences derived from European dances. These led to an interesting number of ironies (lines 20 & 28); "originally" (line 24) the dance was crafted as a parody of the self-important mannerisms of slave holders, but a "further irony" (line 28) was introduced later when European Americans began to parody the cakewalk, adding to its evolution. These layers of irony have the potential to be confusing, but don't get bogged down in them. As you read strategically, get the general gist of what the author is saying and move on. You can always return to this third paragraph and dig into it if a question requires it.

The lengthy fourth paragraph explains that Walker's success in popularizing this complex dance "rested on" (line 47) her ability to make it accessible to different audiences. This idea is followed by specific descriptions of exactly how she brought about acceptance of the cakewalk among different groups of Americans. This passage is descriptive rather than argumentative, so the author's **Purpose** was to describe the origins of the cakewalk and explain how Walker was able to popularize it. The **Main Idea**: The cakewalk evolved into a complex mix of different dance styles and ironic elements, and Walker's understanding of its complexities allowed her to make it accessible to different groups of Americans.

Question Triage: Begin with question 13, a Global question, and then look for straightforward Detail questions. The only one is question 16, so tackle it next. There are two Logic questions here—question 14 (Function) and question 15 (Parallel Reasoning). Since they both provide plenty of research clues it makes sense to complete them before the remaining Inference questions. Of the two Inference questions, 18 provides a slightly more specific reference in its stem than 17, so consider completing them in that order.

13. **(C)**

Which one of the following most accurately expresses the main point of the passage?

(A) Walker, who was especially well known for her success in choreographing, performing, and teaching the cakewalk, was one of the most widely recognized African American performers of the early twentieth century.

(B) In spite of the disparate influences that shaped the cakewalk, Walker was able to give the dance broad appeal because she distilled what was regarded as the most authentic version in an era that valued authenticity highly.

(C) Walker popularized the cakewalk by capitalizing on the complex cultural mix that had developed from the dance's original blend of satire and cultural preservation, together with the effects of later parodies.

(D) Whereas other versions of the cakewalk circulating at the beginning of the twentieth century were primarily parodic in nature, the version popularized by Walker combined both satire and cultural preservation.

(E) Because Walker was able to recognize and preserve the characteristics of the cakewalk as African Americans originally performed it, it became the first popular art form to cross the racial divide in the United States.[14]

Step 2: This Global question asks for the "main point" of the passage.

Step 3: Consult the Main Idea of the passage in order to make your prediction.

Step 4: The correct answer should mention Walker's success in popularizing the cakewalk through her understanding of its complex history.

Step 5: The prediction matches correct choice (C) beautifully. Choice (A) focuses too narrowly on a single detail of the passage. Choice (B) distorts the reason why Walker's approach to the dance was popular, and choice (D) incorrectly suggests that Walker's version of the dance was the only one that contained cultural preservation. Choice (E) also contains a distortion—the cakewalk was identified as "one of the first" (lines 22–23) art forms to cross the racial divide.

[14]PrepTest 54, Sec 1, Q 13

14. **(D)**

The author describes the socioeconomic flux of the turn-of-the-century United States in the third paragraph primarily in order to

(A)   argue that the cakewalk could have become popular only in such complex social circumstances

(B)   detail the social context that prompted performers of the cakewalk to fuse African and European dance forms

(C)   identify the target of the overlapping parodic layers that characterized the cakewalk

(D)   indicate why a particular cultural environment was especially favorable for the success of the cakewalk

(E)   explain why European American parodies of the cakewalk were able to reach wide audiences[15]

Step 2: The words "primarily in order to" identify this as a Logic Function question.

Step 3: The stem directs you to the third paragraph, so glance at your Roadmap in order to get the sense of context that Logic Function questions require. The paragraph as a whole explains that the cakewalk's complex roots are what allowed it to gain the level of popularity it eventually reached.

Step 4: The author mentions the state of flux quoted in the stem while explaining that an art form had to be "many things to many people" (line 43) in order to be popular. The author was providing an example of the kind of environment that led to this requirement, and that in turn allowed the cakewalk to become popular.

Step 5: Correct choice (D) describes the illustration predicted. Choice (A) is extreme; the author never suggests that the cakewalk could *only* have been popular in such times. Choices (B) and (C) are totally out of scope, and choice (E) distorts the author's intent. The third paragraph explained why Walker's version of the cakewalk flourished, not European American parodies.

15. **(C)**

Which one of the following is most analogous to the author's account in the second paragraph of how the cakewalk came to appeal to European Americans?

(A)   Satirical versions of popular music songs are frequently more popular than the songs they parody.

(B)   A style of popular music grows in popularity among young listeners because it parodies the musical styles admired by older listeners.

(C)   A style of music becomes admired among popular music's audience in part because of elements that were introduced in order to parody popular music.

(D)   A once popular style of music wins back its audience by incorporating elements of the style of music that is currently most popular.

(E)   After popular music begins to appropriate elements of a traditional style of music, interest in that traditional music increases.[16]

Step 2: The question asks for an analogous situation to something mentioned in the passage, identifying this as a Parallel Reasoning question.

Step 3: Returning to the second paragraph, you discover that "ironically" (line 20) it was the element of parody (specifically parody of the formal dances held by slave owners) in the cakewalk that led to its popularization among European Americans.

Step 4: The correct answer will describe a situation that follows the general form that you discovered in your research—an art form that, in parodying a cultural group, adopts elements that make it popular among that group.

Step 5: Answer choice (C) is a match of the predicted relationship. It applies this relationship to classical music, but logically it is equivalent, and that's all that counts in a Parallel Reasoning question. Choice (A) misses the point by suggesting a satire that is more popular than the original—such a comparison was absent from the passage. Choice (B) brings in the irrelevant idea of younger vs. older listeners, and choice (D) describes a comeback, not a spreading of popularity. Choice (E) fails to mention the element of parody that was crucial to the prediction.

---

[16]PrepTest 54, Sec 1, Q 15

16. **(E)**

The passage asserts which one of the following about
the cakewalk?
(A)   It was largely unknown outside African
      American culture until Walker popularized it.
(B)   It was mainly a folk dance, and Walker became
      one of only a handful of people to perform it
      professionally.
(C)   Its performance as parody became uncommon
      as a result of Walker's popularization of its
      authentic form.
(D)   Its West African origins became commonly
      known as a result of Walker's work.
(E)   It was one of the first cultural forms to cross
      racial lines in the United States.[17]

Step 2: "The passage asserts" a particular idea, which tells you that this is a Detail question.

Step 3: While the stem doesn't point to a specific area of the text in which to conduct your research, your Roadmap should remind you that, in general, descriptions of the cakewalk were primarily discussed in the first two paragraphs, with paragraphs three and four focused more heavily on Walker's popularization of the dance. So, you can probably find the correct answer in the first half of the passage.

Step 4: With so much text to research, don't waste your time trying to summarize the whole of paragraphs one and two—a brief glance at some key points will suffice. The cakewalk was originally based on West African ceremonial dances, and later went through a series of transformations as its popularity spread among different groups and was subsequently parodied and refined.

Step 5: With such a broad prediction, it may be necessary to go choice by choice. Choice (A) is refuted in the passage (the first paragraph describes the dance's roots in African American culture). Choice (B) also contradicts the passage, which describes the cakewalk as widely popular. Choice (C) distorts the role that parody played in the cakewalk's development, and choice (D) is out of scope. That leaves choice (E), the correct answer, which is directly supported by text in the second paragraph.

Note that, even without highly specific research clues in the stem, a solid knowledge of the author's main ideas can still help you eliminate wrong answer choices quickly and confidently.

---

[17]PrepTest 54, Sec 1, Q 16

17. **(E)**

It can be inferred from the passage that the author would be most likely to agree with which one of the following statements?

(A) Because of the broad appeal of humor, satiric art forms are often among the first to cross racial or cultural divisions.

(B) The interactions between African American and European American cultural forms often result in what is appropriately characterized as "mimetic vertigo."

(C) Middle-class European Americans who valued the cakewalk's authenticity subsequently came to admire other African American dances for the same reason.

(D) Because of the influence of African dance forms, some popular dances that later emerged in the United States featured separate-sex dancing.

(E) Some of Walker's admirers were attracted to her version of the cakewalk as a means for bolstering their social identities.[18]

Step 2: This is an Inference question, so you should be on the lookout for something that *must be true.*

Step 3: The only clue the stem gives you is a reference to the author. By reviewing the author's primary goals in writing the passage, you can make this question easier to work with.

Step 4: The author was most concerned with describing the reasons for Walker's ability to popularize the cakewalk—reasons described in paragraphs three and four. The dance appealed to a disparate audience because Walker was able to present its many layers to people with different cultural expectations. Keep the big picture in mind when evaluating the answer choices.

Step 5: Choice (A) is far too extreme. Just because the cakewalk contained elements of parody doesn't imply that it was a satiric art form, or that such art forms generally cross racial divisions. Choice (B) is also extreme; the author only mentions "mimetic vertigo" (line 36) as a specific description of the cakewalk's layers of parody. Choices (C) and (D) are out of scope and are not supported by the passage. Choice (E), the correct answer, is in line with the author's description of the cakewalk's popularity and is directly supported by examples at the end of the final paragraph.

[18]PrepTest 54, Sec 1, Q 17

18. **(A)**

The passage most strongly suggests that the author would be likely to agree with which one of the following statements about Walker's significance in the history of the cakewalk?

(A) Walker broadened the cakewalk's appeal by highlighting elements that were already present in the dance.

(B) Walker's version of the cakewalk appealed to larger audiences than previous versions did because she accentuated its satiric dimension.

(C) Walker popularized the cakewalk by choreographing various alternative interpretations of it, each tailored to the interests of a different cultural group.

(D) Walker added a "mimetic vertigo" to the cakewalk by inserting imitations of other performers' cakewalking into her dance routines.

(E) Walker revitalized the cakewalk by disentangling its complex admixture of African and European elements.[19]

Step 2: "Most strongly suggests" identifies this as another Inference question.

Step 3: There are some good clues in the stem—you need to find information in the passage reflecting the author's assessment of Walker's significance in the history of the cakewalk. Your Roadmap will indicate that the fourth paragraph contains the text you need.

Step 4: The author emphasizes that Walker's success "rested on" (line 47) her ability to interpret the dance's different demands in such a way that they appealed to diverse audiences. The correct answer should be supported by this central idea.

Step 5: Correct answer choice (A) is true—Walker did popularize the dance by emphasizing diverse elements that were already a part of its evolution. The comparison described in choice (B) is not supported by the passage. Choice (C) is in opposition to the author's Main Idea (and is therefore a 180); Walker didn't recreate the dance for different cultural groups, but rather interpreted the dance as a whole in such a way as to appeal to a large audience. Choice (D) misuses the concept of "mimetic vertigo" (line 36), and choice (E) is never suggested in the passage.

---

[19]PrepTest 54, Sec 1, Q 18

19. **(A)**

The passage provides sufficient information to
answer which one of the following questions?

(A)   What were some of the attributes of African
      dance forms that were preserved in the
      cakewalk?

(B)   Who was the first performer to dance the
      cakewalk professionally?

(C)   What is an aspect of the cakewalk that was
      preserved in other North American dance forms?

(D)   What features were added to the original
      cakewalk by the stage parodies circulating at
      the end of the nineteenth century?

(E)   For about how many years into the twentieth
      century did the cakewalk remain widely
      popular?[20]

Step 2: This oddly worded question doesn't easily fall into a single category. Since you're trying to derive new information from the passage, think of it as an Inference question.

Step 3: The stem provides no clues to help you conduct your research.

Step 4: As with other vague questions, keep the author's Main Idea in mind as you work through the choices.

Step 5: The question in choice (A) asks about the attributes of African dance that were present in the cakewalk, which is addressed in the first paragraph. So, choice (A) is the correct answer. Choice (B) is unanswerable from the passage; the author describes Walker as a very popular performer, but not necessarily the first. The cakewalk's influence on other dances was not addressed in the passage, eliminating choice (C). The specific details asked about in choices (D) and (E) aren't mentioned, so both of these choices can be eliminated as well.

Passage Four: "Group Decision Making"
Step 1:

*Cohesive
groups are
better*

In principle a cohesive group—one whose
members generally agree with one another and
support one another's judgments—can do a much
better job at decision making than it could if it were
(5)   noncohesive. When cohesiveness is low or lacking
entirely, compliance out of fear of recrimination is
likely to be strongest. To overcome this fear,
participants in the group's deliberations need to be
confident that they are members in good standing and
(10) that the others will continue to value their role in the
group, whether or not they agree about a particular
issue under discussion. As members of a group feel
more accepted by the others, they acquire greater

---

[20]PrepTest 54, Sec 1, Q 19

freedom to say what they really think, becoming less
(15) likely to use deceitful arguments or to play it safe by

Members become more vocal/honest

dancing around the issues with vapid or conventional
comments. Typically, then, the more cohesive a group
becomes, the less its members will deliberately censor
what they say out of fear of being punished socially
(20) for antagonizing their fellow members.

But group cohesiveness can have pitfalls as well:
while the members of a highly cohesive group can

Problem: members won't deviate

feel much freer to deviate from the majority, their
desire for genuine concurrence on every important
(25) issue often inclines them not to use this freedom. In a
highly cohesive group of decision makers, the danger
is not that individuals will conceal objections they
harbor regarding a proposal favored by the majority,
but that they will think the proposal is a good one
(30) without attempting to carry out a critical scrutiny that
could reveal grounds for strong objections. Members
may then decide that any misgivings they feel are not
worth pursuing—that the benefit of any doubt should
be given to the group consensus. In this way, they

Groupthink leads to bad decisions

(35) may fall victim to a syndrome known as
"groupthink," which one psychologist concerned with
collective decision making has defined as "a
deterioration of mental efficiency, reality testing, and
moral judgment that results from in-group pressures."
(40)   Based on analyses of major fiascoes of
international diplomacy and military decision making,
researchers have identified groupthink behavior as a
recurring pattern that involves several factors:
overestimation of the group's power and morality,

Groupthink patterns

(45) manifested, for example, in an illusion of
invulnerability, which creates excessive optimism;
closed-mindedness to warnings of problems and to
alternative viewpoints; and unwarranted pressures
toward uniformity, including self-censorship with
(50) respect to doubts about the group's reasoning and a
concomitant shared illusion of unanimity concerning
group decisions. Cohesiveness of the decision-making
group is an essential antecedent condition for this

Other factors besides cohesiveness lead to groupthink

syndrome but not a sufficient one, so it is important
(55) to work toward identifying the additional factors that
determine whether group cohesiveness will deteriorate
into groupthink or allow for effective decision
making.

Passage Structure: This passage discusses decision making in groups (the **Topic**) and asserts that more cohesive groups make better decisions. The author investigates this phenomenon further—in order to "overcome" (line 7) the fear of speaking out, members of a group "need to be" (line 8) confident that they're valued, and "typically" (line 17) they will speak more honestly as a consequence.

The Keyword "but" (line 21) at the onset of paragraph two draws you nearer to the author's primary intentions: There are problems associated with high levels of cohesion as members become more concerned with agreement than with critical thinking. In this way, they may fall "victim" (line 35) to the phenomenon of "groupthink" (line 36), the author's **Scope**. Groupthink is "defined" (line 37) by a psychologist as leading to the deterioration of a group's ability to make sound decisions.

The author begins the third paragraph with some emphatic Keywords, connecting groupthink to a number of "major fiascoes" (line 40) throughout history. The author notes that group cohesiveness is "essential" (line 53) to groupthink, but "not . . . sufficient" (line 54), also stressing the need to understand other factors that may lead to this unfortunate condition.

The author's **Purpose** is to describe the phenomenon of groupthink and examine some of its implications for decision making in groups. The **Main Idea:** Groupthink is a dangerous phenomenon that can sometimes follow from cohesiveness in groups, but other factors may be responsible as well.

Question Triage: Your only Global point is question 20, so score it first. Questions 23 and 25 are natural follow-ups—they're relatively brief Detail questions. Question 26 is also fairly straightforward—a Function question with a specific line reference. Your next stop should probably be question 22, a Strengthen question, because the remaining Inference questions don't look as inviting. Question 24 is Inference, but the stem is fairly specific (asking what the author and certain researchers would agree on), making it a better choice than both 21, which is somewhat convoluted, and 27, which provides less information. Depending on time constraints, you can finish up 21 and 27 in either order, but be ready to guess strategically if you're running low on time.

20. **(A)**

   Which one of the following most accurately expresses
   the main point of the passage?
   (A)   Despite its value in encouraging frank
         discussion, high cohesion can lead to a
         debilitating type of group decision making
         called groupthink.
   (B)   Group members can guard against groupthink
         if they have a good understanding of the
         critical role played by cohesion.
   (C)   Groupthink is a dysfunctional collective
         decision-making pattern that can occur in
         diplomacy and military affairs.
   (D)   Low cohesion in groups is sometimes desirable
         when higher cohesion involves a risk of
         groupthink behavior.
   (E)   Future efforts to guard against groupthink will
         depend on the results of ongoing research
         into the psychology of collective
         decision making.[21]

Step 2: The phrase "main point" alerts you that this is a Global question.

Step 3: Think about the author's Main Idea rather than researching specific text.

Step 4: The author's primary goal is to describe groupthink, a negative consequence that can sometimes follow from high cohesiveness in groups.

Step 5: The correct match is choice (A). Choice (B) is too specific and unsupported by the passage. Choice (C) correctly defines groupthink, but it is too narrow in scope, failing to capture the author's connection of groupthink to cohesiveness. Choice (D) distorts the author's intent, as it's never suggested that low cohesion is desirable. Choice (E) wanders out of scope, since the author never makes any predictions about future analysis of groupthink.

---

[21]PrepTest 54, Sec 1, Q 20

21. **(C)**

A group of closely associated colleagues has made a disastrous diplomatic decision after a series of meetings marked by disagreement over conflicting alternatives. It can be inferred from the passage that the author would be most likely to say that this scenario

(A) provides evidence of chronic indecision, thus indicating a weak level of cohesion in general

(B) indicates that the group's cohesiveness was coupled with some other factor to produce a groupthink fiasco

(C) provides no evidence that groupthink played a role in the group's decision

(D) provides evidence that groupthink can develop even in some groups that do not demonstrate an "illusion of unanimity"

(E) indicates that the group probably could have made its decision-making procedure more efficient by studying the information more thoroughly[22]

Step 2: The words "it can be inferred" tell you that this is an Inference question.

Step 3: Read the question carefully for clues. The stem describes a group making a disastrous decision following a lot of disagreement. This doesn't necessarily guide you directly to a specific part of the text in which to conduct research, but it does relate to the author's definition of "groupthink" and its causes. Recall that the author describes a close relationship between groupthink and cohesiveness—in fact, he states that cohesion is "essential" (line 53) to groupthink.

Step 4: In the hypothetical situation, the group making the decision is argumentative. The author of this passage is not primarily concerned with such groups; they lack the cohesiveness that can lead to groupthink. This may not seem like much to go on, but it does give you enough information to state with certainty that groupthink was probably not a factor in the disastrous decisions made by this group.

Step 5: Choice (C) is a perfect match of the prediction. The hypothetical situation doesn't supply enough information for the deduction described in choice (A), since there's no way to assess whether this group displays "chronic indecision." Choices (B) and (D) suggest that groupthink was at work, in direct opposition to the passage. Choice (E) is completely out of scope; there's no way to know whether more information would have helped this group.

22. **(C)**

Which one of the following, if true, would most support the author's contentions concerning the conditions under which groupthink takes place?

(A)   A study of several groups, each made up of members of various professions, found that most fell victim to groupthink.

(B)   There is strong evidence that respectful dissent is more likely to occur in cohesive groups than in groups in which there is little internal support.

(C)   Extensive analyses of decisions made by a large number of groups found no cases of groupthink in groups whose members generally distrust one another's judgments.

(D)   There is substantial evidence that groupthink is especially likely to take place when members of a group develop factions whose intransigence prolongs the group's deliberations.

(E)   Ample research demonstrates that voluntary deference to group opinion is not a necessary factor for the formation of groupthink behavior.[23]

Step 2: The stem asks you to "support" one of the author's arguments. This is a Logical Reasoning question, and your task is to strengthen the argument.

Step 3: According to the Roadmap, you can find the conditions under which groupthink occurs in the second paragraph. The primary cause that the author is concerned with is a high degree of cohesiveness within a group, which leads to the uncritical acceptance of ideas.

Step 4: How can you best support the author's idea? If it's true that high cohesion leads to groupthink, evidence that groupthink fails to occur in the absence of such cohesiveness would bolster the author's causal assertion. The correct answer will probably reflect this idea.

Step 5: Correct choice (C) is a perfect match, indicating a lack of groupthink where cohesiveness is low. Choices (A) and (B) are totally irrelevant to the comparison of highly cohesive groups to more argumentative groups. Choice (D) suggests that groupthink is likely to occur in fractious groups, but if this were true it would weaken the author's argument. Choice (E) similarly works against the author's hypothesis by suggesting that uncritical acceptance of group ideas doesn't lead to groupthink.

23. **(B)**

The passage mentions which one of the following as
a component of groupthink?
(A)   unjustified suspicions among group members
        regarding an adversary's intentions
(B)   strong belief that the group's decisions are
        right
(C)   group members working under unusually high
        stress, leading to illusions of invulnerability
(D)   the deliberate use of vapid, clichéd arguments
(E)   careful consideration of objections to majority
        positions[24]

Step 2: Since the stem asks for something explicitly mentioned in the passage, this is a Detail
question.

Step 3: Your Roadmap should lead you to the final paragraph, as this is where the author
describes specific patterns of groupthink, including excessive optimism, closed-mindedness
toward opposing viewpoints, and the suppression of any doubts that the group is right.

Step 4: The correct answer will paraphrase one or more of the ideas you uncovered in your
research. If you read them carefully you'll find the match.

Step 5: Choice (B) is the correct answer, paraphrasing the convictions described in the final
paragraph. Choices (A) and (D) are out of scope. Choice (C) distorts the language of the passage, describing a definition of the term "stress" that doesn't comply with author's use of it.
Choice (E) is a 180.

24. **(E)**

It can be inferred from the passage that both the
author of the passage and the researchers mentioned
in the passage would be most likely to agree with
which one of the following statements about
groupthink?
(A)   Groupthink occurs in all strongly cohesive
        groups, but its contribution to collective
        decision making is not fully understood.
(B)   The causal factors that transform group
        cohesion into groupthink are unique to each
        case.
(C)   The continued study of cohesiveness of groups
        is probably fruitless for determining what
        factors elicit groupthink.
(D)   Outside information cannot influence group
        decisions once they have become determined
        by groupthink.
(E)   On balance, groupthink cannot be expected to
        have a beneficial effect in a group's decision
        making.[25]

[24]PrepTest 54, Sec 1, Q 23
[25]PrepTest 54, Sec 1, Q 24

Step 2: Since the stem asks for what can be inferred, this is an Inference question.

Step 3: There are good clues in the question stem. You need to compare the author's point of view with that of the researchers. A scan of the passage leads to paragraph three, where researchers examining "fiascoes" (line 40) have identified specific patterns of behavior in groupthink.

Step 4: How does the author's opinion coincide with that of the researchers? In the second paragraph, the author says that cohesive groups may "fall victim" (line 35) to groupthink. What the researchers and the author seem to agree on is that groupthink is undesirable and leads to poor decision making. The correct answer should reflect this idea.

Step 5: The match is correct answer choice (E). Choice (A) is extreme and voices an idea that neither the author nor the researchers express. Choice (D) is similarly extreme; the researchers suggest that groupthink leads to closed mindedness, but stop short of saying that no outside information can get in. Choice (B) is not supported by any specific text, and the prediction described in choice (C) is never mentioned by the author or the researchers.

25. **(E)**

In the passage, the author says which one of the following about conformity in decision-making groups?
(A) Enforced conformity may be appropriate in some group decision situations.
(B) A high degree of conformity is often expected of military decision-making group members.
(C) Inappropriate group conformity can result from inadequate information.
(D) Voluntary conformity occurs much less frequently than enforced conformity.
(E) Members of noncohesive groups may experience psychological pressure to conform.[26]

Step 2: The stem asks for something the author mentions about conformity. This is a Detail question.

Step 3: The first paragraph describes the author's general pronouncements about conformity in groups. How conformity is achieved is, according to the author, dependent on the level of cohesiveness in the group; if the group lacks cohesiveness, conformity is established through fear. In order to "overcome this fear" (line 7), members of the group need to feel valued.

Step 4: As with other Detail questions, you should expect the correct answer to paraphrase information you've reviewed in your research.

[26]PrepTest 54, Sec 1, Q 25

Step 5: Correct choice (E) accurately describes the fear described in the first paragraph. The author never opines whether such conformity is "appropriate," eliminating choice (A). Choices (B) and (C) are entirely outside the scope of this question, and choice (D) is irrelevant, as the author never compares the frequency of voluntary vs. enforced conformity.

26. **(A)**

In line 5, the author mentions low group cohesiveness primarily in order to

(A) contribute to a claim that cohesiveness can be conducive to a freer exchange of views in groups

(B) establish a comparison between groupthink symptoms and the attributes of low-cohesion groups

(C) suggest that there may be ways to make both cohesive and noncohesive groups more open to dissent

(D) indicate that both cohesive and noncohesive groups may be susceptible to groupthink dynamics

(E) lay the groundwork for a subsequent proposal for overcoming the debilitating effects of low cohesion[27]

Step 2: The key phrase "in order to" identifies this as a Logic Function question.

Step 3: Remember that Logic Function questions rely on your understanding of context. Use your Roadmap to review the main point of the first paragraph as a whole before considering the role that low group cohesiveness plays within it.

Step 4: The author was primarily concerned in the first paragraph with describing the advantages of cohesiveness in group decision making. The brief reference to low cohesion allowed the author to demonstrate how, by contrast, high cohesion is preferable. This context will lead you to the correct answer choice.

Step 5: Choice (A) is the match—the cited text served author's overall claim about cohesive groups. Choices (B) and (D) erroneously refer to groupthink, which is not addressed until paragraph two. Choice (C) is completely out of scope, and choice (E) refers to a proposal that never appears in the passage.

---

[27]PrepTest 54, Sec 1, Q 26

27. **(B)**

Based on the passage, it can be inferred that the author would be most likely to agree with which one of the following?

(A) Highly cohesive groups are more likely to engage in confrontational negotiating styles with adversaries than are those with low cohesion.

(B) It is difficult for a group to examine all relevant options critically in reaching decisions unless it has a fairly high degree of cohesiveness.

(C) A group with varied viewpoints on a given issue is less likely to reach a sound decision regarding that issue than is a group whose members are unified in their outlook.

(D) Intense stress and high expectations are the key factors in the formation of groupthink.

(E) Noncohesive groups can, under certain circumstances, develop all of the symptoms of groupthink.[28]

Step 2: The word "inferred" makes this stem easy to identify as an Inference question.

Step 3: As with other Inference questions that provide little direction for your research, think about the author's main ideas before moving on to the choices.

Step 4: The author opined that groups with a high level of cohesiveness were more apt to make good decisions than groups with low cohesion, although such groups are vulnerable to the debilitating effects of groupthink. Keep these ideas in mind and proceed to the answer choices.

Step 5: The comparison in choice (A) has no support in the passage. Choice (B), the correct answer, is supported by the author's contention that in cohesive groups, members feel freer to express dissenting views—a definite requirement for the examination of all relevant options. Choice (C) might be true in some cases, but overlooks the possibility that a unified group may fall prey to groupthink. Choice (D) confuses the results of groupthink with its causes, and choice (E) has no support in the text of the passage.

---

[28]PrepTest 54, Sec 1, Q 27

CHAPTER 21

FULL-LENGTH SECTION 2[1]

Time—35 minutes
27 Questions

Directions: Each set of questions in this section is based on a single passage or a pair of passages. The questions are to be answered on the basis of what is <u>stated</u> or <u>implied</u> in the passage or pair of passages. For some of the questions, more than one of the choices could conceivably answer the question. However, you are to choose the <u>best</u> answer, that is, the response that most accurately and completely answers the question, and blacken the corresponding space on your answer sheet.

---

[1]PrepTest 55, Sec 2

Often when a highly skilled and experienced
employee leaves one company to work for another,
there is the potential for a transfer of sensitive
information between competitors. Two basic principles
(5)   in such cases appear irreconcilable: the right of the
company to its intellectual property—its proprietary
data and trade secrets—and the right of individuals to
seek gainful employment and to make free use of their
abilities. Nevertheless, the courts have often tried to
(10)   preserve both parties' legal rights by refusing to
prohibit the employee from working for the competitor,
but at the same time providing an injunction against
disclosure of any of the former employer's secrets. It
has been argued that because such measures help
(15)   generate suspicions and similar psychological barriers
to full and free utilization of abilities in the employee's
new situation, they are hardly effective in upholding
the individual's rights to free employment decisions.
But it is also doubtful that they are effective in
(20)   preserving trade secrets.

It is obviously impossible to divest oneself of that
part of one's expertise that one has acquired from
former employers and coworkers. Nor, in general, can
one selectively refrain from its use, given that it has
(25)   become an integral part of one's total intellectual
capacity. Nevertheless, almost any such information
that is not public knowledge may legitimately be
claimed as corporate property: normal employment
agreements provide for corporate ownership of all
(30)   relevant data, including inventions, generated by the
employee in connection with the company's business.

Once an employee takes a position with a
competitor, the trade secrets that have been acquired by
that employee may manifest themselves clearly and
(35)   consciously. This is what court injunctions seek to
prohibit. But they are far more likely to manifest
themselves subconsciously and inconspicuously—for
example, in one's daily decisions at the new post, or in
the many small contributions one might make to a large
(40)   team effort—often in the form of an intuitive sense of
what to do or to avoid. Theoretically, an injunction also
prohibits such inadvertent "leakage." However, the
former employer faces the practical problem of
securing evidence of such leakage, for little will
(45)   usually be apparent from the public activities of the
new employer. And even if the new employee's
activities appear suspicious, there is the further
problem of distinguishing trade secrets from what may
be legitimately asserted as technological skills
(50)   developed independently by the employee or already
possessed by the new employer. This is a major
stumbling block in the attempt to protect trade secrets,
since the proprietor has no recourse against others who
independently generate the same information. It is

(55)   therefore unlikely that an injunction against disclosure
of trade secrets to future employers actually prevents
any transfer of information except for the passage of
documents and other concrete embodiments of the
secrets.

1. Which one of the following most accurately expresses
    the main point of the passage?

    (A)   There are more effective ways than court
          injunctions to preserve both a company's
          right to protect its intellectual property and
          individuals' rights to make free use of their
          abilities.
    (B)   Court injunctions must be strengthened if
          they are to remain a relevant means of
          protecting corporations' trade secrets.
    (C)   Enforcement of court injunctions designed to
          protect proprietary information is impossible
          when employees reveal such information to
          new employers.
    (D)   Court injunctions prohibiting employees from
          disclosing former employers' trade secrets to
          new employers probably do not achieve all of
          their intended objectives.
    (E)   The rights of employees to make full use of
          their talents and previous training are being
          seriously eroded by the prohibitions placed
          on them by court injunctions designed to
          prevent the transfer of trade secrets.

2. Given the passage's content and tone, which one of the following statements would most likely be found elsewhere in a work from which this passage is an excerpt?

    (A) Given the law as it stands, corporations concerned about preserving trade secrets might be best served by giving their employees strong incentives to stay in their current jobs.

    (B) While difficult to enforce and interpret, injunctions are probably the most effective means of halting the inadvertent transfer of trade secrets while simultaneously protecting the rights of employees.

    (C) Means of redress must be made available to companies that suspect, but cannot prove, that former employees are revealing protected information to competitors.

    (D) Even concrete materials such as computer disks are so easy to copy and conceal that it will be a waste of time for courts to try to prevent the spread of information through physical theft.

    (E) The psychological barriers that an injunction can place on an employee in a new workplace are inevitably so subtle that they have no effect on the employee.

3. The author's primary purpose in the passage is to

    (A) suggest that injunctions against the disclosure of trade secrets not only create problems for employees in the workplace, but also are unable to halt the illicit spread of proprietary information

    (B) suggest that the information contained in "documents and other concrete embodiments" is usually so trivial that injunctions do little good in protecting intellectual property

    (C) argue that new methods must be found to address the delicate balance between corporate and individual rights

    (D) support the position that the concept of protecting trade secrets is no longer viable in an age of increasing access to information

    (E) argue that injunctions are not necessary for the protection of trade secrets

4. The passage provides the most support for which one of the following assertions?

    (A) Injunctions should be imposed by the courts only when there is strong reason to believe that an employee will reveal proprietary information.

    (B) There is apparently no reliable way to protect both the rights of companies to protect trade secrets and the rights of employees to seek new employment.

    (C) Employees should not be allowed to take jobs with their former employer's competitors when their new job could compromise trade secrets of their former employers.

    (D) The multiplicity of means for transferring information in the workplace only increases the need for injunctions.

    (E) Some companies seek injunctions as a means of punishing employees who take jobs with their competitors.

5. With which one of the following statements regarding documents and other concrete embodiments mentioned in line 58 would the author be most likely to agree?

    (A) While the transfer of such materials would be damaging, even the seemingly innocuous contributions of an employee to a competitor can do more harm in the long run.

    (B) Such materials are usually less informative than what the employee may recollect about a previous job.

    (C) Injunctions against the disclosure of trade secrets should carefully specify which materials are included in order to focus on the most damaging ones.

    (D) Large-scale transfer of documents and other materials cannot be controlled by injunctions.

    (E) Such concrete materials lend themselves to control and identification more readily than do subtler means of transferring information.

6. In the passage, the author makes which one of the following claims?

   (A) Injunctions against the disclosure of trade secrets limit an employee's chances of being hired by a competitor.

   (B) Measures against the disclosure of trade secrets are unnecessary except in the case of documents and other concrete embodiments of the secrets.

   (C) Employees who switch jobs to work for a competitor usually unintentionally violate the law by doing so.

   (D) Employers are not restricted in the tactics they can use when seeking to secure protected information from new employees.

   (E) What may seem like intellectual theft may in fact be an example of independent innovation.

The following passages concern a plant called purple loosestrife. Passage A is excerpted from a report issued by a prairie research council; passage B from a journal of sociology.

Passage A

Purple loosestrife (*Lythrum salicaria*), an aggressive and invasive perennial of Eurasian origin, arrived with settlers in eastern North America in the early 1800s and has spread across the continent's
(5)   midlatitude wetlands. The impact of purple loosestrife on native vegetation has been disastrous, with more than 50 percent of the biomass of some wetland communities displaced. Monospecific blocks of this weed have maintained themselves for at least 20 years.
(10)   Impacts on wildlife have not been well studied, but serious reductions in waterfowl and aquatic furbearer productivity have been observed. In addition, several endangered species of vertebrates are threatened with further degradation of their
(15)   breeding habitats. Although purple loosestrife can invade relatively undisturbed habitats, the spread and dominance of this weed have been greatly accelerated in disturbed habitats. While digging out the plants can temporarily halt their spread, there has been little
(20)   research on long-term purple loosestrife control. Glyphosate has been used successfully, but no measure of the impact of this herbicide on native plant communities has been made.

With the spread of purple loosestrife growing
(25)   exponentially, some form of integrated control is needed. At present, coping with purple loosestrife hinges on early detection of the weed's arrival in areas, which allows local eradication to be carried out with minimum damage to the native plant community.

Passage B

(30)   The war on purple loosestrife is apparently conducted on behalf of nature, an attempt to liberate the biotic community from the tyrannical influence of a life-destroying invasive weed. Indeed, purple loosestrife control is portrayed by its practitioners as
(35)   an environmental initiative intended to save nature rather than control it. Accordingly, the purple loosestrife literature, scientific and otherwise, dutifully discusses the impacts of the weed on endangered species—and on threatened biodiversity
(40)   more generally. Purple loosestrife is a pollution, according to the scientific community, and all of nature suffers under its pervasive influence.

Regardless of the perceived and actual ecological effects of the purple invader, it is apparent that
(45)   popular pollution ideologies have been extended into the wetlands of North America. Consequently, the scientific effort to liberate nature from purple loosestrife has failed to decouple itself from its philosophical origin as an instrument to control nature
(50)   to the satisfaction of human desires. Birds, particularly game birds and waterfowl, provide the bulk of the justification for loosestrife management. However, no bird species other than the canvasback has been identified in the literature as endangered by
(55)   purple loosestrife. The impact of purple loosestrife on furbearing mammals is discussed at great length, though none of the species highlighted (muskrat, mink) can be considered threatened in North America. What is threatened by purple loosestrife is the
(60)   economics of exploiting such preferred species and the millions of dollars that will be lost to the economies of the United States and Canada from reduced hunting, trapping, and recreation revenues due to a decline in the production of the wetland
(65)   resource.

7. Both passages explicitly mention which one of the following?

    (A)   furbearing animals
    (B)   glyphosate
    (C)   the threat purple loosestrife poses to economies
    (D)   popular pollution ideologies
    (E)   literature on purple loosestrife control

8. Each of the passages contains information sufficient to answer which one of the following questions?

    (A)   Approximately how long ago did purple loosestrife arrive in North America?
    (B)   Is there much literature discussing the potential benefit that hunters might derive from purple loosestrife management?
    (C)   What is an issue regarding purple loosestrife management on which both hunters and farmers agree?
    (D)   Is the canvasback threatened with extinction due to the spread of purple loosestrife?
    (E)   What is a type of terrain that is affected in at least some parts of North America by the presence of purple loosestrife?

9. It can be inferred that the authors would be most likely to disagree about which one of the following?

    (A) Purple loosestrife spreads more quickly in disturbed habitats than in undisturbed habitats.
    (B) The threat posed by purple loosestrife to local aquatic furbearer populations is serious.
    (C) Most people who advocate that eradication measures be taken to control purple loosestrife are not genuine in their concern for the environment.
    (D) The size of the biomass that has been displaced by purple loosestrife is larger than is generally thought.
    (E) Measures should be taken to prevent other non-native plant species from invading North America.

10. Which one of the following most accurately describes the attitude expressed by the author of passage B toward the overall argument represented by passage A?

    (A) enthusiastic agreement
    (B) cautious agreement
    (C) pure neutrality
    (D) general ambivalence
    (E) pointed skepticism

11. It can be inferred that both authors would be most likely to agree with which one of the following statements regarding purple loosestrife?

    (A) As it increases in North America, some wildlife populations tend to decrease.
    (B) Its establishment in North America has had a disastrous effect on native North American wetland vegetation in certain regions.
    (C) It is very difficult to control effectively with herbicides.
    (D) Its introduction into North America was a great ecological blunder.
    (E) When it is eliminated from a given area, it tends to return to that area fairly quickly.

12. Which one of the following is true about the relationship between the two passages?

    (A) Passage A presents evidence that directly counters claims made in passage B.
    (B) Passage B assumes what passage A explicitly argues for.
    (C) Passage B displays an awareness of the arguments touched on in passage A, but not vice versa.
    (D) Passage B advocates a policy that passage A rejects.
    (E) Passage A downplays the seriousness of claims made in passage B.

13. Which one of the following, if true, would cast doubt on the argument in passage B but bolster the argument in passage A?

    (A) Localized population reduction is often a precursor to widespread endangerment of a species.
    (B) Purple loosestrife was barely noticed in North America before the advent of suburban sprawl in the 1950s.
    (C) The amount by which overall hunting, trapping, and recreation revenues would be reduced as a result of the extinction of one or more species threatened by purple loosestrife represents a significant portion of those revenues.
    (D) Some environmentalists who advocate taking measures to eradicate purple loosestrife view such measures as a means of controlling nature.
    (E) Purple loosestrife has never become a problem in its native habitat, even though no effort has been made to eradicate it there.

With their recognition of Maxine Hong Kingston as a major literary figure, some critics have suggested that her works have been produced almost *ex nihilo*, saying that they lack a large traceable body of direct
(5) literary antecedents especially within the Chinese American heritage in which her work is embedded. But these critics, who have examined only the development of written texts, the most visible signs of a culture's narrative production, have overlooked Kingston's
(10) connection to the long Chinese tradition of a highly developed genre of song and spoken narrative known as "talk-story" (*gong gu tsai*).

Traditionally performed in the dialects of various ethnic enclaves, talk-story has been maintained within
(15) the confines of the family and has rarely surfaced into print. The tradition dates back to Sung dynasty (A.D. 970–1279) storytellers in China, and in the United States it is continually revitalized by an overlapping sequence of immigration from China.
(20) Thus, Chinese immigrants to the U.S. had a fully established, sophisticated oral culture, already ancient and capable of producing masterpieces, by the time they began arriving in the early nineteenth century. This transplanted oral heritage simply embraced new
(25) subject matter or new forms of Western discourse, as in the case of Kingston's adaptations written in English.

Kingston herself believes that as a literary artist she is one in a long line of performers shaping a recalcitrant history into talk-story form. She
(30) distinguishes her "thematic" storytelling memory processes, which sift and reconstruct the essential elements of personally remembered stories, from the memory processes of a print-oriented culture that emphasizes the retention of precise sequences of
(35) words. Nor does the entry of print into the storytelling process substantially change her notion of the character of oral tradition. For Kingston, "writer" is synonymous with "singer" or "performer" in the ancient sense of privileged keeper, transmitter, and creator of stories
(40) whose current stage of development can be frozen in print, but which continue to grow both around and from that frozen text.

Kingston's participation in the tradition of talk-story is evidenced in her book *China Men*, which
(45) utilizes forms typical of that genre and common to most oral cultures including: a fixed "grammar" of repetitive themes; a spectrum of stock characters; symmetrical structures, including balanced oppositions (verbal or physical contests, antithetical characters,
(50) dialectical discourse such as question-answer forms and riddles); and repetition. In *China Men*, Kingston also succeeds in investing idiomatic English with the allusive texture and oral-aural qualities of the Chinese language, a language rich in aural and visual puns,
(55) making her work a written form of talk-story.

14. Which one of the following most accurately states the main point of the passage?

(A) Despite some critics' comments, Kingston's writings have significant Chinese American antecedents, which can be found in the traditional oral narrative form known as talk-story.

(B) Analysis of Kingston's writings, especially *China Men*, supports her belief that literary artists can be performers who continue to reconstruct their stories even after they have been frozen in print.

(C) An understanding of Kingston's work and of Chinese American writers in general reveals that critics of ethnic literatures in the United States have been mistaken in examining only written texts.

(D) Throughout her writings Kingston uses techniques typical of the talk-story genre, especially the retention of certain aspects of Chinese speech in the written English text.

(E) The writings of Kingston have rekindled an interest in talk-story, which dates back to the Sung dynasty, and was extended to the United States with the arrival of Chinese immigrants in the nineteenth century.

15. Which one of the following can be most reasonably inferred from the passage?

(A) In the last few years, written forms of talk-story have appeared in Chinese as often as they have in English.

(B) Until very recently, scholars have held that oral storytelling in Chinese ethnic enclaves was a unique oral tradition.

(C) Talk-story has developed in the United States through a process of combining Chinese, Chinese American, and other oral storytelling forms.

(D) Chinese American talk-story relies upon memory processes that do not emphasize the retention of precise sequences of words.

(E) The connection between certain aspects of Kingston's work and talk-story is argued by some critics to be rather tenuous and questionable.

16. It can be inferred from the passage that the author uses the phrase "personally remembered stories" (line 32) primarily to refer to

   (A) a literary genre of first-person storytelling
   (B) a thematically organized personal narrative of one's own past
   (C) partially idiosyncratic memories of narratives
   (D) the retention in memory of precise sequences of words
   (E) easily identifiable thematic issues in literature

17. In which one of the following is the use of cotton fibers or cotton cloth most analogous to Kingston's use of the English language as described in lines 51–55?

   (A) Scraps of plain cotton cloth are used to create a multicolored quilt.
   (B) The surface texture of woolen cloth is simulated in a piece of cotton cloth by a special process of weaving.
   (C) Because of its texture, cotton cloth is used for a certain type of clothes for which linen is inappropriate.
   (D) In making a piece of cloth, cotton fiber is substituted for linen because of the roughly similar texture of the two materials.
   (E) Because of their somewhat similar textures, cotton and linen fibers are woven together in a piece of cloth to achieve a savings in price over a pure linen cloth.

18. The passage most clearly suggests that Kingston believes which one of the following about at least some of the stories contained in her writings?

   (A) Since they are intimately tied to the nature of the Chinese language, they can be approximated, but not adequately expressed, in English.
   (B) They should be thought of primarily as ethnic literature and evaluated accordingly by critics.
   (C) They will likely be retold and altered to some extent in the process.
   (D) Chinese American history is best chronicled by traditional talk-story.
   (E) Their significance and beauty cannot be captured at all in written texts.

19. The author's argument in the passage would be most weakened if which one of the following were true?

   (A) Numerous writers in the United States have been influenced by oral traditions.
   (B) Most Chinese American writers' work is very different from Kingston's.
   (C) Native American storytellers use narrative devices similar to those used in talk-story.
   (D) *China Men* is for the most part atypical of Kingston's literary works.
   (E) Literary critics generally appreciate the authenticity of Kingston's work.

20. The author's specific purpose in detailing typical talk-story forms (lines 43–51) is to

   (A) show why Kingston's book *China Men* establishes her as a major literary figure
   (B) support the claim that Kingston's use of typically oral techniques makes her work a part of the talk-story tradition
   (C) dispute the critics' view that Chinese American literature lacks literary antecedents
   (D) argue for Kingston's view that the literary artist is at best a "privileged keeper" of stories
   (E) provide an alternative to certain critics' view that Kingston's work should be judged primarily as literature

21. Which one of the following most accurately identifies the attitude shown by the author in the passage toward talk-story?

   (A) scholarly appreciation for its longstanding artistic sophistication
   (B) mild disappointment that it has not distinguished itself from other oral traditions
   (C) tentative approval of its resistance to critical evaluations
   (D) clear respect for the diversity of its ancient sources and cultural derivations
   (E) open admiration for the way it uses song to express narrative

In economics, the term "speculative bubble" refers to a large upward move in an asset's price driven not by the asset's fundamentals—that is, by the earnings derivable from the asset—but rather by
(5) mere speculation that someone else will be willing to pay a higher price for it. The price increase is then followed by a dramatic decline in price, due to a loss in confidence that the price will continue to rise, and the "bubble" is said to have burst. According to
(10) Charles Mackay's classic nineteenth-century account, the seventeenth-century Dutch tulip market provides an example of a speculative bubble. But the economist Peter Garber challenges Mackay's view, arguing that there is no evidence that the Dutch tulip
(15) market really involved a speculative bubble.

By the seventeenth century, the Netherlands had become a center of cultivation and development of new tulip varieties, and a market had developed in which rare varieties of bulbs sold at high prices. For
(20) example, a Semper Augustus bulb sold in 1625 for an amount of gold worth about U.S.$11,000 in 1999. Common bulb varieties, on the other hand, sold for very low prices. According to Mackay, by 1636 rapid price rises attracted speculators, and prices of many
(25) varieties surged upward from November 1636 through January 1637. Mackay further states that in February 1637 prices suddenly collapsed; bulbs could not be sold at 10 percent of their peak values. By 1739, the prices of all the most prized kinds of bulbs had fallen
(30) to no more than one two-hundredth of 1 percent of Semper Augustus's peak price.

Garber acknowledges that bulb prices increased dramatically from 1636 to 1637 and eventually reached very low levels. But he argues that this
(35) episode should not be described as a speculative bubble, for the increase and eventual decline in bulb prices can be explained in terms of the fundamentals. Garber argues that a standard pricing pattern occurs for new varieties of flowers. When a particularly
(40) prized variety is developed, its original bulb sells for a high price. Thus, the dramatic rise in the price of some original tulip bulbs could have resulted as tulips in general, and certain varieties in particular, became fashionable. However, as the prized bulbs become
(45) more readily available through reproduction from the original bulb, their price falls rapidly; after less than 30 years, bulbs sell at reproduction cost. But this does not mean that the high prices of original bulbs are irrational, for earnings derivable from the millions
(50) of bulbs descendent from the original bulbs can be

very high, even if each individual descendent bulb commands a very low price. Given that an original bulb can generate a reasonable return on investment even if the price of descendent bulbs decreases
(55) dramatically, a rapid rise and eventual fall of tulip bulb prices need not indicate a speculative bubble.

22. Which one of the following most accurately expresses the main point of the passage?

(A) The seventeenth-century Dutch tulip market is widely but mistakenly believed by economists to provide an example of a speculative bubble.

(B) Mackay did not accurately assess the earnings that could be derived from rare and expensive seventeenth-century Dutch tulip bulbs.

(C) A speculative bubble occurs whenever the price of an asset increases substantially followed by a rapid and dramatic decline.

(D) Garber argues that Mackay's classic account of the seventeenth-century Dutch tulip market as a speculative bubble is not supported by the evidence.

(E) A tulip bulb can generate a reasonable return on investment even if the price starts very high and decreases dramatically.

23. Given Garber's account of the seventeenth-century Dutch tulip market, which one of the following is most analogous to someone who bought a tulip bulb of a certain variety in that market at a very high price, only to sell a bulb of that variety at a much lower price?

(A) someone who, after learning that many others had withdrawn their applications for a particular job, applied for the job in the belief that there would be less competition for it

(B) an art dealer who, after paying a very high price for a new painting, sells it at a very low price because it is now considered to be an inferior work

(C) someone who, after buying a box of rare motorcycle parts at a very high price, is forced to sell them at a much lower price because of the sudden availability of cheap substitute parts

(D) a publisher who pays an extremely high price for a new novel only to sell copies at a price affordable to nearly everyone

(E) an airline that, after selling most of the tickets for seats on a plane at a very high price, must sell the remaining tickets at a very low price

24. The passage most strongly supports the inference that Garber would agree with which one of the following statements?

    (A) If speculative bubbles occur at all, they occur very rarely.
    (B) Many of the owners of high-priced original tulip bulbs could have expected to at least recoup their original investments from sales of the many bulbs propagated from the original bulbs.
    (C) If there is not a speculative bubble in a market, then the level of prices in that market is not irrational.
    (D) Most people who invested in Dutch tulip bulbs in the seventeenth century were generally rational in all their investments.
    (E) Mackay mistakenly infers from the fact that tulip prices dropped rapidly that the very low prices that the bulbs eventually sold for were irrational.

25. The passage states that Mackay claimed which one of the following?

    (A) The rapid rise in price of Dutch tulip bulbs was not due to the fashionability of the flowers they produced.
    (B) The prices of certain varieties of Dutch tulip bulbs during the seventeenth century were, at least for a time, determined by speculation.
    (C) The Netherlands was the only center of cultivation and development of new tulip varieties in the seventeenth century.
    (D) The very high prices of bulbs in the seventeenth-century Dutch tulip market were not irrational.
    (E) Buyers of rare and very expensive Dutch tulip bulbs were ultimately able to derive earnings from bulbs descendent from the original bulbs.

26. The main purpose of the second paragraph is to

    (A) present the facts that are accepted by all experts in the field
    (B) identify the mistake that one scholar alleges another scholar made
    (C) explain the basis on which one scholar makes an inference with which another scholar disagrees
    (D) undermine the case that one scholar makes for the claim with which another scholar disagrees
    (E) outline the factual errors that led one scholar to draw the inference that he drew

27. The phrase "standard pricing pattern" as used in line 38 most nearly means a pricing pattern

    (A) against which other pricing patterns are to be measured
    (B) that conforms to a commonly agreed-upon criterion
    (C) that is merely acceptable
    (D) that regularly recurs in certain types of cases
    (E) that serves as an exemplar

Answer Explanations follow on the next page.

ANSWER KEY

1.	D	10.	E	19.	D
2.	A	11.	A	20.	B
3.	A	12.	C	21.	A
4.	B	13.	A	22.	D
5.	E	14.	A	23.	D
6.	E	15.	D	24.	B
7.	A	16.	C	25.	B
8.	E	17.	B	26.	C
9.	B	18.	C	27.	D

TRIAGE REVIEW

This section provides a number of excellent clues to help you distinguish the simpler passages from the more challenging ones. The first passage is a good place to start your work. Structurally it's very inviting—note that each paragraph contains solid Keyword clues ("often" in line 1, "obviously impossible" in line 21, "therefore unlikely" in line 55) that you can spot with a quick glance at the beginning and end of each paragraph. The language of the passage is comparatively basic, and a glance at the question set reveals two Global questions: 1 and 3.

The fourth passage would be a good place to continue. While the Topic may seem rather esoteric, the opening paragraph begins with a clear definition of the key term "speculative bubble" (line 1) and the third paragraph contains strong opinion language ("Garber acknowledges" in line 32). While question 23 may look a little odd, the others are relatively short and familiar looking.

This leaves the second and third passages as the more formidable challenges. The second passage is the comparative reading pair, and it deals with the natural sciences. While the language of the passages may not look particularly challenging, the majority of the questions are Logic and Inference. Kudos if you noticed that there are no Global questions here, meaning you'll likely need to research every question to earn the points.

The third passage also presents some challenges. Structurally it's not too intimidating, consisting of four short paragraphs and plenty of opinion Keywords. (Pay particular attention to "Kingston herself believes" in line 27 and "Kingston's participation" in line 43, which is enough to tell you that the author is very interested in this Kingston person, whoever she may turn out to be.) That said, most of the questions are Logic and Inference, and therefore likely to be somewhat more challenging.

Ideally, you should complete passages one and four in either order, followed by two and three in either order. This way you're guaranteed to earn the easiest points in the section as quickly as possible, banking time to work with the more challenging passages toward the end. Most of your clues in this section come from the question sets, so don't neglect them when you triage the section; passages that are primarily accompanied by Logic and Inference questions will generally be tougher than those dominated by simpler question types.

Explanations

Passage One: "Nondisclosure Injunctions"

Step 1:

Intell. prop. rights vs. individual rights

(Often) when a highly skilled and experienced employee leaves one company to work for another, (there is) the potential for a transfer of sensitive information between competitors. Two (basic principles)
(5) in such cases appear (irreconcilable:) the right of the company to its intellectual property—its proprietary data and trade secrets—(and) the right of individuals to seek gainful employment and to make free use of their abilities. (Nevertheless,) the courts have (often tried) to
(10) preserve both parties' legal rights by (refusing) to prohibit the employee from working for the competitor, (but) at the same time providing an injunction against disclosure of any of the former employer's secrets. It has been (argued) that (because) such measures help

Some say laws fail to protect either

(15) generate suspicions and similar psychological barriers to full and free utilization of abilities in the employee's new situation, they are (hardly effective) in upholding the individual's rights to free employment decisions. (But) it is also (doubtful) that they are effective in
(20) preserving trade secrets.

Knowledge impossible to lose = corp. property

It is (obviously impossible) to divest oneself of that part of one's expertise that one has acquired from former employers and coworkers. (Nor,) in general, can one selectively refrain from its use, given that it has
(25) become an integral part of one's total intellectual capacity. (Nevertheless,) almost any such information that is not public knowledge may (legitimately) be claimed as corporate property: normal employment agreements (provide for) corporate ownership of all
(30) relevant data, (including) inventions, generated by the employee in connection with the company's business.

Knowledge leaks happen in small ways

Once (an em)ployee takes a position with a competitor, the trade secrets that have been acquired by that employee (may manifest) themselves clearly and
(35) consciously. This is what court injunctions seek to prohibit. (But) they are far (more likely) to manifest themselves subconsciously and inconspicuously—for (example) in one's daily decisions at the new post, (or) in the many small contributions one might make to a large
(40) team effort—(often) in the form the of an intuitive sense of what to do or to avoid. (Theoretically,) an injunction also prohibits such inadvertent "leakage." (However,) the former employer faces the practical problem of securing evidence of such leakage, (for) little will

Hard for employer to prove

(45) usually be apparent from the public activities of the new employer. (And even) if the new employee's activities appear suspicious, there is the (further) (problem) of distinguishing trade secrets (from) what may be legitimately asserted as technological skills

(50) developed independently by the employee (or) already
possessed by the new employer. This is a (major)
stumbling block in the attempt to protect trade secrets,
(since) the proprietor has no recourse against others who
independently generate the same information. It is

Laws can only
stop concrete
exchanges

(55) (therefore unlikely) that an injunction against disclosure
of trade secrets to future employers (actually) prevents
any transfer of information (except) for the passage of
documents and other concrete embodiments of the
secrets.

Paragraph Structure: The author introduces the **Topic** of nondisclosure injunctions in law and then describes two "basic principles" (line 4) that appear to be irreconcilable: the rights of employers to retain their intellectual property, and the rights of individuals to seek employment. This clash of interests forms the author's **Scope**. Despite the problem, courts "nevertheless" (line 9) try to solve the problem through legislation. The author notes that it "has been argued" (line 14) that this legislation fails to protect the rights of either group.

The author expands on this problem in the second paragraph, noting that it's "obviously impossible" (line 21) for an individual to forget learned skills, but that "nevertheless" (line 26) such skills may be considered corporate property.

This leads to the author's notion in the third paragraph that individuals are "more likely" (line 36) to divulge trade secrets in small, unintentional ways rather than ways that are blatantly obvious. While even this kind of violation is "theoretically" (line 41) prohibited by nondisclosure injunctions, it is very difficult for companies to provide evidence that it happens. The author concludes that it is "therefore unlikely" (line 55) that current injunctions will prevent the disclosure of trade secrets except in very obvious cases. The author's **Purpose** was to describe the problems associated with nondisclosure injunctions and the protection of trade secrets. The **Main Idea** of the passage was summarized at the end of the final paragraph: current injunctions are unlikely to prohibit the revealing of trade secrets in many circumstances.

Question Triage: With six relatively simple questions, priorities shouldn't be too tough to determine. Begin with questions 1 and 3, both Global questions, and score these points quickly. Question 6 is a Detail question, but its stem doesn't provide many research clues. Question 5 gives you a specific line reference, so it's better to tackle that one and then move on to question 6. Of the two remaining questions, 4 probably looks more familiar, so answer it next, and finish with question 2, which is oddly worded and may take a little more time to work with.

1. **(D)**

Which one of the following most accurately expresses the main point of the passage?

(A) There are more effective ways than court injunctions to preserve both a company's right to protect its intellectual property and individuals' rights to make free use of their abilities.

(B) Court injunctions must be strengthened if they are to remain a relevant means of protecting corporations' trade secrets.

(C) Enforcement of court injunctions designed to protect proprietary information is impossible when employees reveal such information to new employers.

(D) Court injunctions prohibiting employees from disclosing former employers' trade secrets to new employers probably do not achieve all of their intended objectives.

(E) The rights of employees to make full use of their talents and previous training are being seriously eroded by the prohibitions placed on them by court injunctions designed to prevent the transfer of trade secrets.[2]

Step 2: Since this questions asks you to describe the author's main point, it is a Global question.

Step 3: As is always the case with Global questions, eschew specific passage research and instead think about the author's big ideas to form your prediction. In this case, focus on the author's Main Idea.

Step 4: The author uses a neutral and descriptive tone to express the Main Idea that current injunctions against the revealing of trade secrets aren't likely to be very effective in many cases.

Step 5: Correct choice (D) is the perfect match for your prediction. The "more effective ways" mentioned in choice (A) are never mentioned in the passage. Choice (B) describes a recommendation the author doesn't make, and choice (C) is extreme; the author never suggests that injunctions can never be enforced. Choice (E) is also extreme and too narrow in its focus. The author mentions some difficulties for employees, but they're not the primary focus of the passage.

---

[2]PrepTest 55, Sec 2, Q 1

2. **(A)**

    Given the passage's content and tone, which one of the following statements would most likely be found elsewhere in a work from which this passage is an excerpt?

    (A) Given the law as it stands, corporations concerned about preserving trade secrets might be best served by giving their employees strong incentives to stay in their current jobs.

    (B) While difficult to enforce and interpret, injunctions are probably the most effective means of halting the inadvertent transfer of trade secrets while simultaneously protecting the rights of employees.

    (C) Means of redress must be made available to companies that suspect, but cannot prove, that former employees are revealing protected information to competitors.

    (D) Even concrete materials such as computer disks are so easy to copy and conceal that it will be a waste of time for courts to try to prevent the spread of information through physical theft.

    (E) The psychological barriers that an injunction can place on an employee in a new workplace are inevitably so subtle that they have no effect on the employee.[3]

Step 2: The wording of this stem is less straightforward, but the qualified language "would be most likely to be found" helps you identify this as an Inference question.

Step 3: This stem doesn't provide any specific clues to guide your research; you are simply told to keep the content and tone of the passage in mind.

Step 4: A specific prediction is difficult to come up with here. Think about the content and tone before moving on to evaluate the choices. The author ultimately concludes that current laws designed to protect employees and trade secrets fall short of their goals. The correct answer *must be true* on the basis of these ideas.

Step 5: Choice (A), the correct answer, *must be true*. Its qualified tone (corporations "might best be served") fits in with the tone of the passage, and its suggestion follows from the idea that injunctions against the revelation of trade secrets aren't generally effective. The author never states that injunctions are probably the most effective way of protecting secrets, eliminating choice (B). The author never makes demands such as those in choice (C). Choices (D) and (E) are both too extreme.

---

[3]PrepTest 55, Sec 2, Q 2

3. **(A)**

    The author's primary purpose in the passage is to
    (A) suggest that injunctions against the disclosure
         of trade secrets not only create problems for
         employees in the workplace, but also are
         unable to halt the illicit spread of proprietary
         information
    (B) suggest that the information contained in
         "documents and other concrete
         embodiments" is usually so trivial that
         injunctions do little good in protecting
         intellectual property
    (C) argue that new methods must be found to
         address the delicate balance between
         corporate and individual rights
    (D) support the position that the concept of
         protecting trade secrets is no longer viable in
         an age of increasing access to information
    (E) argue that injunctions are not necessary for
         the protection of trade secrets[4]

Step 2: The key phrase "primary purpose" tells you that this is a Global question.

Step 3: Think back to the author's Purpose to find the correct answer.

Step 4: The author wrote this passage to describe the shortcomings of current injunctions against the revelation of trade secrets. So, find the answer choice that matches this prediction.

Step 5: Correct choice (A) is a perfect match. Choice (B) distorts the author's ideas and is too narrowly focused. Choices (C), (D), and (E) all fail to match the author's tone; this passage wasn't written to support or argue any particular point, but only to suggest that a certain state of affairs is the case. If you find yourself pressed for time on a primary Purpose question, you can use this quick approach to determine which answer choices are likeliest to be correct and focus your attention on them. Scan the beginning of each answer choice, looking for verbs that conform to your prediction, and focus on those choices before looking at any others. This technique can help you hone in on the correct answer quickly without wasting time reading answer traps in their entirety.

[4]PrepTest 55, Sec 2, Q 3

4. **(B)**

The passage provides the most support for which one
of the following assertions?

(A)   Injunctions should be imposed by the courts only
      when there is strong reason to believe that an
      employee will reveal proprietary information.

(B)   There is apparently no reliable way to protect
      both the rights of companies to protect trade
      secrets and the rights of employees to seek
      new employment.

(C)   Employees should not be allowed to take jobs
      with their former employers' competitors
      when their new job could compromise trade
      secrets of their former employers.

(D)   The multiplicity of means for transferring
      information in the workplace only increases
      the need for injunctions.

(E)   Some companies seek injunctions as a means
      of punishing employees who take jobs with
      their competitors.[5]

Step 2: When you're asked to identify an assertion supported by the text, you know you're working with an Inference question.

Step 3: The stem doesn't provide many clues. Think about the author's major goals and prepare to use process of elimination.

Step 4: A concrete prediction isn't easy to make in this case, so bear in mind the author's conviction that current injunctions are ineffective before moving on to the choices.

Step 5: The author never suggests that injunctions should only be imposed in specific situations, but only that they're often hard to enforce. This eliminates choice (A). Correct choice (B), on the other hand, falls directly in line with the author's Main Idea. Choice (C) opposes the author's point of view (recall that the rights of employees are asserted in the first paragraph). The author never calls for more injunctions, eliminating choice (D), and choice (E) is never suggested in the passage.

---

[5]PrepTest 55, Sec 2, Q 4

5. **(E)**

    With which one of the following statements regarding documents and other concrete embodiments mentioned in line 58 would the author be most likely to agree?

    (A)   While the transfer of such materials would be damaging, even the seemingly innocuous contributions of an employee to a competitor can do more harm in the long run.

    (B)   Such materials are usually less informative than what the employee may recollect about a previous job.

    (C)   Injunctions against the disclosure of trade secrets should carefully specify which materials are included in order to focus on the most damaging ones.

    (D)   Large-scale transfer of documents and other materials cannot be controlled by injunctions.

    (E)   Such concrete materials lend themselves to control and identification more readily than do subtler means of transferring information.[6]

Step 2: The stem asks you to find the choice that the author would likely agree with, so this is an Inference question.

Step 3: If you go back to line 54 for proper context, you discover that the author mentions concrete embodiments of information as possible exceptions to the general rule that injunctions are not effective in protecting trade secrets.

Step 4: Based on your research, you should expect the correct answer to refer to the fact that trade secrets passed in the form of concrete media are easier to detect, and therefore more vulnerable to injunction.

Step 5: Correct answer choice (E) is a good paraphrase of the prediction and is the correct answer. Choice (A) presents a comparison of harm never mentioned in the passage. Similarly, the passage never mentions how informative such materials are, eliminating choice (B). The recommendation in choice (C) is not supported by the passage, and choice (D) is out of scope; the author doesn't mention the large-scale transfer of materials.

---

[6]PrepTest 55, Sec 2, Q 5

6. **(E)**

In the passage, the author makes which one of the
following claims?

(A)   Injunctions against the disclosure of trade
       secrets limit an employee's chances of being
       hired by a competitor.

(B)   Measures against the disclosure of trade
       secrets are unnecessary except in the case of
       documents and other concrete embodiments
       of the secrets.

(C)   Employees who switch jobs to work for a
       competitor usually unintentionally violate the
       law by doing so.

(D)   Employers are not restricted in the tactics they
       can use when seeking to secure protected
       information from new employees.

(E)   What may seem like intellectual theft may in fact
       be an example of independent innovation.[7]

Step 2: Since the question asks for a specific claim, it is a Detail question.

Step 3: The only clue you have is that the author is making the claim. That doesn't help much, so a specific prediction will be hard to make.

Step 4: Think through the author's Main Idea and prepare to apply the process of elimination.

Step 5: Be careful with choice (A); it may look tempting at first, but recall that the passage says "it has been argued" (line 14) that injunctions may prohibit an employee from making full use of his or her abilities. Choice (A) claims that injunctions limit an employee's chances of getting a job, so this is a distortion. Choice (B) is also a distortion. The author claims that concrete embodiments are easier to detect and prohibit, not that they represent the only situations in which injunctions are necessary. Choice (C) misses the author's point. Merely switching jobs doesn't violate an injunction. Choice (D) is contradicted by the passage, since injunctions do seek to protect the rights of employees. Only correct choice (E) remains, which is supported in the third paragraph.

Passage Two: "Comparative Passages on Purple Loosestrife"
Step 1:

The following passages concern a plant called purple loosestrife. Passage A is excerpted from a report issued by a prairie research council; passage B from a journal of sociology.

---

[7]PrepTest 55, Sec 2, Q 6

Passage A

P.L. disastrous
for environ.

Purple loosestrife (Lythrum salicaria), an aggressive and invasive perennial of Eurasian origin, arrived with settlers in eastern North America in the early 1800s and has spread across the continent's
(5) midlatitude wetlands. The impact of purple loosestrife on native vegetation has been disastrous, with more than 50 percent of the biomass of some wetland communities displaced. Monospecific blocks of this weed have maintained themselves for at least 20 years.

(10) Impacts on wildlife have not been well studied, but serious reductions in waterfowl and aquatic

Threatens
wildlife

furbearer productivity have been observed. In addition, several endangered species of vertebrates are threatened with further degradation of their
(15) breeding habitats. Although purple loosestrife can invade relatively undisturbed habitats, the spread and dominance of this weed have been greatly accelerated in disturbed habitats. While digging out the plants can temporarily halt their spread, there has been little

little long-
term control
research

(20) research on long-term purple loosestrife control. Glyphosate has been used successfully, but no measure of the impact of this herbicide on native plant communities has been made.

With the spread of purple loosestrife growing
(25) exponentially, some form of integrated control is needed. At present, coping with purple loosestrife

Early detection
best for now

hinges on early detection of the weed's arrival in areas, which allows local eradication to be carried out with minimum damage to the native plant community.

Passage B

(30)   The war on purple loosestrife is apparently conducted on behalf of nature, an attempt to liberate the biotic community from the tyrannical influence of a life-destroying invasive weed. Indeed, purple

People claim
P.L. control
(35)
is for good of
nature

loosestrife control is portrayed by its practitioners as an environmental initiative intended to save nature rather than control it. Accordingly, the purple loosestrife literature, scientific and otherwise, dutifully discusses the impacts of the weed on endangered species—and on threatened biodiversity
(40) more generally. Purple loosestrife is a pollution, according to the scientific community, and all of nature suffers under its pervasive influence.

P.L. control
really about
(45)
controlling
nature

Regardless of the perceived and actual ecological effects of the purple invader, it is apparent that popular pollution ideologies have been extended into the wetlands of North America. Consequently, the scientific effort to liberate nature from purple

loosestrife (has failed) to decouple itself from its
philosophical (origin) as an instrument to control nature
(50) to the satisfaction of human desires. Birds,
(particularly) game birds and waterfowl, (provide) the
bulk of the (justification) for loosestrife management.
(However,) no bird species (other than) the canvasback
has been identified in the literature as endangered by

*Impact
exaggerated*

(55) purple loosestrife. (The impact) of purple loosestrife on
furbearing mammals is discussed at great length,
(though) none of the species highlighted (muskrat,
mink) can be considered threatened in North America.
(What is threatened) by purple loosestrife is the
(60) economics of exploiting such preferred species (and)

*Real threat is to
economy*

the millions of dollars that will be lost to the
economies of the United States and Canada (from)
reduced hunting, trapping, and recreation revenues
(due to) a decline in the production of the wetland
(65) resource.

Paragraph Structure: As always, read and Roadmap each comparative reading passage independently. Be sure to determine the **Topic, Scope, Purpose**, and **Main Idea** for Passage A before moving on to Passage B.

Passage A: You can determine the author's **Topic** (purple loosestrife) and **Scope** (the danger it poses to the environment) from the first paragraph, and you can also find supporting examples of this danger. The author notes that "while" (line 18) certain measures can temporarily halt the advance of purple loosestrife, little research has been conducted on its long-term effects on ecosystems. The brief second paragraph indicates that "at present" (line 26) the best known way to combat the infestation is to detect it early and take quick action. The author's **Purpose** in this passage was to describe the dangers posed by loosestrife and current prevention measures. The **Main Idea** is that loosestrife poses a clear threat to wetland ecosystems, and integrated control is necessary to combat the threat.

Passage B: This author also writes on the **Topic** of purple loosestrife, but with a decidedly different tone. The **Scope** of Passage B is the motivations of those who seek to control loosestrife. This becomes evident with the author's use of subtle opinion Keywords. Proponents of waging "war" (line 30) on purple loosestrife do so "apparently" (line 30) to defend nature, and their efforts are "portrayed" (line 34) as an attempt to save nature "rather than" (line 36) control it. All of this qualification implies that the author holds an opposing viewpoint, a prediction that is borne out in the second paragraph. The author indicates that loosestrife-control proponents have failed to separate themselves from "popular...ideologies" (line 45) and are "consequently" (line 46) seeking to control nature, not to defend it. Their "justification[s]" (line 52) aren't supported by evidence. The author finally concludes that "what is threatened" (line 59) by the purple loosestrife is the economic benefit provided by the wetlands that are being invaded. Taken in total, the author's **Purpose** is to question the motives of the proponents of loosestrife control, and the **Main Idea** is that these proponents are not truly interested in defending nature, but in controlling it for their own economic benefit.

Both of these authors are concerned with the invasion of purple loosestrife into certain eco-systems, but their goals are very different. Passage A presents evidence for the highly destruc-tive nature of loosestrife and urges its control, whereas Passage B suggests that the damage loosestrife causes has been exaggerated and questions the motives underlying its control. Being aware of these differences will certainly help you answer the questions accurately.

Question Triage: As I noted in the section overview, this comparative passage set contains no Global questions, so you should begin by looking for straightforward Detail questions. The first two questions, 7 and 8, are good starting candidates. The remaining questions are a mix of Logical Reasoning and Inference. While it's generally a good idea to bypass Inference questions in favor of simpler points, questions 9 and 10 are both amenable to your understanding of the authors' Main Ideas; question 9 asks for a central point of disagreement, and question 10 asks for an author's attitude. These are concepts you should already have a good understanding of by the time you've finish reading strategically. Question 11 asks for a point of agreement between the two authors and is therefore similarly amenable to the comparison strategy you've learned to apply to these passages. That leaves questions 12 and 13, both Logical Reasoning questions, which you can tackle in any order as time allows.

7.　**(A)**
　　Both passages explicitly mention which one of the
　　following?
　　(A)　furbearing animals
　　(B)　glyphosate
　　(C)　the threat purple loosestrife poses to economies
　　(D)　popular pollution ideologies
　　(E)　literature on purple loosestrife control[8]

Step 2: The stem asks for explicit information, a clear indication of a Detail question.

Step 3: Although the stem doesn't provide any specific research cues, you can still think about the general ideas mentioned in both passages in order to make the choices easier to evaluate.

Step 4: Both passages deal with evidence that purple loosestrife is invasive to local ecosystems, though they disagree about the legitimacy of such evidence. The correct answer is likely to refer to this kind of evidence.

Step 5: Choice (A) is correct—both passages mentioned the claim that purple loosestrife nega-tively affects populations of furbearing animals. Choice (B) is only mentioned in Passage A, and choices (C), (D), and (E) are specific to Passage B.

[8]PrepTest 55, Sec 2, Q 7

8. **(E)**

    Each of the passages contains information sufficient
    to answer which one of the following questions?
    (A)   Approximately how long ago did purple
          loosestrife arrive in North America?
    (B)   Is there much literature discussing the
          potential benefit that hunters might derive
          from purple loosestrife management?
    (C)   What is an issue regarding purple loosestrife
          management on which both hunters and
          farmers agree?
    (D)   Is the canvasback threatened with extinction
          due to the spread of purple loosestrife?
    (E)   What is a type of terrain that is affected in at
          least some parts of North America by the
          presence of purple loosestrife?[9]

Step 2: The question is asking for a specific Detail that can be found in either source.

Step 3: Since there aren't any specific clues to help your research, think about your comparison of the two passages before moving on to the choices.

Step 4: Much like question 7, you must seek information common to both passages. Since both passages considered much of the same evidence, focus your attention there while employing the process of elimination.

Step 5: Choice (A) is mentioned in Passage A but not in Passage B. References to game hunting are particular to Passage B, eliminating choices (B) and (C). The canvasback was also specific to Passage B, so choice (D) is out. Since both passages refer to the loosestrife's invasion of the wetlands of North America, choice (E) must be correct.

9. **(B)**

    It can be inferred that the authors would be most
    likely to disagree about which one of the following?
    (A)   Purple loosestrife spreads more quickly in
          disturbed habitats than in undisturbed
          habitats.
    (B)   The threat posed by purple loosestrife to local
          aquatic furbearer populations is serious.
    (C)   Most people who advocate that eradication
          measures be taken to control purple
          loosestrife are not genuine in their concern
          for the environment.
    (D)   The size of the biomass that has been displaced
          by purple loosestrife is larger than is generally
          thought.
    (E)   Measures should be taken to prevent other
          non-native plant species from invading North
          America.[10]

[9]PrepTest 55, Sec 2, Q 8
[10]PrepTest 55, Sec 2, Q 9

Step 2: The question stem asks for an Inference, in this case one that the authors would disagree about.

Step 3: The question stem doesn't give many specific research clues, but you can still make a solid prediction based on your understanding of the big ideas.

Step 4: Think about each author's Main Idea and the tonal differences in the passages. The author of Passage A asserted that local ecosystems are gravely threatened by loosestrife, while the author of Passage B downplays the threat, suggesting that few endangered species are threatened. The correct answer is likely to reflect this core disagreement.

Step 5: The match for your prediction is correct choice (B). Choice (A) is specific to Passage A, choice (C) is specific to Passage B, and choices (D) and (E) are not supported by either author. Only an idea that is mentioned in *both* passages can be a source of disagreement, so you can eliminate all of the choices that refer to ideas specific to one passage.

10. **(E)**

   Which one of the following most accurately describes
   the attitude expressed by the author of passage B
   toward the overall argument represented by passage A?
   (A)   enthusiastic agreement
   (B)   cautious agreement
   (C)   pure neutrality
   (D)   general ambivalence
   (E)   pointed skepticism[11]

Step 2: The phrase "most accurately describes" tells you that this is an Inference question. You need to infer the attitude of author B toward the argument made in Passage A.

Step 3: Once again, this question focuses on the larger ideas of both passages rather than specific details. Think about contrasts between the passages to make your prediction.

Step 4: All the clues you need for a solid prediction are right there in the passages. From the beginning of Passage B, the author expresses disagreement with the views presented in Passage A, using terms like "apparently" (line 30) and "dutifully" (line 38) to cast doubt on them. In the final sentences of Passage B, the author explicitly denies the motivations stated by those who seek to control purple loosestrife. The correct answer must demonstrate this clear disagreement.

Step 5: This should be an easy match if you've made a good prediction, since the only answer choice that expresses disagreement is correct choice (E). The remaining choices describe either agreement or neutrality, making them wrong.

---

[11]PrepTest 55, Sec 2, Q 10

11. **(A)**

It can be inferred that both authors would be most
likely to agree with which one of the following
statements regarding purple loosestrife?
- (A) As it increases in North America, some wildlife
  populations tend to decrease.
- (B) Its establishment in North America has had a
  disastrous effect on native North American
  wetland vegetation in certain regions.
- (C) It is very difficult to control effectively with
  herbicides.
- (D) Its introduction into North America was a
  great ecological blunder.
- (E) When it is eliminated from a given area, it
  tends to return to that area fairly quickly.[12]

Step 2: This Inference question asks you to identify something that the two authors would agree on.

Step 3: As with question 10, compare the authors' Main Ideas to reach a solid prediction.

Step 4: While the authors disagree about the big issues, there is some agreement on the smaller details. Both authors agree that loosestrife is invasive in certain ecosystems, and that it negatively affects some wildlife. The authors clearly disagree on the degree of this effect, but they both acknowledge that it exists. Expect the correct choice to reflect one of these points of agreement.

Step 5: Choice (A) is a direct match for the prediction. As is commonly the case in comparative-reading wrong-answer choices, choices (B), (C), and (E) all refer to ideas present in only one of the passages (Passage A), and choice (C) is also extreme. Choice (D) is never explicitly stated in either passage, and though the author of Passage A probably would agree with it, there's no agreement from the author of Passage B.

12. **(C)**

Which one of the following is true about the
relationship between the two passages?
- (A) Passage A presents evidence that directly
  counters claims made in passage B.
- (B) Passage B assumes what passage A explicitly
  argues for.
- (C) Passage B displays an awareness of the
  arguments touched on in passage A, but not
  vice versa.
- (D) Passage B advocates a policy that passage A
  rejects.
- (E) Passage A downplays the seriousness of claims
  made in passage B.[13]

---

[12]PrepTest 55, Sec 2, Q 11

[13]PrepTest 55, Sec 2, Q 12

Step 2: This is a rare form of Logical Reasoning question, known as Method of Argument. The stem asks you to provide a structural analysis of how one passage relates to the other.

Step 3: This is another big picture question. Instead of conducting specific research, compare the primary Purpose of Passage A to that of Passage B.

Step 4: Passage A presents a specific argument for the control of purple loosestrife, and Passage B calls the conclusions and motivations of this argument into question. The correct answer will reflect some aspect of this relationship.

Step 5: Correct choice (C) may not have jumped out at you at first. It doesn't explicitly describe the adversarial relationship between the passages, but it *does* remark on the fact that Passage B responds to the arguments made in Passage A, demonstrating that the author of Passage B is aware of those arguments. (Note that this is different than asserting that the author of Passage B is aware of the specific *author* of Passage A; the authors of paired passages never refer to one another directly, though they may refer to the same ideas.) It is equally true that the author of Passage A demonstrates no awareness of the arguments made in Passage B. Choice (A) is off base, since Passage A doesn't respond in any way to the claims made in Passage B. Choice (B) implies an agreement that doesn't exist. Choices (D) and (E) reverse the relationships between the two passages—wrong answer traps you'll avoid as long as you read the choices carefully.

13. **(A)**

Which one of the following, if true, would cast doubt on the argument in passage B but bolster the argument in passage A?

(A) Localized population reduction is often a precursor to widespread endangerment of a species.

(B) Purple loosestrife was barely noticed in North America before the advent of suburban sprawl in the 1950s.

(C) The amount by which overall hunting, trapping, and recreation revenues would be reduced as a result of the extinction of one or more species threatened by purple loosestrife represents a significant portion of those revenues.

(D) Some environmentalists who advocate taking measures to eradicate purple loosestrife view such measures as a means of controlling nature.

(E) Purple loosestrife has never become a problem in its native habitat, even though no effort has been made to eradicate it there.[14]

Step 2: The words "cast doubt" and "bolster" tell you that this is a Logical Reasoning question. You must strengthen the argument made by one passage and weaken the argument of the other.

---

[14]PrepTest 55, Sec 2, Q 13

Step 3: Once more, rather than conducting specific passage research, think about the big ideas. The argument of Passage A (the one you need to strengthen) is that purple loosestrife is ecologically dangerous and should be controlled. Passage B claims that the danger is exaggerated and that calls for such control are motivated by economic concerns rather than a true desire to protect the environment.

Step 4: Since Passage B calls the evidence presented by Passage A into question, you should seek to bolster A's evidence. The author of Passage B downplays the threat posed to wetland wildlife, so a good prediction would suggest that the threat is more serious than Passage B acknowledges. This would make the author of Passage A more likely to be correct while casting doubt on the central argument of Passage B.

Step 5: Correct choice (A) fulfills the prediction. If population reduction can lead to species endangerment, then the evidence of such reduction present in Passage B becomes support for Passage A's central assertion that wildlife is endangered. Choices (B) and (C) are outside the scope of the argument, and therefore can neither strengthen nor weaken it. Choice (D) is a 180; it supports Passage B over Passage A. Choice (E) introduces irrelevant information, since the behavior of purple loosestrife in its own environment has no bearing on how it affects the wetlands of North America.

Passage Three: "Kingston and 'Talk-Story'"
Step 1:

Critics: Kingston's work not influenced by previous work

With their recognition of Maxine Hong Kingston as a major literary figure, some critics have suggested that her works have been produced almost *ex nihilo*, saying that they lack a large traceable body of direct
(5) literary antecedent especially within the Chinese American heritage in which her work is embedded. But these critics, who have examined only the development of written texts, the most visible signs of a culture's narrative production, have overlooked Kingston's

Auth: Kingston connected to talk-story

(10) connection to the long Chinese tradition of a highly developed genre of song and spoken narrative known as "talk-story" (*gong gu tsai*).

Traditionally performed in the dialects of various ethnic enclaves, talk-story has been maintained within
(15) the confines of the family and has rarely surfaced into print. The tradition dates back to Sung dynasty

History of talk-story

(A.D. 970–1279) storytellers in China, and in the United States it is continually revitalized by an overlapping sequence of immigration from China.
(20) Thus Chinese immigrants to the U.S. had a fully established, sophisticated oral culture, already ancient and capable of producing masterpieces, by the time they began arriving in the early nineteenth century. This transplanted oral heritage simply embraced new
(25) subject matter or new forms of Western discourse, as in the case of Kingston's adaptations written in English.

Kingston herself believes that as a literary artist she
is one in a long line of performers shaping a
recalcitrant history into talk-story form. She

(30)   distinguishes her "thematic" storytelling memory
processes, which sift and reconstruct the essential
elements of personally remembered stories from the
memory processes of a print-oriented culture that
emphasizes the retention of precise sequences of

(35)   words. Nor does the entry of print into the storytelling
process substantially change her notion of the character
of oral tradition. For Kingston, "writer" is synonymous
with "singer" or "performer" in the ancient sense of
privileged keeper, transmitter, and creator of stories

(40)   whose current stage of development can be frozen in
print, but which continue to grow both around and
from that frozen text.

Kingston's participation in the tradition of
talk-story is evidenced in her book *China Men*, which

(45)   utilizes forms typical of that genre and common to
most oral cultures including: a fixed "grammar" of
repetitive themes; a spectrum of stock characters;
symmetrical structures, including balanced oppositions
(verbal or physical contests, antithetical characters,

(50)   dialectical discourse such as question-answer forms
and riddles); and repetition. In *China Men*, Kingston
also succeeds in investing idiomatic English with the
allusive texture and oral-aural qualities of the Chinese
language, a language rich in aural and visual puns,

(55)   making her work a written form of talk-story.

Margin notes:

How Kingston adapts talk-story

Example: China Men

Paragraph Structure: The author's **Topic** (the work of Kingston) and **Scope** (her use of talk-story) are presented in the first paragraph by way of a dichotomy between how "some critics" (line 2) view Kingston's work and how the author interprets it. The critics suggest that Kingston's work is not essentially influenced by previous literary works or by her own cultural background, "but" (line 6) they've "overlooked" (line 9) her connection to the tradition of the talk-story.

The second paragraph provides some background on the talk-story, describing both its history and how it has been "maintained" (line 14) within families and from generation to generation, finally producing an established and "already ancient" (line 21) art form in the Chinese American community. This new form of talk-story "embraced" (line 24) forms of western storytelling, and the author uses this connection as a way to bring Kingston back into the conversation.

The third paragraph presents Kingston's own point of view: She "believes" (line 27) that she's employing the talk-story form in her own work and has "distinguished" (line 30) the elements of talk-story in her work from those of the "print-oriented" (line 33) culture in which she lives. This idea is summarized in her view that a writer is "synonymous" (line 37) with a "singer" (line 38) or "poet" (line 38).

The author completes the passage with a specific example, "China Men" (line 44), demonstrating how this work "utilizes" (line 45) elements of oral culture. As always, note the presence of this lengthy example without wasting time trying to memorize it; it will probably show up in the questions, but proper research will allow you to come back to this paragraph when necessary.

The author's ultimate **Purpose** was to describe the influence of talk-story in Kingston's work, and the **Main Idea** follows suit: Despite the opinions of some critics, Kingston's work is rooted in the tradition of the talk-story.

Question Triage: Begin by grabbing the sole Global point: question 14. The remaining seven questions are a mix of Inference and Logic, so it's best to approach them one at a time and skip the ones that are likely to be time-consuming. Questions 15 and 16 are both Inference questions, but 16 provides a specific line reference, so tackle it next. Question 17, a Parallel Reasoning question, also directs you to a specific portion of the passage, so it shouldn't be too tough to make a prediction and score the point. Question 18 asks you to consider Kingston's opinions, which were primarily located in a single paragraph, so consider answering it next. Questions 19 and 20 both contain enough contextual information in their stems to be worth a look at this point—since question 19 asks you to weaken the author's argument, you should be able to work with this one easily if you've understood the Main Idea (which embodies the author's argument), and 20 is a Function question with specific line references. Question 21 asks for the author's attitude toward a particular concept, so depending on time constraints, consider tackling it before returning to question 15, an Inference question that provides you with no clues to guide your research (and is therefore likely to be challenging).

14. **(A)**

Which one of the following most accurately states the main point of the passage?

(A)   Despite some critics' comments, Kingston's writings have significant Chinese American antecedents, which can be found in the traditional oral narrative form known as talk-story.

(B)   Analysis of Kingston's writings, especially *China Men*, supports her belief that literary artists can be performers who continue to reconstruct their stories even after they have been frozen in print.

(C)   An understanding of Kingston's work and of Chinese American writers in general reveals that critics of ethnic literatures in the United States have been mistaken in examining only written texts.

(D)   Throughout her writings Kingston uses techniques typical of the talk-story genre, especially the retention of certain aspects of Chinese speech in the written English text.

(E)   The writings of Kingston have rekindled an interest in talk-story, which dates back to the Sung dynasty, and was extended to the United States with the arrival of Chinese immigrants in the nineteenth century.[15]

Step 2: The phrase "Main point" signals a Global question in which you will identify the Main Idea of the passage.

Step 3: No specific research is necessary.

Step 4: Recall and paraphrase the Main Point: Kingston's work is rooted in the tradition of the talk-story, despite what some critics have suggested.

Step 5: Choice (A) is a perfect match. Choices (B) and (D) focus to specifically on details to capture the author's Main Idea, and choices (C) and (E) produce ideas that are out of scope.

---

[15]PrepTest 55, Sec 2, Q 14

15. **(D)**

Which one of the following can be most reasonably inferred from the passage?

(A)   In the last few years, written forms of talk-story have appeared in Chinese as often as they have in English.

(B)   Until very recently, scholars have held that oral storytelling in Chinese ethnic enclaves was a unique oral tradition.

(C)   Talk-story has developed in the United States through a process of combining Chinese, Chinese American, and other oral storytelling forms.

(D)   Chinese American talk-story relies upon memory processes that do not emphasize the retention of precise sequences of words.

(E)   The connection between certain aspects of Kingston's work and talk-story is argued by some critics to be rather tenuous and questionable.[16]

Step 2: The key language "inferred" identifies this as an Inference question.

Step 3: There aren't any specific clues to guide your research, so think about the author's main concerns and be prepared to proceed by process of elimination.

Step 4: The author is most concerned with describing the deep connection between Kingston's work and the tradition of the talk-story. Use this knowledge to guide your assessment of the answer choices.

Step 5: Choice (A) generalizes far beyond the scope of the passage, which only concerns the work of one author. Choice (B) is not supported by the passage. Choice (C) distorts information from the second paragraph, incorrectly suggesting that talk-story combined with storytelling forms outside of the Chinese and Chinese American communities. Choice (D), the correct answer, is referenced in lines 30–35, in which Kingston describes key differences between Western and talk-story traditions. Choice (E) presents another distortion; the critics mentioned in the beginning of the passage don't argue that Kingston's connection to talk-story is tenuous, they completely ignore its existence.

---

[16]PrepTest 55, Sec 2, Q 15

16. **(C)**

It can be inferred from the passage that the author uses the phrase "personally remembered stories" (line 32) primarily to refer to

(A)   a literary genre of first-person storytelling
(B)   a thematically organized personal narrative of one's own past
(C)   partially idiosyncratic memories of narratives
(D)   the retention in memory of precise sequences of words
(E)   easily identifiable thematic issues in literature[17]

Step 2: The question asks what a specific phrase refers to, telling you that it is a Logic Function question.

Step 3: As with any Logic Function question, be sure to research for context. In the third paragraph, the author presents Kingston's description of the way she merges talk-story with Western forms of writing. This paragraph describes important contrasts, specifically a contrast between the personally remembered stories mentioned in the stem and the "memory processes of a print-oriented culture" (line 33) that emphasizes precise sequences of words.

Step 4: The correct answer must take the dichotomy described by the contrast Keywords in the third paragraph into account. Since the personally remembered stories serve as a contrast to specific retention, the correct answer should describe these stories as a looser form of memory.

Step 5: Although it uses language that is perhaps surprising, the only choice that matches the prediction is correct choice (C)—"partially idiosyncratic memories" is another way of describing the looser form of narrative predicted. Always remember that the correct answer must match the *concept* of your prediction, even though it may not use the same words. None of the other choices describe the less-precise form of narrative that the structure of the paragraph led you to expect.

---

[17]PrepTest 55, Sec 2, Q 16

17. **(B)**

In which one of the following is the use of cotton fibers or cotton cloth most analogous to Kingston's use of the English language as described in lines 51–55?

(A)   Scraps of plain cotton cloth are used to create a multicolored quilt.

(B)   The surface texture of woolen cloth is simulated in a piece of cotton cloth by a special process of weaving.

(C)   Because of its texture, cotton cloth is used for a certain type of clothes for which linen is inappropriate.

(D)   In making a piece of cloth, cotton fiber is substituted for linen because of the roughly similar texture of the two materials.

(E)   Because of their somewhat similar textures, cotton and linen fibers are woven together in a piece of cloth to achieve a savings in price over a pure linen cloth.[18]

Step 2: The stem asks you to identify an analogous situation based on the text, so this is a Logical Reasoning question, specifically Parallel Reasoning.

Step 3: Reviewing the lines referenced in the question stem tells you that Kingston's use of English in *China Men* was primarily important because she infused it with qualities of the Chinese language.

Step 4: The correct answer must reflect the relationship described in the text; specifically, one type of language taking on the attributes of another very different language. Since the stem refers to cotton cloth, you should expect the correct answer to describe cotton cloth taking on the properties of some other, different kind of cloth.

Step 5: Choice (B) perfectly matches the prediction—cotton cloth takes on the properties of woolen cloth. Choice (A) fails to refer to two different types of cloth and is therefore not properly analogous. Choice (C) refers to a substitution, which doesn't match the relationship described in the passage. Choice (D) refers to types of cloth that are similar rather than dissimilar, as does choice (E).

It is worth noting that, even in a rather abstract question like this one, a strong prediction always helps you score the point.

[18]PrepTest 55, Sec 2, Q 17

18. **(C)**

The passage most clearly suggests that Kingston believes which one of the following about at least some of the stories contained in her writings?

(A) Since they are intimately tied to the nature of the Chinese language, they can be approximated, but not adequately expressed, in English.

(B) They should be thought of primarily as ethnic literature and evaluated accordingly by critics.

(C) They will likely be retold and altered to some extent in the process.

(D) Chinese American history is best chronicled by traditional talk-story.

(E) Their significance and beauty cannot be captured at all in written texts.[19]

Step 2: You are asked to identify what the passage "suggests" that Kingston believes. The qualified language is indicative of an Inference question.

Step 3: Your Roadmap should lead you back to paragraph three to research Kingston's description of her own work. Toward the end of the paragraph, signaled by "for Kingston" in line 37, she states that the stories she tells can be "frozen in print" (lines 40–41) but continue to grow outside of the text.

Step 4: Based on your research, you should expect the correct answer to refer to the process of change beyond the printed page described in the text.

Step 5: Correct choice (C) does indeed describe the process of change predicted. Choice (A) distorts Kingston's view, as she never suggests that the stories are "[in]adequately expressed" in English. Choice (B) is never mentioned and is therefore out of scope. Choice (D) runs counter to Kingston's attempts to express elements of talk-story in English, as does the extreme view of choice (E).

19. **(D)**

The author's argument in the passage would be most weakened if which one of the following were true?

(A) Numerous writers in the United States have been influenced by oral traditions.

(B) Most Chinese American writers' work is very different from Kingston's.

(C) Native American storytellers use narrative devices similar to those used in talk-story.

(D) *China Men* is for the most part atypical of Kingston's literary works.

(E) Literary critics generally appreciate the authenticity of Kingston's work.[20]

---

[19]PrepTest 55, Sec 2, Q 18
[20]PrepTest 55, Sec 2, Q 19

Step 2: The stem asks you to weaken the author's argument, so this is a Logical Reasoning question.

Step 3: The author argues that Kingston's work is rooted in the tradition of talk-story. To weaken this argument, you can undermine the evidence the author provides. Where in the passage is this evidence provided? According to your Roadmap, the author's primary example was the novel *China Men* as described in the final paragraph. A quick review of this paragraph shows that the author indicates that *China Men* contains a number of elements specific to oral culture generally.

Step 4: Now that you've identified the chief evidence for the author's case, the hard work is over. The correct answer should show that *China Men* is not representative of Kingston's work, thus casting doubt on her argument.

Step 5: Choice (D), the correct answer, is the clear match. Choice (A) is out of scope; other authors are irrelevant to this argument. The same goes for choice (B). Choice (C) isn't any better, since the practices of Native American storytellers have no bearing on Kingston's work. Choice (E) is also irrelevant. Whatever the critics may think, the author's argument isn't about Kingston's authenticity.

20. **(B)**

   The author's specific purpose in detailing typical talk-story forms (lines 43–51) is to
   (A)   show why Kingston's book *China Men*
           establishes her as a major literary figure
   (B)   support the claim that Kingston's use of
           typically oral techniques makes her work a
           part of the talk-story tradition
   (C)   dispute the critics' view that Chinese American
           literature lacks literary antecedents
   (D)   argue for Kingston's view that the literary
           artist is at best a "privileged keeper" of stories
   (E)   provide an alternative to certain critics' view
           that Kingston's work should be judged
           primarily as literature[21]

Step 2: The word "purpose" helps you identify this as a Logic Function question.

Step 3: Lines 43–51 encompass most of the final paragraph. A glance at your Roadmap should remind you of the function of this paragraph as a whole—to provide a supporting example of the author's argument that Kingston's work is rooted in the tradition of talk-story.

Step 4: You've already got the prediction in hand; the lines quoted were in support of the author's Main Idea.

[21]PrepTest 55, Sec 2, Q 20

Step 5: Choice (A) misunderstands the reason why *China Men* was discussed. However, choice (B) matches the prediction exactly and is the correct answer. Choice (C) is a little trickier; the author does argue against the critics' claim that Kingston in particular lacks literary antecedents, but the critics never claim that Chinese American literature as a whole lacks such antecedents. Choice (D) is too narrow in focus, and choice (E) misinterprets both the function of the quoted text and the viewpoint of the critics.

21. **(A)**

Which one of the following most accurately identifies
the attitude shown by the author in the passage
toward talk-story?

(A)   scholarly appreciation for its longstanding
         artistic sophistication
(B)   mild disappointment that it has not
         distinguished itself from other oral traditions
(C)   tentative approval of its resistance to critical
         evaluations
(D)   clear respect for the diversity of its ancient
         sources and cultural derivations
(E)   open admiration for the way it uses song to
         express narrative[22]

Step 2: This is an Inference question, as identified by a request for the author's attitude.

Step 3: The stem asks for the author's attitude regarding talk-story. According to the Roadmap, this was most generally discussed in the second paragraph, in which the author describes the history of talk-story and then discusses its evolution in the Chinese American community. Be sure to note Keywords of emphasis in this paragraph; the author describes talk-story as a "sophisticated oral culture" (line 21) that is "capable of producing masterpieces" (line 22).

Step 4: Based on the author's language, the correct answer should reflect a respect for talk-story's history and artistry.

Step 5: Your prediction should lead you straight to correct choice (A). Choices (B) and (C) describe disappointment and tentative approval, neither of which match the author's tone. Choice (D) starts off well with "clear respect" for talk-story but gets the details wrong, since the author doesn't show particular interest in the "diversity of its ancient sources." Choice (E) introduces the out of scope notion of song.

---

[22]PrepTest 55, Sec 2, Q 21

Passage Four: "Speculative Bubbles"

Step 1:

Def. of bubble

(In economics,) the term "speculative bubble" (refers to) a large upward move in an asset's price driven (not by) the asset's fundamentals—(that is,) by the earnings derivable from the asset—(but rather by)
(5) mere speculation that someone else will be willing to pay a higher price for it. The price increase is (then) (followed) by a dramatic decline in price (due to) a loss in confidence that the price will continue to rise, (and) the "bubble" is said to have burst. (According to)

Mackay: tulip market= bubble

(10) Charles Mackay's classic nineteenth-century account, the seventeenth-century Dutch tulip market (provides) (an example) of a speculative bubble. (But) the economist Peter Garber (challenges) Mackay's view, (arguing) that there is (no evidence) that the Dutch tulip

Garber: no bubble

(15) market really involved a speculative bubble.

Dutch tulip sales

(By) the seventeenth century, the Netherlands had (become) a center of cultivation and development of new tulip varieties, and a market (had developed) in which rare varieties of bulbs sold at high prices. For
(20) (example,) a Semper Augustus bulb sold in 1625 for an amount of gold worth about U.S.$11,000 in 1999. Common bulb varieties, (on the other hand,) sold for very low prices. (According to Mackay,) by 1636 rapid price rises attracted speculator (and) prices of many
(25) varieties surged upward from November 1636 (through) January 1637. (Mackay further) states that in February

Mackay's argument

1637 prices suddenly (collapsed;) bulbs could not be sold at 10 percent of their peak values. (By) 1739, the prices of all the (most prized) kinds of bulbs had (fallen)
(30) to no more than one two-hundredth of 1 percent of Semper Augustus's peak price.

(Garber acknowledges) that bulb prices increased dramatically from 1636 to 1637 and eventually reached very low levels. (But he argues) that this
(35) episode (should not) be described as a speculative

Garber 's argument

bubble, (for) the increase and eventual decline in bulb prices (can be explained) in terms of the fundamentals. (Garber argues) that a standard pricing pattern occurs for new varieties of flowers. (When) a particularly
(40) prized variety is developed, its original bulb sells for a high price. (Thus,) the (dramatic rise) in the price of some original tulip bulbs could have (resulted) as tulips in general, (and) certain varieties in particular, (became) fashionable. (However,) as the prized bulbs (become)
(45) more readily available through reproduction from the original bulb, their price (falls) rapidly; (after) less than 30 years, bulbs sell at reproduction cost. (But) this does (not mean) that the high prices of original bulbs are irrational, (for) earnings derivable from the millions
(50) of bulbs descendent from the original bulbs (can be) very high, (even) if each individual descendent bulb

commands a very low price. (Given) that an original
bulbs can generate a reasonable return on investment
(even if) the price of descendent bulbs decreases
(55)   dramatically, a rapid rise and eventual fall of tulip
bulb prices (need not indicate) a speculative bubble.

Paragraph Structure: The author introduces the **Topic** right away by defining the concept of speculative bubbles: The price of a commodity is driven up not by its actual value, "but rather by" (line 4) what speculators guess that others are willing to pay for it. When this speculation reaches its peak, the bubble "burst[s]" (line 9) and prices fall precipitously. The **Scope** becomes apparent in the second half of the paragraph as the author introduces two opposed views of the Dutch tulip market: Mackay believes the tulip market "provides an example" (lines 11–12) of such a bubble, whereas Garber argues that there is "no evidence" (line 14) that such a bubble existed. The author is most concerned with exploring these conflicting views.

The second and third paragraphs describe Mackay's and Garber's theses respectively. Mackay points out that a Semper Augustus bulb sold for an astonishing amount of money. Common bulbs, "on the other hand" (line 22), were not nearly so expensive. "According to Mackay" (line 23) speculators inflated the price of new tulip varieties, and he "further states" (line 26) that soon thereafter prices collapsed.

In the third paragraph, Garber "argues" (line 34) the price fluctuations described by Mackay can be described in rational terms. He suggests that the sudden rise in price of certain bulbs "could have resulted" (line 42) from their fashionable status at the time. "However" (line 44), he notes, as a rare bulb becomes more common, their prices fall rapidly. "But" (line 47) this price decrease "does not mean" (line 48) that the original prices were based on speculation, given that the total sales of a particular type of tulip represent a significant return on investment. He concludes that the price fluctuations "need not indicate a speculative bubble" (line 56).

Don't lose sight of the author's Purpose and **Main Idea** amidst all these details; the author's tone was neutral, and the **Purpose** of the passage was to describe two different interpretations of a particular phenomenon (the price fluctuations in the Dutch tulip market). The **Main Idea**, similarly, is that while Mackay believes the tulip market is evidence of a speculative bubble, Garber argues that no such bubble was present and that the price changes were based on rational principles.

Question Triage: With only six questions of common types, this group of questions isn't terribly challenging to triage. Answer Global question 22 immediately, then move on to Detail question 25. From here, questions 26 and 27 are both good options: question 26 is a paragraph Function question, amenable to a quick glance at your Roadmap, and 27 is a Vocab-in-Context complete with a line reference. With only two questions left, 24 is the better choice. It's an Inference question, but it refers to a specific point of view, simplifying your research. Save 23, the oddly worded Parallel Reasoning question, for last.

22. **(D)**

Which one of the following most accurately expresses
the main point of the passage?

(A)   The seventeenth-century Dutch tulip market is
widely but mistakenly believed by economists
to provide an example of a speculative bubble.

(B)   Mackay did not accurately assess the earnings
that could be derived from rare and expensive
seventeenth-century Dutch tulip bulbs.

(C)   A speculative bubble occurs whenever the
price of an asset increases substantially
followed by a rapid and dramatic decline.

(D)   Garber argues that Mackay's classic account of
the seventeenth-century Dutch tulip market
as a speculative bubble is not supported by
the evidence.

(E)   A tulip bulb can generate a reasonable return
on investment even if the price starts very
high and decreases dramatically.[23]

Step 2: This Global question asks you to identify the main point of the passage.

Step 3: As always, paraphrase the author's Main Idea before scanning the choices.

Step 4: The author's Main Idea was purely descriptive: Mackay believes a bubble occurred in the Dutch tulip market, and Garber doesn't.

Step 5: Choice (D) correctly describes the point of contention between Mackay and Garber. Choice (A) wrongly describes Mackay's ideas as widely believed and also refers to them as mistaken, something the author never does. Choice (B) is similarly flawed, as it focuses too much on detail and assumes that Mackay is wrong. Choice (C) misses the larger issues at work in the passage by only mentioning the definition of a speculative bubble, and choice (E) is similarly focused on a single detail. Wrong answer choices in Global questions frequently obsess over small details to the exclusion of major ideas—watch for this trap on test day.

---

[23]PrepTest 55, Sec 2, Q 22

23. **(D)**

Given Garber's account of the seventeenth-century Dutch tulip market, which one of the following is most analogous to someone who bought a tulip bulb of a certain variety in that market at a very high price, only to sell a bulb of that variety at a much lower price?

(A) someone who, after learning that many others had withdrawn their applications for a particular job, applied for the job in the belief that there would be less competition for it

(B) an art dealer who, after paying a very high price for a new painting, sells it at a very low price because it is now considered to be an inferior work

(C) someone who, after buying a box of rare motorcycle parts at a very high price, is forced to sell them at a much lower price because of the sudden availability of cheap substitute parts

(D) a publisher who pays an extremely high price for a new novel only to sell copies at a price affordable to nearly everyone

(E) an airline that, after selling most of the tickets for seats on a plane at a very high price, must sell the remaining tickets at a very low price[24]

Step 2: The stem asks for a situation analogous to a specific situation. This is a Logical Reasoning question, specifically Parallel Reasoning.

Step 3: There's plenty of information in this stem, so be sure to read it carefully. You must review Garber's account of a person buying at a high price and selling low. According to the Roadmap, this information is in the third paragraph. Garber describes the devaluation of the tulip bulb in terms of market fundamentals; a buyer might invest in a rare bulb on the expectation that the sale of millions of bulbs descendent from the original would provide a return on the original investment.

Step 4: Although you can't predict the specific subject matter of the correct answer, the logic will match Garber's as described in the third paragraph. You should look for an example of someone investing in a rare item in order to profit on reproductions sold at a lower price.

Step 5: Correct choice (D) describes the same kind of logic that Garber describes in the passage. None of the other choices reference the sale of reproductions from an original, and they all can be eliminated for that reason. Once again, a strong prediction makes the correct choice much easier to find.

---

[24]PrepTest 55, Sec 2, Q 23

24. **(B)**

The passage most strongly supports the inference that Garber would agree with which one of the following statements?

(A)   If speculative bubbles occur at all, they occur very rarely.

(B)   Many of the owners of high-priced original tulip bulbs could have expected to at least recoup their original investments from sales of the many bulbs propagated from the original bulbs.

(C)   If there is not a speculative bubble in a market, then the level of prices in that market is not irrational.

(D)   Most people who invested in Dutch tulip bulbs in the seventeenth century were generally rational in all their investments.

(E)   Mackay mistakenly infers from the fact that tulip prices dropped rapidly that the very low prices that the bulbs eventually sold for were irrational.[25]

Step 2: This time you're looking for an Inference that Garber would agree with.

Step 3: As with question 23, a review of Garber's description of the Dutch tulip market is in order. Garber bases his views on market fundamentals—the price fluctuations he observes are rational, because a person who purchases a rare bulb at a high price can expect to sell reproductions at lower prices in order to make a profit.

Step 4: The correct answer should reflect Garber's assessment of the tulip market, so look for a choice that conforms to his description of market fundamentals.

Step 5: Choice (B) is an almost exact paraphrase of Garber's viewpoint and is therefore the correct answer. Choice (A) is extreme. Just because Garber doesn't believe a bubble occurred in this case you can't assert that he believes bubbles are generally rare. Choice (C) sets up a false dichotomy, as Garber never claims that the absence of a bubble implies a rational market. Choice (D) is also extreme; there's not enough information to make an inference about the investments of "most people." Finally, choice (E) misrepresents Garber's disagreement with Mackay.

---

[25]PrepTest 55, Sec 2, Q 24

25. **(B)**

The passage states that Mackay claimed which one of the following?

(A)   The rapid rise in price of Dutch tulip bulbs was not due to the fashionability of the flowers they produced.

(B)   The prices of certain varieties of Dutch tulip bulbs during the seventeenth century were, at least for a time, determined by speculation.

(C)   The Netherlands was the only center of cultivation and development of new tulip varieties in the seventeenth century.

(D)   The very high prices of bulbs in the seventeenth-century Dutch tulip market were not irrational.

(E)   Buyers of rare and very expensive Dutch tulip bulbs were ultimately able to derive earnings from bulbs descendent from the original bulbs.[26]

Step 2: The phrase "the passage states" identifies this as a straightforward Detail question.

Step 3: Mackay's claims are detailed in the second paragraph in which he suggests that the price fluctuations in the Dutch tulip market were based on speculation and were therefore indicative of a bubble.

Step 4: The correct answer should paraphrase the details you've already researched.

Step 5: Correct choice (B) reflects Mackay's belief that the tulip market was affected by speculation. Mackay never denies the effect of fashionability on price as suggested in choice (A), and choice (C) has no support in the passage. Choice (D) is a 180; Mackay believes that the price increases *were* irrational, at least in part. This sounds more like something Garber would have said, as does choice (E). Beware of wrong answer traps that confuse one point of view for another. Careful research will help you avoid losing points to this common error.

---

[26]PrepTest 55, Sec 2, Q 25

26. **(C)**

The main purpose of the second paragraph is to
- (A) present the facts that are accepted by all experts in the field
- (B) identify the mistake that one scholar alleges another scholar made
- (C) explain the basis on which one scholar makes an inference with which another scholar disagrees
- (D) undermine the case that one scholar makes for the claim with which another scholar disagrees
- (E) outline the factual errors that led one scholar to draw the inference that he drew[27]

Step 2: This is a Logic Function question. You must describe how the second paragraph functions within the passage as a whole.

Step 3: Refer to your Roadmap to get the context you need.

Step 4: Paragraph two describes the price fluctuations in that occurred in the Dutch tulip market as well as Mackay's interpretation of them. The correct answer should assert that this paragraph demonstrates evidence for one of two conflicting viewpoints present in the passage.

Step 5: Correct choice (C) is the match. Choice (A) is extreme (how can we know how all experts in the field feel about this?) and choice (B) misinterprets the function of the paragraph. It was intended to describe Mackay's position, not identify his mistakes. No undermining occurs in the second paragraph, eliminating choice (D), and choice (E) makes a completely out of scope reference to factual errors.

27. **(D)**

The phrase "standard pricing pattern" as used in line 38 most nearly means a pricing pattern
- (A) against which other pricing patterns are to be measured
- (B) that conforms to a commonly agreed-upon criterion
- (C) that is merely acceptable
- (D) that regularly recurs in certain types of cases
- (E) that serves as an exemplar[28]

Step 2: This is another Logic Function question, this time asking you to define a phrase in context.

Step 3: Start your research at the beginning of paragraph three in order to establish the context you need. Garber's position is that the price fluctuations are based on market fundamentals, leading to his assertion that a standard pricing pattern occurs for new types of flowers.

---

[27]PrepTest 55, Sec 2, Q 26
[28]PrepTest 55, Sec 2, Q 27

Step 4: In context, Garber's reference to a standard pricing pattern is quoted as support for his central idea, that the price fluctuations described in the passage are representative of ordinary changes in the market and not indicative of a bubble. The correct answer should show that a standard pricing pattern is one that is expected.

Step 5: Correct choice (D) describes a predictable pattern. The remaining choices all describe varying everyday usages of the word "standard," none of which make sense in the context of this passage. As always, Logic Function questions rely completely on your sense of context within the passage. Be sure to research this context carefully before examining the answer choices.

PART IV

THE TEST DAY EXPERIENCE

CHAPTER 22

GET READY FOR TEST DAY

Congratulations. Your work with the Kaplan Method and strategies gives you the knowledge and practice you need for LSAT success. Now, it's time for you to schedule a test date, register for the exam (if you haven't done so already), and put yourself in the right frame of mind to take the next step on the road to law school.

The details of registering for the test are covered in "An Introduction to the LSAT" at the beginning of the book. Follow the steps and recommendations mentioned there to ensure that you have a spot at the next test administration or on the test date that's best for you. In the remainder of this chapter, I'll cover what you need to do to have yourself mentally and emotionally ready for the rigors and rewards of test day.

YOU ARE PREPARED

First, remember (and remind yourself) that you are prepared. By learning the lessons and doing the work from this book, you can know, with confidence, that there is nothing else you need to *know* about LSAT reading comprehension. The Kaplan Method, the specific strategies, and the analysis that I've presented in this book are the result not only of my own tenure as an LSAT instructor; they're the summation of five decades of Kaplan expertise and research. Hundreds of great LSAT minds—including those of perfect scorers, legal scholars, and psychometricians—have contributed to the development, testing, and refinement of Kaplan's LSAT pedagogy. If we know it, you now know it. So strike from your mind any concern that there's one more secret to uncover or a mysterious LSAT Rosetta Stone to search for. You have the most complete, proven system for LSAT Reading Comprehension success available. If you've already studied and practiced from this book's companion volumes—*Kaplan LSAT Logic Games: Strategies and Tactics* and *Kaplan LSAT Logical Reasoning: Strategies and Tactics*—you can say the same thing about the entire exam.

Now, saying that you *know* everything you need to about the Reading Comprehension section doesn't mean you're ready to *do* everything you need to do to achieve your goal score. You need to continue to practice and review. Indeed, I'll cover that in the next section of this chapter. But first, I want to make sure you're translating your comprehensive knowledge of reading comprehension into confidence on test day. From now until the day you sit for your official administration of the LSAT, you need to exhibit the confidence your preparation has earned you.

There are some very practical steps you can take to reinforce your test day confidence. Once you're registered for the test, visit your test site. You may even want to take a reading comprehension passage to practice in the very room where you'll be sitting for the real test. At a minimum, know where you're going to be, how you'll get there, and where you'll park or where public transportation will drop you off. You want no surprises on the morning of your official LSAT.

The day before your test, relax. There's no way to cram for a skills-based exam. While your competition is scrambling and fretting, go to the gym, watch your favorite movie, or have a nice dinner. Gather what you need for the next day, and keep yourself one step ahead of everything you need to do. It sounds a little corny, but acting confident will actually make you feel more confident. Get to bed relatively early, have a good night's sleep, and wake ready to have the best day of your (test-taking) life.

The following is a list of what you'll need to have with you on test day:

LSAT SURVIVAL KIT

You MUST have the following:

- Admissions ticket
- Photo ID
- Passport-style photos
- Several sharpened #2 pencils
- 1-gallon transparent zip-top bag

You SHOULD also have:

- Pencil sharpener
- Eraser
- Analog wristwatch
- Aspirin
- Snack and drink for the break

You CANNOT have:

- Cell phone
- MP3 player
- Computer or electronic reader
- Electronic or digital timers
- Weapons
- Papers other than your admission ticket

That list conforms to the rules for the test site as they stand at the time of this writing. You should check www.lsac.org periodically before your test date to make sure there haven't been any changes or amendments to the Law School Administration Council's (LSAC) policies.

Of course, the "MUSTs" are non-negotiable. You need those to be allowed entry to the testing room. Some of the "SHOULDs," on the other hand, you may not need at all. But if you begin to feel a little headache coming on, or if you find your stomach grumbling midway through Section 3 of the test, you'll be awfully glad you took along those "just in case" items. As for the "CANNOTs," do yourself a favor and avoid any conflict with the proctors or test administrators. Just leave your phone or electronics in the car or at home.

One other very practical thing you can do is to dress in layers. The LSAT is usually administered during the weekend and almost always in a large, institutional building. It's really tough to predict whether the room will be too hot or too cold or whether it will fluctuate throughout the day. Take the Goldilocks approach and make sure the temperature is always "just right" for you by wearing or taking the kind of sweater or light jacket that's easy (and quiet) to slip on or off.

The stress levels of test takers around you will be high. But if you demonstrate nothing but preparation and confidence on the morning of the test, you'll feel calmer, more clear-headed, and ready for the real challenges of the test itself.

CHAMPIONS PRACTICE. VIRTUOSOS PRACTICE. YOU PRACTICE.

To put my earlier point about practice into formal logic terms, knowledge of the test is necessary, but not sufficient, for test day success. Mistaking this relationship is something that leads a lot of test takers off track. They haven't achieved the score they want, so they say, "There must be something I don't know yet," or, "What am I missing?" The fact is that many of these test takers know all about the test, but they haven't practiced taking the test. Ask almost any great performer, musician, public speaker, or athlete and they'll tell you that the key to their success is practice. A great violinist may study a composer's compositional theory, historical context, or even personal life in order to better understand a piece before performing it. But all of that will mean little if the performer hasn't practiced. The audience would be pretty disappointed if the violinist showed up to give a lecture about the composer instead of playing a concert. It's the same with the LSAT. Your audience, law school admissions officers, won't care what you know about the exam, just how well you perform on it.

So how can you best practice? First, lay out a study and practice schedule for yourself that runs from now until test day—one that's ambitious but practical. Fill in as much as you can about which sections or question types you'll be practicing each day or week. If you're working on different parts of the test, vary the sections you're practicing and the materials you're using.

If you haven't completed and reviewed the full-section practice in this book, make sure you do so. Leave time for review of your work. Remember that you're not just checking to see whether you produced the correct answer, you're asking whether you did so as efficiently and effectively as you could have. That means that you should always be reviewing the questions you got right as well as those you got wrong. Look for what features and patterns in a question or passage you're likely to see again on test day. You won't see the passages from this book on your test, but every question on your test will have similarities to those you've practiced here.

If you're looking for additional practice, consider the following additional resources:

OTHER KAPLAN LSAT RESOURCES

Logic Games On Demand
Logical Reasoning On Demand
Reading Comprehension On Demand
Comprehensive, section-specific courses for in-depth instruction and targeted practice.

LSAT Advantage—On Site, Anywhere or On Demand
Our most popular option—complete, targeted, and focused prep designed for busy students.

LSAT Extreme—On Site or Anywhere
Maximum in-class instruction plus tutoring for students who want extra time, review, and more practice.

LSAT One on One—On Site or Anywhere
An expert tutor designs a one-on-one, custom program around your individual needs, goals, and schedule.

LSAT Summer Intensive
Six weeks of total LSAT immersion in a residential academic program at Boston University

Check out *www.kaplanlsat.com* for courses and free events in live, online and in your area.

All of those additional resources will provide the outstanding instruction, coaching, and practice you expect from Kaplan test prep. Consider which ones work best for your schedule, learning style, and admissions timeline. Kaplan is committed to helping you achieve your educational and career goals.

THE PSYCHOLOGICAL DIMENSIONS OF TEST DAY

There's no doubt that taking your official LSAT is one of the most important steps (maybe *the* most important) you'll take on the road to law school. That's a lot of pressure. It's natural to have a little excitement and some extra adrenaline for such a big event. Those are actually healthy things to feel, provided that you channel your emotions into energy and concentration, rather than anxiety and confusion. I'd be pretty disappointed if, after weeks or months of practice and preparation, one of my students said, "Eh, I don't really care what happens on the test." Of course you care. That's why you're reading this book and working so hard. So embrace the big day.

I've already talked about how you can begin to foster an attitude of confidence and act in ways that support and sustain it. Here are a couple of practical steps you can take to carry your confidence right into the testing room.

Know What to Expect

It is easy to lay out the order of events on test day. Here's a chart that shows you what will happen from the time you arrive at the test site.

Event	What Happens	Time
Check-In	Show admissions ticket, ID, fingerprints, room and seat assignment	10–30 minutes
Rules and Procedures	Test booklets distributed, proctor reads the rules, test takers fill out grid information	30 minutes
LSAT Administration		
Section 1	Logic Games, Logical Reasoning, or Reading Comprehension Section	35 minutes
Section 2	Logic Games, Logical Reasoning, or Reading Comprehension Section	35 minutes
Section 3	Logic Games, Logical Reasoning, or Reading Comprehension Section	35 minutes

Break	Test booklets and grids collected, test takers have break, return to seats, booklets and grids redistributed	12–20 minutes (10 minute break with additional time for administrative tasks)
Section 4	Logic Games, Logical Reasoning, or Reading Comprehension Section	35 minutes
Section 5	Logic Games, Logical Reasoning, or Reading Comprehension Section	35 minutes
Prepare for Writing Sample	Test booklets and grids collected, test takers given a chance to cancel scores, Writing Sample booklets distributed	5–10 minutes
Writing Sample	Test takers produce Writing Samples	35 minutes

You can see that even if everything goes as smoothly as possible, you're in for around five hours from start to finish. This is another reason that it's so important to be rested, comfortable, and nourished. Students who are too groggy to be at their best in Section 1 or too exhausted and hungry to keep up their performance in Section 5 will have trouble competing with someone like you, who's prepared for the entire testing day, from start to finish.

One thing that star performers do—I don't care if you're thinking of singers, actors, athletes, or even great trial lawyers—is to warm up before they "go on." You can do the same on the morning of your test by reviewing a Logic Game, Logical Reasoning question, or Reading Comprehension passage that you've done before. As you revisit the game or question, go over the steps in the Kaplan Method that allowed you to be successful with the item before. This will get your brain warmed up just as a quarterback would loosen his arm or a singer would warm up her vocal cords. Don't try new material, and certainly don't try a full section. Just start reading and thinking—calmly and confidently—in the LSAT way. You'll be miles ahead of the unprepared test taker who looks shell-shocked for most of Section 1.

In order to maintain a high level of performance, it's important to stay hydrated and nourished. Mental work makes most people hungry. So drink water at the break and have a small, healthy snack. Don't, however, eat a sleep-inducing turkey sandwich or gobble sugar that will have you crashing out during Section 5.

Knowing what to expect also helps you manage your mental preparation for test day in other small, but important, ways. A lot of test takers don't know that the proctors will ask whether anyone in the room wants to cancel his or her score right after Section 5 is completed and the test booklets are collected. If you're not expecting that question, it can throw you into a moment of self-doubt. It's human nature to underestimate your performance on the test. You will remember the handful of questions that gave you trouble while ignoring the dozens of questions you answered routinely with no problem. I've personally known students who canceled their scores when they shouldn't have. The LSAC allows you a number of days after the test to cancel your score, so don't worry about it during the exam. Complete the Writing Sample to the best of your ability. You can always consider things that might have caused you to underperform—illness, a personal crisis—after you've completed the test.

You Will Panic, but Don't Panic

Over the course of four to five hours of rigorous, detailed, strictly timed test taking, you're going to reach a point at which you lose focus, feel overwhelmed, or just downright panic for a moment. It's normal. So first thing, don't feed the panic by blaming yourself or saying, "Oh, I knew this would happen." There's nothing wrong with you for having those feelings. In fact, panic is a physical response to high-pressure situations. It's related to the autonomic nervous system, the "flight or fight" response we've adapted to survive danger. Your heart beats faster; blood leaves your brain to go to your extremities; your breathing gets rapid and shallow. That's all very important when the danger you face is a predator or enemy. It's just not very helpful when you're facing a standardized test.

If—when—you face a point of doubt, confusion, or panic on test day, take a moment. Collect yourself physically first. Take a deep breath; sit up in a straight, comfortable posture; put both feet flat on the floor and lower your shoulders; even close your eyes for a second while you breathe. Then open your eyes and remind yourself that whatever you're looking at, it's just an LSAT question. The fact is that you've seen one like it and done one like it before. You know that's the case because of your preparation. Get your concentration back by reciting the Kaplan Method as you work through the problem. You know that will provide a strategic, purposeful approach every time.

Worry Only about What's in Your Control

When I have students in LSAT prep courses, they often ask a lot of questions about what to do if things go wrong on test day. "What if the proctor doesn't give us a verbal five minute warning?" "What if someone is being noisy right behind me?" "What if the school marching band is rehearsing in the courtyard under the window?" All of those and a few weirder, more distracting things have happened to test takers. But my students' concern about such occurrences before test day is misplaced. They should be taking care of the things that are within their control—learning the Kaplan Method, practicing reading comprehension passages—not worrying about the things that aren't. The vast majority of LSAT administrations go off without more than a minor hitch. Your job is to be ready to have a peak performance on a routine test day.

When the unexpected happens, stay calm. If there is something that you notice before the test begins—a window is open, letting in cold air or street noise; the lights in the back of the room aren't turned on, making it dark where you're sitting—just let the proctor know (politely) and ask if it can be remedied. If something happens during a section—another test taker is unconsciously tapping his pencil; the proctor forgets the five-minute announcement—keep working. Raise your hand and get a proctor's attention. When they come to your seat, quickly and quietly explain the situation. Most of the time, they'll take action to remedy the situation. But don't let those things throw you off your game. If something truly bizarre happens that seriously impedes your performance—a fire alarm goes off, a wrecking crew starts to jack-hammer the building—follow the proctor's instructions, keep a record of what happened, and follow up with the LSAC by telephone or in writing after the test concludes. You are welcome to contact 1-800-KAPTEST and ask for advice from one of our LSAT experts, too. A word to the wise: The LSAC will not add points to a score as a remedy for a distracting test administration, but they have found other ways to accommodate test takers who, through no fault of their own, have been unable to complete the test or who encountered unmanageable distractions.

GET READY FOR TEST DAY

This chapter really boils down to one message: Prepare yourself for the perfect test day. Display confidence and preparation in all that you do. Get ready for a consistent, focused performance from start to finish. When that's the attitude you take into the test, you're more likely to outperform your competition and have your best day regardless of what else does or doesn't happen.

CHAPTER 23

SECRETS OF THE LSAT

The "secrets" of the LSAT aren't really secrets at all. They're well-known facts that many test takers fail to take full advantage of. The best test takers use the structure and format of the test to their advantage. Just as a great football or basketball coach adjusts the team's strategy when time is running out on the clock, or just as a great conductor rearranges an orchestra to take advantage of the acoustics in a new venue, you can learn to adjust your approach to the test you're taking. We might well laud the insightful coach or conductor by saying, "Wow, he really knows the 'secrets' of this game (or stadium or theater)." But in fact, he's simply taking account of all the circumstances and making the right strategic decisions for that time and place. Consider a handful of facts that make the LSAT a unique testing experience, and see how you can use them to your advantage.

EVERY QUESTION IS WORTH THE SAME AMOUNT TO YOUR SCORE

Many tests you've taken (even some standardized tests) rewarded you more for certain questions or sections than for others. In school, it's common for a professor to say, "The essay counts for half of your score," or to make a section of harder questions worth five points each while easier ones are worth less. With such exams, you may simply be unable to get a top score without performing well on a given question or topic. It makes sense, then, to target the areas the professor will reward most highly.

As you well know, that's not the case on the LSAT. Every question—easy or hard, short or long, common or rare—is worth exactly the same amount as every other question. That means that you should seek out the questions, games, and passages that are the easiest for you to handle. Far too many test takers get their teeth into a tough question and won't let go. That hurts them in two ways. First, they spend too much time—sometimes three or four minutes—on such a question, sacrificing their chances with other, easier questions. Second, since questions like these are tough or confusing, they're less likely to produce a right answer no matter how much time you spend. Learn to skip questions when it's in your interest to do so. Mark questions that you skip by circling the entire question in your test booklet. That way, those questions will be easy to spot if you have time left after you complete the other questions in the section. If you've eliminated one or two obviously incorrect answer choicess, strike them through completely so that you don't spend time rethinking them when you come back to the question.

When schools receive your score report, the only thing they see is your score. They don't know—and they don't care—whether you've answered the easiest or the toughest questions on the LSAT. They only care that you answered more questions correctly than the other applicants. Becoming a good manager of the test sections is invaluable. You'll do that, in part, by triaging the games or passages and choosing to put off the toughest for last. Even more often, you'll manage the section by skipping and guessing strategically. Don't slug it out with a tough question for minutes and then grudgingly move on. Boldly seek out questions on which you can exert your strengths, and be clearheaded and decisive in your decisions to move past questions you know are targeted at your weaknesses. Take the test; don't let it take you.

ONE RIGHT, FOUR ROTTEN

I'm sure you've had the experience, on a multiple-choice test in school, of having a teacher tell you, "More than one answer may be correct, but pick the best answer for each question." Given that you're a future law student, I wouldn't be surprised to learn that you may even have debated with your instructor, making a case for why a certain answer should receive credit. As a result, you're used to comparing answer choices to one another. On the LSAT, however, that's a recipe for wasted time and effort. The test makers design the correct answer to be unequivocally correct; it will respond to the call of the question stem precisely. Likewise, the four wrong answers are demonstrably wrong, not just "less good."

For the well-trained test taker—for you, that is—this leads to an important, practical adjustment in strategy. Throughout the test, you should seek to predict the correct answer before assessing the answer choices. In Logical Reasoning, you will, on most questions, be able to anticipate the content of the correct answer, sometimes almost word for word. In Reading Comprehension and Logic Games, you should spend the time up front to have a clear passage road map or game sketch. At a minimum, you must characterize the correct and incorrect answers (if the correct answer *must be true*, for example, each of the wrong answers *could be false*). Then seek out the one answer that matches your prediction or characterization.

The bottom line is that, on the LSAT, you are always comparing the answers against what you know must be correct, not against one another. When locating the correct choice is difficult or time-consuming, you can always turn the tables on the test maker and eliminate the wrong ones.

Because you know that there will always be one correct choice and that you can always identify the characteristics that make wrong answers wrong, you can always take the most direct route to the LSAT point.

THERE'S NO WRONG-ANSWER PENALTY

This point is easy to understand, but sometimes hard to remember when you're working quickly through an LSAT section. The LSAT is scored only by counting the number of correct responses you bubble in. Unlike some standardized tests—the SAT is the most notorious example—you're not penalized for marking incorrect responses. Simply put, there's nothing to lose, so mark a response, even if it's a blind guess, for every answer.

Of course, strategic guessing is better than just taking a wild stab at the correct answer. Even if a question gives you a lot of trouble, see if you can eliminate one or more answer choices as clearly wrong. When you can, take your guess from the remaining choices. Removing even one clearly incorrect choice improves your chances of hitting on the right one from 20 percent to 25 percent; getting rid of two wrong answers, of course, gives you a one-in-three chance of guessing correctly. Provided that you do it quickly (not taking time away from questions you can handle with little trouble), strategic guessing can improve your score.

Students ask another question related to this point about the answer choices. They want to know if a particular answer choice—(A), (B), (C), (D), or (E)—shows up more often than others, or whether it's better, when guessing, to pick a particular choice for all guesses. The answer to both questions is no. Over the course of a full LSAT, all five answer choices show up just about equally. There's no pattern associated with particular question types. You're no more likely to see any particular answer early or late in a section. Thus, when you're blind guessing, you have a one-in-five chance of hitting the correct answer whatever you choose. And there's no benefit from guessing choice (C) or choice (D) over and over. It's far more valuable to spend your limited time trying to eliminate one or more wrong answers than it is to fret over any illusory patterns within the choices.

THE LSAT IS A MARATHON . . . MADE UP OF SPRINTS

At this point in your academic career, you've had long tests and you've had tests that put time pressure on you. But chances are, you've never encountered as intense a combination of the two as you will on the LSAT. In the last chapter, I already talked about the importance of stamina. Including the administrative tasks at the beginning, the breaks, and the collection and distribution of your testing materials, you're in for around a five-hour test day. It's important to remember that, over the course of that marathon, the first and fifth sections are just as valuable as those in the middle. Unsurprisingly, Kaplan's research has shown that, for the untrained test taker, those sections are likely to produce the poorest performance. You can counteract the inherent difficulties in the schedule by doing a little warm-up so that you're ready to hit the ground running at the start of Section 1, and by staying relaxed and having a healthy snack at the break so that you're still going strong at the end of Section 5. Just taking these simple steps could add several points to your score.

At the same time that you're striving to maintain focus and sustain your performance, you're trying to manage a very fast 35 minutes in each section. Attack each section with confident, strategic guessing and you'll be outperforming many test takers who succumb to the "ego battle" with tough or time-consuming questions. But there's one more thing that you have to add to your repertoire of test day tactics: You have to learn to not look back. Over the years, I've talked to many students who could tell me how they thought they performed on each of the test's sections. To be honest with you, I find that a little disappointing. Sure, you may remember that the game with the Cowboys and Horses or the passage on Nanotechnology was really challenging, but it's a waste of time and mental capacity to try and assess your performance as you're taking the test. Once you've answered a question, leave it behind. Give your full concentration to what you're working on. This is even more important when it comes to sections. Once time is called, you may no longer work on the section, not even to bubble in the answers to questions you completed in your test booklet. If a proctor sees you continuing to work on a section for which the time has expired, he or she can issue you a misconduct slip, and the violation will be reported to all of the schools to which you apply. More importantly, you're harming your work on the current section.

There's no rearview mirror on the LSAT. Work diligently, mark the correct answers, and move on to the next question. Keep this in mind: Even if you could accurately assess your performance as you worked (you can't, but imagine it for a moment), it wouldn't change anything. You'd still need to get the remaining questions right. So learn this lesson—and the other "secrets" of the LSAT—now. Be like those seemingly brilliant coaches and performers. By knowing how the LSAT test day works, you can gain an edge over test takers who treat this just as they have every other exam in their academic careers.

CHAPTER 24

LSAT STRATEGIES AND TACTICS

At last, I'll bring you full circle back to the premise at the start of this book. The LSAT may be unlike any other test you've studied or prepared for, but it need not be mysterious or overwhelming. The underlying principle that has informed this book is that **every question has an answer.** The twist is that you're not expected to know the answers. How could you? This is a test that rewards what you can do, not what you've learned. In that sense, you can't *study* for the test. And you certainly can't cram for it. What you can do, indeed what you've been doing throughout this book, is to *practice* for the test. Instead of thinking of the LSAT as a test, think of it as your law school audition or tryout. A play's director or a team's coach doesn't ask you what you know; she wants to see what you can do. And just as the director or coach will give you everything you need to demonstrate your skill, the test makers always give you everything you need to produce the correct answers on the LSAT.

THE LSAT REWARDS THE CORE 4 SKILLS

Law schools don't expect incoming students to know the law. Indeed, much as the LSAT does, your professors may try to use your outside knowledge and assumptions against you. What the schools are looking for is incoming students who have the skills they'll need to succeed through the coming three years of rigorous legal training. That, at least in part, is what they're looking for your LSAT score to indicate. That's why the LSAT is a skills-based, rather than a knowledge-based, exam. Back near the beginning of this book, you learned the central skills rewarded on the test.

THE CORE 4 LSAT SKILLS

1. Strategic Reading
2. Analyzing Arguments
3. Understanding Formal Logic
4. Making Deductions

USE WHAT YOU'VE LEARNED THROUGHOUT THE TEST

One nice thing to realize is that much of the work you've done here, preparing for the Reading Comprehension section specifically, will translate to exceptional performance throughout the test. To be successful on the LSAT, you must make deductions and draw valid inferences from related rules and statements dozens of times in every scored section.

So let me leave you with this: The LSAT is designed to reward the skills that will make you a successful law student. You know that you have those skills. You are, after all, seeking this path with passion and focus. The work you've done in this book is all about honing your skills and preparing you for a successful test day. Take the insights you've gathered about LSAT reading comprehension and apply them throughout the exam. Take what you've learned about yourself as a test taker, and use it not only for a stronger, more confident performance on test day, but also throughout your law school endeavor, during your bar exam, and into your legal career. Best of luck to you. Now, go out and accomplish great things.

NOTES

NOTES

NOTES

NOTES

NOTES

NOTES

NOTES

NOTES

NOTES

NOTES